ISBN 978-1-330-38845-7
PIBN 10048320

1 MONTH OF
FREE
READING

at

www.ForgottenBooks.com

By purchasing this book you are
eligible for one month membership to
ForgottenBooks.com, giving you
unlimited access to our entire
collection of over 1,000,000 titles via
our web site and mobile apps.

To claim your free month visit:

www.forgottenbooks.com/free48320

HISTORY *of* BOKHARA

FROM THE EARLIEST PERIOD

·DOWN TO THE PRESENT

COMPOSED FOR THE FIRST TIME AFTER ORIENTAL KNOWN

AND UNKNOWN HISTORICAL MANUSCRIPTS

BY

ARMINIUS VÁMBÉRY

ORDINARY PROFESSOR OF ORIENTAL LANGUAGES AND LITERATURES

IN THE ROYAL UNIVERSITY OF PESTH

SECOND EDITION

LONDON

HENRY S. KING & CO. ·

65 CORNHILL & 12 PATERNOSTER ROW

1873

TO

LORD AND LADY HOUGHTON

WITH

THE AUTHOR'S

RESPECT AND CONSIDERATION.

PREFACE.

OUR INFORMATION concerning the past history of the different peoples of Asia becomes more extensive in proportion as the researches of science into the geography, ethnography, and philology of the countries in question are pushed farther and farther. The Ottoman Empire, though long since in constant communication with all parts of Europe, only occupied the attention of historians for the first time in the last century, and even then their information was so superficial that the writings of Petis de la Croix and Cantemir only became really trustworthy when confirmed by the later investigations of Hammer and Zinkeisen. The enormous industry of G. Weil sufficed to do ample justice to the annals of Arabia and Egypt, where he had the past alone to deal with; but the muse of Persian history found no adequate representative until the accomplished General Malcolm, following up the subjects first broached by Thevenot, Chardin, and Niebuhr, came forward to interpret her, after having himself several times traversed the whole of Persia, studied and learnt to know it thoroughly. The country beyond the Oxus still remains a soil comparatively unknown to history. In the beginning of this century, a few streaks of light first penetrated to us through the darkness enveloping the whole region; but since then the sword of conquest has lifted the veil considerably, and although our knowledge both of the country and its inhabitants is still very imperfect, it is easy to imagine that great eagerness exists amongst cultivated Europeans for a better acquaintance with the present conditions of existence, and, if possible, for some insight into the early history of that nation of Central Asia which, though geographically so far removed from us, has been brought into close relations with us by recent political events.

To satisfy this curiosity, I have ventured on attempting, with small sources of information and still smaller abilities, the somewhat arduous task of writing the *first history of Bokhara*. But for the circumstances that from my earliest years my imagination was excited by the thoughts of that distant region, and that my whole youth was spent first in laborious preparations, and then in more laborious journeys, I should not now, in my maturer years, have had the courage to risk myself in so considerable a literary enterprise. It seems, however, to be the lot ordained for me to traverse regions where I have had scarcely any, or absolutely no predecessors; and having now to explore with the pen an entirely new field, I will, in the place of further apologies, content myself with enumerating the scanty sources of information without which the utmost determination to learn must have proved fruitless.

The history of Bokhara is divided into two parts—the ancient history, or history of Transoxania, and the modern, or history of the khanate of Bokhara. During the first period, ending with the fall of Emir Timour, Central Asia, though never the subject of special historical works, could not be left entirely unnoticed. Her annals were at that time inextricably mixed up with those of the rest of the interior of the world of Islam, and sometimes with those of the Western Mohammedans; and, although the historians of the time did not bestow the same attention on political events in Transoxania as on those in Khorasan, Irak and Arabistan, we are still enabled to glean from them the most important features of the past. The epochs in which, for instance, the Samanides and Emir Timour issued from Bokhara and Samarkand, the decrees by which half (and at times the whole) of Islamite Asia was governed, fall within this period ; but in spite of this, even at those very moments, the history of Transoxania proper has never had adequate attention given to it. The second period, commencing with the appearance of the Özbegs, has so far some scanty special history of its own, simply for the reason that the politically insignificant khanate of Bokhara was isolated from its neighbours, who scarcely regarded the very slight and transitory influence it exercised amongst them. In accordance with these two periods, the authorities for this history may be divided into two separate classes :—

I. Older and better known histories ; i.e., historical works partly edited and translated by Orientalists, partly consulted in the original manuscripts for the elucidation of particular questions.

II. New or unknown manuscripts, brought back from Central Asia by the most recent travellers, and consequently unknown hitherto to the great mass of Orientalists.

As regards the first class, the works I have made the most use of, so far as they bear on the history of Transoxania, are the following :—

1. *Tarikhi Tabari*, following the Turkish translation which has appeared in print, more especially for the period of the Arab invasions beyond the Oxus ; for although Narshakhi's history is the most useful for this chapter, the data of the Mohammedan author of universal history are still of much value, both from the variations of some of his versions and the novelty of some of his details.

2. *Tarikhi Baihaki*, from the edition by W. H. Morley and

Captain W. Nassau Lees, published in the 'Bibliotheca Indica,' Calcutta, 1862. Its value as a contribution to the history of Transoxania consists in the details it gives of the early career of Mahmud Sebuktekin, and of the diplomatic relations between Mes'ud Sultan and the independent princes of Kashgar and Samarkand. This book contains, however, only certain parts of the Tarikhi Ali-i-Sebuktekin (History of the Family of Sebuktekin), by Ebul Fazl Baihaki.

3. The *Rauzat es Sefa*, by Mirkhond, and the continuation of that book down to modern times, compiled from the works of Khondemir, Alem araj Abbasi, Tarikhi Sefevi, Tarikhi Nadir Shah, and others, lithographed together with the author's original work at Teheran, in the year 1274 (1857), and published in two volumes. In addition to this, I have also had at my disposal the fragments of Mirkhond, edited by Vullers and Quatremère; but I have only been able to make any special use of Mirkhond in the chapter on the Seldjukides, for his book is a compilation of other well-known works;[1] and, wherever practicable, I have preferred using the originals.

4. *Tarikhi Djihankusha*, by Ala-eddin Ata Melik Djuveini. This is known as the principal authority used by Rashid-eddin, Vassaf, Hafiz Abru, and other historians of the Mongolians; and, although the two former surpass him in detail, his work is of very great value to the history of Transoxania and of the Turkish people generally. I have made use of the copy in the Imperial Library at Vienna—the same used by Hammer in his 'History of the Golden Horde.'

5. *Zafernameh* (Book of Victories), by Sherefeddin Ali Yezdi. The well-known biography of Timour, translated

---

[1] Mirkhond carried this practice of compiling so far, that he frequently copies word for word whole sentences from his authorities. His history of the wars of Djenghiz, for instance, is nothing more than a copy of Djuveini, leaving out simply a few ornamental passages of the original text.

(not very perfectly) into French by Petis de la Croix, Paris, 1722. I have also seen at Khiva a Tchaghataian translation of this ' Zafernameh.'

6. *Matlaa es Saadein*, (Rise of the Two Lucky Stars, supposed by some to point to Djenghiz and Timour ; by others, more probably, to Timour and Shahrukh), by Sheïkh Kemaleddin Abdurrezak, who lived at Herat and Samarkand during the most flourishing period of the Timouride rule : one of the most interesting and instructive books ever written on the history of any single epoch in the annals of the Islamite nations of Asia. The second volume, from the death of Timour to that of Ebusaïd Mirza, is especially of very great value, giving in great detail, and with still greater literary ability, a striking picture of the life and deeds of Timour's scientific and artistic successor. Abdurrezak was born at Herat in 816 (1423), and died in 887 (1482) at Samarkand.

7. *Babernameh*, from the original version in the well-known Ilminsky edition. I afterwards also saw the excellent French translation, published only last year by Pavet de la Courteille.

8. *Sheïbani-nameh*, from the edition published by Berezin, with a Russian translation. The Tchaghataian text, consisting only of a few sheets, gives some details as to the origin, family circumstances, and earlier career of the Özbeg hero, from the time of his wanderings on the lower courses of the Yaxartes. The book ends with his death,. but the principal wars and the tragic fate of Sheïbani are only cursorily mentioned.

9. *Shedjre-i-turki* (Turkish Genealogy), by Abulgazi Bahadoor Khan, the original edition published by Count Romanzoff at Kasan, in 1825. This book, taken altogether, is a mediocre copy of Rashid-eddin's, especially of the portion dealing with the origin of the Turks ; and the only chapters of any

historical value are those dealing with the time of Abulgazi, and with his own personal adventures.

10. *Tarikhi Nadir Shah,* by Mirza Mohammed Mehdi Khan, from a lithographed copy published at Teheran in 1260 (1844).

11. *Nasikh et tevarikh. Tarikhi Kadjarie.* The history of the dynasty now reigning in Persia, in which a few scanty notices of Bokhara in the end of the last and beginning of the present century are to be found. According to the references used by Malcolm, it appears that the annalists of Persia have given a few special accounts of this period in the history of Iran, but I have not succeeded in obtaining a sight of any of them.

In addition to these principal sources of information, I have of course also made use of all I could find relating to the past history of Transoxania in Oriental works, both printed and in manuscript, or in European histories, biographies, or books of travel ; as extensive a knowledge as can possibly be obtained of all literature bearing on this subject is nowadays the first requisite for an author attempting any work. I have, however, spared the reader the whole long list of books of reference, more especially as they will all be found indicated in their proper places in the text.

As regards the second class of my authorities, new and un- known manuscripts chiefly, relating to the domestic history of Bokhara, they consist unfortunately only of five :—

1. *Kitab-i-Narshakhi* (the Book of Narshakhi) was written by Ebu Bekir Mohammed bin Djafar un Narshakhi (accord- ing to one account in the year 337, according to others in 332), under the title Kitab-i-Akhbar-i-Bokhara (Book of News of. Bokhara), by order of the Samanide Nuh bin Nasr, who reigned in Bokhara under the name of Emir Hamid, 331–343. The

original was written in Arabic, and translated into Persian 190 years afterwards. The existing Persian translation bought by Sir Alexander Burnes in 1832 at Bokhara, now the property of the Royal Asiatic Society of Great Britain and Ireland, deals first with the earliest history of the town and neighbourhood of Bokhara; the author's attention seems to have been more especially bestowed on the investigation of the walls, gates, palaces, and canals, and also on that of the system of taxes and the official administration of Bokhara. The manuscript proceeds with a detailed account of this portion of Transoxania under the Samanides in their prosperity, or rather, strictly speaking, of the town and adjacent parts, for the districts of Miyankal and Sogd are not mentioned.

The second part describes the Arabic occupation of the country, with more details than are to be found anywhere else. The accounts of the first century of the Arabic administration are somewhat confused, but the descriptions of the false prophet Mokanna, and of some other incidents of the period, are all the more interesting. This part is followed by the history of the Samanides, which the author was only enabled to carry down to the commencement of the reign of Emir Hamid, but which his translator has continued to the fall of the dynasty. At the end of the book is a separate treatise on the holy shrines of Bokhara, and the saints and scholars who lie there. As I am informed, a second copy exists in Europe in the possession of the Russian scholar Khanikoff. Unfortunately, both the copies which have been handed down to us are written in a bad, almost illegible handwriting, in the Nes'khi character.

2. *Sheïbani-nameh*, a Tchaghataian heroic poem, by Prince Mehemmed Salih of Khahrezm, which, in a manuscript of 218 pages, rehearses and describes the deeds of

Sherbani Mehemmed Khan, from the time when he first appeared before Samarkand to the date of his march on the
capital of Khorasan, embracing a period of only about eight
years of his life. As all our previous information about Sherbani was derived either from the book of Baber or from Persian annals, both alike inimical to him, this description is
all the more welcome, as the first that is really authentic, for
Prince Mehemmed Salih acted as secretary to the Özbeg hero,
of whom he occasionally speaks in exaggerated terms, but on
the whole he gives us a picture of the ethical, social, and political condition of Transoxania at that time, the value of
which cannot be overestimated, and which I trust as soon as
possible to publish in the original text, with a translation
and notes. The copy at my disposal, which is unique in
Europe, and of which I have never seen another even in Central Asia, belongs to the Imperial Library at Vienna ; Flügel
mentions it in his Catalogue, vol. ii. p. 323, but he seems to
have been unacquainted with Tchaghataian, as otherwise his
notice of it would surely have been less scanty and less defective.

3. *Tarikhi Seïd Rakim*, a collection of chronograms from the
year 700 to 1055 of the Hidjra, brought down to 1013 (1604)
by Seïd Rakim (the name appears apocryphal), and subsequently carried on to 1055 (1645). Though, in fact, nothing
more than a persian chronology of certain events, the historical explanations appended to these quatrains or distiches are
of considerable value, more especially the allusions to scholars
and celebrated sheïkhs of the period of whom we should otherwise have no record. These Tarikh are in chronological order,
but the lives of some personages, such as Timour, Sherbani,
Abdullah Khan, and Abdul Mumin Khan, are given at length
and faithfully described. The manuscript, which is my own

property, occasionally mentions some of the celebrities of Khorasan, but it deals principally with the countries beyond the Oxus, and belongs, therefore, properly to the list of authorities for the special history of Bokhara and Transoxania.

4. *Tarikhi Mekim Khani*, by Mehemmed Yusuf, the munshi (secretary) to Mekim Khan, a son of Subhankuli Khan, who was attended by the author whilst Viceroy of the province of Belkh. The Persian manuscript, bought at Bokhara by Burnes, and now the property of the Asiatic Society of Great Britain, commences with Djenghiz Khan, as the ancestor of the Ashtarkhanides, and goes on from him to Ebulkhair Khan, the progenitor of the Sherbanides. This dynasty has been already tolerably well described, but this manuscript, written in cramped Taalik, gives most important details regarding the extraction of the Ashtarkhanides, and concerning the best known princes of their house, viz., Baki Mehemmed Khan, Imamkuli Khan, Nezr Mehemmed Khan, Abdulaziz Khan, Subhankuli Khan, and finally Mehemmed Mekim Khan, who, however, never actually succeeded to the throne of Bokhara. This manuscript embraces a period of nearly two hundred years, and its style, although not free from the usual Oriental glosses, is a tolerably fluent one.

5. *Dakhme-i-Shahan* (The King's Grave), by Munshi Sadik Mirza, who appears to have been in the service of Emir Maasum. It begins with a song of praise of the last Ashtarkhanides, whom the poet represents as moralising from their graves on the fleeting character of all earthly things, and on the virtues of princes. This is followed by a history in verse of the principal campaigns of Emir Maasum against the Persians and Afghans, unfortunately not of much historical value; and the last part consists of occasional poems celebrating different festivities and the births and circumcisions of the

sons and grandsons of the sovereign. I bought the beauti-
fully-finished Persian manuscript written in Taalik, at Samarkand, and it is now my property.

As the nature of the authorities I have made use of is very
various, so various is the literary value of my work. The
first part contains, with the exception of a few data taken
from Narshakhi's manuscript, little that will be new to Orientalists, though much of it may be so to the general public, as
the manuscript authorities concerning Central Asia have never
before been so largely made use of. The second, however, deals almost entirely with data hitherto little known,
or entirely unknown even to the world of scholars, for they
bring before us a *series of princes and even whole dynasties
regarding whom scarcely anything has as yet been written in
Asia, and not a single word in Europe.* As regards the
execution of the work, I have striven to keep before me clear-
ness of style and uniformity of treatment.[1] Considering
the great difference in the amount of references at my command, it might have been possible for me to go into much
greater detail in some portions of the book; for instance, I
could have followed out much more fully Mirkhond's description of the Seldjukides, the account of Timour's life given by
Sherefeddin, and that of the period of the Timourides in
Abdurrezak's excellent manuscript; but I would not venture
to do this, as from the want of equally full authorities for other

---

[1] With this view I have been careful also to adopt the simplest possible method
in transcribing foreign words. Instead of following one or the other system of
transcribing, I have simply endeavoured to reproduce the foreign words with the
letters (in English) most akin to their proper pronunciation. Thus I have *dj* for
چ, *tch* for چ, *sh* for ش, *s* for س, *z* for ز, and *th* for ث. The apostrophised
vowels always represent the Arabic ع. In general I have probably differed somewhat from other Orientalists by always transcribing the Arabic words as I heard
them from the lips of Persians and Turkestanis.

periods, the symmetry of the book would have been disturbed, and the baldness and dryness of certain of the chapters would have been more painfully apparent by the contrast. For the same reason I have for the present abstained from any detailed account of events in the neighbouring khanates. I am in possession of some data for the history of Khokand and Khiva, and when I have added a little more to the stock at my command, I purpose giving an historical *précis* of these eastern and western parts of Central Asia.

In conclusion, I beg here to express my most grateful thanks to all those who have, in different ways, assisted me in the execution of this work. To Colonel H. Yule, the greatest of authorities on all matters relating to mediæval Asia, I would offer my thanks for the information I have derived from his private letters as well as from his admirable works ; and I have further to thank Baron Ottokar v. Schlechta, Secretary of Legation ; M. A. Barb ; M. E. Birk ; the Royal Asiatic Society of Great Britain ; and Mr. J. Wussin, for their great courtesy in placing materials at my disposition here at Pesth, where the necessary books of reference would have otherwise been unattainable to me.

And now I commit the fruits of many years' toil to a benevolent public. Would that they were less full of imperfections and faults ! But it must always be a difficult task to write the *first* history of any country, and it becomes doubly so, when the country in question has only emerged in the present generation from the thick mist of darkness in which its annals had for centuries been shrouded.

THE AUTHOR.

PESTH : *April* 28, 1872.

CONTENTS.

INTRODUCTION.

GENERAL notions of the geography of Central Asia may be assumed to be as a rule very indefinite and uncertain, and the political significance of the word Transoxania appears equally vague. Taken literally, the name is a translation of the Arabic Mavera-un-nehr (that which lies beyond or across the river), and it might therefore be supposed that Transoxania meant the country lying beyond or on the right shore of the Oxus. But this is not strictly speaking the case, for even in Belkhi's [1] geographical manuscript a portion of the left shore of the upper course is included in the definition of Transoxania; and quite correctly so, as far as the political frontier is concerned, for from the period of the Samanides down to modern times, the districts of Talkan, Tokharistan, and Zem, although all lying partly or entirely on the left bank of the Oxus, have been looked on as integral portions

---

[1] The exact similarity in treatment and identity of dates observable in the descriptions given by the earliest Arabian geographers of certain portions of Islamite Asia, have caused the scientific men of Europe to doubt exceedingly which of the three oldest geographers, Belkhi, Istakhri, or Ibn Haukal, should be set down as the author of this work, undoubtedly the product of one pen. The learned Dutchman, Mr. M. J. de Goeje, has recently discussed the question fully in the *Journal of the German Oriental Society* (vol. xxv. pp. 42-95), and, as the result of his investigations, has led me to assume that Ebn Zaid El Belkhi, who died in 322 (933), was the author of the oldest Arabic geographical manuscript. The copy of this work belonging to the Imperial Library at Vienna, and entitled *Mesalik u Memalik* (Roads and Countries), has been placed at my disposal, and considering the highly interesting character of its contents all the friends of Asiatic literature will rejoice to hear that it appears from the essay above alluded to that M. de Goeje is engaged on bringing out an edition of the original. Istakhri's account of Central Asia or Transoxania (I am speaking here of Mordtmann's translation) is but a meagre extract from the original.

of Bokhara. Our historical researches seem to prove that this arrangement dates from the Samanides, who were themselves originally natives of that part of Khorasan. On obtaining possession of Transoxania they incorporated their own heritage with their new dominions, and thus it remained until the fall of the dynasty. Under the first Ghaznevides, Mahmud and his son Mes'ud, the whole of the left shore of the Oxus formed part of Khorasan, and things remained the same under the Seldjukides, Djenghizides and Timourides, who, as masters of all Iran, were able to restore the old natural frontier of Khorasan without imperilling their own interests. Under the Sheïbanides and Ashtarkhanides, that is, during the space of about three centuries, the whole of the left shore of the Oxus, from Bedak'hshan to Tchihardjui was subject to Bokhara, and remained so, (with few interruptions) to the house of Manghit, until quite recent times, when Transoxania appeared about to fall to pieces, and the ruler of Kabul was thus enabled to seize for himself all the doubtful possessions of Bokhara. We gather, therefore, from all this that the political frontier of Transoxania in the south must be fixed on a line extending along the cis-oxanian territory, in latitude 71° to longitude 35°, from Bedak'hshan to the left bank of the Murghab ; a tract of country divided in ancient times into the following provinces: 1. Khatlan and Wakhsh ;[1] 2. Udjan, perhaps more correctly Wadjan ; 3. Tokharistan, with the capital of Belkh ; Kunduz and Khulm are now the principal places there ; 4. Zem, comprising the modern Ḳerki, Andkhoï and Meïmene ; and finally, 5. Amul, later Amuye, the modern Tchihardjui, which borders on the east and south on the desert of Khahrezm.[2]

---

[1] The Greek Ὦκος seems derived from Wakhsh or Uakhsh, the name of a province and a tributary of the Oxus. But, according to another view entertained by some, the name of this river, which was known to the Arabs by the name of Djihun, is derived from the Turkish Œgüs or Œküs = river. The natives to this day call it Derya or Amu, both which words simply mean *the river*.

[2] I spell this word *Khahrezm* and not Khowarezm or Chowarezm as Mordtmann and other Orientalists have it, for the following reasons : 1. I have always

It is no less difficult to fix precisely the northern frontier of Transoxania. In ancient times, the country of Osrushna lay here, which, according to Belkhi, bordered eastwards on Fergana, southwards on Kesh, northwards on Djadj, and westwards, or rather south-westwards, on Sogd. Osrushna was the name of that mountainous part of the present khanate of Bokhara commencing east of Samarkand and running up, under different designations,[1] to the Thien-Shan. The principal places in it were Bu Mekhet, the capital (now unknown), Sabad od Savat (now Sarvad, far east in the mountains), Dizek (now Djizzak), and Zamin, bordering on the ancient Fergana, and now on the confines of the khanate of Khokand. In the north, beyond Osrushna, lay the country of Djadj, in the valley of the Yaxartes, with many towns, amongst which Khodjend, Binaket, Otrar, Siganak, Sirem, Sarban and Taraz, can be identified at the present day. I have never heard any mention made of the Great Wall, which Belkhi describes as having been built, by Abdullah bin Hamid, between the mountains and the Yaxartes, probably as a protection against the invasions of the nomads. Although this most ancient of all geographical works includes these two countries under the head of Transoxania, the history of their subjection to the capital on the Zerefshan is not more clearly made out than that of the other integral portions of the country in the

---

heard the word pronounced in this way in Iran and in Khahrezm itself, and I can no more believe that the Khahrezmians can be systematically wrong in pronouncing the name of their own country than I could conceive that Frenchmen or Englishmen would pronounce German names more correctly than Germans themselves. 2. There are several words in Persian with a similar orthography, which are invariably pronounced with an a or oa. Such, for instance, are خواه khah = willing; خواهر khaher = sister; خوار khar = miserable, contemptible, etc. 3. Yakut has shown by a line in his *Mudjem ul Buldan*, vol. ii. p. 480, that the first syllable of Khahrezm should be written with a *fatha*, consequently with an a. As regards the meaning of the word, I adhere to the opinion I have already expressed that Khahrezm signifies *ready to fight, warlike*.

[1] The best known are Botm (the ancient Asfera), Ak Tau, Fan and Altaba (in the south), then Tchunkartag, Sultan Hazrettag and Suzenghiran.

south. Osrushna always belonged to Bokhara, but Djadj
very frequently changed hands. In the pre-Islamite period
these northern shores of the Yaxartes formed an independent
state governed by Turks, which, however, was annexed to
Bokhara during the Arabic rule there, in the time of the
Samanides. It asserted its independence again under the
Seldjukides, and the Turkish prince Kadr Khan rose to
considerable power. From the date of the Mongolian invasion Djadj became a bone of contention between Khahrezmians in the west and Uigurs in the east; and after the
death of Djenghiz, Kadr and his successors waged a long
fratricidal war with the Tchaghataides about this very territory.
Even Timour himself only effected the incorporation of this
part of Transoxania at the price of bloody battles with both
his south-eastern and north-western neighbours—battles
which were renewed oftener and more fiercely after his death;
and although the mighty princes of the dynasties of the
Sheïbanides and Ashtarkhanides remained occasionally for a
time in undisputed possession of all that portion of Turkestan
known as Transoxania, two decades were scarcely ever
suffered to elapse without the Mongolian, Kalmuck and the
Kirghiz princes of the neighbourhood interfering here by force
of arms. In fact, it is only since the middle of the last
century (of the Christian era) down to the present day that
the valley of the Yaxartes, with its capital Tashkend, has
really, with only passing interruptions, remained peaceably
subject to Fergana or the modern khanate of Khokand.

It follows from all this that it is almost impossible in
dealing geographically with Transoxania to assign definitely
an accurate frontier. We can and will therefore comprehend
in our definition of Transoxania solely Bokhara, or the khanate
of Bokhara; for, although it has only been known by the latter
name since the time of Sheïbani and of the Özbegs, the shores
of the Zerefshan and the tract of country stretching southwards
to the Oxus and northwards to the desert of Kizil Kum, represent the only parts of the territory which have remained

uninterruptedly portions of the original undivided state of Transoxania from the earliest historical times. The following districts have been celebrated from the very commencement of its history :—

Bokhara, the capital from the time of the Samanides, and at the date of the very earliest geographical reports concerning Transoxania, is said, during its prosperity, to have been the largest city of the Islamite world. The inner town, surrounded by a wall with seven gates, was not particularly remarkable, but the suburbs, watered by innumerable canals, and enriched with buildings whose splendour vied with the natural beauties of the scenery, were all the more magnificent. The earliest Arab travellers are loud in their praises of the extensive gardens, studded with small but luxuriant fruit trees, and the Alui-Bokhara (Bokhariot plums), celebrated a thousand years ago, still retain their reputation as the most delicate of their kind in Asia. Bokhara was not, however, merely a luxurious city, distinguished by great natural advantages, it was also the principal emporium for the trade between China and Western Asia, in addition to the vast warehouses for silks, brocades, and cotton stuffs, for the finest carpets, and all kinds of gold and silversmiths' work; it boasted of a great money-market, being in fact the Exchange of all the population of Eastern and Western Asia ; and there is a proverb current to this day: 'As wide awake as a broker of Bokhara.' The other principal towns were : *Tavaïs*, seven *fersakhs* north-east of Bokhara, on the road to Samarkand ; previous to the Arab invasion it had been called Kut (in Turkish, fortunate, or good-fortune). It was a strongly-fortified place, and celebrated for its yearly fairs, lasting ten days and often visited by upwards of 10,000 people. In the south, *Beïkend*, the second great trading city of Bokhara, whose inhabitants traded with China in the east and with the sea-coast in the west; this town lay on the high road to Amul and Merv, and enjoyed the reputation of great wealth. In the time of the Seldjukides, Arslan Khan did much for the road leading thither through the desert from Tarab, by erecting various public buldings, and constructing canals; but the Arabs had given Berkend a death-blow, and, although it revived for a short time, its further decay could not be long delayed, and at the present day the traces of its ruins are barely recognisable. In the north, *Zendine*, now Zindani, where cotton was cultivated, and the cotton stuffs of the town were exported to all parts of Western Asia; and Vardanzi, Rametin and Nur, all now insignificant places. The second district was called *Miyankal*, —the *middle country*, lying between Bokhara and Samarkand. It received this designation in the time of the Samanides, and has retained it to the present day. The principal town was, and is, *Kermineh*, lying in a fertile neighbourhood, celebrated at all periods of Islamite history, and said to have been the birth-place of several eminent poets, whose names have, however, not been preserved to us. *Nur*, north of Kermineh (the modern Nurata) was at all times a frequented place of pilgrimage, and is still visited by devotees. East of Kermineh lay Ferakhsha, the place mentioned by Narshakhi, celebrated for its fairs; and north-east, on the borders of the desert, lay the strong city of Sertak, with her citadel perched on a height whence the eye rested on all sides on luxuriant gardens, with houses and palaces peeping out between the foliage. North-west, about the same spot now occupied by Gidjdovan, lay the considerable town of Djend, the frontier fortress towards Khahrezm, a country commanding the whole of the western steppe, and itself containing an industrious agricultural and pastoral population; eastward of Djend lay the towns of Ashnas, Özkend[1] and Signak. *Sogd* was the third province, and comprised the mountainous part of Transoxania (which may be described as the extreme western spurs of the Thien-Shan), with no definite frontier on the east, but bordering westward on Miyankal, southwards on

---

[1] Not to be confounded with the Özkend lying in the east of Fergana.

Kesh, and northwards on Osrushna. The capital was Samarkand, undoubtedly the Maracanda of the Greeks, which they specify as the capital of Sogdia. This city has, throughout the history of Transoxania, been the rival of Bokhara. Before the time of the Samanides, Samarkand was the largest city beyond the Oxus, and only began to decline from its former importance when Ismail chose Bokhara for his own residence. Under the Khahrezmians it is said to have raised itself again, and become much larger than its rival, and under Timour to have reached the culminating point of its prosperity.

. With the fall of the Timourides its decay commenced ; Bokhara became from this time the only official capital, and the princes of the house of the Sheïbanides, the Ashtarkhanides and the Manghits, only visited Samarkand as a summer excursion for the sake of its natural beauties. According to the oldest geographical works, the beauty of this town also lay in its suburbs, for within the fortress, which was surrounded with a strong wall, the houses were mostly built of wood and clay, and so crowded together that Istakhri maintains the atmosphere would have been positively unhealthy, but for the great quantity of *willow trees*.[1] Samarkand, lying much higher than Bokhara, has always been distinguished for a bracing, healthy climate, but it owes its reputation, as the proverbial Paradise of Islam, to the wealth of water brought from the neighbouring mountains by numerous canals and streams into the plain. According to Belkhi, all this water comes from the river Sogd,[2] which rises in the hills above Djighanian. A reservoir existed not far from the sources of the river, whence the water was conveyed to Vargas (also called Bargas or Burgas) to the weir, whence it flowed in canals eastward and westward. The principal reservoir was like a small lake, the margin studded with

---

[1] So translated by Mordtmann, p. 131.

[2] In the Vienna manuscript of *Mesalik u Memalik*, p. 143, Sogd is erroneously spelt Sind.

villages; and the principal canals, such as those of Barmish
and Dekish, fertilised a tract of country to a distance of six
days' journey.   Samarkand lay a little on one side of the
great high-road to India; and as the caravans invariably
passed either through Belkh, Karshi and Bokhara, or else
by Nishabur, Amul and Berkend, it never became a centre of
inland commerce, and was always known more as a city of
pleasure.   Its inhabitants are described as handsome, cleanly,
modest and hospitable people, and Ibn Batutah,[1] though
enchanted with the saintly Bokhara, places Samarkand
higher as regards natural virtues; and, strangely enough, this
estimate is justified by modern experience, for I myself met
with far more kindliness and warm-heartedness at Samarkand
than at Bokhara.   The Mongolians stripped Samarkand of
the splendour it had enjoyed in the pre-Islamite period and
in the time of the Samanides, for Ibn Batutah saw nothing
but ruins; the prosperity which returned to it under the
Timourides, chiefly through the instrumentality of Ulug Mirza,
and of which Baber has left us a glowing description in his
Memoirs, was in its turn destroyed by the barbarous Özbeg
warriors of the Sheïbanides.   There were a few other remarkable places in this district, such as Debus, later converted into the fortress of Debusie, lying westward on the
road to Bokhara; further east, Vargas, Sarvas, Famury, and
the flourishing town of Rebud, where Akhshid, a former
prince of Samarkand, had built some villas; and, finally, in the
south the town and district of Sarvan, lying amongst the
hills, with a rather severe climate, but inhabited by a very
hardy and healthy race.   Zerdeghird, the well-known abode
of the Christians in the time of the Samanides, lay about ten
fersakhs beyond this.

The fourth district was *Kesh*, now Shehri Sebz. Up to
the time of the Samanides it was chiefly inhabited by Arabs
of the tribe of Bekr bin Vail.   The town was fortified,

---

[1] *Voyages d'Ibn Batoutah*, par C. Defrémery et le Dr. B. R. Sanguinetti, Paris,
1855, p. 52.

and had four gates :—1. Dervaze Ahenin (the Iron Gate) ; 2. Dervaze Abdullah ; 3. D. Kassaban (Butcher's Gate) ; 4. D. Sharistan (Town Gate). The crop of fruit at Kesh was greater than in any other part of Transoxania ; this is no longer the case, and was probably then due to the excellent system of irrigation. Two rivers, the Rud-i-Kassaban and the Rud-i-Khushk, flowed through here to the plain of Nakh'sheb. Kesh was full of villages, such as Werd, Bala Bedrin, Rasum, Sam, with the hills of the same name, celebrated as the last refuge of Mokanna, Ozghan, Djarudan, etc., etc.

The fifth district was *Nakh'sheb*, always a principal station on the road between Belkh and Bokhara, but comparatively less cultivated than the parts of Transoxania we have just enumerated, in consequence of the streams which flowed down from Kesh becoming dried up in the sand of this part of the country in summer, so that the inhabitants were entirely dependent on wells even for water to drink. Nakh'-sheb received the Mongolian name of Karshi = Palace, from the Tchaghataian Prince Kebek, who built a palace there in the year 708 (1318), after which the whole town was after-wards called. Berke and Keshie [1] were also important places. We should also notice the districts lying near the sources of the Oxus, such as Wakhsh, Khatlan, Djighanian (called by Istakhri, Sighanian) and Kulab, where Hissar-i-Shaduman afterwards became celebrated in the north-west; but, un-fortunately, our information concerning the whole of that mountainous region is so scanty and confused, that even in modern times we know but little of its geography. The only fact which can be affirmed with certainty is, that Ter-

---

[1] It is remarkable that the Mongolians have left more traces of their ' rule ' beyond Transoxania proper, that is on the left bank of the Oxus, than in Trans-oxania itself. Judging by their names, the following list of places must all have been originally Mongolian colonies :—Andkhoï, formerly Andakhod (in Mongolian Anda-kud = united fortunes), also Tchitchektu and Almar (the modern Meïmene). They have even left a living record of themselves in the persons of the Mongolians inhabiting the hills south-east of Herat.

med, also called Termez, was the oldest ferry across the
Oxus to India. In the time of the Samanides it seems to
have been a flourishing place with a 'Friday mosque' (which
of itself indicates a large population), and a large bazaar
paved with tiles. Termed declined in importance under the
Mongolians, and in latter times the ferry traffic across into
Afghanistan was partially diverted to Kilif and Khodja Salu.

As regards the present political subdivisions of Transoxania, which was first recognised as the 'Khanate of Bokhara'
under the Timourides, there have been perpetual changes ever
since the time of the Özbegs, and nothing, save the general
outline of the country, has remained as it was. At present,
there are the following provinces, which are again sub-divided
into 'tömens' or districts :—1. Bokhara, the town and its
suburbs, such as Bahaeddin, Shehri Islam, Miten and Miri
Kulel. 2. Bokhara, the district, with the towns of Vardanzi,
Vafkend, Rametin, Vanghazi and Khairabad. 3. Miyankal, with its capital, Kermineh and the towns of Zia-eddin,
Mir Khatirdja, Nur Ata, and Yenghi Kurghan. 4. Kette
Kurghan, with the towns of Karasu, Pendj-shembe and
Tshelek. 5. Samarkand, with Pendj-Kend, Karatepe, Soyüd
and Umkend. 6. Hissar, with Shirabad. 7. Shehri Sebz,
with the fortresses of Kitab, Tchiraktchi, and Yekebagh.
8. Karshi, with Feïzabad. 9. Lebab, with its capital Kerkhi.
10. Tchihardjui. 11. Karaköl, with Betik and Eltchik.
To these were added until lately, the districts of Djizzak, Zamin and Oratepe, which have, however, since the last Russian
conquests been lost to Bokhara. Judging from the present
features of modern Bokhara, one would be inclined to think
the reports of the ancient geographers grossly exaggerated, if
not actually pure inventions, for everything beyond the Oxus
seems now sunk into decay ; everything on the sites of former
splendour expresses only poverty and insignificance. Bokhara
itself, the capital, the seat of government, and of all learning,
and the centre of considerable trade and manufactures, is
one of the dirtiest and most unhealthy places in all Asia,

numbering at the outside 30,000 inhabitants, of which the larger proportion still belong to the Iranian race, which has maintained so far the commercial and industrial reputation of the city. The only traces of former splendour are to be found in the foundations of a few mosques and remains of the Palace, dating from the pre-Islamite period. Karshi is the second city of the khanate, both for trade and manufactures, and also for the number of its inhabitants. Next to Karshi, Samarkand, which is rich in ruins, used to be pointed out especially as the resting-place of many hundred saints. It is celebrated for fruit, for leather and cotton manufactories, for cream, and for skilfully-enamelled *wooden* saddles. According to Fedjenko's estimate, it contains 30,000 inhabitants, and 86 mosques, 23 colleges, 1,846 shops, and 27 caravanserais. But Samarkand and Kette Kurghan, where the best boots in the khanate are manufactured, have both fallen under foreign dominion, so that Kermineh must now be reckoned the third in rank of the cities of Bokhara. A few others have a certain reputation, for example, Hissar for its excellent cutlery—particularly knives and sword-blades; Tchihardjui for its horse-fairs, Karaköl for its extensive market for Persian slaves. And, finally, a few little villages in the north where those peculiarly strong and active donkies are to be found, with whom the fleetest of the long-eared Egyptian asses would compete in vain.

As regards its physical conformation, Transoxania, or the northern half of the tract of country vaguely known as 'Central Asia,' is chiefly a plain country extending from those eastern chain of hills, which, as the extreme spurs of the Thien-Shan, reach nearly to Samarkand, and sink with a rapid declension down to the shores of the Caspian Sea. With the exception of a few table-lands, and some bits of hard clay, or loam—called by the inhabitants *Takir*=dry, barren country—the soil consists chiefly of black or yellow sand, and the only land really fit for cultivation is that lying

on the slopes of the hills or on the banks of rivers and canals.
As is the case throughout Asia, Nature left to herself pro-
duces scarcely anything, and ten years of warlike disturbance
are sufficient to turn the most fertile neighbourhood into a
desert. Even the most persevering industry often proves a
failure, especially where there is a strip of sand all the
deeper for being narrow. These strips of sandy soil intersect
all the cultivated districts, and are to be found in the immediate neighbourhood of the cities of Bokhara and Samarkand ;
on the road between these two places, the traveller passes
through several miles of a sandy waste—the desert of Melik,
lying in the heart of a cultivated district ; there is a tradition
that 300 years ago a salt lake existed here. In spite of this,
the fertility of Bòkhara and of the two other khanates has
passed into a proverb, for their products are both excellent
and various. Bokhara has grain, fruit, silk, cotton and dyes,
all unrivalled of their kind. The same may be said of its
cattle, for besides their horses, which are celebrated throughout Asia, their camels surpass all the other sorts of this most
useful domestic animal, in the south and west of Asia; and
their mutton, finally, is equal to any in the world. The hilly
country east and south of Samarkand is rich in minerals,
which have, however, hitherto been neglected and unknown.
Even Belkhi, however, mentions iron, ammoniac quick-
silver, tin, slate, gold, naphtha, pitch, vitriol, and a stone used
for fuel, i.e., coal, which has lately been re-discovered by the
Russians in the same neighbourhood.

The cause of the fertility of this comparatively waste
country of Bokhara is, no doubt, in the first place the 'blessed'
river, formerly called Sogd, afterwards Kohik, and now
Zerefshan, 'scatterer of gold.' The German savant Dr. Radloff,
and Russian traveller Fedjenko, have lately given us some
information regarding the sources of this river. According to
the latter, the river *Fan*, so called from the hills in which it
springs, is the principal of the four streams which rise a
a height of 7,000 feet above the level of the sea, and flow

down into the plain under the name of Zerefshan. The
principal stream divides north-east of Samarkand, and
flows in different arms westward and south-westward towards
the steppe country. The largest arm flows north-west of
Samarkand by Pendj-shembe and Khatirdja to the lake of
Karaköl, whilst a smaller arm of the same loses itself
in a lake on the borders of the desert of Khalata, between
Khodja Oban and the village of Khakemir. The second
of the principal arms of the river flows south-westward
from Samarkand, by Kette Kurghan and Bokhara, towards
the desert ; and, if we take into consideration that it feeds a
large number of both natural and artificial canals in its comparatively short course, the volume of water in this river is
amazing. The only other river of any importance besides
the Zerefshan is the small rivulet of Shehri Sebz. It is only
occasionally full as far as Karshi, but with very little care
might be made of inestimable use to the whole neighbourhood. Experience shows that irrigation carried on for
several years creates an alluvial soil, which is the whole secret
of fertility. This is still more the case with the waters of the
Oxus ; but Bokhara gains comparatively nothing by this
river, for the right bank from Termez towards Tchihardjui is,
almost uninhabited, and indeed could not be inhabited, as
the banks rise almost invariably considerably above the
level of the river, and the irrigation of the country would
consequently be difficult, if not impossible. The climate,
which can scarcely be called mild but yet is not severe,
is favourable for production. The different variations
of temperature may be roughly catalogued as follows :—
Up to the point where the undulations of the eastern
hills cease, the climate is moderate ; in the lowlands, more
especially in the neighbourhood of the steppes, i.e., in
Bokhara, Kerki and Karaköl, the extremes of heat and cold
are well nigh insupportable ; but with the exception of the
first-named city, the atmosphere is nowhere unhealthy, and
the diseases which prevail are rather to be traced to un-

wholesome habits and deficient clothing than to the influence of climate.

The remarks just made concerning the productive powers of the khanate of Bokhara, apply equally to the neighbouring countries, both in the east and west, and this may assist in explaining the astonishing rapidity with which these countries recover from the ravages of war. Belkhi notices this fact, remarking that a beaten army recovers itself nowhere so quickly as in Transoxania. In connection with this remark, he places the number of cities in that country at 300,000, which is, of course, a gross exaggeration, and a monstrous improbability, but still there is not the least doubt that the number of the inhabitants of Transoxania, and especially of Bokhara, was very much larger in ancient times than it is now. In the Arab conquest each city had *several tribes* quartered on it, and yet the inhabitants were not homeless. The suburbs of the capital are said to have been so densely populated in the time of the Samanides, that a man might ride for miles either southwards or northwards between rows of houses, and the 360 large mosques, the tradition of which still survives among the Bokhariots, appear really to have existed. Bokhara suffered most in the Mongolian invasion, and yet within a few years she could boast again of 16,000 *male* *inhabitants*,[1] and 1,000 students were enrolled in her colleges within a quarter of a century of the destruction of the city. Bokhara regained all her former prosperity for a short time under the Ashtarkhanides, especially under Imamkuli Khan, but after the fall of that dynasty the number of the inhabitants dwindled gradually away, until it amounts in modern times barely to 35,000 souls. What is here said of the capital applies equally to the whole country. The population of Transoxania must formerly have been five or six

---

[1] Vassaf, from whom this note is taken, only speaks of inhabitants generally. We must not forget that Eastern statistics of this kind refer solely to men capable of bearing arms ; women and children (*Ehli ayal*) are never taken into consideration.

times as large as it is now; for although the large armies which, from the time of the foundation of the khalifate, streamed almost uninterruptedly, either as mercenaries or as independent conquerors, forth into Western Asia and onwards towards the Nile, were principally drawn from the neighbouring steppes, yet the shores of the Oxus and the Yaxartes must have furnished contingents such as could only have been contributed by a populous country. The great majority of the inhabitants of Transoxania were Iranians, and Persian was the ordinary language of Bokhara, Fergana and Khahrezm under the Arab, Samanide, Seldjukide and Khahrezmian Princes, till long after the Mongolian invasion; later, as we shall see, Turkish gained the upper hand. The character of the Transoxanians has also undergone great changes. The first Arabian geographers are never tired of praising the nobility of mind, the frankness, generosity and hospitality of the natives. At present the latter is the only one of these virtues which still flourishes in the country, but not even that in the towns; of the others no trace is to be found anywhere. Transoxania was exposed for centuries to the onward roll of the stream of the neighbouring Turanian races, and the disruption of both her political and social condition was in consequence fearful. The tyranny of conquest here, as elsewhere, has not only devastated flourishing plains, but has also uprooted all the finer qualities of the human mind. Central Asia is, at the present day, the foul ditch in which flourish together all the rank vices which are to be found scattered singly throughout the Mohammedan countries of Western Asia.

HISTORY

OF

BOKHARA.

I.

WHILE the most important lands of Asia have veiled the beginning of their history in the grey mist of myths and fables, Bokhara attaches to the beginning of her existence as a state a legend whose probability can be easily explained by the physical peculiarities of its soil. It is as follows :—

'Bokhara was in old time a hollow, which was covered with swamps and marshes,[1] with woods and reeds. The rivers and brooks were swollen by the snow of the eastern mountain-range in the neighbourhood of the present Samarkand, and inundated every year the low-lying country, which, unsuitable for agriculture, was all the more profitable for hunters and fishers.

'Even from the distant Turkestan came sportsmen, who gradually established themselves here, and thus gave rise to

[1] These lakes and marshes extended themselves in a south-westerly direction beyond the old Barkenti Ferrakh and the modern Karaköl. They appear to have extended twenty fersakhs in length, and abounded in water-fowl and fish above all other parts of Khorasan. This was even in the time of Djenghiz a favourite spot for killing swans, and his sons Tchagatai and Oktai sent fifty camel-loads of water-fowl, the booty of one season, as a present to their father. In later times, Timur also spent the autumn in the pursuit of swans. The lake of Karaköl even now abounds in fish.

B

the villages Tarkamrud, Bervane, Asvane, and Nur.[1] These chose them a prince from among themselves, Aberzi by name, who dwelt in Berkend, i.e. Princetown, for Bokhara, the present residence of the sovereign, did not then exist. This Aberzi, however, became more and more tyrannical as his power increased, so that the wealthier classes fled from his violence into the northern part of the Turkish country, where they built the city of Djemuket, or Djemkent, which in the speech of that day signified the "fair and good city."[2] The poorer classes, feeling their own inability to resist him, invoked the aid of a neighbouring Turkish prince, by name Karadjurin, who sent the oppressed an army under the command of his son, Shirkishver. Aberzi was taken prisoner, put into a sack full of spikes, and rolled about on the ground until he died.

'After the tyrant had been thus got rid of, Shirkishver recalled the exiled rich, to whom was given the privilege of forming a class of nobles under the name of Khudat, while the poor who had remained behind were characterised as subjects. Shirkishver is said to have ruled about thirty years, and was succeeded by a prince of the name of Sekedjket (?), to whom is attributed the building of the cities Rametin and Ferakhsha. When he afterwards brought home as his bride the daughter of the Emperor of China, the idols which she brought with her as her portion were deposited in the first-named city.'

The historical source[3] from which we have taken this extract further informs us that the ruler of Bokhara, whose government was contemporary with the beginning of the Moham-

---

[1] Owing to the illegibility of the manuscript, the correctness of these, as of many other proper names in Narshakhi, can hardly be guaranteed.

[2] Djemkent is even now the name of an unimportant place on the Lower Yaxartes. In another passage of Narshakhi this word is given as the name of Bokhara. The learned Fr. Spiegel, in a private letter, most obligingly suggested that this word is identical with the Huzvaresh Djem kent = 'made by Djem,' observing at the same time, that according to Abulfeda Djem kot, which has passed into Sanscrit under the form Yama kota, was considered as the eastern end of the habitable world.

[3] Narshakhi.

medan era, was called Bendun, who made himself a name by rebuilding the castle founded by Efrasiab, or, according to others, by Siaush.[1] He had his name engraved on an iron tablet which was fastened above the castle gate, a monument which was still existing in the time of our authority, that is, 500 years later, when both it and the castle went to ruin. The legend relates, that when Bendun was building the castle it several times fell down without apparent cause. The counsel of the wise men was enquired of, who answered that they should raise seven stone columns in imitation of the seven stars. After that the castle stood firm. No sovereign was ever overcome nor died therein.

Bendun left behind him a son, by name Tugshade, who was a minor. The reins of government consequently passed into the hands of his wife, whom our authority names Khatun.[2] The period of her government, during which time the Arabs appeared in the land, is said to have lasted over fifty years. The lofty wisdom of this lady and the respect that was paid to her are especially celebrated. Every day after sunrise she left her castle on horseback, came to the gate of the Righistan, then called the place of the sellers of provender, where she seated herself upon a throne, and, surrounded by the officers of her house and the great men of the land, administered justice. Two hundred youths, with golden girdles and swords, formed her guard daily during the audience. These were relieved on the following day by others, and thus each tribe came four times a year on duty.[3] With this lady the actual sovereignty of the earlier dynasty in Bokhara came to an

---

[1] The legend relates that when Siaush, the son of Keïkaus, fled from Iran over the Oxus and came to Bokhara, Efrasiab honoured him greatly, and gave him his daughter to wife. Siaush wished to leave a memorial behind him, and built Bokhara. According to others, Efrasiab built it himself.

[2] Khatun, which most lexicographers consider to be Persian, is in my opinion a Turkish word, and derived from the root *kat*, which contains the idea of mixture, amalgamation.

[3] The principality of Bokhara must consequently have contained ninety tribes, perhaps more correctly, families of distinction.

end. Its later members received from the Mohammedan conquerors the title, but not the power, of a prince.

Tugshade, who appears to have maintained himself for thirty
years in tolerable independence, at the price of conversion to
Islam, was engaged in war with the Turks, and especially with
a certain Vervan or Derdan. In all probability he engaged in
this war in the interest of the Arabs, for when he departed
this life his son Kuterbe, so named in honour of the Arab
conqueror, was confirmed in the dignity of his father. Kuterbe, whose nominal sovereignty coincided with the rule of
Ebu Muslim, in Khorasan, did not show the fidelity of his
father either towards the Arabs or towards their religion, and
as he only ostensibly belonged to Islam, while in secret he
acknowledged the old faith of Parseeism, he was executed as
an apostate, by command of Ebu Muslim, in the year 166 (782),
and his son Nenat, or Binyat, was set up in his place. The
latter was, at first, of course when his establishment was in
question, a good Mohammedan, but he afterwards inclined all
the more conspicuously to the old faith, and even became a
zealous disciple of the false prophet Mokanna, of whom more
hereafter. When this came to the knowledge of the Khalif
Mehdi, he ordered a band of horsemen to fall upon him in his
house at Ferakhsha and cut him to pieces. After this event
we find scarcely any further notice of the old reigning family
of Bokhara. The last titular prince of this house, whose name
was Ebu Ishak,[1] is only known from his sale of his fief to
Ismail the Samanide for a yearly allowance of twenty thousand
direms. He died 301 (914), and his sons passed their time in
miserable poverty.[2]

---

[1] He is said to have been a grandson of Ninat, or Binjat.

[2] Ahmed bin Leith, to whom the shadow of authority enjoyed by this scion of
the old dynasty of Bokhara was a thorn in the side, asked Ismail why he endured
him any longer. As the great Samanide declared the conduct suggested to him
as unjust, Ebu Ishak himself appeared before them. 'Baba,' asked Ismail,
'how much corn do thy estates bring thee in yearly?' 'It is with great trouble,'
answered Ebu Ishak, 'that I raise twenty thousand direms a year.' With that
Ismail promised him the sum named as a pension, which the other gladly
accepted.

To these meagre, but by no means uninteresting, historical data we would add the observations which, in conjunction with the dim light afforded us from other quarters, help us to some degree of knowledge respecting the Præ-Islamite period of Transoxania. That the lands on the other side of the Oxus were already in the period of grey antiquity the home of a people of pure Iranian descent, is proved to us in the first place by the oldest monument of the Iranian people, i.e. the Vendidad.

The first chapter, relating to the Creation, which has been so often commented upon by the learned men of modern times, treats of sixteen localities called into being by the creative power of Ormuzd. We find there, under 2, Gau together with Sughda, i.e. the Sogd or Sogdia of modern times; 3, Muru, i.e. the older Meru or Merv; 4, Bakhdi, i.e. Bactria; 5,. Nisayu, i.e. Nisa, or perhaps more correctly, Nesa;[1] 6, Haroyu, i.e. Heri or Herat; 9, Verkhana, i.e. Hyrkana;[2] and 16, the eastern Ragha, which is held to be the Yaxartes.[3]

Although the discussion and identification of this important list of names gives room to much speculation, so much is certain, that the earliest traces of Iranian culture are not to be sought in the south and west of modern Iran, where monuments and cuneiform inscriptions attract the attention of the

---

[1] Spiegel (*Eranische Alterthumskunde*, p. 194) is of opinion that this place is no longer to be discovered, and as it is stated to have been situated between Muru and Bakhdi, it is to be looked for near Andkhui Shiborgan and Meïmene.

[2] In identifying Verkhana with Hyrkana, I follow the statements of recognised authorities, although I should be disposed to discover under the name Verkhana, Fergana, were it only for the reason that I consider the word Hyrkana as of later, i.e. Turkish origin. Hyrkana is the Greek corruption of the word Körken or Görghen, the name of a river which rises in the Kurdish mountains, traverses this region, and falls into the Caspian Sea. The word Görghen is to be recognised in the Djordjan (both province and city) of the Arabs, whose ruins the Turkomans even now designate as Görghen; further, in the name of the wilderness Görghen Tcbölü, and in the appellation of the land on the northern border of this wilderness Görghendj, as Khahrezm, the modern Khiva, is called in the oldest geographical manuscript.

[3] Khanikoff (*Mémoire sur l'Ethnographie de la Perse*, p. 37) names this place under '16° l'est de Ragha (d'après Spiegel);' while Spiegel himself (*Eranische Alterthümer*, p. 195) puts this place under No. 12, and identifies it not with the Yaxartes, but with Rhages in Media.

enquirer, but in the east and north-east. The Greeks had
heard of civilised life and even of a great empire in Central
Asia long before the expedition of Alexander, probably at
the court of the Achæmenids.[1] It was in Bactria that
Zoroaster appeared with his new religion after his own
country, the province of Atropatene, the modern Azerbaidjan,
had refused him a hearing. From this land of the thousand
cities, as Justin names it, the worship of fire was spread over
Sogdia and Khahrezm ; and from the celebrated temple in
Nubehar, in which, according to Maçoudi, served the family of
the Barmekides before their migration to Bagdad, the light of
the new doctrine was carried into the ancient Persia and Media.
Thus we find the cradle of the historical romance of ancient
Iran—whose elaboration was attempted by Hamza of Isfahan
and the poet Dakiki, and which later was completed by the
master-hand of Firdusi—not in the west and south, but in
the eastern districts of modern Persia.

To be sure, the historical value of the wars against Turan
and its most powerful prince, Efrasiab, is but small, but ethnography finds important evidence in the descriptions given by
the ' king's book ' of the language, the manners, and the external appearance of the ancient foes of Iran, a picture from
which the early existences of Iranian elements may be safely
concluded. The high antiquity of the civilisation in these
parts is asserted in a no less convincing manner by the Arabic
author Ebu Rihan el Biruni, a native of Central Asia, and the
only critical investigator of the antiquities of Central Asia.
Among other things, he tells us that the solar calendar of
Khahrezm was more perfect than that of the Greeks and
Arabs ; he gives us an insight into the old dialect of Sogdia
and Khahrezm, by communicating the names of the twelve
months, the thirty days of each month, and the signs of the
Zodiac—a nomenclature for the most part Zend and of a
purer form than those preserved by the Parsees. He speaks

[1] Sir Henry Rawlinson, in an anonymous article in the *Quarterly Review*,
1868, p. 488.

further of Khahrezmian inscriptions which the first Arab conquerors of the land are said to have carefully perused.[1]

These were in all probability composed in Zend, a language which might well have maintained itself longer on the banks of the Oxus than in Iran, although even in the first-named district the ancient language and alphabet had already fallen into oblivion in the second century of the Hidjra. We hear of two such enigmatical, illegible inscriptions, which had come down from Præ-Islamite times, and which may be supposed to have been written in Zend or Bactrian Pali. One of them was found on an iron-plated gate of Samarkand, and as the gate was destroyed by a conflagration the inscription also perished. The second was, as Narshakhi relates, placed above the entrance of the old royal palace at Righistan in Bokhara, and probably contained more than the mere name of the founder as that author hints. But apart from these conjectures, the Persian dialect of modern Central Asia contains, both in its words and forms, more traces of the old Persian language, before it was disfigured by Semitic and Turanian elements, than all the other dialects of the language put together. And this, too, although the first has for centuries been in the closest contact with an overwhelming Turanian majority, while the latter are only in the extreme south in occasional contact with their Semitic neighbours.[2]

The physical characteristics of the Eastern and Western Iranians stand, when compared together, in similar relations to each other. In the physiognomies of the Tadjiks, Galtchas, Vakhanis, Djemshidis, and Parsevans, which now make up the east Iranian population, more traces of the Iranian race are to be found than even on the bas-reliefs which date from the

---

[1] Sir Henry Rawlinson in *Quarterly Review*, 1868, p. 491.

[2] The Persian dialect of Central Asia as spoken by the Tadjiks has hitherto failed to attract the attention of Iranian philologists, which in consequence of the Russian occupation it doubtless soon will do. This dialect has many peculiarities, both in grammatical forms and in words, which remind us of the language of Firdusi, and it is really remarkable that the pronoun and verb appear to be less influenced by the Turkish language than is the Persian or modern Iran.

period of the Sasanides.[1] The theory of the learned ethno-
grapher Khanikoff, that the scene of the earliest activity of
the Iranian people lay in the fertile valleys between the Hindu
Kush and the mountain-chain of Pughman and Kuhi Baba,
should be accepted, if we extend this supposed cradle of the
Iranian people to the fertile banks of the Kohik or Zerefshan.
In what way the Iranian race spread itself from the above-
named region to the south and west, is a question which lies
outside the sphere of our researches.   For us it is all the more
interesting to know how far the Iranian element of Transoxania extended towards the north and east ; for although in this
endeavour we have only the assistance of a geographical
nomenclature, the individual names render us all the more
valuable service when we take into consideration that on the
other side of the Oxus the settled civilised population was
always composed of Iranians.

As the oldest colony we may point to that piece of land which
stretches from the old Akhsiket on the eastern frontier of
Fergana as far as Bokhara.   This forms the most fertile portion
of Transoxania, is traversed by numerous natural and artificial
streams, and the names of its mountains, brooks, and rivers,
as well as its towns, districts, and villages, as we find them set
down in Belkhi's geographical manuscript, are all of old
Persian origin.   From this central point their civilisation could
never extend itself farther west than Bokhara, as it was stopped
in that direction by the sandy tract of Khodja Oban, a projec-
tion of the Desert of Khalata.   Karaköl (the black lake), as
also Berkend (the prince's city), arose later, as their Turkish
names show.   Towards the north their civilisation extended
itself beyond Khodjend (khosh djend, or khob djend = lovely
city [?]) as far as Djadj (the name of the Yaxartes and of a
town on its banks), and Binaket (also Penaket, probably

<hr>

[1] See on this subject the excellent work of Khanikoff, already referred to. He
attributes to the Tadjiks the character of the greatest purity of race. Rawlinson
attributes it to the Vakhanis, the wild mountaineers of Bedakhshan. In Central
Asia itself the Galtchas are regarded as the oldest Persians (Iranians) of the land.

from Penah ket=place of refuge), while in the east it extended itself, though only sporadically, far into the valleys of the Heavenly Mountain, for no one can doubt that Khoten, Turfan, and the names of other places point to earlier Iranian colonies.[1]

Wherever the capabilities of the soil permitted it, and the danger of Turanian inroads was not too threatening, culture-loving Iranians established themselves. Whether it was the innate love of peaceful industry, or the neighbourhood of the ingenious Chinese, it is well known that the silk trade, which was carried on between the Chinese Empire and Rome in the days of Augustus, found zealous promoters amongst the Central Asiatics, and these were certainly not Turanians. Narshakhi relates that the merchants of Beïkend served as a medium of communication between China and the Western Sea (Caspian).[2] From the Byzantine authorities we learn that in the fifth and sixth centuries of the Christian era, the inhabitants of Bokhara and Sogdia led large silk caravans through the empire of the Sasanides to that of Eastern Rome, and lastly, that the Arabs when they forced their way over the Oxus found there important manufacturing and agricultural industry. It is true that no monuments such as those of Persepolis and Susa, no cuneiform have as yet afforded eloquent evidence of the ancient civilisation of Central Asia.

But we should not forget that the Iranian genius had even in the earliest times to contend beyond the Oxus with the neighbouring Turanian hordes ; for we may assume with certainty that, however ancient may be the establishment of the

---

[1] Abel Rémusat, in his *Histoire de la Ville de Khoten*, considers the word Khoten to be a corruption of the Sanscrit Kou-stana, i.e. ' breast of the earth' (*mamelle de la terre*). The Central Asiatics derive the word from the Persian khob-ten, i.e. ' beautiful body,' with reference to the handsomer race of men, which, owing to its constant communication with Cashmere, distinguishes Khoten from the other cities of Eastern Turkestan.

[2] I say Caspian, but it is not impossible that by the expression in the text the Sea of Aral may be meant, for the geographical manuscript of Belkhi in the third century of the Hidjra notices the opinion that the Derya-i Khahrezm, or Sea of Aral, communicated with the Derya-i Khozar, i.e. the Caspian.

Iranians in the cities built on the banks of the Oxus and
Yaxartes, even then the Turanian nomads wandered in the
neighbouring steppes.

With regard to the time when the first inroads of the
Turanians into the cultivated regions of Transoxania, it is
impossible to form the faintest conjecture. Their supremacy
and settlement properly so called took place during the Mongolian occupation. We know just as little about the ethno-
logical relations of the nomads who wandered on the edge
of the steppe, for the name Guzz, or Ghïzz, was applied to
them sometimes north of the Yaxartes, sometimes north of
the Oxus. In Belkhi's geographical work the nomads north of
Djadj, where civilisation and Islam ended, are named Guzz,
while Persian authorities many centuries later apply the same
name to those Turkish nomads who kept Sultan Sandjar in
captivity in the neighbourhood of the modern Andkhoï.
There is also but little certainty in the conjecture that fixes
700 B.C. as the date [1] when the Turks poured over the Oxus,

[1] Rawlinson, in the article referred to above, says: 'It must suffice then to
explain, that for about 1,000 years, from 700 B.C. to 300 A.D., a succession of
Scythian tribes, belonging apparently to the same family as the Uralian tribes of
Russia, and the Finns, Lapps, and Hungarians of Europe, burst in from the Yaxartes
and swept over the western portion of the continent of Asia, extending to India in
one direction, to Syria and Asia Minor in another.' Regarded from the standpoint
of history, I can make no objection to this theory. But the philological proofs are
exceedingly feeble. What are given as Turanian decipherings are exceedingly
doubtful, and I must at the outset frankly declare that I find very little Turanian
in the so-called Turanian words discovered by Oppert, Norris, and Mordtmann.
As of these last-named works I have this moment at hand only Mordtmann's
communication on the cuneiform inscriptions of the second class, in the twenty-
fourth volume of the *Zeitschrift der deutschen morgenländischen Gesellschaft*, I will
only cite some of the instances there brought forward of similarity of Turanian
words by way of proving how unsound the whole theory is, and that the last-named
Iranian antiquary is by no means at home in Turanian philology. For instance,
on p. 9, *Ango* = mare, is compared with the Turkish tengiz ; why not with the
Turkish engin = the open sea, or has Herr Mordtmann discovered that the latter
word is derived from the old Turkish eng, signifying breadth, extension? Again,
Anira = volui is compared with the Turkish onamak, but unfortunately the last
does not mean 'to wish,' but 'to be contented.' On p. 15, artak = habitans with
the Turkish oturmak = to inhabit, more correctly olturmak = 'to sit.' Does he
mean to compare the root *art* with the root *oltur*? Again, p. 18, atzaka = vastus,
with the Turkish uzun = long. Why not rather with atchik = broad, open?
Avarras = castrum, with the Hungarian vár = fortress, and the Turkish (*sic !*)

the old boundary line between Iran and Turan, as far as India.

What is told us later about the Scythians of the Romans, about the Sacæ of the Greeks, about the Hephtalites, or White Huns, of the Byzantines, and about the Yue-tchi of the Chinese, has more probability in its favour. For that the Turks under some name or other pressed into Bactria about the second century B.C., and there erected an empire on the ruins of the Greek kingdom of Bactria, which, according to Reinaud,[1] lasted till the middle of the sixth century of the Christian era, finds confirmation, besides the testimony of the names of the kings on the Bactrian coins, in the word Belkh or Balkh. This word is nothing else but the old Turkish balik or balikh=city, capital, as the Turks called the residence of the sovereign, the town *par excellence,* just as the Mongols did many centuries later when they called the residence of the great Kaan, *Kaan Balikhi* (the Cambalec or Kambalu of the Europeans), to wit ' the city of the kaan.'

Another proof of the early existence of Turanian elements south of the Oxus is afforded by the first Arabic geographers, according to whom in earlier times Turks belonging to the tribe Khaladj [2] (more correctly Khilidj, Kilidj=a sword), dwelt

varush = town. It is scarcely necessary to say that the first word is derived from the Persian baru = a rampart or dam, and the last is formed from vár, a genuine Hungarian word which the Osmanlis borrowed from them on the banks of the Danube. On p. 21 eviduva = eripui with the Turkish tutmak = to grasp hold ; *lucus a non lucendo.* On p. 24 git = afferre, with the Turkish götürrnek. Herr Mordtmann has probably forgotten that this word originally means ' to bear,' ' to raise,' and is connected with the word kütch = burden. But the Turkish ghetirmak, ' to bring,' would not be of service, for the original form is gheltirmek = to cause to come. On p. 25 I = river, with the Turkish irmak. Equally amusing is the comparison of the Turkish ayak = foot with yagi uig ; yaki = enemy. The words, it is well known, are derived from two entirely different roots. The root ay has the signification of an opening, cleft, and yag, also ' yao,' signifies wicked, malicious. In order to elucidate the remains that have been handed down from præ-historic times, one must not turn to the Osmanli or any other more modern dialect of the Turkish people, but to the language of the Kudatku Bilik, and even this is at the most only 900 years old.

[1] *Relations politiques et commerciales de l'Empire romain avec l'Asie orientale.* Paris, 1863, p. 227.

[2] They are mentioned under the name Khaladj, more correctly Khilidj, a word which can be identified with the Turkish kilidj, a sword.

on the banks of the Hilmend. These were probably the remains of those Sacæ from whom is derived the name Saka-stene, Seghistan, at present Sistan.

On the other side of the Oxus we find a similar proof of the early existence of the Turkish element in the designation of the capital Bokhara, a word whose Turanian origin is beyond doubt, as also in the word Berkend already mentioned. Even the Amu, as the natives call the Oxus, is Turkish, and signifies river. Whether the Turks at their earliest appearance in Transoxania played the part of rulers or served as auxiliary troops of the Iranian princes, is difficult to decide ; but I am inclined to accept the first view, and that from the following considerations. First, the Turks, as a warrior class *par excellence*, soon arrived at dominion wherever they made their appearance—a rule of which we find many instances both in the middle ages and in modern times. Secondly, this view is borne out by the relations between the Byzantine Empire with the Turks in the far East. For when the inhabitants of Sogdia found the silk trade, for them so profitable, interfered with, which interference they attributed to the policy of the Persians, the *Turkish* prince of Sogdia first of all applied for assistance to the Great Kaan, Dizabul.[1]

When he, too, was unable to effect anything in a peaceful manner with the King of the Persians, he put himself into communication with Justin II., Emperor of Constantinople. In order to reach the shores of the Bosphorus, starting from the court of Dizabul, the Turkish ambassador, as he was obliged to avoid Persian territory, had to travel along the northern coast of the Caspian Sea and through the most secret passes of the Caucasus. This circumstance favours the supposition that the powerful Turkish prince was established in the mountains of Altai, or on the banks of the Yaxartes. Further, the Prince of

[1] Dizabul, as the Byzantine historians call him, seems to be the Greek form of the Turkish dizavul or dizaul, which from the root diz^{m•k} and tiz^{m•k}, to set in order, arrange, range, is to be translated, an orderer or arranger (for instance, in battle). It thus designates a dignity, like the new word Yasaul, a member of the body-guard in China, from Yas^{•m•k}, to order, to make ready.

Sogdia, whom the Greeks called Maniakh, was, to judge from his name, not an Iranian but a Turanian. Maniak is a Turkish word meaning prince, noble, distinguished, and with a slight variation is still to be found among the Kirghises, who give their princes the title Manap.[1] Thirdly, the first historical notices of Transoxania make frequent mention of individual tarkhans, which is a well-known Turkish dignity. These ruled in Samarkand, Belkend, and Vafkend, and were individually conquered by the Arab invaders. But, taken all in all, our knowledge of the Turks in Middle Asia before the times of Islam is unfortunately very small. If the Byzantine Christians had only had so much education and desire for knowledge as the Mohammedan savants of the first centuries of the Hidjra, the journey of the Byzantine ambassador Zemarchus, who visited the coast of Dizabul about the end of the sixth century of the Christian era, would have been of great benefit to science. But Christian ignorance and Greek pride prevented this result, so that the diplomatist of Justin II. has left us, instead of notices of his route and specimens of the languages of the barbarians, only an uninstructive account of manners and ceremonies.

As regards the earliest religious conditions of Central Asia, we have before observed that among the Iranian population the doctrines of Zoroaster had assumed the position of a national religion. The neighbourhood of Belkh makes this intelligible; and when we take into consideration the firmness with which the Iranian population resisted the later assaults of Islam, we shall not be surprised to find that the teaching of Zoroaster spread from the fire-altars of Transoxania eastward to the Turkish nomads of the mountains of Tien-Shan,[2] and to

---

[1] See 'Observations sur le Kirghis par M. Radloff,' *Journal asiatique*, extrait no. 9 (1863), where it is expressly said, 'Leurs Manaps de l'hérédité comme les sultans des Khazaks.' If I am not mistaken, I myself have heard the title Manap among the Karakalpaks.

[2] Fr. Spiegel asserts, in an article which appeared in the *Ausland*, under the title 'Das östliche Turkestan,' that in the seventh century after Christ, Turkish tribes in the north of the Tien-Shan were fire-worshippers.

the north-west as far as the shores of the Sea of Aral. But
still Parseeism even in Transoxania had long before the
beginning of history received a dangerous blow by the spread
of Buddhism from the East—a circumstance which is clearly
hinted at in the myths of the Shahnameh. The learned
enquirer into Iranian antiquities [1] writes on this subject in his
discussion of the 'king's book' as follows :—'From this time
forward,' that is, from the death of Keikhosru, 'emphasis was
laid upon the fact that the Turanians were worshippers of
idols. The Turanian king is called Peghu nežad, that is,
derived from Peghu, and, it is added, he writes with Peghu
letters, which has doubtless reference to his Buddhistic origin.'

It is highly probable that in Transoxania the war between
Buddhism and Parseeism had the character of a struggle not
only between religions but between races. The supporters of
the former faith were the Turanians, who had received it from
Thibet, while the Iranians, on the other hand, defended with
natural zeal the national religion of their country. We do not
know at what date the old Iranian city Djemu-ket received
the Turanian name of Bokhara, for Bukhar [2] is even now the
Mongolian word for a Buddhistic temple or monastery. But
from the influence exercised by China over the Turks of the
north, from the Desert of Gobi to the Caspian Sea, even before
the Christian era, for instance during the Han dynasty (163
B.C. to 196 A.D.), we may conclude that the doctrines of Buddha
found adherents on the banks of the Zerefshan in the first
centuries after Christ.

In connection with this may be brought the already cited
statement of Narshakhi about the daughter of the Emperor of China, whose dowry consisted of idols which were
deposited in Rametin. We may besides refer to the report
of the Buddhistic travellers Fa-Hian and Hiuen-Tsang,

---

[1] Professor Dr. Fr. Spiegel in his *Eranische Alterthumskunde*, p. 663.

[2] The Mohammedan authors give a similar etymology, asserting that Bukhar
in the language of the idolaters meant medjma-i-ilm, i.e. a place for the collection
of knowledge, that is, a college or school. Even now the Turks pronounce the
word quite correctly Bukhara, while the Persians say Bokhara.

about the flourishing condition of Buddhism in Eastern Turkestan in the fifth century of our era, which could not fail to have an influence on the lands about the Oxus. Lastly, the traces of Buddhism in Transoxania can be found at the time of the Mohammedan conquest ; for when the Arabs took Beïkend, and plundered it, among many other idols, one peculiarly large golden idol attracted their attention, which had in the place of eyes two valuable pearls, which were sent as a present to Haddjadj. Nay, long after the spread of Islam Buddhism lingered in the memory of the inhabitants of Central Asia. Narshakhi tells us that two great fairs of dolls or images were held yearly at Bokhara, and that often at one of these fairs as much as fifty thousand direms worth of toys changed hands. This, the Arabic author observes, comes from the old practice that prevailed, in the times when the Bokhariots were idolaters, of purchasing their idols at these fairs.

Our sketch of the religious condition of Central Asia in the Præ-Islamite period would be even more imperfect than it is if we were to leave unnoticed the Christianity of the Nestorians, which very early spread far into Inner Asia and reached the lands bordering on the Oxus and the Yaxartes. As the learned Colonel H. Yule, in his remarkable work 'Cathay and the Way Thither,' rightly observes,[1] the legend of the apostolic activity of St. Thomas extending as far as China, as well as the report of the diffusion in the third century of the doctrines of Christ among the Persians, Medes, and Chinese, must not be unconditionally accepted. But that this was partially the case in the following century is proved by the persecutions of the Christians under Shapor, and the existence of the archbishoprics of Tus and Merv in 334, of which the latter was raised, in 420, to the dignity of a metropolitan see. Driven from the Byzantine Empire by the bitterness of sectarian animosity, the Nestorian separatists

---

[1] See p. lxxxviii. of that work.

were early led to seek in the far East a field for their feverish
activity. Their hatred of Byzantium occasionally procured
for them the favour of the Sasanides, and before the appearance of Islam their missionary efforts must have had a special
measure of success in those parts where the contact of Buddhism and Parseeism had loosened the hold of either faith on
men's minds, and disposed them to religious speculations.

This was especially the case in Central Asia. The Christianity of Transoxania had its centre at Samarkand, where a
bishop's see was established, according to the accounts of the
Syrians, about 411–415 ; according to the opinion of Yule,
about 503–520. Cosmas speaks of Christians on the banks
of the Oxus in the middle of the sixth century. That the
Arabs found such in Bokhara is plain from the account given
by Narshakhi of the *Keshkushan,* of whom we are told that
they were neither Arabs nor inhabitants of the land, neither
Moslems nor Fire-worshippers, but had immigrated from the
West, occupied themselves for the most part with commerce,
and were held by the Bokhariots in universal esteem. When,
by order of Kuteïbe, the Bokhariots had to abandon half their
houses to the Arab immigrants, the Keshkushan had to give
up the whole of theirs. They had consequently to build new
ones outside the city, where they had beautiful gardens and
kiosks, which, when they were at a later day expelled from
the country, were sold at high prices. ·

From the above it will be easily understood that, as the
rule of Islam grew ever stricter in the cities of Transoxania
after the Arab conquest of the country, the Keshkushan
(according to the etymology of the word ' Wanderers ') could
not long maintain themselves. In the third century of the
Hidjra it was only in the mountainous neighbourhood of
Samarkand that an important Christian community was to be
found, named Zerdeghird.[1] In the east of Turkestan, however, they lived for a long time unmolested ; but although

---

[1] See Belkhi's Geographical Manuscript in the Kaiserliche Hofbibliothek, at
Vienna, p. 145.

under the rule of the Buddhistic Mongols they triumphed over their Mohammedan oppressors,[1] at the end of the thirteenth century there were but few Christians to be found in Central Asia.

After the foregoing attempt to lift the thick veil of secrecy which conceals from our gaze the national and social life of Transoxania during the Præ-Islamite period, no one will be surprised that we are not able to report anything about its political circumstances. Even with respect to the last century before the Arab conquest, when the wars and political relations between the Sasanides and the Eastern Roman Empire had brought the interior of Asia into somewhat closer connection with the West—even from that period we hear nothing about the land beyond the Oxus which could serve as the starting-point of an historical discussion. We read, it is true, that in the reign of Behram V., or Varanes, as he is called by the Byzantines, the Khan or Khakan of the Turks poured out of Transoxania into Iran with a powerful host of 150,000 men and laid waste Khorasan, but was nevertheless defeated with great loss by the Persian king and driven beyond the Oxus. Not less vague is the account of the war between Firuz, the Peroses of the Greeks, and the Prince of the Turks, to whom the Persian historians give the good Iranian name of Khoshnuvaz, i.e. the 'good-natured,' which has reference rather to the noble character of the Tatar than to his actual name. The story goes that Firuz displayed his gratitude towards the noble Turk who had helped him to mount the throne, by making an inroad into Transoxania. Firuz was defeated,

---

[1] The Mohammedan historians deny this, but we read on this subject in Colonel H. Yule's *Travels of Marco Polo* (London, 1871), vol. i. p. 172, as follows:—
'Prince Sempad, High Constable of Armenia, in a letter written from Samarkand in 1246 or 1247, mentions, &c. I tell you that we have found many Christians scattered all over the East, and many fine churches, lofty, ancient, and of good architecture, which have been spoilt by the Turks. Hence when the Christians of these countries came to the presence of the reigning Khan's grandfather (i.e. Chingiz), he received them most honourably and granted them liberty of worship, and issued orders to prevent their having any just cause of complaint by word or deed. *And so the Saracens, who used to treat them with contempt, have now the like treatment in double measure.*'

and Khoshnuvaz showed his generosity by pardoning the black ingratitude, while he sought to secure himself by a treaty of peace against another attack.

But the Sasanide could not rest ; he repeated the attempt, and lost, in one fatal encounter, his army and his life. The Persian chroniclers do not inform us whether this Khoshnuvaz of theirs was really Khakan over all the Turkish tribes of Central Asia, or merely the prince of some district beyond the Oxus. In Narshakhi and Tabari we only hear of individual tarkhans, who at the time of the Arab invasion ruled in Beïkend, Rametin, Vardanzi, Samarkand, and Fergana. But they leave us in doubt as to whether these were independent of one another or under the suzerainty of a Khakan. The original and correct definition of the title tarkhan [1] certainly implies the existence of such a suzerain or superior lord. The history of the Arab conquest seems to point to mutual independence, for, when the tarkhan of Samarkand was engaged in war with Kuteïbe, he was obliged to call in the aid of his kindred allies from Turkestan and Fergana. Besides, an united defence on the part of the warlike Turanians would have rendered, at the very least, doubtful the success of a handful of Arabian adventurers, in spite of all their religious enthusiasm.

But whether divided or united, whether independent or in vassalage, it is certain that the Turks in the sixth and seventh centuries of our era had possessed themselves of the dominion of many places in Transoxania. The stream of fresh immigration from the great steppe of the north had on its side, in no long time, swollen to such a mass as already to crush the original Iranian inhabitants under the exclusive dominion of the Turks, were it not that at the very same time Mohammed in the steppe of south-western Asia brought about that revolution which was to give a new form to more than the half of that vast continent.

[1] *Tarkhan* is an old Turkish dignity, and distinguishes such persons as were free from taxation. In the oldest Turkish documents *tarku* means 'a letter of protection, a letter of nobility,' and in Mongolian (*Kowalewsky*, p. 1768a), *tarkha lakhu* means 'to grant anyone a privilege.'

II.

THE INROADS OF THE ARABS AND THE CONVERSION TO ISLAM.

46 (666)—96 (714).

THE foundation pillars of the gigantic structure of Islam were scarcely set up in Western Asia, when the victorious columns of the Arabian adventurers pressed into Transoxania, following in the track of the great Macedonian. In the year 46 (666), Ziad bin Ebu Sufian sent the valiant general Rebi Ibn ul Harith from Irak to Khorasan, who in consequence of the consternation produced by the fall of the last of the Sasanides overthrew all whom he encountered in Eastern Iran and carried his victorious banner as far as Belkh. Belkh had always been the southern gate of Transoxania ; no wonder then that the fame of the wealthy Sogdia induced the covetous Arabs to make an inroad. They seem on the first occasion to have penetrated without any systematic plan of invasion as far as the banks of the Yaxartes. How rich were the treasures with which they returned laden, how enticing was their success, is best seen from the circumstance that four years later, when Ziad died, 50 (670), his son Obeïdullah was sent by Muavie on a new expedition to Bokhara.

This time the undertaking was of a more serious character. Obeïdullah bin Ziad first attacked the wealthy Beïkend, the seat of government and of commerce, which he reduced after a long struggle. With great booty and more than 4,000 captives he proceeded to Bokhara. This was about the end of 53 (672). Queen Khatun, of whom we have already spoken, called her Turkish neighbours to her aid, and the Arabs, who

had set up their *balistæ* and were engaged in the operations of
the siege, were fallen upon in the rear by her allies. Obeïdullah
bin Ziad defended himself bravely, and is even said to have
inflicted a defeat upon the infidels, but was obliged this time
to return to Merv without reducing Bokhara.[1]   The Moslems,
in possession of treasures, weapons, garments, gold and silver
utensils—amongst the latter the boots of the queen, set with
precious stones of the value of 20,000 direms,[2] excited in the
highest degree the wonder of the primitive inhabitants of the
Arabian desert—laid waste in their rage all the places through
which they passed during their retreat, and even cut down
the trees.

The Arabic historians tell us that Queen Khatun, to save
her country from the destruction which threatened it, made
peace with Obeïdullah and engaged to pay a yearly tribute of
a million of direms.   Nevertheless, we find that after an
interval of hardly three years the Arabs again commenced
hostilities against Khatun under Said bin Osman.   The royal
lady, relying on her treaty with Obeïdullah, attempted to
soothe the leader of the perjured Arabs with presents, but in
vain.   Said disallowed the treaty made by his predecessor,
sent the presents back, and pressed relentlessly forward against
Bokhara.   Weakened by the long struggle, still more by the
disobedience of her own subjects, the princess could not this
time maintain the conflict.   She made peace, and, as Said
required hostages as guarantees for her good behaviour during
his absence, she sent into his camp eighty of the most
rebellious nobles, and thus disencumbered herself of her most
dangerous enemies.   After peace was concluded, the proud
Arab required that the princess should appear in person
before him.   Khatun,[3] who is said to have been of surpassing

---

[1] According to Tabari, Abdullah advanced as far as Tashkend.

[2] A direm, according to Johnson's Persian Dictionary, is worth about twopence.

[3] With regard to Queen Khatun, Arabian or rather Mohammedan slander
relates that even during the lifetime of her husband she carried on an illicit amour
with one of his servants, to which Tugshade owed his birth.   On the death of
her husband, some were disposed to set the chief of the army on the throne ; but
she succeeded in securing the sovereignty to her bastard son, in spite of the
tumults that ensued.

beauty, presented herself in her robes of state, and produced on the stern warrior such an effect that his heart was at once inflamed with passion, which gave rise to relations celebrated in songs which centuries afterwards still lived in the mouths of the people of Bokhara.[1]

Thus established in tolerable security in Bokhara, Said turned his arms eastward against Sogdia, that is, the cities of Sogd and Samarkand. The last-named place had not at that time an independent ruler. It was the Turkish tarkhan of Sogd whom the Arabs encountered and in the end overcame. As Said passed through Bokhara on his way back to Khorasan the Bokhariots required him to give up the hostages he had taken with him. He promised to do so when on the other side of the Oxus. There the demand was repeated, but he put off their liberation until his arrival at Merv. After Merv Nishabur, after Nishabur Kufa, was designated as the place where they were to be set free, till at last the nobles of Transoxania were carried far from the pleasant banks of the Zerefshan into the sunburnt wastes of Arabia, there to serve as trophies of their returning conqueror. In Medina Said had them deprived of their swords, their girdles set with precious stones, of their clothes and jewels, and the proud sons of princes were degraded to the condition of slaves. This irritated them so much that with one accord they determined to prefer an heroic death to a life of ignominy. Inspired with feelings of vengeance, they fell upon Said in his palace, killed him, and then destroyed themselves. This happened during the khalifate of Yezid bin Mervan.

The Arabs had on their return home scarcely recounted all the wonders of the distant and rich Sogdia, when Bokhara

[1] Narshakhi tells the following remarkable anecdote of the first meeting of Khatun and Said. In order to present a terrible spectacle to the Princess of Bokhara, a certain Abidullah bin Hazim was ordered to place himself in the midst of a tent warmed by a fire. This man was of robust frame, and had very red hair and eyes. The glare of the flame heightened their colour, with which at that time the inhabitants of Bokhara were unacquainted, to such a degree, that the queen was so terrified by his appearance that she started up and ran away, nor was she induced to return without great difficulty.

again freed itself from their yoke, and Muslim [1] bin Ziad, who had succeeded Said in the governorship of Khorasan, was compelled to march with an army towards the Oxus. Again the queen called on her neighbours of Sogd for aid, while she is reported to have received succours from the northern Turks to the extent of 120,000 men. This enormous host did not, however, terrify the Arabs, who trusted to the usual good fortune of their weapons. They laid siege to Bokhara, and only delayed the assault until they should receive information regarding the number and position of their enemies. Muslim bin Ziad entrusted Mohallab, an officer of his suite, with the work of reconnoitring. He urged that a less highly placed officer might undertake the office ; but on Muslim repeating his command, Mohallab complied. He required one man from each regiment,[2] and set out secretly by night.

The next morning, when Muslim informed the rest of his troops of the mission of Mohallab, the Arabs began to murmur and to say : ' Thou hast sent the Emir Mohallab on before us, so that he may snatch the best of the booty out of our mouths ; if a battle had been in question, no doubt we should have been the foremost.'   In fact many of them, inspired by the basest greed, hurried after Mohallab, and overtook him. As soon as he perceived their approach, he exclaimed : ' Ye have done wrong ; we have come as far as this unperceived ; now ye have aroused the attention of the enemy, and the affair can but end ill.'   Nevertheless Mohallab took courage. He numbered the Arabs he had with him and found they were 900 in number. Scarcely had he set them in battle-array when the enemy's trumpet sounded, and the Turks in their first onset cut down 400 of the Musulmans ; the rest took to flight in the wildest confusion. Mohallab, with a few of his followers, was surrounded by the enemy. In the utmost peril he shouted aloud, and his

---

[1] Tabari names him اسلم but the statement of Narshakhi, which we have followed, seems to be correct.

[2] The Persian text says علم ' banner.'

powerful voice was, according to the statement of Narshakhi, heard in the Arab camp, distant about half a fersakh. Thence a body of troops under Abdullah bin Djudan at once hastened to his assistance.[1] Seeing their countrymen approach, Mohallab and his comrades roused themselves for one final effort. In the meantime the whole Arab army took part in the battle; the Turks were defeated, and so great was the booty that fell into the hands of the Mohammedans that the share of each soldier was worth 10,000 direms, or about 20l. Of course under such circumstances Queen Khatun had no alternative but to submit to the victors, with whom she made peace.

The Arabs returned to Merv, not to leave the harassed dwellers in Transoxánia at rest, but on the contrary to prepare a new expedition under the guidance of a leader, to whose caution, courage, and perseverance it was granted to extinguish the last sparks of ancient Persian civilisation in the region in which it had first arisen, and to plant the doctrines of the Arabian Prophet in the distant valleys of the Thien-Shan.

This leader was Kuteïbe bin Muslim, who in 86 (704) received from Haddjadj the command to conquer Transoxania. As he did not intend to carry on mere robber expeditions, but to effect the thorough conquest and conversion of the country, it was for him of the highest importance to make himself master of the southern Belkh. His army was collected in Merv, and stimulated by sermons and recitations of the Koran. He then descended from the pulpit to mount his war-horse, and had not yet arrived within the limits of the ancient Bactria, when the inhabitants of Belkh came out to meet him and conducted him with honour into their city. . He secured the dominion of the Khalifs in the city, made a circuit over the

---

[1] According to Narshakhi, the very time that Mohallab's cry for aid filled every one with consternation, Abdulla bin Ziad called for his dinner, on which Abdullah Djudan observed : 'May God satisfy thee ! Thou seemest to have no idea of the danger of war.' A very characteristic reproof addressed to his commander by a subordinate officer.

Oxus, and returned by the present Tchihardjui [1] to Merv.
From the last-named place Kuteïbe commenced in 87 (705)
his campaign against Transoxania. He first of all marched
toward Beïkend.

Arrived on the edge of the desert, he found himself opposed
by a superior force, which surrounded him in such sort that
months passed without anything being known of him, and
Haddjadj had public prayers offered up for the safety of one
encompassed with danger while fighting for the faith. Nevertheless Kuteïbe contrived to escape from the perils which
surrounded him. Neither the numerical superiority of the
Bokhariots, nor the stratagem by which the Bokhariots
sought to induce him to retreat by diffusing a rumour of the
death of Haddjadj, availed to break his iron courage.[2] He
accepted battle ; the Turks were defeated in one day's engagement ; one portion of them were dispersed in the wildest
confusion, the rest threw themselves into the strongly fortified
Beïkend. This town was at once besieged ; its resistance
cost the Arabs many a severe struggle. For fifty days all the
efforts of the Mohammedans seemed without results ; at last
a breach was made in the walls. Kuteïbe promised a rich
reward to the soldier who first effected it, which in the case of
his death was to be given to his children. The promise had
its effect, and the fortress was taken and occupied by the
Arabs.

Scarcely, however, had Kuteïbe departed, when he received the intelligence that the people of Beïkend had openly
revolted, and had killed Varka bin Nasr el Bahili, whom he
had left behind as governor. It is true, the Arabs had brought
the catastrophe upon themselves by their own misconduct ; for
Varka is said to have carried off beautiful girls, whose father

---

[1] According to Tabari, Kuteïbe, on his way back to Merv, conquered the towns
of Kumsek and Veramishe, but was afterwards hard pressed by the allied forces
of the Turks of Sogd and Ferghana.

[2] Kuteïbe's own spy, a Persian by birth, of the name of Tender, who was
employed by the Beïkenders. He brought the false news to Kuteïbe, who had
him immediately put to death.

avenged the dishonour of his family by stabbing the ravisher. Nevertheless the anger of Kuteïbe knew no bounds. He hastily returned, and ordered the city to be plundered and burned. All the men of age to bear arms were massacred, and the women and children were made slaves. Not even the one-eyed chieftain of the Turks was allowed to ransom his life.

We are told that the people of Beïkend, properly so called, were for the most part merchants, who traded with China and other parts of the world. They had been absent during the war, and when they returned they ransomed their wives and children. Gradually the city itself was rebuilt, and Beïkend was the only place which recovered from the ruin brought on the country by the Arab conquest. The fall of Beïkend was of so much the greater importance for the Arabs, as the place had always been regarded as the south-western gate of Transoxania. It was besides the most flourishing place in that country after Sogd and Rametin, and the booty which fell into the hands of the victors was immense. Especial mention is made of an idol-temple which contained several statues of massive gold and silver 40,000 drachmæ in weight. Two pearls of the size of pigeons' eggs [1] served as eyes for one of these idols. Kuteïbe sent both these pearls, together with a large quantity of booty, to Haddjadj, who expressed his admiration in a letter of thanks.

We can easily imagine with what haste the covetous nomads of the Arabian Desert seized on the accumulated treasures of the conquered. The first things most eagerly appropriated by the visitors were arms, the best of which had always been made in this part of Asia. Although the great store of arms in Beïkend had been distributed among the soldiers, yet so great was the demand for such articles that a lance was sold for 70 drachmæ, a cuirass for 200, and a shield for even higher prices. Although the Arabs had no want of warriors, for the tribes of Beni Temim, Bekri, and Abdul Kais, which played

---

[1] When asked whence came these valuable pearls, the people of Beïkend answered that two birds had brought them thither from a distant country.

the principal part in the conquest of Transoxania, alone
numbered 21,000 men,[1] it is certain the Arab army had not
the numerical superiority.   This circumstance is perhaps the
reason why the conquest conducted by Kuteïbe, although he
had made himself master of the southern border of the steppes
of Turkestan, progressed so slowly.   Kuteïbe had as yet engaged in no hostile operations against Bokhara itself.   It was
his policy to cut off that city, by no means strong in means of
defence, from its Turkish allies.   Consequently he began by
reducing the small independent states of Vardan (at present
Vardanzi), Rametin, and Sogd, with the intention of afterwards
operating with greater success against Bokhara.   This plan
had been enjoined on him by Haddjadj.   In the year 89 (698)
he subdued Kesh (Shehri Sebz) and Nakhsheb (Karshi).   Ten
years later he proceeded to attack Vardan, but encountered un-
foreseen obstacles in carrying out his design, as it had been
anticipated by the Turkish princes.   They had formed an
alliance among themselves, and set themselves and their united
forces in his way.   This time all the princes of Transoxania
and Sogdia had ranged themselves on the side of Bokhara.
They had been joined by the ruler of Fergana. and a certain
Kurmogan[2] from the farther East, who is described as nephew
of the Emperor of China.   It seemed as if the Turkish chiefs
had become aware of their danger, and were determined by
united efforts to repel the Arabian invaders.

To what extremities Kuteïbe, who was engaged in the siege
of Vardan,[3] was reduced, appears from the description given
by Tabari.   This author relates that the Arabs, surrounded

---

[1] According to Tabari, the Arab forces in Khorasan during the time of
Kuteïbe were as follows :—the tribe Beni Alie, with 9,000 men ; Bekri, under the
leadership of Hasim Elmunzir, with 7,000 ; Beni Temim, with 10,000 ; Abdul
Kais, under the leadership of Abdullah bin Djudan, with 4,000 ; besides these the
Kufites, 7,000 in number, and a branch of the tribe Abdul Kais, with 4,000 men ;
in all, 41,000.

[2] Tabari calls him Kuriganun, but both forms of the name seem to be
erroneous.   By the supposed relation of the Chinese Emperor, some Mongol or
Uigur must be meant, whose name could not have had so strange a sound.

[3] Narshakhi calls this place Vardan and Vardun ; Tabari, on the contrary,
Vardandjzat.   Its modern name is Vardanzi.

on all sides, saw themselves already in danger of total dis-
comfiture; their women broke out into terrible lamentations
and tore their faces. Nevertheless the exhortations and en-
couragements of Kuteïbe prevented the Arabs entirely losing
courage. 'Up, my children, ye *must* discomfit these Turks,'
was his address to the several tribes. He especially inspired
the tribe of Temim, from whose ranks a warlike chieftain,
Kezim by name, chosen to fill that position by the supreme
chieftain of the tribe,[1] Veki' bin Ebul Esvad, was the first to
throw himself upon the enemy. Although we have great reason to doubt the glorious victory attributed by Tabari to the
Arabs, so much at any rate is certain, that they successfully
broke through the chain thrown round them by the Turks.
They were, however, unable to save themselves without having
recourse to the wiles of diplomacy. Perceiving that, under the
circumstances, it was impossible to renew the battle, Kuteïbe
attempted to dissolve the union of the allies; and as permanent concord was never a distinguishing feature of the
Turkish character, his design was in a short time successfully
carried out.

The ruler[2] of Sogd led into the field a proportionally
larger number of troops than any of the allies. It was consequently most important to induce him to separate himself from
them. A Nabathæan of the name of Hoyan, to whom
Kuteïbe entrusted the accomplishment of this design, contrived
during a skirmish to convey to the prince a confidential communication to the effect that his allies intended to deprive him
of his dominions as soon as the Arabs had left the country.
'We can remain here only as long as the hot season lasts,'
observed the crafty Arab; 'as soon as winter commences we

---

[1] From this passage in Tabari, it appears that the Arab nomads had two
superior chiefs in each tribe. One was the Sheïkh or Reïs, properly so called;
while the other was at the head of the men of war. The first of these was in
this case Veki' bin Ebul Esvad.

[2] Terkhun, according to Narshakhi and Tabari, who suppose it to be a proper
name; Terkhun, Tarkhan (Magyar tarkhán), is a word designating a rank among
the Turanian populations. See note 1, p. 18.

must retreat southward ; do not forget that thy allies, coming,
as they do, from the north, will not be disposed to leave the
charming Sogdia so lightly.   It were better for thee to conclude a peace with us, and to excuse thyself to thy allies, that
thou didst so from fear of the fresh forces which Haddjadj is
sending us by way of Kesh and Nakhsheb.   This thou wilt
say merely as an excuse, for of us thou hast no reason to fear.'
It is difficult to decide whether Turkish simplicity or some
well-founded reason influenced the Sogdian.   It is sufficient to
say that he fell into the snare, and concluded a secret peace
with the Arabs, to whom he promised to pay a yearly tribute
of two millions of direms.   As he at once desisted from hostilities, the rest were compelled to retreat, and Kuteïbe escaped
from the danger which had menaced him for four months.

It is scarcely necessary to observe that in these negotiations
the tarkhan of Samarkand was duped.   In spite of the conclusion of peace, Kuteïbe, under pretence of hastening the
building of the mosques prescribed by the treaty, sent instead
of masons 4,000 armed Arabs, who took up their quarters in
the city.   When the tarkhan would avenge this disgraceful
treachery, he, together with his faithful adherents, was surprised and slain.   According to another account, his people,
irritated by the ignominy of having to pay a yearly tribute,
rose tumultuously and deposed him.   Unable to endure such
disgrace, he fell by his own sword.   Samarkand was plundered.
Among the captives was a daughter of Yezdedjird, the last of
the Sasanides.   She was presented to the Khalif Velid.   The
idols and other articles made of gold are said to have weighed
more than 50,000 miskal.

It was now time to allow the Arab army the repose which
it had earned so well.   Kuteïbe therefore led them back to
Merv, where they remained during the winter.   Having received powerful reinforcements, he the next spring advanced
against Bokhara, determined by one final successful effort to
set the crown on his own exertions and those of his predeces-

sors. According to Narshakhi, Queen Khatun still held the reins of government in the royal city on the Zerefshan. Considering the advanced age to which she must have attained, this is scarcely credible. But whoever it was that then stood at the head of affairs considered all further resistance unavailing. Bokhara, that had been three times conquered and converted to Mohammedanism, and had yet always fallen back into its old national religion, now for the fourth time opened its gates to receive along with its conquerors the doctrines of their prophet. These doctrines, which had at first been violently opposed in that city, were in later times as zealously studied; and at the present day Islam, which is evidently falling to ruin in all other parts of Asia, is still to be found at Bokhara in the same guise as under the first Khalifs.

And yet how long and various were the struggles which Kuterbe had to maintain against the obstinate adherents of the doctrines of Buddha and of Zoroaster! The political changes do not seem to have occasioned the Arab much trouble; for after the occupation of the city the reigning khudat (prince) was confirmed in his dignity on condition that an inferior official named by the Khalif should be associated with him in the government. Later, under the title of Emir, this official became the sole depository of power, and threw the prince into the shade. A further condition was that the Khudat had to pay a yearly tribute of 200,000 direms to the Khalif, and 10,000 direms to the governor of Khorasan, and besides one half of the net profit of the public baths to the Arabs settled in the city. Taken all in all, these are less severe exactions than those which Mohammedan Bokhara had to submit to at the hand of other Mohammedan conquerors. On the other hand, the proud Bokhariots must have found it particularly hard to bear the measures employed to force on them the doctrines of the Arabian prophet.

As the conquerors observed that many, whom the terrors of the conquest had compelled to an open profession of Islam,

exercised in the most profound secrecy,[1] or in the stillness of
the night, their old worship with still greater zeal than before,
every Bokhariot was commanded to give up half his house to
an Arab.   These new inmates played the part of spies in the
midst of the family, watched over the newly converted, imparted to them instruction in ritual matters, and in cases of
backsliding denounced the obstinate offenders to the authorities. Religious conduct received even pecuniary reward. Whoever appeared at Friday prayers in the mesdjid-i-Kuterbe,
built 94 (742), received two direms. In this mosque, and in
the open places for prayers (mosalla) which were formed out of
the Righistan, the worshippers were at first accustomed to
make the ritual prostrations, &c., in obedience to the word of
command given by the imam. In order to render the holy
word of the book of God accessible to everybody, the Koran
was recited not in Arabic but in Persian,[2] a proceeding which
at the present day would excite the greatest horror amongst
Mohammedans, who, according to an opinion widely spread
amongst them, regard the translation of that wonderful work,
the Koran, as the greatest possible presumption. The struggle
maintained by the adherents of Parseeism against the aggressive doctrines of Mohammed seems to have been both violent
and obstinate.

The scanty reports of that period tell us that for many
years the Mohammedans of Bokhara dared not appear
unarmed either in the mosque or in other public places. Although the natives were not allowed to carry arms unless they
embraced Islam, severe encounters continually took place.
The patricians of Bokhara are represented as being the most
obstinate in the resistance to the new faith. When they were
summoned to attendance at the mosque, they answered with

---

[1] As a monument of this secret worship, there exists at the present day in
Bokhara a subterranean mosque called mesdjid-i mogan, the mosque of the Fire-
worshippers.

[2] Up to the present time it is only in Bombay that the Koran has been
lithographed with a Persian interlinear translation, which, rejected by the Western
Mohammedans, is purchased by the inexperienced Turkestanis.

a shower of stones, which conduct so incensed the Arabs, that at last, falling upon them, they plundered and destroyed their palaces. The building materials thus obtained were employed in the erection of mosques, so that many of the Mohammedan houses of prayer had, according to Narshakhi, gates adorned with idolatrous sculptures (?) ; nay, what is even more wonderful, these gates existed for 300 years, to the great scandal of Sunnite Islam. When it was found that even the above severe measures failed to produce the expected results, Bokhara was actually wrested out of the hands of the natives and divided among the Arabs. Thus the portion of the city extending from the gate of the spice-merchants [1] to that of the fortress was assigned to the Nossairi tribe; another portion again to the men of Yemen ; while others obtained a portion of the suburbs together with a Christian church, which was of course transformed into a mosque. A like severity was displayed in Samarkand. Here, too, everybody had to give up his arms. The strangers that came into the town had, so Tabari relates, their hands sealed up for a fixed time, and whoever went out of his house by night was put to death.

As for Kuteïbe, instead of waiting until the state of things in Bokhara had got somewhat settled. he hastened to continue his career of conquest eastward. In the year 95 (711) he attacked Fergana, the present khanate of Khokand. Having conquered it, he pressed along the old road through the Terek Pass in Eastern Turkestan, which we are accustomed to call Chinese Tartary. Here he encountered the princes of the Uigurs, who in default of union among themselves were easily conquered one after another, although several of them had called in Kalmuck auxiliaries from Northern Dzungaria. We are told that the Arabs extended their incursions into the

---

[1] Der-i-Attaran is the expression used in the text of the original. It seems to have been situate to the south-west, in which direction there exists at the present day, in the neighbourhood of the Karaköl gate, a Mahalle-i-Attaran, or quarter of the spice merchants.

province of Kansu. Although the doctrines of the Arabian prophet did not take firm root in Kashgar Khoten and Turfan until long afterwards, for many centuries later both Buddhism and Christianity counted numerous adherents in these countries, it is nevertheless a remarkable fact, and a source of no little pride to the present inhabitants of Eastern Turkestan, that Turfan on the very first appearance of the Arabs embraced Islam, in spite of the fact that the most zealous Buddhists were then to be found in the valleys of the Tien-Shan.

From this, the farthest eastern frontier of Islam, Kuteïbe presently returned through Fergana to Merv. He was recalled by the report of the death of the Khalif Velid. He had reason to fear the anger of the new Khalif, Suleïman bin Abdul Melik, and in order not to become the victim of his resentment he anticipated him by open rebellion. It seems that Kuteïbe entered on this course with reluctance, and only when he perceived that the new Khalif, not daring to brave the powerful governor of Khorasan, sought in secret to make himself a party among Kuteïbe's troops. Even in rebellion the governor showed his foresight. The messenger who carried his letter of defiance took with him two other epistles. The first of these contained assurances of his loyalty ; the second expressions of contempt towards Yezid the son of Mohallab, whom Kuteïbe especially feared as his rival, and in this he openly avowed that in case the latter were put in his place he would offer open resistance. As Kuteïbe rightly conjectured that Yezid was always to be found close to the Khalif's person, he told his messenger, ' Give him the first letter alone; but if thou seest that Suleïman hands it over to the son of Mohallab, then give him the second also ; and if he lets Yezid read that, then hand over to him the third also.' [1]

The messenger, who found Yezid in the presence of the Khalif, acted according to his instructions. Suleïman made as

---

[1] See Weil, *Geschichte der Chalifen*, vol. i. p. 556. Mannheim, 1856.

if nothing had happened, and allowed the man to depart in peace. He had not yet returned to his master when the latter, conjecturing how his mission had ended, or, as is probable, informed of it beforehand, set up the standard of revolt. Kuteïbe, however, had greatly deceived himself with regard to the army which had under his leadership gained so many brilliant victories, and acquired so much wealth. If he had followed the advice of his brother, Abdurrahman, to retire into Transoxania, and there found an independent kingdom, the spirit of rebellion, the desire of adventure which prevailed in these districts, would have materially assisted him. But he persisted in his determination to remain at Merv, while he relied on the devotion of his troops. In the decisive moment he addressed himself to them in a speech in which he referred to his prosperous administration of the province of Khorasan, and to the misery and disorder which would result from the rule of his incompetent and profligate successor. In vain did he remind them that he had taken them as beggars into his army, and had enriched them with the treasures of Turkish and Persian princes—he spoke to deaf ears. His words only roused to greater activity those who had conspired against him, at whose head stood Veki' bin Ebul Esvad and Hasan bin Iyas. On his discovery of the plot, and attempting to seize the person of the latter, the conspirators fell upon him and murdered him after a severe struggle, in which several of his brothers sacrificed their lives at the head of a few faithful adherents, who had hastened to the defence of his palace.[1]

[1] Tabari relates, in a manner equally interesting and pathetic, the details of Kuteïbe's unfortunate end. Abandoned by the warriors with whom he had shared so many dangers and hardships, by his own people whom he had enriched, nay, even by his own relations, who naturally shrank from the idea of revolting against the Khalif, but few stood by his side at the last hour of his life. His palace was surrounded by his enemies, his stables were already in flames, and in the last struggle, left without a horse, he opposed his opponents on foot. As he observed one of his kinsmen among his foremost assailants, he is said to have uttered the following verse :—

'Alas! such to-day is the spirit of the people,
Where the sun shines thither do they turn themselves.'

A certain Djehm first wounded him with an arrow, and another then cut him to pieces with his sword.

D

Thus died in the month Zilhidje, of the year 96 (714), in the forty-seventh year of his eventful life, the man who founded for the Mohammedan faith a great and mighty empire in the distant East, who gave the final blow to the religion of Zoroaster, after the mortal wounds it received at Kadesia and Nahrevan, who had planted Islam upon a soil that had ever been most fertile in fanaticism and devotion.

III.

POLITICAL AND RELIGIOUS TROUBLES DURING THE RULE OF THE ARABS.

96 (714)—261 (874).

THROUGHOUT the whole period of the Arab occupation, Bokhara and the whole of Turkestan were degraded to the position of parts of the province of Khorasan. The proud capital on the Zerefshan, the wealthy Beïkend, and the industrious Fergana, obeyed the commands issued from Mervi-Shah-Djihan, 'Merv the queen of the world.' Although Bokhara and Samarkand had their emirs, these officers were entirely dependent upon the governor of Khorasan, and their sphere of action was extremely limited. The history of Transoxania is from this time that of the administration of the Arab authorities deputed by the Khalifs of Damascus and Bagdad to govern this the eastern border province of their empire.

The province did not recover its political independence until the dynasty of the Samanides set up their throne on the farther side of the Oxus, and only retained the title of vassals of the khalifs from religious considerations. The period of Arab rule, extending over nearly 150 years, forms one uninterrupted series of troubles, internal party discord, and insurrections, caused either by the governor of Khorasan himself or by the restless population of the province. Boundless cupidity, inspired partly by the desire for mere personal wealth, partly by the desire to fortify their position at the court of the Khalif by the expenditure of money, enabled the governors of Khorasan [1] in no long time to accumulate immense sums. At the same time the distance of the province from the central government awoke in the breasts of its governors a wish to make themselves independent, while the warlike character of the population of Transoxania made them ready to enlist in the service of the rebels. It is consequently easy to explain why Khorasan from the first gave the khalifs so much trouble, and why it was so difficult permanently to maintain the peace of that province.

In the place of Kuteïbe, whose splendid successes, as we have seen, only seemed to plunge him into ruin, the Khalif Suleïman appointed Yezid bin Mohallab, 97 (715). Of course the very first thing he did was to deprive the officials appointed by Kuteïbe, first of their posts, and afterwards of their property and their liberty. No one dared to check his arbitrary conduct during the reign of Suleïman. But on the death of the latter, his successor in the khalifate, Omar bin Abdul Aziz, treated Yezid in the same way in which Suleïman had treated Kuteïbe. The power and riches to which Yezid bin Mohallab had attained in the course of two years awakened the suspicions of the Khalif. As his fears of an insurrection were to a great extent justified, he wished to anticipate the designs of the governor, and entrusted to Moslema, who was at that time conducting the war against the Greeks, the office of deposing Yezid. The Khalif, however, subsequently summoned Yezid to his court.[2] Yezid obeyed the summons, but

---

[1] As an instance of the colossal fortunes acquired by the Arab officials in Khorasan, we may cite the account of Tabari, who tells us that when, during the revolt of Rafi' bin Leïth, the insurgents plundered the house of the governor of Samarkand, they found there nearly three million drachmas.

[2] The letter of summons ran as follows:—'In the name of the Merciful and Gracious God. I, the servant of God, Omar, the Prince of the Faithful, to Yezid bin Mohallab. O Yezid, know that Suleïman,' i.e. his predecessor, 'a servant among the servants of God, to whom the Almighty gave favour and dominion, hath withdrawn from this transitory world into eternity. He hath appointed me to be his successor, and, after me, Yezid Abdul Melik, should he remain in life. The duties imposed on me are no trifles, for I have to attend to all the affairs of the Mussulmans. Well, as yet, have all the Moslems done me homage. Do thou also do me homage, and call on the people entrusted to thy care that they too may do

was seized at Bæsra and thrown into prison. He did not regain his liberty until the death of Omar in 101 (719), and only after a long struggle, maintained against him by Moslema during the khalifate of Yezid bin Abdul Melik, was he defeated and slain. In his stead came Moslema, who entrusted the administration of Bokhara and Samarkand to Said bin Amru ul Djarshi.

As Fergana had, during the recent confusion, shaken off the rule of the Arabs, Said marched with an army against their prince, who was called Khilidj,[1] after varying success, totally defeated him, and returned with rich booty to Bokhara. Nevertheless, in the course of a few years, under the reign of the Khalif Hisham, 106 (724), the restless Turks again rose in insurrection in Transoxania, gained possession of Samarkand, and rendered necessary the appearance of a large Arab army. Khalid bin Abdullah, at that time the governor of Khorasan, sent against them his brother Esed, a man of a benevolent rather than of a warlike disposition. For three years Esed endeavoured to re-establish order, but in vain. He was even compelled to retire with great loss. Irritated by the defeats which Esed had experienced, Hisham deposed him, and sent in his stead Esresh bin Abdullah,[2] who did not, however, succeed any better.

The Turks of Samarkand, in all probability supported by the Khakans of Fergana and Eastern Turkestan, had collected a force of more than 100,000 men, and Djendeb, the newly-appointed governor of Khorasan, was obliged to proceed against them in person. The vanguard of his army was

---

me homage. Then set a lieutenant in thy office in Khorasan and come hither to me.' How great is the difference between the simplicity and terseness of this document, written when the Mohammedan princes were at the zenith of their greatness, and the ridiculous bombast of future sovereigns!

[1] See note in the first chapter. Here also the Arabic authors take the name of the Turkish tribe for that of their prince.

[2] According to Tabari, Esresh lost at the beginning 1,000 men, who belonged to the tribe Beni Temim, which had settled at Bokhara. He is said to have afterwards defeated the Turks, and yet to have retired to Belkh—a contradiction, which is best explained by supposing his undertaking to have failed.

led by Sevret bin Ebu Bahr el Darimi, who was sent with
10,000 men towards Samarkand, by way of Beïkend, while
Djendeb himself marched by way of Belkh. The Khakan of
Samarkand, who, according to Tabari's account, had 120,000
men around his standards, did not venture to attack the main
body of the Arab army. He avoided an encounter with
Djendeb, but threw himself all the more fiercely on Sevret,
who came in his way, on whom he inflicted a terrible defeat.
Sevret himself fell, and of the 20,000 Mohammedans who followed him not one escaped. Djendeb wept bitter tears when
he heard of this catastrophe. Although he consoled himself
with the verse of the Koran, 'They came from God and to
God must they return,' he did not fail to raise a new levy in
the larger cities of Khorasan and Tokharistan. Having thus
collected an army of 43,000 men, he attacked and totally
defeated them.[1] He then left Nasr bin Seyyar behind him in
Samarkand, and returned in triumph to Merv, where he soon
after died. Esed bin Abdullah became governor of Khorasan
in his stead. Esed had, however, to clear out of his way his
rival, Harith bin Sherih, and in his expedition against the
latter he was surprised by death in Belkh.

The power of the Turks was to a certain extent broken by
this last campaign of the Arabs, but party strife still prevailed
in Transoxania, until the reins of government in Khorasan
were entrusted to the iron arm of Nasr bin Seyyar. This
man, distinguished by remarkable energy and caution, had,
as we have seen, held command in Samarkand, and Hisham
shortly before his death in 125 (742) appointed him to the
governorship in Khorasan. The best proof of his abilities
is afforded by the circumstance that he succeeded in maintaining himself in that office during the reigns of five successive khalifs, namely, Hisham, Velid, Yezid, Ibrahim, and

---

[1] The Turkish Khakan was already engaged in investing Samarkand, where the
wives and children of the Mohammedans had taken refuge. So that Djendeb
came just at the right time, and by his defeat of the Turks acquired a large
quantity of booty.

Mervan bin Mehemmed, the last of whom died in 133 (749). In fact, the governor was only overthrown by Ebu Muslim in 129 (746), when the dynasty of the Ommeyyads, of whom he was a faithful adherent, came to an end. The first step taken by Nasr in his new office was the complete subjection of the Turkish hordes of Transoxania and Fergana, who had always formed the most warlike portion of the population and had given the Arabs most trouble. This expedition of his, which extended to the eastern boundaries of Fergana and even as far as Kashgar,[1] was marked by signal success. He triumphed not only by the force of arms but also by his affability and sense of justice; and it is perhaps to be attributed to these qualities of his, that Ebu Muslim,[2] who raised himself from a

[1] Narshakhi relates that Nasr-i-Seyyar, in his expedition against Khokand, passed through Bokhara, and there married the daughter of Tugshade. As during the Ramazan he sat with Tugshade in front of his tent, two noble inhabitants of Bokhara came to him to complain of the injustice committed by Tugshade and by the Emir of Bokhara, Fazil bin Omar. As Nasr had converted both these men to Islam and took great interest in them, he quietly enquired of Tugshade concerning the matter. The complainants imagined that Tugshade blackened their characters and caused their ruin. They meditated revenge, and fell upon Tugshade and Fazil in front of Nasr's tent. Tugshade fell mortally wounded. Nasr gave him his own pillow to support him, and caused his own physician Karadja to attend him. Tugshade, however, died, and Narshakhi adds the *bizarre* observation, that after his death, his servants separated his flesh from his bones.

[2] Ebu Muslim, whose proper name was Abdurrahman bin Muslim, derived his origin from Khorasan, belonged to the tribe of Beni Adjel, and in his youth worked as a saddler. As certain notorious Shiites from Khorasan made a pilgrimage to Mecca, he joined himself to them. In the last-named city the chief of the Abbasides, Mehemmed Ali ben Abdullah, pointed him out as the man who by his intelligence and courage should bring that family to the throne, and enjoined the companions of Ebu Muslim that they should assist him in time of need. Returned to Khorasan, Ebu Muslim waited until Kermani, a powerful prince in the south of Persia, engaged in open hostilities against Nasr. As Ebu Muslim knew that the former would gain the victory, he allied himself to him, and declaring war not only against Nasr bin Seyyar, but also against the Ommeyyads, invited the people of Khorasan to do homage to the Abbasides. At first about a thousand warriors joined themselves to him, but his party soon increased in power to such an extent, that Nasr bin Seyyar, unable to contend against him, and seeking in vain for assistance, was at last compelled to retire from the contest, and died in the neighbourhood of the present Teheran. Ebu Muslim found a valiant lieutenant in the person of Kahtaba, Emir of Isfahan, who conquered for him the provinces of Görghen, Kum, Kashan, and Isfahan—indeed, almost all Persia—everywhere annihilating the adherents of the Ommeyyads, and proclaim-

saddler's apprentice to be the founder of a dynasty, did not gain the whole of Transoxania for his party.

That the Turks of Mavera un Nehr as well as those of Kharezm were easily won for the black banner of the Abbasides—nay, adopted its cause with enthusiasm, is evident from the deep respect with which even now the Özbegs and Turkomans mention the name of Ebu Muslim.[1] But it is plain from the historical sources before us that the original Iranian population of the land, viz. the Tadjiks, fought under the banner of Nasr, and long remained true to the cause of the Ommeyyads. The resistance which Nasr bin Sayyar offered, not only to the superior force but also to the allurements of Ebu Muslim, deserves our respect, for it was only by the death that overtook him in his flight that the rule of the Ommeyyads fell in Khorasan. On the other hand, the adroitness of Ebu Muslim deserves our admiration, who in an astonishingly short space of time gained over to his side all the Turks of Transoxania, and attached them to himself to such a degree that the myths which even now live in the mouths of the Özbegs and Turkomans compare him to the Khalif Ali for valour and wondrous works. At all events the influential individuality of Ebu Muslim first made the warlike supremacy of the Turks, although only mediately, felt in Western Asia.[2] Nay, it seems that fate would have it that as the black banner of the Abbasides was set up by

ing Ebu Muslim as the rightful Emir of the Abbasides. Kahtaba then pressed forward towards Kufa, and on the banks of the Euphrates a decisive engagement took place between him and the Ommeyyads, in which he lost his life, but by the brilliant victory of his troops placed the Abbasides on the throne of the khalifate.

[1] I have seen in Central Asia an historical manuscript full of details regarding the life and actions of Ebu Muslim (see my *Cagataische Sprachstudien*, p. 37, and my *Travels in Central Asia*, p. 358), and will only add that the Turkomans consider him one of their own race, who, endowed with the gifts of a prophet, saved at a critical period the doctrines of Islam from ruin. In the ballads which Turkish minstrels chant in his praise, he is represented as a hero like Rustem, who for the most part is engaged with unbelieving Persians.

[2] According to the work about Ebu Muslim, mentioned in the preceding note, the army which, under the leadership of Kahtaba, defeated the Ommeyyads, was for the most part composed of Turks—a fact easily explained by the great influence exercised by Ebu Muslim in Khorasan and Transoxania.

Turanian aid, it should again be trampled in the dust by the might of a Turanian prince.

Although men of the stamp of Nasr bin Seyyar and Ebu Muslim held Transoxania completely in check, yet the whole of Islam was shaken partly by the sectarian struggles of the Shiites and Kharidjites, partly by the change of dynasty in the khalifate—a change resting on a religious foundation ; and it was not to be expected that the inflammable spirits of Turkestan should remain unaffected by the commotion. As the oppressed national feelings of Persia, disguised in the sectarian zeal of the Shiites, took the field against Arab domination, so was religion used in Transoxania as a lever by which men attempted to overthrow the arbitrary tyranny of the Arabs. The first manifestation of these feelings took place in Bokhara, and, as among their kinsmen in Iran, assumed the form of a revolt in favour of the Shiite sect. During the rule of Ebu Muslim in Khorasan, a certain Sherik bin Sheikh ul Mehdi, a fanatical Shiite, raised the standard of revolt in favour of a khalif of the direct line of Ali. In his proclamation he announced as follows :—' We have had enough of misery brought upon us by the descendants of Mervan : now that we are, thank God ! free of them, why should we submit to the yoke of the Abbasides ? We will now have a true descendant of the Prophet.' It is remarkable that not only the greatest part of the population of the capital on the Zerefshan joined themselves to him, but even the prefect Abdul-Djebbar bin Shaib and the Emir of Khahrezm were among his partizans.

The movement headed by Sherik was, as may be supposed, supported by a powerful army. As soon as Ebu Muslim heard of what had happened, he at once sent the general Ziad bin Salih with 10,000 men to Bokhara ; he encountered the insurgents before the city, and during a battle that lasted thirty-seven days suffered considerable loss from the superior numbers of Sherik's followers. The partizans of the Shiite were at last compelled by hunger to abandon their strong position ; they were driven towards Nukende, a place celebrated for the abundance of its fruit, and totally defeated with great slaughter. Nukende was given over to the flames, and without turning aside to Bokhara, Ziad continued his march to Samarkand, probably for the purpose of extirpating the Shiites, who had greatly increased in that city.

But although the sect of the Shiites in Turkestan was thus nipped in the bud, and the body politic of Islam did not suffer any schism in the far East, in the course of scarcely twenty-five years so great a storm arose as had almost succeeded in tearing up the slight roots of the plant of Islam set only a century before with so much blood in the loose sandy soil of the steppes of Turkestan. This storm was the appearance of the false prophet Mokanna, the so-called 'veiled prophet' of Khorasan, who first promulgated his peculiar doctrines in Transoxania in the year 150 (767). This was the commencement of a struggle which lasted more than fifteen years, and excited a commotion that was felt many centuries later.

Mokanna, or Hashim bin Hekim,[1] to call him by his proper name, was a native of Gheze, a place situated in the district of Merv. He early distinguished himself by the keenness of his intellect, and enjoyed the reputation of being acquainted with secret arts. As his father filled the post of a serheng or general under Ebu Djafar Revaneki Belkhi, Mokanna at first served in the same capacity[2] under Ebu Muslim. Whether it was that in the service of this mighty vassal of the khalifate his imagination was heated by his experiences in Western Asia—for that was the period when eccentricities of all kinds were in full bloom in the world of Islam[3]—or that

---

[1] Weil, *History of the Khalifs*, vol. ii. p. 101, a fuller from Merv, who was called Atta.

[2] Weil says he had been secretary to Ebu Muslim.

[3] The reign of the Khalif Mehdi was, as Tabari rightly observes, the period in which Mohammedan heresies were in full bloom. Tabari relates with horror that there were people who did not believe in Mohammed and the Koran, and made themselves merry over fasting and prayer. He says that these heretics were worse than Jews, idolaters, or fire-worshippers, who had at any rate some belief or other, while the heretics asserted that this world had no beginning and will also

he was excited by the stirring times in which he lived to imagine himself in the possession of supernatural powers, we do not know, but it is certain that he asserted his prophetic character under Ebu Muslim.   As, however, he knew that the latter would endure no other greatness beside his own, he at first kept comparatively quiet.   But when Ebu Muslim's death had loosened the bands of order and discipline in Khorasan, Mokanna believed that a favourable moment had arrived.   He proclaimed his religion openly, but was at once seized and sent as a prisoner to Bagdad.   As to how long he remained there we have no certain information; we only know that he came back from Bagdad, as did Bab [1] in more modern days, strengthened in his delusions of a prophetic mission. In Merv he collected the remains of his former secret adherents, and proclaimed his doctrines with all the greater zeal.

The first time that he appeared amongst them, about the year 150 (670), he asked them, 'Do ye know who I am?' They told him that he was Hashim bin Hekim, to which he answered, 'Ye are in error; I am your God and the God of all worlds; I name myself as I will.   I appeared before under the forms of Adam, Ibrahim, Musa, Jesus, Mohammed, Ebu Muslim, and now in the form in which ye see me.' 'How comes it then,' they replied, 'that they only proclaimed themselves prophets, whereas thou wilt be God himself?' 'They were merely sensual,' was his answer, 'but I am altogether spiritual, and have the power to assume whatever form I will.' At first he remained in the neighbourhood of Merv, and sent his apostles throughout Turkestan with a summons to conver-

---

have no end ; men and beasts spring up like plants, no one knows whence they come nor whither they go ; that there is no life after death, nor any other world but this.

[1] Bab, who in recent times brought all Persia into an uproar through his new religion, in like manner commenced his career after his return from Bagdad.   As Mokanna from his rocky nest communicated his delusions to his adherents without once coming into personal contact with them, so also were the adherents of Bab carried away to the most daring enterprises, while their master was for years in prison in the fortress of Tcherig.

sion, worded as follows :—' In the name of the merciful and
all-gracious God, I, Hashim, son of Hekim, Lord of all Lords.
Praised be God the Only One, who formerly revealed himself
in Adam, Noah, Ibrahim, Musa, Christ, Mohammed, Ebu
Muslim. Namely, I, Mokanna, Lord of Might, of Glory, and
of Truth. Band yourselves together around me, and know
that mine is the Dominion of the World, mine the Glory and
the Omnipotence. Beside me there is no God. He that
goeth with me cometh into Paradise, he that fleeth from me
falleth into Hell.'

The hostile spirit of sectarianism which at that time per-
vaded all Islam, especially the great excitement which was
caused by the change of dynasty, may have largely contributed to lead the lower classes of Turkestan, in whose bosoms
still glimmered some sparks of the old national fire-worship,
to apostatise from Islam and to receive the doctrines of
Mokanna in masses. When Hamid, at that time governor of
Khorasan, attempted to seize him, there were whole villages
which afforded a secure asylum to the fugitive prophet.
Nevertheless, the majority of his adherents, who, on account
of their white clothing, were called Sefid-djameghian, or ' the
White-robed,' were to be found on the other side of the Oxus
in Bokhara, Samarkand, Kesh, and Nakhsheb.[1] Mokanna,
who did not feel himself sufficiently secure in the neighbourhood of Merv, sought to reach one of those places, and
although his purpose was discovered and the river was guarded
at several points, he nevertheless succeeded, with thirty-six of
his faithful followers, in reaching the opposite bank, and
escaping to a strong fortress belonging to Kesh, situated on
the mountain Sam (?).[2] In this place of careful conceal-

[1] Here it was that, to gratify the wish of some of his followers who desired to
see a miracle, he drew out of a well a shining body in the form of a moon. The
Mah-i-Nakh'sheb, or ' moon of Nakh'sheb,' is even now a favourite metaphor of
the Persian poets. Curiously enough, Narshakhi, who gives a very detailed
account of Mokanna's life, makes no mention of this episode.

[2] Tabari calls this fortress Nevakid ; and as it was situated to the north of
Kesh (for we are told that the Arab general Daud, who would march from this
fortress to Belkh, had to pass Kesh on his way), it must have been either Yemeni

ment the pseudo-prophet, who still kept his face covered with
a green veil, or, according to others, a golden mask, and was
therefore called Mokanna, or 'the veiled,'[1] remained throughout the whole of the fourteen years of the religious war, without once leaving his hiding-place. Withdrawing himself from
publicity, he carried out his objects for the most part through
his powerful representatives, who were at the same time
generals. An Arab from Bokhara named Hekim and three
commanders of armies—Hashri, Bagi, and Kirdek[2]—were at
the head of a movement which first broke into revolt in a
village not far from Bokhara. The Sefid-djameghian attacked
a mosque, killed the muezzin and fifteen true believers, and
by their acts of violence against the Mussulmans soon spread
terror and anxiety throughout the whole of Turkestan.
Alarmed at the increasing peril, the Emir of Bokhara, Husein
bin Mu'az, made the first attempt to put them down. He
marched with all his available troops, accompanied by the
inhabitants of Bokhara, who were led by the kazi, Amir bin
Omran, against the village of Narshakh, where the adherents
of Mokanna had concentrated their chief forces ; the kazi
wished at first to employ persuasion and reproof, but finding
these fail had recourse to arms. According to Narshakhi's
account, the result of the first encounter was favourable to the
Arabs, and 700 of the Sefid-djameghian were said to have
remained on the field of battle. This advantage, however,
had but little influence on the state of affairs, for it soon appeared that the local authorities of Transoxania could not

or Kitab, both accounted strong fortresses and situated to the north of the modern Shehri-Sebz. Weil, *History of the Khalifs*, vol. ii. p. 103, calls this place
Sanam.

[1] Narshakhi and Tabari both relate that he used the veil to conceal his hideous
one-eyed countenance. If we decline to attribute this explanation to Mohammedan
hatred (which is very possible), we might believe that he wished to imitate
Kaliph Ali, who went about generally veiled, and whose picture is thus represented
by the Shiites.

[2] Tabari names the principal *confidant* of Mokanna, Tokhardje, while he gives
the three generals the names Serkhume, Habubi, and Gheyek, or Kiyek. I have
placed in the text the names mentioned by Narshakhi, as this author is more
reliable in all that relates to Mokanna.

cope with the rebels, and that energetic action on the part of the governor of Khorasan was imperatively necessary.

While on the one hand the mysterious individuality of Mokanna, enveloped in a halo of sanctity, believed by many to be clothed in the very light of the Godhead, had the strongest influence in exciting his adherents to deeds of bravery and to the most reckless contempt of death, on the other hand the cause of the veiled prophet had gained an equally firm support in the alliance of the Turks. A Turkish chieftain, named Khulukh, or Kuluk,[1] had taken part in the insurrection with many thousands of his people. In the first place the Mohammedanism of the Turks was at that time by no means beyond suspicion, in the second place Mokanna offered them the best opportunity for plunder and rapine, and it was in fact by their hordes only that the Arab troops were so long kept at bay. At the urgent commands of the Khalif Mehdi, Abdul Melik, at that time governor of Khorasan, had sent the general Djebrail bin Yahya to Bokhara. He contended, with varying fortunes, against the main body of the Sefid-djameghian before Samarkand,[2] until he was so severely crippled that 7,000 men, under the command of Ukbe bin Muslim, had to be sent to his assistance from Belkh. The last, terrified by a successful stratagem,[3]

[1] Khulukh or Kuluk, according to the orthography of our documents. But it is possible that ڬلڂ has arisen in consequence in the points from the old Turkish or Uigur ڬلڂ khilidj, according to the modern pronunciation kilidj. The Khakan of Khokand, who in the year 101 (719) defeated Said bin Amru úl Djarshi, had a similar Turkish name.

[2] It is not clear from our authorities whether Samarkand was garrisoned by the Sefid-djameghian or by the Moslims. Narshakhi would lead us to conjecture that the former was the case, since he makes Djebrail bin Yahya to encamp before Samarkand ; Tabari, however, hints at the contrary, and asserts that the struggles of the Arabs before Samarkand were directed against the besieging army of the ' White-robed.'

[3] The stratagem was as follows. A messenger was sent to Mokanna with instructions that he should purposely fall into the hands of Ukbe. The man was taken prisoner, and on being searched a letter was found on him, which contained congratulations on account of the victory gained by Mokanna's general over Djebrail, further intimating that the army, after plundering Samarkand, would proceed

according to Tabari, turned back when he had proceeded
half way.   Even when 14,000 additional troops were sent by
the governor of Khorasan and the Arab forces concentrated
themselves in Termez, they were unable to resist the fanatical
adherents of Mokanna, who stamped armies out of the ground.
Even before they could cross the Oxus the Arabs suffered a
severe defeat.   Deprived of the necessary auxiliaries, and cut
off from all communication either with Belkh or with Merv,
the position of Djebrail bin Yahya before Samarkand became
extremely critical.

By dint of great exertions he succeeded in gaining possession of the strongly-fortified Narshakh.   After a siege of four
months, in which catapults, mines, fire, and all other imaginable means [1] were employed, a large breach had been made.
The Arabs penetrated into the place and promised to treat
the Sefid-djameghian with forbearance on condition that they
would return to the bosom of Islam and give up their leaders
and their arms to the Khalif.   A long procession of the ' White-
robed,' said to carry arms concealed beneath their garments,
betook themselves, under the leadership of Hekim, into the
Arab camp.   Hekim was conducted, before the eyes of his
followers, into the tent of Djebrail.   His long stay therein
excited their suspicion ; and as Hashri,[2] on demanding an
explanation of his continued absence from a son of Djebrail,
was without further reason cut down, the irritated fanatics,[3]

southward against Ukbe.   Ukbe supposing the letter to be authentic, and fearing
the superior numbers of the enemy, hastily retired.

[1] Narshakhi speaks of *arade* or waggons.   Can these have been the war
chariots mentioned in the Bible, provided on either side with a row of sharp
scythes?

[2] Narshakhi relates that Hashri rode up to the son of Djebrail in golden boots.
Of Queen Khatun we are told that she had like coverings for her feet—an article
of luxury which we never encounter in the subsequent, i.e. Mohammedan period
of Asiatic history.

[3] A proof of the fanaticism of the followers of Mokanna, and at the same time
of the cruelty of the Arabs, is contained in the following episode related by
Narshakhi.   After the battle, one of the prisoners, the widow of a soldier named
Seru, was brought before Djebrail, who asked her, ' Thou recognisest Ebu
Muslim as the father of the Moslims?'   'No,' answered the woman, ' that he is
not, for he hath slain my husband.'   She was hewn in pieces, and her son, who
was with her, was beheaded.

inflamed with a spirit of revenge, seized on their concealed weapons. The struggle was renewed with increased bitterness, and the followers of Mokanna who had almost been made prisoners again found themselves free, and the victory of Djebrail rendered of no avail. It is true that Narshakhi tells us that Baghi was killed in this action, and Kirdek alone escaped back to Mokanna ; but the tame resistance encountered by the ' White-robed,' and the power they continued to develope in the whole of Transoxania, contradict all the bombastic reports of victory given by the Mohammedan historians. There could be no doubt that the power of Mokanna was on the increase, and the existence of Islam was seriously threatened.

It is therefore no wonder that the Khalif Mehdi, in his alarm, came to Nishabur in order to avert the evil by a change in the governorship of Khorasan. Hence Abdul Melik was superseded in the year 161 (777) and Mu'az bin Muslim set in his place. The latter at once took more energetic measures, collected a vast army in the desert between Merv and Bokhara on the banks of the Oxus, and set 3,000 armourers to work to prepare the weapons required. He then joined Said ul Djarshi, the brave Emir of Herat, and hastened to the assistance of the Arabs before Samarkand. On the way thither, he was surprised by Sefid-djameghian lying in ambush on the plain of Berkend. Although, according to Tabari's account, the Mohammedans gained the victory, the contrary seems to have taken place; for Mu'az, instead of continuing his road to Samarkand, retired in haste to Bokhara. He attributed the failure of his undertaking to the Emir of Herat, having in spite of all remonstrances insisted on carrying with him several thousand sheep, which aroused the cupidity of the Turks, and tempted them to the most daring actions. Nothing therefore remained for the Arab general but to wait in Bokhara for a more favourable moment. As has been already observed, the cultivators of the fields, consequently the lowest class of the people, had for the most part gathered around the standard of Mokanna, they were joined by the plundering nomadic Turks; and as the wild anarchy with which the warfare was conducted horrified the peaceable Iranian natives, it was impossible for the cause of Mokanna long to prosper on the banks of the Zerefshan, where the settled population was more attached to Mohammedan civilisation.

The Sefid-djameghian were soon everywhere hunted down, and at the moment their camp before Samarkand was weakened Mu'az made a second attempt, which proved successful, to make himself master of that city. The leader of the 'White-robed' having fallen in the battle, his followers dispersed. Mu'az placed Djebrail bin Yahya in Samarkand, and led the main body of his army against the fortress in which Mokanna, as already stated, had taken up his abode, inhabiting himself the innermost citadel, while the outer fortifications were occupied by his devoted soldiery. Narshakhi tells us the following interesting episode of Mokanna's retirement. About 50,000 of his adherents were encamped before the gate of the fortress, and earnestly requested to be allowed a single glimpse of his glorious presence. He declined, and sent his page with a message: 'Tell my servants that Musa also wanted to see my divinity, but could not look on the radiancy of my glory; to behold me is death to the earth-born.' His enthusiastic adherents declared they would gladly sacrifice their lives if only this supreme favour was granted.

As they would take no denial, Mokanna granted their prayer, and appointed them a certain time when he promised to show himself at the gate of the fortress. On the evening of the appointed day he placed all his wives in a row within the fortress with mirrors in their hands, held so that the rays of the setting sun were reflected in the glasses, and at the moment the reflection was most brilliant the gates were thrown open. The strong light dazzled the eyes of the fervent believers, who fell to the ground amazed and crying out, 'O God! this glory suffices us: if we gaze longer we shall all be

E

annihilated l'   They remained some time prostrate in the
dust, till at last Mokanna sent to them his page with a
message that they might arise : God was well pleased with
them, and had given them the good things of all the world.

Mu'az surrounded the hiding-place of Mokanna with a
formidable army, composed mostly of Arabs.   He first tried
to induce him to surrender peaceably.   A messenger was sent
into the fortress.   Mokanna asked who he was and what he
wanted.   'As thou givest thyself out to be a god,' answered
the messenger, 'thou shouldst know all things ; why, then,
dost thou ask ?'   This bold behaviour on the part of a
Mohammedan in the stronghold of Mokanna is related by
Tabari, but is much to be doubted.   At any rate the latter
made it evident in his reply that notwithstanding the reverses
of his followers he intended to persevere to the last in the
character he had assumed.   The question now was to take the
fortress at any price.   Mu'az prepared to lay siege to it, but
the cold season [1] setting in, which is especially severe in the
district of Shehri-Sebz, it became necessary to send the Arab
troops, for shelter from frost and cold, to the more southern
Belkh, and the siege in consequence progressed very slowly.
The Khalif Mehdi, anxious and impatient as to the result of
this most serious matter, removed Mu'az bin Muslim, after
two years' service, and appointed in his place as governor of
Khorasan in the year 163 (779) Said ul Djarshi, who was
equally well acquainted with the local circumstances.   He
proved more energetic than his predecessor, and commenced
by building houses for the Arab troops, so as to continue the
operations of the siege uninterruptedly.   Nevertheless he had
to spend two more years before the walls of this formidable fortress.   Kizum, a brother of Mokanna,[2] was the
first to surrender with 30,000 of his men, in consequence of

[1] Shehri-Sebz and the neighbourhood have the same climate as Samarkand.
Both places are situated on the slopes of the Karatau mountains, and have a
severe and long winter.

[2] Tabari says kardash, but it is not to be forgotten that this word in the older
Turkish writings and in Central Asia is used to designate a relation.

which the followers of Mokanna were driven back within a
much smaller space, and having besides suffered greatly from
hunger, at length surrendered unconditionally with three
thousand eight hundred fanatics from Kesh, who had been
looked on as the bitterest opponents of the Moslims; Mokanna
alone still held out in the inner citadel, which was placed on
the point of a rock and held to be impregnable.

We are told that Mokanna during these last days, after his
most faithful adherents had abandoned him and all hope of
escape was gone, assembled his wives around him to a banquet. He there invited them to drink his health in wine in which
he had previously mingled poison. All drank of it with the
exception of one named Banuka, who, having perceived the
atrocious deed, spilt the wine into her bosom, and feigning to
be dead, afterwards repeated as the sole surviving witness the
details of the last moments of the false prophet. According
to the account which a certain Ebu Ali Mohammed, from
Kesh, heard from her, Mokanna, after the wives were all dead,
cut off the head of his faithful page, the only male among
his immediate attendants, and then flung himself into a
burning furnace which had been heated for three days together, and whence he never came out. He is said to have announced this intention to his wives before the deed. He
told them he should take this step at the last moment in
order to accuse those who had deserted him before the
throne of God, and that with the help of the angels whom
he would bring with him he should still triumph after all.
Banuka [1] added, ' I watched the furnace a long time, but he
never came out of it.' Banuka was the person who gave up
the citadel to the general Said ul Djarshi, but not until she
had been promised ten thousand aktche from the treasury of
Mokanna. The Arabs took possession of the citadel with all
the treasures it contained, and by this successful conclusion

[1] Such is the name given to this woman by Tabari. It is, however, not a
proper name, but rather derived from the Persian *banu*, 'a woman.'

of a war that had lasted many years delivered the eastern frontier of Islam from a great peril.

We must be content to remain in the dark as to Mokanna's teaching, and even as to the fact whether or not he asserted or intended to assert any positive dogmas. His commencements seem to indicate that he intended to include in his religion the doctrine of the Incarnation, and that on the whole he was under the influence not only of Indian but also of old Persian notions of religion. It would be difficult to maintain anything positive on the subject. Narshakhi, who gave 300 years later the most detailed account of the strange sect that had run riot in his native city, accuses the adherents of Mokanna of the same vices which the modern Mohammedans attribute to the Druses in the Lebanon and the Babis in Persia. For instance, we are told that they abstained from prayer and from outward religious acts, practised community of women, and regarded the murder of a Mohammedan as a work most pleasing to God. All this, however, as well as the speeches ascribed by Islamite historians to the Veiled Prophet, seems based on pure invention. This uncertainty with regard to the teaching of Mokanna is the more to be regretted as his doctrine survived him several centuries. The translator of Narshakhi relates that so late as the year 512 (1128) secret adherents of Mokanna, who only professed Islamism outwardly from fear, were still to be found in the neighbourhood of Kesh and Nakh'sheb, and even in some of the villages around Bokhara, for instance in Kushki Bunar.

After the overthrow of Mokanna the religious doubts came to an end in Turkestan, and the agitated waves of fanaticism gradually subsided, but the tendency to political disturbances among the warlike inhabitants of Transoxania could be checked but for a short time, notwithstanding the iron rule of the earlier Abbasides, and the much-praised administration of the Barmekedes. Towards the end of the reign of Harun ar Rashid we find Rafi' bin Leïth, the grandson of Nasr bin

Seyyar, taking the field in open rebellion against the Khalif. Though not actually intending to avenge the blood of his grandfather, slain in the cause of the Ommeyyads, he was nevertheless the cause of the early death of the greatest of the Abbasides.[1]   Rafi', a young soldier of remarkable personal beauty, is said to have raised the standard of revolt in consequence of the severity with which his illicit intercourse with a woman had been punished by the Khalif.[2]   Harun ar Rashid had given orders to Ali bin Isa, the governor of Khorasan, which he in turn' transmitted to Suleïman, the prefect of Samarkand, to have Rafi' paraded through the town on a donkey, with his face to the tail,[3] to separate him from his wife, and to throw him into prison.   Rafi' escaped this disgraceful punishment by flight, but he presently returned in secret, and as Ali bin Isa was universally detested for his inordinate exactions and tyranny, Rafi' had no difficulty in instigating the people of Samarkand to revolt first against Ali, and lastly against Harun ar Rashid himself.   For a long time the Turkestanis had made repeated complaints to the Khalif against Ali, but the latter had succeeded by means of his immense riches[4] in allaying the displeasure of the rapacious Harun.   Even when the latter finally determined to remove him he was still afraid of his vassal's power, and enjoined the greatest caution and stratagem on the African general Horthuma bin Ayan.   Horthuma advanced with an army supposed to be auxiliaries against the insurgent Rafi', and when

---

[1] Harun ar Rashid is said to have caught the illness of which he died on his way from Bagdad to Khorasan, whither he was going in order to suppress the revolt of Rafi'.

[2] The object of his affections was the wife of a certain Yahya bin ul Asháth. She had apostatised from Islam, and was in consequence divorced from her husband.   Afterwards Rafi' reconverted her to Islam, and married her, to the great scandal of the Mohammedans.

[3] This way of punishing superior officers was for a long time in vogue among the Mohammedan peoples.   Thus Murad II., after the battle of Varna, condemned a pasha, for cowardice, to have half his beard shaved off, and to be paraded round the camp, dressed in woman's clothes, and seated on an ass, with his head to the tail.

[4] See note, p. 36.

Ali, suspecting no danger, came to meet him, he handed over to him the decree of removal,[1] took him prisoner, and sent him to the Khalif. In the meantime Rafi' bin Leïth had increased his strength in Samarkand, had won over all Transoxania to his cause, and established his camp in Bokhara, so that Horthuma, advancing against him across the Oxus, found himself entirely forsaken. Awed by the superior power of Rafi', no one would listen to Horthuma.

Under such circumstances Meemun, in order to overpower Rafi', addressed himself to the family of the Samanides. The general Khozeïma ibn Khazim was not fortunate in the attempt he made to bring back the rebels to their allegiance. The result of this failure was to transplant into Turkestan the dynasty to whom the most brilliant period of the countries of the Oxus, and especially the independent history of Bokhara, were mainly due.

[1] The letter of Harun ar Rashid was as follows :—'In the Name of the Merciful and Gracious God ! O Ali bin Isa, thou unworthy bastard ! Is this the return made by my favour which I showed in raising thee from the rank of a porter to that of a prince, that I now hear all the viziers speak of thy incapacity? Formerly I gave no credence to their words, and for this thy thanks are that thou oppressest the Moslims and hast deserted me. I have now sent Horthuma that he should bind thee and take thee prisoner, and administer justice unto everyone. Therefore deliver up the government to him and obey all his words.'

IV.

THE SAMANIDES AND EMIR ISMAIL.
261 (874)—295 (907).

ESED BIN ABDULLAH (surnamed the Good and Friend of
the Oppressed), being Viceroy of Khorasan, was implored by a
nobleman[1] of Belkh, named Saman, one of the remaining
followers of Zoroaster, to assist him against his enemies who
had expelled him from the above-named city. Esed took up
his cause warmly and reinstated him in his former home, upon
which Saman out of gratitude embraced the religion of Islam,[2]
and named his first-born son Esed, after his protector. This
Esed had four sons, Nuh, Ahmed, Yahya, and Ilias, who,
following their father's example, were all entirely devoted to
the cause of the Arabs, so that Khalif Meemun was fully
justified in his recommendation of them to the governor of
Khorasan[3] as 'men of high lineage and well-fitted for the
highest posts.' As already mentioned, their services were
required in the war against Rafi' bin Leïth, and as the valuable assistance they rendered soon compelled Rafi' to submit,
Meemun recompensed each of Esed's sons separately, granting Nuh Samarkand, Ahmed Fergana, Yahya Djadj (Tashkend) and Osrushna, and Ilias Herat. The succeeding

---

[1] Saman traced his descent from the Sasanide Behram Tchubin; hence his
reputation among the Arabs as being of aristocratic birth.

[2] The fact that Saman whilst still a heretic had held a command in Belkh long
after the Arab conquest, proves the small progress Islamism had at first made
among the followers of Zoroaster.

[3] Gasan bin Abbad, a nephew of the celebrated Fazl bin Sahl, who as
Meemun's vizier bore the title of Zulriasetein—i.e. controller of both civil and
military departments.

khalifs confirmed these grants, and upon Nuh's death the government of Samarkand passed to his brother Ahmed, whose son, Nasr, succeeded him and was confirmed in his office by a diploma of Khalif Vathik's. Whilst, on the one hand, the open favour with which the Samanides were treated by the Arabs materially strengthened the rising dynasty, the connection with them proved, on the other hand, an advantage to all Transoxania. In those countries about the Oxus and Yaxartes which had suffered most from constant convulsions, order began to be restored, and it very soon became evident that under the Samanides a new era would dawn on Transoxania.

Nasr bin Ahmed, a man with many virtues but of a weak and suspicious nature, would, however, scarcely have found it possible in the face of the confusion caused in one quarter by the Tahirides (though their power was declining), and in another by the revolt of Yakub bin Leïth at Khorasan, to establish his throne on a firm basis, had it not been for the steadfast support he received from his younger brother Ismail. This Ismail, born at Fergana in the month Shevval of the year 234 (848), was only fifteen years old at the time of his father's death. He clung to his elder brother with devoted affection and respect, which were not even shaken when the latter went to war with him. The first occasion on which Ismail distinguished himself as a young man of twenty-five was at Bokhara, where the inhabitants were split up into fractions of the different parties then existing in the east of Islam, and exposed to the greatest dangers by their own internal divisions. Huseïn bin Tahir of Khahrezm invaded the country in the year 259 (872), plundering and laying waste the whole of Bokhara.[1] Some of the nobles of the country, following the advice of Obeïdullah el Fikih, a man

[1] On one occasion, under pretext of collecting taxes, he called in all the *Esrefi* coins for the purpose of changing them into silver. He had to fly suddenly during the night, leaving behind him the treasure. It fell into the hands of the poor of the city. They enriched themselves so, that long after any very wealthy person was nicknamed 'a sharer of Huseïn bin Tahir's treasure.'

of great learning and consideration, applied to Nasr the
Samanide at Samarkand for help and protection. He proposed to send them his brother Ismail, and despatched him
at once to Bokhara; on hearing of his arrival the enemy
opened negotiations for peace. Bokhara was placed under the
command of the Samanides, and the name of Nasr inserted in
the Khutbe in the place of that of Yakub bin Leïth. Ismail
made his solemn entry as Nasr's representative into the city,
which was decorated in his honour, on the 1st Ramazan, 260,
and in spite of the division of parties his reception was
cordial. Gold and precious offerings were poured forth to
welcome the guest, whose virtues were well known by reputation. Bokhara had good reason to keep the day as a festival,
for the unity of the whole of Transoxania, indeed of all
Turkestan, was now accomplished, and in the diploma sent
the same year by Khalif Mu'temid investing Nasr with the
viceroyalty of Transoxania, his dominion is described as
extending over all countries *from the banks of the Oxus to the
extreme East.*[1]

Notwithstanding the critical circumstances under which
Ismail first appeared in Bokhara, he soon succeeded in making
himself universally beloved. The most difficult person to
conciliate was his brother Nasr himself, who was annoyed
with him at the very outset, because during a temporary
absence from Bokhara he had left a deputy in charge whom
Nasr disapproved of.[2] He wished in consequence to depose
him, and was only prevented doing so by the intervention of
mutual friends. With many misgivings he allowed him to
return to Bokhara, where Ismail was again received with
every mark of distinction. His return was welcome to all,
as it was hoped that with his well-known love of order and
strict justice he would put an end to the system of brigandage

---

[1] The original says, ' *Es abi Djeihun Ta akza Bilad Meshrik.*'

[2] Mirkhond, in his *History of the Samanides,* ascribes the beginning of the
misunderstanding with Nasr to the intimate friendship between Ismail and Rafi'
bin Horthuma ; there were not wanting mischievous persons who persuaded Nasr
that Ismail was conspiring with Rafi' to drive him from his throne.

which had grown up in his absence—nearly 4,000 brigands
lurking between Rametin and Barket alone. Ismail at once
sent out troops and almost entirely annihilated them, leaving
only a small number of prisoners to be sent to Samarkand.
Scarcely had this danger been overcome when news arrived
that Huseïn bin Tahir had again crossed the Oxus and was
advancing on Bokhara with 2,000 Khahrezmians. Ismail
hurried to meet him and entirely overthrew him. This was
the first opportunity he had had of showing his personal
bravery, and his popularity with his soldiers was further increased by his munificent gifts [1] to them.

On his return to Bokhara Ismail attempted to resume the
reins of government, but again encountered obstacles. The
principal men of the city on the Zerefshan, who had profited
largely by the preceding confusion, and saw that the establishment of order would curtail their privileges, got up an
opposition. It was necessary to get rid of them, and the
chiefs were therefore sent to Samarkand under pretext of
an embassy to Nasr, who, according to a previous understanding, seized them and threw them into prison. Ismail
found himself nevertheless still unable to govern with the
tranquillity he desired. His brother Nasr, jealous of his
success and always full of groundless suspicion, sought a new
cause of quarrel in an alleged unpunctuality in the payment of taxes. Bokhara at that time possessed a revenue of
500,000 direms, only a small portion of which belonged to
Ismail, and as after repeated demands he still delayed to
pay over the remainder, the dispute between the two brothers
soon culminated in open war. In the year 272 (885) we find
Nasr, always easily roused, advancing with an army against
Bokhara. Ismail, unprepared, made his escape through
Tarab to Beïkend, whence he sent a messenger named
Hamuye to solicit the help of his friend and ally Rafi' bin
Leïth (who from being a rebellious vassal, advanced to the

[1] His presents to his officers consisted of *linen* dresses, far more highly valued at
that time in Central Asia than silk.

post of Viceroy of Khorasan). Rafi' hurried over the Oxus, and, having joined Ismail, their united forces were on the point of attacking Nasr when they found they had been circumvented by him, their communications with the inhabited portion of Bokhara interrupted at Tavaïs, and themselves cut off in the desert. There had been a failure of crops that year, and the want of provisions soon reduced the troops to the utmost extremity. Rafi', perceiving the critical position he would be in should the two brothers come to an understanding and join in attacking him, suddenly changed his tactics and came forward as a peacemaker between Nasr and Ismail.[1] He succeeded in bringing about an agreement, on the condition that Ismail should in future only take the position of a *Muhasil*, i.e. a collector of taxes, at Bokhara,— whilst the actual government of the town should be committed to other hands. This was done in 273 (885); but within fifteen months the old dispute about the payment of taxes revived. Nasr, as usual, first commenced hostilities. His army, supported by a strong contingent from Khokand, was commanded by General Ebul Asha'th. But Ismail was better prepared on this occasion; he had brought up auxiliary troops from Khahrezm, and in the latter part of the year 275 (888) entirely defeated Ebul Asha'th in a decisive battle.

---

[1] Mirkhond ascribes the bringing about of this peaceable understanding to a different cause, for in p. 115 of Defrémery's translation we find the following passage relating to it :—' Lorsque Hamouieh fut arrivé au terme de son ambassade, Rafi se dirigea en personne vers le Mavérannahr. Quand il eut passé le fleuve Oxus, Hamouieh conçut quelques craintes et se dit : "Rafi, avec cette armée qui l'accompagne, pourra réduire sous sa puissance la totalité de Mavérannahr. Il est à présumer que, tandis qu'il repoussera Nasr, il s'emparera d'Ismaïl, et de la manière dont il lui donnera la principauté il faudra désormais qu'Ismaïl lui soit soumis ; et ce sera une grande honte." Hamouieh ayant consacré sa prudence à prévenir cet événement fâcheux, dit à Rafi : "O Émir, ce qui convient est que tu fasses des efforts afin que la paix soit conclue entre les frères ; car si tu persistes à combattre, il est possible que les deux frères fassent ensemble un accord, et que tu éprouves un sujet d'affliction sur la terre étrangère." Le conseil d'Hamouieh se trouvant conforme aux dispositions de Rafi, celui-ci envoya des députés auprès de Nasr et d'Ismaïl et leur fit dire : L'avantage de chacun se trouve dans la paix. Il montra tant d'insistance à ce sujet que les deux frères conclurent un accommodement et Rafi retourna dans le Khoraçan.'

Nasr himself narrowly escaped being killed by a charge of Khahrezmians, who were only halted with difficulty just in time to save him; he thereupon threw himself off his horse and surrendered. Ismail, hearing what had occurred, hurried to the spot and treated his captive brother with the profoundest marks of respect. Kissing the cushion on which Nasr sat, he said, 'O Emir, it was the will of God that my eyes should this day behold thee captive.' 'It was *thine own will*, Ismail,' replied Nasr; 'thou hast rebelled against thy superior and sinned before God.' 'I confess thou art right,' returned Ismail; 'but be thou magnanimous and forgive me.' While this conversation (the whole of which is most creditable to the great Samanide's noble and generous character) was going on, the younger brother, Is'hak, who had taken part in the battle against Nasr, appeared on the scene and remained some time quietly looking on, on horseback. Ismail angrily reproved him for his insolence in not dismounting in the presence of his elder brother and the head of the family. Is'hak excused himself on the ground that his horse was too restive; but he was lifted from his saddle, and, having kissed the feet of the captive, remained standing before him in an attitude of the deepest humility. Ismail continued : 'O Emir, thou wilt do well to return at once to thy great capital before this news reaches it, which might damage thy reputation at Mavera un nehr.' 'What, Ismail!' said Nasr, 'thou proposest to me thyself to send me back to my own home?' 'What else should I do,' replied Ismail, 'but fulfil thy wishes?'

Nasr, moved to tears by these words, could not refrain from expressing his deep remorse at the bloodshed he had caused. He remounted his horse, and set off for Samarkand, his two brothers accompanying him the first league. He spent the next four years quietly at Samarkand, and died there on the 22nd Djemazi ul evvel of the year 279 (892–3).

Upon the death of his brother, Ismail assumed in the year 280 (893–4) the sovereignty of all Transoxania and Khahrezm ; he confided the government of Samarkand to Nasr's son, but chose Bokhara for his own residence, and it was there that he received from Khalif Mu'tasid Billah the diploma of investiture with the usual banners and robes. Ismail looked upon this sign of submission to the Prince of the Faithful as an act well pleasing to the Almighty, although, practically, the recognition of the Court of Bagdad was a matter of indifference to him, and the Khalif himself was perfectly aware that the document by which he made over to him the right of ' Khutbe and money-coinage '(?) was a mere formality. The khalifate had by this time been completely undermined by the burdens of all kinds resting on it, and only maintained itself by relying on a network of small intrigues. The degenerate successors of Mohammed lived in dread of the new dynasties rising up in the east of the empire, and we accordingly find Khalif Mu'tasid, at the same time that he was appointing the Emir Ismail as ' his accredited representative at Mavera un nehr and Defender of the Faith and of the Khalifate against all their enemies,' sending secret orders to Amru bin Leïth, the former rebel and now Viceroy of Khorasan, to attack Ismail and overthrow him.[1] The latter of course appeared unconscious of anything, and immediately after ascending the throne undertook, as a mark of gratitude for his investiture, a *gaza* (i.e. a religious war) against the Christian settlement of Taraz, which lay to the north of his dominions, near the modern Hazreti Turkestan. He defeated the Christians, turning their principal church[2] into a

---

[1] The Khalif granted his request, and encouraged him to go to war with Ismail, at the very time probably that he was confirming the latter as Viceroy of Transoxania, and inviting him to oppose Amru. (Weil, *History of the Khalifs*, vol. ii. p. 485.)

[2] Narshakhi expressly says, ' Kilisa-i-Buzurk ' ▬ Great Church, and as the same author always calls the Parsee meeting-houses *Ateshkhane* ▬ fire-temples, it may be assumed almost with certainty that the Turkish prince conquered by Ismail was a Christian, and that the church which was converted into a mosque belonged to a body of Nestorian Christians. In Colonel Yule's excellent work, *Cathay and the Way Thither* (London, 1866), it is clearly shown that so late as the fourteenth century, a Nestorian bishopric existed in the neighbourhood of the modern Hazreti Turkestan, north of Samarkand, and that, as is well known, this sect had been established in that district since the fourth century.

mosque, and then returned home with such an amount of booty that the share of each trooper amounted to 1,000 direms. On his return to Bokhara, Ismail hoped to devote himself to the work of internal administration, but before long the war broke out with Amru bin Leïth which occupied all his attention for seven years. Amru, as we have said, had been secretly incited by the Khalif to attack Ismail; he had defeated Rafi' bin Horthuma, but found the Samanide, with his increasing power and popularity, a rival he was anxious to get rid of at any price. The intimate relations which had existed between Rafi' and Ismail convinced Amru that the latter's feelings towards himself were not likely to be very friendly; and as he was seeking an occasion to quarrel, the circumstance that a fugitive servant of his had been well received at Bokhara seemed to give him a pretext for a rupture. He tried at first a paper war, being probably unprepared for any other; on Ismail sending a sharp answer, he feigned conciliation, and wrote, ' Why this quarrel ? The Khalif has entrusted these countries to us ; we are colleagues, let us also be friends and confidants. No gossip shall in future disturb our union ; my former expressions were unguarded, but that is all over now, and in future thou shalt never be interfered with, and enjoy thy power undisturbed.' Ismail was already encamped on the Oxus, where he received this letter, which was brought to him by an embassy from Amru headed by the celebrated Sheikh Nishabur ; he saw through the trick, and wrote a short cold answer, whereupon the astute Saffaride ordered his general, Ali bin Shervin,[1] to advance on Bokhara, desiring him to spare the Bokhariots themselves as much as possible, and to endeavour to win them over by fair means rather than foul. Hearing of this, Ismail at once crossed the Oxus. Ali bin Shervin took the offen-

---

[1] Other authorities state that Ismail was the first to propose peaceable negotiations, and that Amru replied, ' Thou art Lord of a great continent, I only possess the land beyond this river (Oxus), and am surrounded by heretics. Be content with that thou hast, and leave this frontier territory to me.' (Weil, *History of the K'halifs*, vol. ii. p. 485.)

sive with a strong body of artillery, but, although both sides fought desperately, Ismail's troopers gained the victory. These children of the desert, riding with uncouth wooden stirrups, inflicted a crushing defeat on Amru's army, and took both the generals, Beshr and Ali bin Shervin himself, prisoners. As usual, Ismail displayed wonderful magnanimity to his fallen enemies. Instead of taking the whole army prisoners, according to the usual custom, he loaded the men with presents, and set them free to return home; and when his own people expressed their astonishment at this proceeding, he said, 'Why, what would you do with these poor men? Let them go quietly home, and they will never fight us again.'

Amru bin Leïth was filled with rage on the news of the defeat arriving at Nishabur, and thought of nothing but revenge. He began by demanding the release of his generals, and on this being refused, marched with a fresh body of men on Bokhara. Ismail, however, was well prepared, and had gained over the neighbouring provinces to his cause; he immediately crossed the Oxus, and attacked the fortress of Belkh which Amru held. He failed in his attempts to induce the inhabitants of Belkh to deliver up Amru to him, and had just determined on active operations when Amru forestalled him by a sortie, which resulted in a pitched battle. Amru's army was totally defeated, and he himself, with only two attendants, had great difficulty in escaping from the field, and was soon after taken prisoner and brought before Ismail, on Wednesday, the 9th Djemazi ul akhir of the year 288 (900).[1] Ismail was deeply moved

Narshakhi also mentions a second general, Mohammed bin Leïth, who was sent in another direction with 5,000 men. According to the *Zinet et Tevarikh*, Amru had 70,000 men, and Ismail only 20,000.

[1] The *Zinet et Tevarikh* gives an anecdote of Amru's sudden reverse of fortune, which illustrates the fatalist notions of the Orientals. On the first evening of his captivity, he sat on the ground watching one of his guards preparing for him a frugal meal; the only cooking utensil at hand being a pail such as is used in watering horses. Just as it had been put on the fire, a dog ran up and dipped his nose in, but the opening was so narrow that he could not draw his head back, and

at the sight of his captive enemy; as Amru was about to dismount to salute him, he prevented him, saying, ' To-day it is my duty to pay thee respect.'   He sent him to a country palace in the neighbourhood, visited him again at the end of four days, and sought by every possible attention to alleviate the misfortunes of his former adversary.   Upon enquiring how he came to be taken prisoner, Amru related to him the following story :—' As I was escaping, my horse fell under me. I got off and laid down exhausted by fatigue and exertion. All at once I became aware of two troopers levelling their lances at me ; I asked what they wanted from an old man like me, and begged them to spare my life.   Upon that they came up to me, took pity on me, and one of them even set me on his own horse.   In the mean time more people had gathered round ; I was asked what valuables I had about me, and upon my showing a few pearls worth about 80,000 direms, they were taken from me as well as my signet-ring and my embroidered boots.'   He went on to say that since then, in obedience to Ismail's orders, he had been treated with distinction, and many of his things had been returned to him. Ismail's magnanimity had made a profound impression on Amru, and he went on to reveal to him that he had concealed at Belkh ten asses' load of gold, which he was ready to make over to him as a mark of his gratitude.   Ismail sent for the treasure and returned it to Amru.[1]

ran off with both pot and dinner.   Amru laughed heartily at the absurd accident, and on his guard asking how in his situation he had the spirits to laugh, he said, ' My steward complained this morning that three hundred camels were not sufficient to carry my cooking apparatus; this evening one dog carries off the cooking apparatus and the dinner too.'

[1] According to some Oriental historians, Ismail indignantly rejected the proffered treasure, saying, ' Whence didst thou and thy brother amass this treasure? All the world knows ye were the sons of a coppersmith ; a few days' good luck, which was in truth your undoing, brought you to power, and you have gained your riches by tyranny and injustice.   Would you now shift the burden of your ill-gotten gains from your own shoulders to mine ?   No, you will find I am not the man to be taken in by fine speeches.'   Ismail most certainly never used such language as this to his enemies, and the whole story is as much an invention of Oriental historians as the fable of the discovery of Amru's treasure near Herat by a bird of prey, related in the above-mentioned work of Defrémery, p. 121.

The generous Samanide would doubtless have continued to heap benefits on his fallen enemy, had not the Khalif Mu'-tasid Billah, on hearing of his victory, written to demand that Amru should be given up to him : he alleged that, as Prince of the Faithful, he alone had power to mete out punishment to the offender, whom he had himself incited to war. It may easily be imagined how painful this order was to Ismail. Though well acquainted with the Khalif's malicious intrigues, his sentiments of piety forbade him to disregard the commands of the Prince of the Faithful. He therefore obeyed, and had Amru brought in a litter to Bokhara, but had not courage personally to acquaint him with the terrible order. He afterwards pointed out to him the inevitable though bitter necessity of acquiescence, prayed his forgiveness, and asked what more he could do for him. Amru recommended his sons and his faithful servants to the protection of his benefactor, and then set out for Bagdad, surrounded by all the luxuries of regal state. On his arrival there, the Khalif made him over to the eunuch Safi, who threw him into prison, and after a captivity of two years he was beheaded by order of the Vizir Muktafi, in Djemazi ul evvel of the year 290 (903).

Immediately after Amru's arrival at Bagdad, the Khalif sent Ismail the diploma investing him with the sovereignty of Khorasan, which extended at that time from Bestam (the modern Shahrud) eastwards as far as Belkh, and northwards from Kain, by Sistan, Irak, and Mazendran, to the Oxus. The envoy also brought splendid robes of office, and was received by Ismail with every mark of distinction, and pre-sented with costly gifts.[1] Ismail was on the point of taking formal possession of his dominions, when he heard that the Alide Mohammed bin Zeïd, Prince of Tabaristan, was marching against him. He first tried to ward off the attack

---

[1] Ismail made the envoy a present of 100,000 direms. His pious veneration for the Khalif is shown by the fact that before assuming any one of the robes of office, he repeated two prayers with 'rikaats.' A rikaat consists of two genu-flexions and one prostration, with appropriate prayers.

by peaceful negotiation; but as this attempt failed, Mohammed bin Harun was sent against the enemy. A battle was
fought which at first seemed favourable to the Alide, but in consequence of his presuming rashly on his supposed advantage,
the tide turned, and the Prince of Tabaristan lost both his
throne and his life. Ismail made over the province to his
successful general; the latter, however, rewarded him with
the basest ingratitude, and rose against him; but Ismail
soon regained possession of Tabaristan, and sent his nephew
Ebu Salih Mansur there as governor, whilst the rebel expiated his guilt with his blood.

Having returned from Irak, Ismail was obliged again to
take the field in the year 291 (903) to repel a threatened invasion of the Turks on his northern frontier, in the neighbourhood of the modern Hazreti Turkestan. The Turks had
always been the plague of Transoxania, and, according to an
Arab authority, appeared on this occasion in unusual numbers.[1]
This, however, did not prevent their being defeated and driven
back in confusion. Ismail's army returned to Bokhara laden
with booty; and thus ended the last of the series of campaigns
by which the great Samanide had, since his accession to
power, added so many rich provinces to his hereditary dominions on the Oxus, and created a mighty empire out of
Mavera ul nehr, which under the Arab rule had been only a
dependency of the province of Khorasan.

Bokhara was now virtually the capital of all the states of
Central Asia, for the power of the ruler on the Zerefshan extended northwards to the confines of the great desert, eastwards to the valleys of the Thien-Shan mountains, southwards to the Persian Gulf and the northern frontier of India,[2]

---

[1] Defrémery quotes a statement of Ibn el Athir, according to which the
Turkish camp contained 700 *large tents*; and as these tents were used by the chiefs
alone, the Arabian author concludes the total number of Turks to have been
enormous.

[2] Narshakhi mentions Scinde and Hind; but this must have been a random
boast, for it was reserved for Sultan Mahmud, the Ghaznevide, first to assert his
authority beyond the chain of Suleïman.

and westwards beyond Irak to within a few days' journey
of the Khalif's residence. Ismail's representatives governed
the towns of Merv, Nishabur, Rei, Amol, Kazvin, Isfahan,
Shiraz, Herat, and Belkh. He first succeeded in uniting the
Iranians of the East and those of the West, and the fusion of
states brought about by his administrative talent and military
success proved more stable than the Arab Empire, which was
consolidated but for a short time by all the blood shed in the
early religious wars. In order to comprehend this political
triumph, we must remember that during the 250 years which
had elapsed since the Arab invasion, Mohammedan-Persian
habits of thought had taken the place of the ancient Persian
culture both in Iran and in Transoxania. Religion was the
chief cause of this change, which had not however as yet entirely obliterated the sentiment of nationality amongst the
Iranian people, for the Arab officials of the Khalif were as
much hated as native officers were popular and beloved. This
was the real reason that a few lucky soldiers, on once showing
signs of breaking with the Khalif, were enabled to rise successfully and found new dynasties ; and this is also the explanation
of the ease with which Ismail succeeded in establishing an
independent kingdom, which, in spite of his apparent deference to the Khalif, had really been his object from the first.
Besides all this, Bokhara became, in consequence of Ismail's
predilection for the place, not only his habitual residence, but
the centre of all the intellectual movement and mental activity
then stirring in the eastern portion of Islam. After the national
existence of Iran had been apparently blotted out by the
unfortunate battle of Kadesia, and Persia had been overrun
and devastated by the naked barbarians of the Arabian Desert,
some sparks of Persian civilisation still smouldered beneath
the desecrated altars in Eastern Iran, especially about Belkh
and in Transoxania. These sparks were rekindled by the
Samanides into a beneficent flame : the direction it took was
purely Islamite, but the origin of the movement was clearly
traceable to the fire-temples of Zoroaster.

Bokhara, celebrated in the days of the Parsees as 'the seat of all the sciences,' wished to maintain its former reputation under the Islamite *régime*, and soon succeeded in meriting the title of ' the noble and pious city Bokhara '—a title it certainly does not deserve at the present day.   The intellectual activity of the time was entirely directed to theological science, and accordingly the first celebrities who adorned the city on the Zerefshan were eminent religious characters whose graves are to this day objects of the greatest reverence.[1]   Such, for instance, was the great *Khodja Ebu Hifz el Bokhari*, born in 150 (767), a learned man, long the leader of thought in the city of Bokhara.   He was a pupil of the Imam Mohammed ·Sheïbani, and reckoned by him his most distinguished scholar.   Ebu Hifz died in 227 (841), and left behind him a brilliant memorial of his intellectual labours in the person of his pupil *Abdullah al Fikih*, surnamed *Al Bokhari*, the greatest of Mohammedan jurisconsults, who first saw the light in 194 (809) in the last-mentioned town, and whose great work, ' Djami es Sahih,' i.e. ' Collection of the Truth,' is said to be the most frequently quoted and most largely commented book in the whole literature of Islam.   Ibn Khallikan relates that upwards of 70,000 pupils were taught from this book by the author ; the work is based on 600,000 traditions, and took sixteen years to compile.   He died in the neighbourhood of Samarkand in the year 256 (869).   Next we have *Mohammed el Sebdemuni*, the learned supreme judge in Ismail's reign, who died 304 (916); then *Mohammed bin ul Fazl*, the greatest exegetical theologian of his time, and many others, on whose account Bokhara was, even at that time, a subject of envy to all the other cities of Islam.[2]   Ismail's panegyrists say it was

---

[1] See the volume at the end of the *Tarikhi Narshakhi*, on the celebrated shrines of the holy graves at Bokhara.   The grave of Ebu Hifz el Bokhari is in the burying-ground known as *Tel Khodja*.   The same burial-ground contains the grave of the Sheikh Bidar, of whom it is said that he had never slept for forty years, but spent all his nights in acts of worship.

[2] The *Zikr-i-Ulemai Bokhara*, of which the above-mentioned volume is an extract, mentions several hundred saints who are buried in and around Bokhara, more than half of whom lived during the time of the Samanides.

this reputation of sanctity that caused the great Samanide to prefer Bokhara to Samarkand. He was known himself as a strictly religious and pious prince,[1] and one who protected learned men and treated them liberally,[2] and in consequence many came to his capital from considerable distances either to pursue their studies in his splendid *Medresses*, or to devote themselves to a contemplative life in the endowed 'Reading houses' (or *Kirâtkhanes*). History also tells us of a certain Hashid Sofi, a former Emir of Damascus and great dignitary, who settled at Bokhara to spend his days in solitude and religious contemplation, and died there in the year 246 (809).[3] The national feeling aroused in Iran under the Samanides, in addition to its religious tendencies, gave the first impulse to the revival of the Persian language and literature. After having been suppressed by the Arab rulers for more than 200 years, the harmonious tongue of Iran flourished once more under Nasr and Ismail's reigns. In contradistinction to the later Islamite peoples of Asia who imported with Mohammedan culture a quantity of Arabic words and idioms into their own languages, the Persian poets were strict purists; the works of Ebul Hasan Rudeki derive their principal charm from this peculiarity, which also constitutes the great merit of the immortal Firdusi's masterly epic. Unfortunately, this patriotic tendency was soon departed from, for under the Seldjukides their literature was already full of superfluous expressions borrowed from foreign languages. The first Samanides deserve more credit for their exertions in favour of the original language of Iran than any princes who have ruled over the Persian-speaking peoples of Asia from that day to this.

[1] It is mentioned as an instance of Ismail's piety, that when riding through the streets, he invariably got off his horse on hearing prayers chanted, and only returned to his saddle when the Muezzin had ended his call.

[2] As a proof of Ismail's generosity to the Mollahs, it may be mentioned that Mohammed bin el Fazl el Bokhari left at his death 400,000 ducats!

[3] A story is told of Hashid, that in crossing the Oxus, he threw all his worldly goods into the river, retaining only a comb (to this day the principal item of a dervish's dressing-case), on which was engraved on one side a verse from the Koran, and on the other,

'It is easier to sin than to do penance.'

Ismail (or more properly Emir Ismail, as he is called by oriental historians, in token of his apparent independence of Bagdad) was the very man to mould this remarkable crisis in the history of Central Asia. He was no less brave than the founders of the Soffaride, Deïlemite, and Buyyide dynasties, and his character was further remarkable for piety, love of justice, humanity, and a taste for learning. Hearing, on one occasion, that the tax-collectors of Reï were using loaded weights, he instantly sent off a messenger to seize all the weights and bring them sealed up to Bokhara, and the collector of taxes at Reï was suspended and the office closed until Ismail had had all the weights rectified by removing the superfluous metal, and had sent them back. The following anecdote is also very characteristic. His son Ahmed had a tutor, who one day being with his pupil, exclaimed in his father's presence: ' May God never bless thee nor him that begot thee !' Ismail left the room, and pacified the tutor by a handsome present. Emir Ismail's memory was handed down to later centuries in Khorasan, indeed throughout Iran, in connection with these and similar anecdotes which all Orientals love to enlarge on; it is therefore not surprising that his name should to this day be venerated as that of a saint by the Tadjiks of Bokhara.

We have already alluded to his predilection for the city on the Zerefshan, and, although it was not in his power to do as much for it as, for instance, Timour did for Samarkand, his memory will be cherished for ever by the original inhabitants of Bokhara as that of the only really great prince of Iranian blood. Amongst the buildings erected by Ismail, the first to be mentioned is the palace on the Righistan, which had been begun in præ-Islamite times, but was enlarged and ornamented by him so as to become a fit residence for the reigning prince and for the high officers of state. Secondly, the Serai Molian, which Ismail erected on the banks of the canal of the same name, and fitted up luxuriously and with princely splendour. It is described as a most charming habitation, surrounded by gardens, lawns, flower-beds, fountains, and running brooks. He took especial pains about the water-supply,[1] which was brought in well-contrived canals from the river above down into the town; he also fortified and extended the wall[2] of the town, which had been built in the time of Khalif Mehdi by the governor Ebulabbas Tusi.

The number of high class schools in Bokhara under Emir Ismail is said to have been greater than in any of the other cities of Eastern Asia, for Belkh, surnamed *Kubbet ul Islam*— the cupola (or pinnacle) of Islam—did not rise to the position of a rival till much later. The city on the Zerefshan, the centre of nearly half Mohammedan Asia, flourished and increased more and more as the seat of wealth and learning, and also of the far-famed silk-manufactory. Ismail was amply rewarded for his protracted wars, although he did not long enjoy the pleasures of sovereignty. He fell ill in his palace on the Molian Canal. The doctors thought the damp of the place injurious, and recommended him to move to his hunting-seat—Zerman; he did so, but died soon after on a

---

[1] Though the very unhealthy water supplied to the modern town of Bokhara is brought from the Zerefshan (which flows north of the town), by a few miserable canals which are in fact no better than gutters, the old capital of Mavera ul nehr boasted at the time of the Samanides of no less than eleven broad canals named as follows :—1. *Djuy Molian*, which flowed through the finest part of Bokhara, its banks being bordered by fine palaces in splendid gardens. This part of the town was called *Molian* because Ismail had made it over to the Mollahs as a *Vakf*, i.e. *pious foundation*. 2. *Rudi-i-Shapur*, commonly called Shafirghiam, also *Kiafirgam* (by Mesalik u Memalik), owes its origin to a prince of the house of Saman, a great sportsman, who lived near Bokhara and made this canal. 3. *Furkan ul Aya*. 4. *Furkanrud*. 5. *Gar Gatferrud*, a very large one. 6. *Samtchin*, also large. 7. *Peikanrud*. 8. *Feraiviz ul ulya*,[*] much used for watering the neighbourhood. 9. *Feraivis ul Sefli*, sometimes called Zimun. 10. *Keif* or *Kif*. 11. *Rudi Zer*. All these canals, says Narshakhi, from whom we quote this list, were made artificially, excepting the fifth, which was formed from a natural stream.

[2] The first wall of the town was built in consequence of the frequent invasions and ravages of the neighbouring Turks. The first wall was built in the year 215 (837). It had already been extensively repaired before Ismail's time in the year 235 (849). And again after Ismail by Kilitch Tamgan, in the year 560 (1164), until it was eventually entirely destroyed by Djenghiz in 610 (1213).

---

[*] The MS. of Mesalik u Memalik mentions Feravan ul Sefli and Feravan ul ulya as villages about Bokhara.

Tuesday evening in the month Sefer of the year 295 (907), in the' sixty-first year of his age, having reigned thirty-four years—part of the time as his brother's representative at Bokhara, and the remainder as the independent ruler of the eastern portion of the Mohammedan Asia.[1]

[1] He governed Bokhara for twenty years as representative of his brother Nasr; he then ruled Mavera ul nehr seven years, and Khorasan seven years, which makes up the thirty-four years.

V.

IN the East, as in the West, empires and dynasties have only been able to maintain themselves on the pinnacle of greatness so long as they have been animated by a spirit of unity amongst themselves, leading them steadily to work together for the good of the commonwealth. Where this has been wanting, even the most brilliant talents of individuals have availed little, and thus we see the house of Saman declining rapidly from the moment that some of its members, and some of the dignitaries of the state, forgetting the respect and obedience due to their chief, began to intrigue to seize the reins of government themselves.

In the confusion created by the decaying authority of the Khalifs in this part of Asia, a strong governing hand in Transoxania, commanding the services of all the Turkish hordes, might have done great things, but the Samanides who succeeded Emir Ismail were, with few exceptions, helpless puppets in the hands of their own officials ; and thus it came about that the Turks, instead of being servants, soon came forward as leaders, and rapidly attained to a power which enabled them not only to overthrow the Samanides in Transoxania, but to break loose in every direction, obtain possession of many other Asiatic thrones, and assert their claim to the title of ‘the dominant race,’ which they have retained to this day.

Emir Ismail was succeeded by his son Ahmed, a prince of an ungovernable temper and warlike tastes, but without a trace of his father's pacific virtues. His first act on assuming the government was to seize his uncle, the governor of Samarkand, whom he suspected as a secret rival, and cause him to be imprisoned at Bokhara. He then proceeded to Tabaristan to punish the Viceroy there, Paris Kebir, for the extortions by which he had amassed enormous wealth.[1] The Viceroy took refuge at Bagdad, having beforehand obtained the Khalif Muktafi's permission to do so, and Ahmed, more annoyed at the loss of the treasure than at the escape of his subordinate, appointed in his place another governor of Tabaristan, Ebul Abbas bin Abdullah, a worthy man, who soon became so popular that the Alide Nasir el Utrush (the Dumb Conqueror[2]) could effect nothing against the Samanide government. Ahmed returned to his capital, but his love of conquest would not allow him to remain long quiet. He next cast his eyes on Sistan, and marched in 298 (910, 911) with a considerable army, commanded by his ablest generals, against the Saffaride Muadil, then ruler of Sistan, conquered him, and carried him prisoner to Bokhara, after entrusting the conquered province to his nephew Ebu Salih Mansur, whose father had been released from prison, and reinstated in his former office.

In the year 301 (913) Ahmed was hunting on the banks of the Yaxartes, when he received the information that the Alide Utrush had taken possession of Tabaristan, and driven out the governor Saluk. He was deeply distressed, and is said to have exclaimed: 'O God! if it should be thy will to take my kingdom from me, take my life as well.'[3] His prayer was soon granted. He had for some time lived in fear of his immediate followers, and was in the habit of sleeping with two lions, stationed like watch-dogs, outside his chamber; this precaution was forgotten one night

[1] Mirkhond relates that Paris escaped to Bagdad with 4,000 troopers and a large treasure. While he was on his way there, Khalif Muktafi died, and his successor, Muktadir Pares, looking on Paris and his treasure as a lucky prize, poisoned him and took possession of his earthly goods.

[2] His real name was Hasan ibu Ali, a son of Husein ibu Ali, who had been wandering amongst the Deïlemites since 287 (900), and converting many to Islamism. His zeal for proselytising, like that of all the Alides, was however merely as a means to his real end—the increase of his own worldly power. (Weil, *History of the Khalifs*, vol. ii. p. 613.)

[3] Defrémery, *Histoire des Samanides*, p. 130.

in camp, and his own servants seized the opportunity of attacking him, and murdered him in the night of January 23–24, 914.[1] He had reigned six years, four months, and seven days. In consequence of his tragical death he was surnamed Emir Shehid Ahmed (Ahmed the Martyr).

His son Ebul Hasan Nasr (afterwards known as Said the Fortunate) ascended the throne as a boy of ten years old. When the nobles of Bokhara were introduced to do homage to him, the child cried, and exclaimed in terror, 'Are you come to kill me like my father ?' He was reassured and took courage. During the first years of his reign the government was conducted by a regency, but afterwards his fortunate star led him to successes for which his reign is glorified beyond every other by oriental historians. Emir Said, as he is usually called, was certainly not without talent, and singularly fortunate in all his undertakings ; but nevertheless the brilliancy of his reign resembled the flickers of an expiring flame rather than a steady light, for though he obtained undisturbed possession of the whole territory of his grandfather, and even added new conquests [2] to it, he contributed in the long run next to nothing to the stability of the Samanide dynasty. He had in the beginning to defend himself against his uncle Is'hak, who, backed by a considerable party, asserted his own right to the throne as the oldest member of the family. Hamuye, Emir Said's commander, had to conduct two campaigns against him before he succeeded in taking him prisoner to Bokhara, where he shortly afterwards died. Next, Mansur, the son of Is'hak, encouraged by the disaffected Husein, raised the standard of revolt at Nishabur. Hamuye marched against him, but as he died just at that critical moment the campaign had to be carried on against Husein. Ahmed bin Sahl, a faithful partisan of the Samanides, at that time Emir of Herat, offered his services in quashing the rebellion. Husein was carried prisoner to Bokhara, but was afterwards pardoned, and even given a

---

[1] Weil, *History of the Khalifs*, p. 614.

[2] Malcolm, in his *History of Persia*, includes amongst these the towns of Reï, Isfahan, and Kum.

place at court.[1]   Nasr was often guilty of ingratitude, and on
this occasion too broke his promise to Ahmed bin Sahl, in consequence of which the latter rose against him in the year 370
(919, 920).   Hamuye, however, laid siege to Herat and took
Ahmed, whom he sent to Bokhara, where he also died in prison.

The most important of all these campaigns, however, was the
one Nasr had to carry on against the Alides in Tabaristan.
These had not only recovered from their defeats since the
death of Ahmed, but had actually extended their authority
over a part of Khorasan, thanks principally to the exertions
of their brave general Leile bin Numan, who had advanced by
Damghan as far as Nishabur.   Hamuye marched against him
and defeated him, and Leile retreated and was killed during
the retreat in the year 309 (921) ; but peace was not thereby
restored to Tabaristan, fresh partisans of the Alides had to
be dislodged, now in one quarter, then in another, and the
Khalif had to be assisted in controlling his turbulent officials,
such as the former slave Fatik, who actually took possession of
the town of Rei.   Emir Said found himself, however, quite
equal to cope with all these difficulties, thanks to the vigilance
with which he watched even the most distant frontiers of his
dominions, and thanks also to the respect and blind obedience
the dynasty of the Samanides was at that time still able to
command.[2]   His reign lasted twenty-eight years, and was rich

[1] One day Emir Said asked for some water, which was brought to him in a
common jug.   Husein expressed his astonishment at this to the son of Hamuye
as follows :—' Thy father is governor of Nishabur, where such beautiful jugs are
made ; * why does he not send some specimens here ? '   But the son of the famous
general replied wittily, ' When my father sends presents from Khorasan they are
generally specimens of such articles as thyself.'

[2] Mirkhond relates the following anecdote as a proof of extraordinary respect
and obedience.   Makan bin Kaki was trying by force to possess himself of
Khorasan, and the generalissimo Emir Ali Muhtadj was sent against him.
During his last audience of the prince, to receive his final instructions before
leaving, some of his followers noticed that he showed signs of great uneasiness
and pain.   When the audience was over and the prince had retired, Emir Ali
drew a scorpion from within his clothes which had bitten him in seven places.
The prince was afterwards told of this, and on his enquiring of the general why

* The pottery of Nishabur is celebrated to this day.

in instances of truly princely virtues, and the generosity lavished by him on the great poet of his age, Ebul Hasan Rudeki, deserves to be held in remembrance.[1] He died of consumption at the early age of thirty-eight years, in Sha'ban of the year 331 (943).

Nasr had named his younger son as his successor, but as he had died before him, the government passed to the elder brother, Nuh, whose fine qualities earned him the name of Emir Hamid, i.e. the Favoured Prince. He began his reign by an act of magnanimity, pardoning Ebul Fazl Mohammed, the chief partisan of his deceased rival, and appointing him Viceroy of Samarkand. The long list of wars and revolts which makes up the history of his reign, as well as of that of his predecessors, commenced towards the end of the year 332 (943) with the campaign against the Deïlemite Rukn-ed-dowleh, who had seized on Reï. Ebu Ali, grandson of the general Muhtadj, a very brave and very ambitious man, was at that time in command of the Samanide prince's troops. His first attack on Rukn-ed-dowleh, in the neighbourhood of Reï, failed, owing to the treachery of the Kurdish soldiers,[2] but the following year he put his opponent to flight, and restored order in the province. This service, and possibly also the fact that he had carried out Nuh's wishes in assisting Vashmeghir to get possession of the government of Tabaristan, caused Ebu Ali to assert with much arrogance inordinate pretensions to recompenses from Nuh ;

he had not retired on first becoming aware of the insect, received the following reply: 'If a servant cannot stand a few bites of a scorpion when in his master's presence, how is he to endure sword-cuts in his absence ?'

[1] Ebul Hasan Rudeki, the oldest of the Persian poets, still well known and popular in Central Asia, is remarkable for the fertility of his pen and the purity of his language. Hammer states that, according to the commentators of the *Yemini*, his history of Persian poetry, he is said to have written one million three hundred distiches collected in a hundred books. His magnificence was princely. He went about preceded by two hundred boys, who were his slaves, and followed by four hundred camels laden with valuables.

[2] It appears from this that the Kurds, who to this day inhabit the district of Khorasan, from Nishabur up towards Astrabad along the northern frontier of Iran, were not transplanted by the Seffevides from Kurdestan proper, as modern Persians assert, but had long been established in this locality, and always constituted a principal portion of the forces of Khorasan.

and upon finding that the viceroyalty of Khorasan, which
he believed himself entitled to, had been given to another, he
broke into open rebellion against his master. He joined
Ibrahim the Samanide, Nuh's uncle and rival, and the two
together made themselves masters of Irak; Khorasan also
went over to them. Ibrahim caused the Khutbe to be everywhere read in his own name, and Nuh, who had left Bokhara
and fled to Samarkand, would certainly have lost his throne,
if, fortunately for him, his enemies had not begun to quarrel
with each other. In consequence of these quarrels a reconciliation was effected between him and his uncle Ibrahim, and he
returned in triumph to Bokhara, the inhabitants of which
were sincerely devoted to him. Ebu Ali seemed willing also
to return to his allegiance, and even took service again under
Nuh in a campaign against Rukn-ed-dowleh, but their relations
soon again became unsatisfactory, and the end was that Ebu
Ali went over and joined Rukn-ed-dowleh in a fresh revolt
against Nuh, and, assisted by Rukn-ed-dowleh, obtained from
the Khalif his own investiture as independent ruler of Khorasan. In the year 343, Ebu Ali caused the Khutbe to be read
in the mosques of Khorasan in the name of the Khalif Muthi,
and thus, in conjunction with the Deilemites, who had extended
their power as far as Shiraz, drove back the Samanides within
the original frontiers of Transoxania.

Nuh, or Emir Hamid, died in the year 343 (954), after a
reign of thirteen years. His son Abdul Melik, commonly
called Emir Reshid (the Brave Prince), succeeded him as a
boy of ten years old. He subsequently did everything in his
power to restore the influence of the Samanides in the west of
the empire, but in vain. His commander, Asha'th bin Mohammed, one of the best generals of his day, only succeeded
in obtaining tolerable conditions of peace from the Deilemite
Rukn-ed-dowleh, but no submission. Abdul Melik was passionately devoted to field sports and chivalrous amusements,
for which reason he was often nicknamed Ebul Fewaris, i.e.
Father of Knights. He died, after a reign of seven years, on

the 8 Shevval of the year 350 (961), from the consequences of a fall from his horse.[1] He was succeeded by his brother Mansur bin Nuh, surnamed Emir Shedid—the Just Prince; and the decay into which the reputation of the Samanides had fallen may be estimated by the fact that Alptekin, a former slave[2] who had raised himself to the rank of Vizir, and was at that moment commanding at Nishabur, was able to declare this election null and void, and to bring a considerable force into the field against his lawful sovereign. However, the Oxus was defended by a strong body of Mansur's adherents, who prevented his advance, and he had to retire to Ghazna;[3] his second attempt was more successful. Mansur was forced to enter into negotiations, and Alptekin, having agreed to pay a yearly tribute of 50,000 dinars to Nishabur, was reinstated in his former office. Mansur's campaign against Rukn-ed-dowleh came to a similar termination. The dynasty of the Deïlemites, masters of nearly half Iran, was a power with which the decaying house of the Samanides could not pretend to cope. Mansur had to give in at last; he made peace with Rukn-ed-dowleh, and married his grand-daughter, the daughter of Azed-ed-dowleh. This occurred in the year 361 (971, 972).

Mansur remained at peace from this time forward, and died, after a reign of fifteen years, on the 4 Shevval of the year 365[4] (976), at Bokhara. His son Nuh bin Mansur, known at

---

[1] He met with this fall whilst playing at *djukan*, or ball on horseback. The player while riding at full gallop has to catch up the ball from the ground with a bat, and send it in two strokes through two hoops affixed to poles one behind the other. This game requires more gymnastic cleverness than the Turkish game of *djirid*. Both are now gone out of fashion.

[2] Alptekin is a word compounded of *Alp* (hero) and *tekin* (called, named). The latter word, more correctly *tiken*, *tegen*, *tiyen*, is still used among the Turkomans to express a proper name, and if a person is asked his name, he will answer, for instance, *Oraz-tegen-men*, I am he who is called Oraz. *Tekin* is a common termination of many Turkish names, as: Karatekin, Nushtekin, Ainaltekin, Sebuktekin (more properly Sevüktetiñ), &c. It is also possible that *tekin* or *degin* is used in the sense of *like*, *resembling*.

[3] Mirkhond says that Alptekin completely routed Mansur's troops at Belkh, but afterwards retired nevertheless on Ghaznee.

[4] I follow the authority of Narshakhi. Mirkhond gives the 11th Redjeb as the date of Mansur's death.

Bokhara under the name of Emir Seïd Ebul Kasim, found even more stormy days and harder fights in store for him before he could assert his hereditary rights. The power of the great Samanide had by this time fallen low indeed.

The successors of Vashmeghir in Djordjan and Tabaristan had all but proclaimed their independence, and Azed-ed-dowleh held both the Iraks; and whilst these great party leaders, in their arrogant self-assertion, were either rising against their common suzerain or quarrelling with each other, Ebul Kasim's own vizirs were doing their best, by their mutual quarrels and jealousies, to destroy the remnants of power left him. The most serious of these disputes was that between Ebul Abbas Tash, surnamed Hussam-ed-dowleh (the Sword of the Kingdom), and Ebul Huseïn Simdjuri. The former had been made Viceroy of Khorasan by Ebul Kasim in the year 371 (980, 981). He was a man of noble disposition and upright character, but his adversary was a covetous intriguer, who succeeded in deceiving the weak-minded sovereign, and inducing him to degrade his faithful servant. Tash, burning with indignation at this unjust treatment, flew to arms to defend himself against his rival, in which he at first succeeded, thanks to the assistance rendered him by the Deïlemite Fakhr-ed-dowleh.[1] Ebul Huseïn was for a short time driven out of Khorasan, but he returned with reinforcements from Kerman, against which Tash was unable to maintain himself. He was defeated and fled to his excellent friend Fakhr-ed-dowleh to Djordjan, where he died universally beloved, in the year 379 (989, 990). The friendship existing between Tash and Fakhr-ed-dowleh was singularly warm and deep. It is refreshing first to see Tash receiving the fugitive Fakhr-ed-dowleh, in the day of his adversity, and making many sacrifices to protect him, and later on we are touched to see Fakhr saving his unhappy friend at his own imminent peril, and then sustaining him with princely magnificence for the rest of his life. Ebul Huseïn did not

---

[1] Tash had put Fakhr-ed-dowleh under obligations by the assistance he had once given him in his campaign against Muvejed-ed-dowleh.

long enjoy the honour he had won through base treachery. He was struck with apoplexy in the arms of one of his concubines, and died a year earlier than his unfortunate rival, leaving the government of Khorasan to his son Ebu Ali. The character of the latter was even baser than his father's; he had scarcely entered on his office before he behaved in the most disgraceful manner to Nuh. It was evident from the first that his object was to shake off altogether the authority of the Samanides, and that he would stick at nothing to accomplish this object. The farthest east, the country now known as Eastern Turkestan, was at that time inhabited by the Uigurs,[1] a Turkish tribe who had been the first to separate from the great nomadic main body of the Turkish race and to settle down in a home on the slopes of the Thien-Shan mountains.

We find amongst them the first traces of social and political institutions of purely Turkish growth; although they existed from the earliest period of the Christian epoch, as small isolated states scattered about the region lying between the modern Chinese province of Kansu and the eastern frontier of Khokand, the existence of a great compact Uiguric kingdom only dates from the decay of the Samanides. It appears

[1] The only authentic information we have concerning the Uigurs is contained in a MS. in Uigurian, in the possession of the Imperial Library at Vienna. The title of it is the *Kudatku Bilik*, i.e. fortunate science, and it treats of the ethics as well as of the political and social condition of Turkish society at that time. The great importance of this MS. is chiefly owing to two points: in the first place, it dates from the year 462 (1069), and is in consequence the oldest Turkish document we possess. The author wrote the first part of his work on the extreme eastern frontier of Turkish territory, in the neighbourhood of Komul, the second part was written in Kashgar, and it is expressly stated that this *was the first book ever written in the Turkish language*; we have therefore here an authentic document from which we may gather information respecting the earlier condition of those Turkish tribes now scattered far and wide, and which gives us most important assistance in tracing out their mutual historical development. In the second place, we learn from the *Kudatku Bilik* that the Uigurs possessed from the earliest times a by no means contemptible civilisation, which was afterwards moulded by Christian and Mohammedan influences, but certainly did not owe its existence to the latter, which is the more noticeable as the revival of the Persian language, and with it the new Iranian culture, were just then beginning to spread. There are further details of the Uigurs to be found in my work, *Uigurische Sprachmonumente und das Kudatku Bilik*. Innsbruck, 1870.

that Ilik[1] Khan was the first to complete the work of uniting the scattered parts; next to him Boghra or Kara Boghra [2] Khan was the most celebrated for his successful religious wars, in which he converted thousands of Buddhists and Christians to Islamism. He had united all the different Turkish tribes in the East under his sceptre, and pushing forward his conquests westwards, he sought to enrich himself with some of the fragments of the Samanide empire, but he thereby got into hostilities with the puppet ruling at Bokhara, and struck up an alliance with Ebu Ali, the rebellious vassal of Ebul Kasim.

Whilst Ebu Ali was quietly working against Nuh in Khorasan, Boghra Khan advanced with a large army, to which the Turks of Khokand had joined themselves, from Kashgar to the banks of the Zerefshan. Inandj [3] Hadjib, the first general sent against him, was beaten and carried prisoner into Turkestan. Faik was then put at the head of the army, but repaid his master's favour by the basest treachery, so that when Boghra Khan took possession of Samarkand, there was nothing left for the unhappy Samanide prince but to take to flight in disguise, and, accompanied only by a few faithful servants, Ebul Kasim, seeking help on all sides, first addressed himself to Ebu Ali, but that base creature feigned innocence and regret that, in consequence of the critical state of his own province, it was impossible for him to do anything. Fortunately for Ebul Kasim, just at this juncture Boghra Khan died of an illness caused by the unhealthy climate of Bokhara. He was therefore enabled to return to his faithful capital, but as the hostile sentiments of the departed Uiguric prince were now taken up by his own

---

[1] Ilik, or Ilek, as some of my predecessors have erroneously spelt it, is a Uiguric word signifying prince, ruler, regent, and is therefore no more a proper name than Turkan or Tarkhan, Khatun or the other titles by which Arabic and Persian authors designate the Turkish authorities of the time. In the absence of more precise information we here use Ilik in place of a proper name.

[2] Boghra, or more properly Bokra or Bokhra, means in eastern Turkish a male camel. Before Islamism had thoroughly taken root amongst the Turks it was by no means uncommon to designate grave and distinguished personages by the names of animals.

[3] Not Inanedj, as Defrémery has it. Inandj is a Turkish word signifying faith, trust.

rebellious vassals Ebu Ali and Faik, he was forced to seek
strength by uniting himself with some powerful ally. Such a
one he met with in the founder of the dynasty of the Ghaznevides. Sebuktekin, at that time ruler of the whole district
between Ghaznee and the shores of the Indus, and celebrated .
besides for the riches he had amassed in his frequent invasions
of India,[1] was devotedly attached to the house of Saman and
joyfully granted Ebul Kasim the help required. He marched
to the Oxus with a large army and 200 elephants, to chastise
the rebels Ebu Ali and Faik. Ebul Kasim met him at Kesh,
and on seeing him, Sebuktekin, though many years his senior,
at once dismounted, and reverentially kissed his stirrup.

This alliance was most advantageous for the Samanide prince,
for although Ebu Ali was powerfully supported by the rulers of
Djordjan and Irak, he could not withstand the united forces of
Ebul Kasim and Sebuktekin, who was also accompanied by
his son Mahmud. A battle was fought on the plain of Herat,
in which the rebels were routed and forced to flee to Nishabur.
Ebul Kasim entered Bokhara in triumph. The aged Sebuktekin received the title of Nasir-ed-dowleh (Succourer of the
Kingdom), and his son that of Seïf-ed-dowleh (Sword of the
Kingdom), but they had no sooner returned to Ghaznee than
Ebu Ali, who had taken refuge at the court of the Deïlemites,
reappeared, and hoping that the departure of Sebuktekin had
left the field open to him, once more attacked Nishabur. He
had, however, grievously miscalculated. The care of the re-
conquered province had been entrusted to Mahmud, who had
shown unmistakeable signs of future greatness, but before he
could even send his father word of the invasion, he was attacked by Ebu Ali, put to flight, and all his treasure taken
from him. Sebuktekin, however, soon arrived on the scene,
met Ebu Ali at Tus, and defeated him utterly, driving him
back at last into Khahrezm. Ebul Kasim behaved with
wonderful magnanimity, for he took compassion on Ebu Ali
and actually interceded with Ebu Abdullah, the Shah of

---

[1] Narshaski. Others ascribe the Indian campaigns only to his son Mahomed.

Khahrezm, to receive him kindly. But his intercession was unsuccessful, for the Shah of Khahrezm put his guest in irons ; but this breach of hospitality excited such indignation on the part of the Viceroy Meemun bin Mohammed (who was also influenced by certain private motives), that he attacked the Shah, and having defeated him, had him put into the identical irons from which Ebu Ali had just been released. After this success, Meemun returned with Ebu Ali to Djordjan, and the captive Shah was brought out and put to death during a festivity.[1] But Ebu Ali himself came to no better end. Ebul Kasim had formally pardoned him at the intercession of Meemun, but he was afterwards persuaded by others to throw him again into prison. Sebuktekin desired to have him given up to him, and he died in prison under him in the year 387 (997). The government of Ebul Kasim continued for a short time disturbed by the invasion of the Turkish chief Ilik,[2] whom the rebel Faik had summoned from Kashgar, but Sebuktekin averted this danger also, and Nuh bin Mansur or Ebul Kasim, as we have called him, died quietly in the year 387, after a reign of twenty-two years.

Ebul Harith Mansur, the son of Nuh, ascended the throne as a raw, inexperienced youth, and committed the great mistake of quarrelling with Mahmud, the successor of the powerful Sebuktekin, although the latter, from good feeling for the house of the Samanides, took no notice of his unfriendliness, and simply held aloof. Ebul Harith soon fell a victim to the malice of a discontented courtier named Bektözün, who invited him to his house, and there put out his eyes.[3] His brother, Abdul Melik, quite a young child, was put in his place. Faik and Bektözün, the two really powerful men in the state, supported him, and he succeeded in eluding the anger of the deeply insulted Mahmud, whose star was then in the ascend-

[1] Mirkhond states that on this occasion Ebu Ali, who had hitherto abstained from all spirituous liquors, for the first time 'allowed the apparently firmly-built edifice of his temperance to be overthrown by the fragile glass of a wine-flagon.'

[2] See note 1, p. 82.

[3] Bektözün is a Uiguric word signifying very just, very honest.

ant, but soon after fell a victim to the treacherous protection of Ilik Khan.[1] The latter moved uninvited with his army from Kashgar on Bokhara, in order, as he said, to chastise the enemies of his beloved neighbour ; but he soon betrayed his real object by seizing the Bokhariots who had gone out to receive him, and putting them in irons ; he then entered Bokhara in 389 (999) and threw Abdul Melik himself into prison, where he died.[2] Muntasir,[3] the third son of Ebul Kasim, having fortunately escaped from the prison into which Ilik had thrown the whole family, made one last attempt to restore the fallen fortunes of his dynasty. He escaped from Khahrezm in the disguise of a young female slave, and his intention was, with a few faithful followers, to take up arms against the usurpers of his throne. He met with warm sympathy from several of the former vassals of his family, especially from Shemsel Maali Kabus, the son of Vashmeghir, but this alone was of little service. He succeeded, however, with the help of the Guzz-Turkomans, in twice defeating Ilik's troops, but these were but fitful gleams of light from the declining sun of the Samanides' fortunes. It was vain for him to seek to cope with such an adversary as Ilik Khan, whose territory after the conquest of Bokhara extended from the interior of China to the Caspian Sea. Supported by a few old friends of his family, he wandered for a long time about Taburistan, Sistan, and Khorasan, and actually succeeded in the year 391 (1001) in getting possession of Nishabur ; but he was driven out again by Nasr, the son of Mahmud and grandson of Sebuktekin, and after further wanderings was at last betrayed by his own people into the hands of Ilik and utterly routed. His family and attendants were taken prisoners, but he himself escaped, only however to meet his death in the camp of the tribe of

---

[1] Abdul Melik had retreated to Bokhara with Faik after Mahmud had thoroughly defeated the army of the Samanides concentrated in the neighbourhood of Merv from all parts of Transoxania.

[2] According to Mirkhond, he was imprisoned at Özkend (not Uzkend, as stated by Defrémery). Özkend was a town, now reduced to a village, in the neighbourhood of Mergholan in Khokand.

[3] His real name was Ebu Ibrahim.

Ibn Behidj, where he was murdered by a certain Mehrui, who was himself executed for the crime shortly after.

Thus ended, in the month of Rebiul evvel of the year 395 (1004, 1005), the last of the Samanides. With him a family became extinct which had reigned in certain parts of Transoxania and Fergana from the earliest times, and afterwards from the time of Nasr—that is for a space of some 145 years—had ruled absolutely over all Central Asia, and whose members may therefore with truth be regarded as the founders of that religious and social polity which was regarded in former centuries, by the Mohammedans of three continents, as the nearest approach to the ideal of the golden age of Islam, and is in consequence still to this day held in high veneration. The capital of the Abbasides and other cities of Western Asia were open to all manner of sects and of free-thinkers, but Bokhara, Belkh, and Samarkand were, under the Samanides, so to speak, the special refuge of the Mohammedan scholars and zealots, who adhered scrupulously to the most minute observance of the Sheriaat (religious law) and the sunna (traditions), and thereby caused the branches of Islamism to flourish in the whole of Western Asia as vigorously as in Mekka and Medina themselves. The political supremacy of Bokhara over the different tribes of Central Asia, which has been maintained up to modern times by the rulers of the Zerefshan, may be traced to a similar origin. The deference paid by the mighty Sebuktekin to Bokhara, a deference imitated in later times by Afghans, Indians, and Özbegs, began during the period of the greatness of the Samanides. They represented the last Iranian dynasty in the land of the ancient Iranian civilisation, and the importance of the legacy left by them to their Turco-Tartaric successors on the throne of Transoxania cannot be overrated. It is no cause for astonishment that after the fall of the Samanides, Transoxania should have become a prey to the greatest anarchy. Two different nationalities had from the earliest times made their mark in the country. The Iranians, representatives of ancient civilisation, had, as already stated, lost very little of their original nationality by the adoption of Islamism. They were still addicted to trade, to science, and to peaceful occupations generally ; the military element, and consequently the actual power, thus necessarily fell almost exclusively to the second great division of the people, the Turks. Turks had from the earliest times been placed in military commands, and often entrusted with the highest posts ; during the time of the latter Samanides they had acquired more and more power, and when the dynasty died out the only change to them was that they carried out their policy in their own name, and assumed the position of independent rulers.

Bokhara, the seat of government, was nominally held by Ilik Khan from Kashgar, but his authority was barely recognised in the districts of Kesh, Samarkand, and Khokand, where every man did what was right in his own eyes. Some banded themselves together to drive out Ilik Khan, others sought assistance from the mighty Sultan Mahmud. It was an epoch in every way favourable for a brave and determined soldier to seize on the opportunity ; such a soldier had already appeared on the scene before the final catastrophe, and the effect of his influence on the political condition of Transoxania soon became apparent.

VI.

THE SELDJUKIDES.

395 (1004)—528 (1133).

THE course of the history of Central Asia was from the earliest times considerably influenced by the part played in it by these tribes of Turkish nomads, known to the Arabs and Persians by the generic name of 'Guzz,' who lived in the wide desert or steppes, commencing on the Chinese frontier, and extending to the shores of the Caspian Sea. For a long time before and after the Arab occupation, in fact during the whole period of the Samanide rule, the stream of Turkish migration to the banks of the Oxus had flowed downwards south-east, principally from Khokand and Eastern Turkestan. But, after the power of the Samanides was broken, the Turks in the north began to move, and advanced freely, with their flocks and herds in search of pasture, into the inhabited portion of the khanate of Bokhara.

The history of the origin of the Seldjukides is obscured by numerous myths, but it appears from it that Seldjuk, or more correctly Seldjik,[1] the son of Tokmak and Subash, commander of the army of a prince named Pigu or Bogu,[2]

---

[1] All rules for the pronunciation of Turkish are set at defiance by the word Seldjuk. It should be either Seldjik or Saldjuk ; *djik* or *djuk* are diminutives, the first is used with words where the vowel *e* or *i* occurs in the last syllable, but the latter only after *a o* or *u*. The spelling of Turkish words, as handed down to us by Arabic and Persian authors, is almost invariably wrong, as they were generally quite ignorant of the language, and could not, and to this day cannot master the different pronunciations of Turkish words.

[2] Bogu means 'stag.'* We have already noticed the habit amongst the Turks of using the names of strong or handsome animals as proper names.

---

* It seems probable that we also have to do here with Pigu, the Persian name for Buddhists and for eastern Turks.

were expelled from their native steppes for some crime, and forced to seek their fortunes in strange countries. Seldjuk, with 100 horsemen, 1,000 camels, and 50,000 sheep, migrated to a place on the southern confines of the desert, in the neighbourhood of Djend.[1] He settled there and, with all his followers, embraced Islamism.[2] His religious zeal showed itself by his endeavours to protect the peaceable inhabitants of the neighbourhood against the incursions of his heathen kinsmen. His reputation and power increased from day to day, and his court became the refuge of all the oppressed ; Muntasir himself, the last of the Samanides, coming to him for help against Ilik Khan. Seldjuk took compassion on the hardly pressed Samanide, and went to war with Ilik Khan ; the result was that he obtained possession of the whole of one of the most cultivated districts of the khanate, and was thus enabled to take his place as one of the independent princes of Transoxania, rousing thereby great jealousy and indignation in all the others.

We have scarcely any reliable details of the extent to which Seldjuk, who lived to a very advanced age, succeeded in pushing his influence forward in Bokhara. We only know for certain that he took the greatest pains with the military training of his two grandsons, Togrul and Tchakar,[3] and that

---

[1] Ibn Khallikan describes Djend as distant twenty 'fersakhs' from Bokhara. I have been unable to discover any mention of the place in the oldest geographical documents.

[2] The names of the first Seldjukides, Musa, Junis, Michal, and Israil, have a strong resemblance to Biblical names, and there can be no doubt that Christianity had at this period made far more progress in Central Asia than Mahommedan historians are willing to allow. Taking these circumstances into consideration, there appears every probability that the Turkish nomads when Seldjuk parted from them were nominally disciples of the Nestorian Christians rather than of Shamism or Buddhism, and this supposition gains ground from the fact that certain Turkish tribes, such as those of Naiman and Kangli, are expressly stated by Djuveini in his *Djihankuska* to have embraced Christianity. This fact is further attested by the list of the Alanite officers who sent in from the court of the Great Khan their submission to the Pope at Avignon as faithful Christians in the year 739 (1338). Col. Yule gives a detailed account of this embassy in the second volume of his *Cathay, &c.*

[3] Togrul and Tchakar are two Turkish words : the former is a contraction of Tograul, the slaughterer, from the verb togramak, to slaughter ; the latter means the brilliant, the glittering one, from tchakmak, to glitter. Our European

after his death they were constantly at war with the principal potentates of the time in Central Asia, such as with Ilik Khan in Bokhara, and Boghra Khan in Kashgar. It appeared even then to be foreseen that these young offshoots of the tribe of Seldjuk would in time grow into the mighty race whose branches would reach from the interior of China to the shores of the Mediterranean, and from the Sea of Aral to the Persian Gulf, and under the shadow of which so many of the celebrated nations of antiquity, and the spiritual chief of Islamism himself, would find shelter. The two brothers, united by the bonds of the tenderest affection for each other, and pursuing always the same objects, spent their lives alternately in flying before the malice or the superior strength of their adversaries, and again in asserting themselves by force of arms. Though living in the midst of a settled population, they remained true to the habits of nomads, and it was thus easy for them to move house and home from one spot to another, or in moments of more than usually pressing danger to send off their wives and children with their treasures and stores to some safe hiding-places in the desert, whilst they themselves, trusting only to their swift little horses, risked the fortune of war.[1] By these means they contrived to lay the foundation of their future power, under the very eyes of so powerful a conqueror as Mahmud the Ghaznevide, who, although much alarmed at the numbers and increasing strength of these redoubtable sons of the desert,[2] found himself powerless to check them, or to drive them from the scene. Alitekin,

Orientalists have by mistake identified tograul with togru, straight, and as the significance of Tchakar was unknown to them, they erroneously thought that it was a misspelling for Djaafar.

[1] The modern Turkomans to this day carry on war in this fashion, and, in consequence of this, many have mistaken the Seldjukides for Turkomans.

[2] In connection with this it is stated that when Israil appeared at the court of Sultan Mahmud on a mission from the Seldjukides, the latter, while discussing with him his plans against India, enquired the number of Seldjukides capable of bearing arms ; the envoy drew an arrow from his quiver and replied, ' Send this arrow to my kinsmen, and thou wilt receive 10,000 horsemen.' ' And if I should want more ?' asked Mahmud. ' Then,' said Israil, ' send this second arrow, and thou wilt receive 50,000.' ' But, if this should not be enough,' said the Ghaznevide,

ruler of Samarkand and an ally of Ilik Khan, had, in consequence of his desire for conquest, quarrelled with Kadr Khan,
the son and successor of Boghra Khan of Kashgar; Sultan
Mahmud, as a friend of Kadr Khan, crossed the Oxus with
an army, drove out Ilik, and, determined equally to protect his
ally from the Seldjukides, offered the two brothers a settlement
in Khorasan, in the hope that by separating them from their
clansmen it might prove easier to overcome them. Togrul and
Tchakar were at first disposed to listen to the friendly insinu-
ations of the great Ghaznevide, and sent their uncle Israil, also
called Boghu, to his court, but hearing that he had been ill-
treated there, some even affirming that he had died in prison,
they determined, in spite of the enmity of the neighbouring
princes, especially of Alitekin, who had meantime returned to
Samarkand, to remain in their former position in Transoxania.
Ilik endeavoured again to betray them, by trying to sow the
seeds of internal discord amongst the Seldjukides, but this
failed, as well as the open attack made on them by his troops
under the command of Alpkara. Though repulsed at first, the
two brothers soon recovered themselves, annihilated Alpkara's
army, and killed him, but brought on themselves by this brilliant success a fresh enemy, the ruler of Khahrezm, who
attacked them with an overwhelming force on the right bank
of the Oxus, in the desert between Bokhara and Khiva, utterly
routed them, and forced them to retreat hurriedly.[1] Under these
circumstances the brave grandsons of Seldjuk bade adieu to
the country between the Oxus and Yaxartes, the land inherited

---

' Then,' replied Israil, ' send my bow, and 200,000 warriors will join thee.' This
story has gone the round of nearly all eastern and western historians, but we must
describe it as a myth, for the part played in a peaceful mission by the bow and
arrows is not in accordance with the habits of the time.

[1] The defeat of the Seldjukides was owing less to the weakness of their own
arms than to a trick of. the Khahrezmians. The Prince of Khahrezm began by
feigning friendship, and offered the two brothers and their followers a home in his .
own country, of course only for the sake of luring them out of reach of their own
clansmen on the left bank of the Yaxartes. The Seldjukides suspected no evil ;
they knew that the Prince of Khahrezm was at enmity with Sultan Mes'ud, the
successor of Mahmud, the Ghaznevide, and thought their alliance might be
necessary to him to help him against the latter.

from their fathers, and set forth by the eastern extremity of
the Hyrcanian desert for Khorasan, where, on the ancient
classical soil of Iran, they were destined to reap the fruits of
their active youth, hardly-fought battles, and marvellous perseverance. And they did reap these fruits in their fullest
measure.

In the year 422 (1030), that is, within a year of the death
of Sultan Mahmud, we find the Seldjukides west of Merv,
on the ground now occupied by the Tekke-Turkomans, in
the neighbourhood of the southern cities of Nisa and Abiverd,[1] from which point they molested the rich province of
Khorasan by constant raids, as grievously as is done by the
Turkomans to this very day.[2] On first taking possession of
that country, they are said to have sent an embassy to Sultan
Mes'ud, the son and successor of Mahmud, to offer the expression of their devotion and friendship, and solicit in return the
permission to settle in Khorasan. According to most historians, Mes'ud returned a grossly insulting answer, flatly refusing,
in a manner which so stirred up the pride of Togrul Beg and
Tchakar Beg that they sent off their families and flocks to
the interior of the great sandy desert of Karakum, and prepared with the assistance of their warlike followers to take by
force what the scornful Ghaznevides had refused to grant them
by fair means. It seems, however, improbable that, even if
circumstances had been different, the plunder-loving sons of
the desert would have remained quiet with the rich cities of
Khorasan before them. Not only the north-western district
of Iran, but every tract of country bordering on steppes in-

---

[1] Abiverd and Nisa still exist on the northern border of Iran, but are of course
now no better than miserable settlements, constantly exposed to the incursions of
Tekke-Turkomans. The road for caravans between Deregöz and Khiva passes
by the former place.

[2] The Seldjukides were, as is well known, the first Turks who settled on
the north-eastern border of Iran. There were nomads in the neighbourhood of
Merv both during the Arab occupation and in the time of the Samanides, but they
were not Turks. The same was the case in the north-west of Iran; the Guzz-
Turks from the north of the Caspian Sea did not descend to the Balkan (in the
Hyrcanian desert) until the commencement of the 10th century of the Christian
era.

habited by nomads, has invariably been exposed to similar visitations. It was the first time, however, that Khorasan had experienced one, and the extent of the desolation wrought by these turbulent neighbours is evident from the woeful complaints addressed by the Khorasanians to the court of Mes'ud. The proud Ghaznevide was indignant. He sent out his general, Begtogdi,[1] with an army provided with 1,000 camel-loads of arms, 100 camel-loads of gold, and several elephants, to confront the terrible sons of the desert. But the effeminate southerners from the Hilmend and the Indus were utterly powerless to cope with the hardy nomads. Begtogdi was routed in the first battle, and Mes'ud now took the command himself. A council of war was held at Nishabur, in which it was determined to come to terms with the Seldjukides,[2] but the latter sent back word to Mes'ud that 'as he had not thought their friendship worth having when they offered it, they would now have none of his.'

They remained quiet through the winter of 423 (1031), but in the spring recommenced their raids on a larger scale than ever. Mes'ud, mistrusting his own military capacity, gave back the command of his forces to his Subashi[3] (generalissimo), who proved however as powerless as himself to check the sudden incursions from the desert, and equally sudden retreats of the Turkomans. For three years Khorasan was exposed to constant plunderings and devastation, and, in the end, in the year 427 (1035) the Subashi was driven out of the northern districts of Khorasan, and Tchakar Beg

---

[1] Begtogdi is a Turkish word, and signifies princely, royal, born of princes.

[2] The proud Ghaznevide actually humbled himself so far as to propose to form a matrimonial connection with these rough soldiers of the desert. He offered to give princesses of his own house in marriage to the three Seldjukide princes, but they naturally declined to accept.

[3] Subashi is a Uiguric word, signifying commander-in-chief of the army. Vullers, in his original edition of *Mirkhondi Historia Seldjukidarum*, p. 28, spells the word Siashi سیاشی, and says in a note, سباشی subaschi *mendose* ut videtur pro سیاشی quod proprie significat *dux exercitus*. The etymology of the word is to be found in the dictionary of my *Uigurische Sprachn onumente*.

obtained possession of the wealthy and flourishing city of Merv, becoming thereby virtually lord of all North Khorasan. Mirkhond states that the inhabitants of Merv, perceiving the utter impotence of the Ghaznevides, opened their gates of their own accord to the Turkish chieftains, and placed themselves under their protection. The two brothers made their solemn entry into the ancient capital of Khorasan, and divided their rule in such a way that Togrul Beg undertook the administration, and Tchakar Beg the defence of the country. The results of their success had, however, after a time to be given up again, in consequence of the strenuous exertions made by Sultan Mes'ud to recover his authority ; he advanced by Belkh upon Merv in the year 429 (1037) with a force of 70,000 cavalry and 30,000 infantry, and the Seldjukides, deeming discretion the better part of valour, very wisely retired before these overwhelming numbers. Sultan Mes'ud regained possession of the cities of Belkh and Nishabur, but only for a short time ; for as soon as the brothers, operating singly, had had leisure to collect their forces, Tchakar Beg reappeared from the desert in the neighbourhood of Damghan, and vigorously recommenced hostilities. A decisive battle ensued in the neighbourhood of the latter place in Ramazan of the year 431 (1039). Mes'ud was completely beaten and fled to Ghaznee, where he died shortly after.

The two brothers had now gained undisturbed possession of Khorasan, the keystone of all operations in Islamite Asia, and were able to set to work unmolested to lay the foundations of their future greatness. The chief strongholds of the Seldjukides' power were Belkh in the east and Nishabur in the west, and from these two points their influence gradually extended farther and farther. They were summoned to Khahrezm to settle the disputes which had broken out there between the prince and the commander of the forces,[1] and

---

[1] The commander of the forces in Khahrezm had rebelled against the prince of the country, and forced the latter to address himself to the Seldjukides for help. Tchakar Beg did replace the dispossessed prince on his throne, but only on condition of his becoming a vassal of the Seldjukides.

without further ado they took possession of the country, and incorporated it with their own dominions. They then pushed forward over the ruins of the former power of the Buyyides to Azerbaïdjan, and in the year 446 (1054) the skirmishers of the Turkish army, led by Togrul Beg, penetrated into the interior of the eastern Roman Empire ;[1] and although the bold inhabitants of the desert in their raid on the land of the Cæsars were bent rather on plunder than on actual conquest, yet even their temporary success against the great name of Rome—so long one of awe to the ancient Asiatic—increased enormously the prestige and reputation of the Seldjukides. Togrul Beg was said to meditate a pilgrimage to Mecca with the object at the same time of clearing the road thither, which the state of anarchy in Bagdad had long rendered unsafe. He appeared in the ancient city of the Khalifs at once as a conqueror and as a humble servant.[2] Having upset the Deïlemite Melik Rehim, and assisted to place El-Kaim-bi-emri-Allah on the throne of the Khalifs, he pushed onwards in 450 (1058) against his rebellious uncle Ibrahim Ainal:[3] he was accompanied in this expedition by Alp Arslan, the son of Tchakar Beg, who had died shortly before at his own home. The quarrel with Ibrahim was soon made up, and Togrul Beg returned to Bagdad to restore Kaim (who had in the meantime been driven out) from the prison into which he had been thrown to the seat of the Khalifs.

In the year 451 (1059) the bold leader of the Turkish hordes was for the first time received in a solemn audience by the Prince of the Faithful, ' God's shadow on earth.' At their first meeting the Khalif would not profane his majesty by

---

[1] Gibbon (Murray, 1862, vol. viii. p. 154) relates, on the authority of some Greek statement, that Togrul sent an envoy to Constantinople to demand tribute and submission.

[2] At the first meeting of the Turkish chief and the Khalif, the latter appeared veiled, the black mantle of the Abbasides hanging from his shoulders, and in his right hand the staff of Mohammed. Togrul Beg was deeply moved by the majestic appearance of the Ruler of all the Faithful, and approached him humbly on foot, not venturing to mount his horse again until the Khalif called to him, ' Get on again, Togrul.'

[3] Perhaps more correctly spelt *Inal*, a name still common in Central Asia.

lifting his Burka (veil), and Togrul had to content himself with humbly kissing his hand. But Kaim's majestic demeanour was but a hollow symbol, for Togrul forced him to give him his daughter in marriage, and was occupied with preparations for the wedding, when he was himself overtaken by death at Reï in 455 (1063), in the seventieth year of a turbulent life, and the twenty-sixth of his reign. His successor, Alp Arslan, was a soldier endowed with a majestic presence and great mental abilities, who carried on his uncle's conquests with still greater activity and success. Some of his oriental panegyrists inform us that his head from the tip of his cap to the end of his beard measured two yards in length,[1] others speak of his enthusiasm for the heroic deeds of Alexander and Ali, whose lives he was never tired of studying. Alp Arslan was the first Turkish chieftain who led Turkish cavalry across the Euphrates, and brought the classic and sacred ground of Western Asia under the dominion of the race which rules it to this day.[2]

Some oriental historians tell us that the Emperor of Rome, Romanus Diogenes, inflamed with self-confidence and enthusiasm, had determined to plant the cross itself in the holy city of Islam, at the seat of the Khalifs, to burn all Korans, and not to return till he had made his way as far as Samarkand. But the origin of these reports is easy to trace. The wild sons of the desert having tried their strength against the rotten edifices in Iran and Arabistan, could not resist the temptation of measuring themselves with the Roman Empire, still famed for its power and wealth. Alp Arslan carried on the work begun by Togrul Beg. The Byzantine army, numbering in its ranks Franks and Normans, and representatives of various Christian people, could not withstand the furious onslaughts of the Turkish mul-

---

[1] Mirkhond, *History of the Seldjukides*, Vullers' edition, p. 46.

[2] *Ibn Khallikan* (in the Turkish translation printed at Constantinople in the year of the Hegira 1280), vol. ii. p. 222. Gibbon says : ' He passed the Euphrates at the head of the Turkish cavalry, and entered Cæsarea, the metropolis of Cappadocia, to which he had been attracted by the fame and wealth of the temple of St. Basil.'

titudes, and suffered a terrible defeat.[1] Romanus himself was taken prisoner,[2] and, although Alp Arslan behaved to him with the greatest magnanimity,[3] this reverse of the Roman arms proved the commencement of the long series of Turkish victories over the Byzantine Empire which culminated in the capture of Constantinople 500 years later. The victorious Turk having forced Byzantium to render him tribute, returned, spreading destruction around him, by Kerman and Tebbes, and across the desert,[4] to his own capital of Nishabur, which he reached just in time to receive the bride of his son Melikshah, a daughter of the great Khakan [5] of Samarkand, and to celebrate the wedding [6] with all due splendour. The leisure he granted himself was however but brief. Having nominated Melikshah his successor, and entrusted the administration of the various provinces of his great empire to his

[1] Alp Arslan endeavoured at first to bring matters to a peaceable issue, but in vain. The tenor of the messages exchanged is very characteristic, though we do not gather from them a much higher opinion of the civilisation of the Byzantine Christians than of that of the Tartaric hordes. Alp Arslan's message to Romanus was, according to Mirkhond, as follows :—' Although thine army is numerous, remember, thou art opposed by a prince whose victories are known far and wide. If thou wilt repent of thy rashness, render tribute, and abstain from hostilities, the Sultan will confirm thee in all thy possessions, and no harm shall happen to thee. But if not, thou wilt bring ruin on thine own head.' According to Gibbon, Romanus replied, ' If the barbarian wishes for peace, let him evacuate the ground which he occupies for the encampment of the Romans, and surrender his city and palace of Reï as a pledge of his sincerity.'

[2] One of the soldiers of the Sultan's bodyguard struck at him, but at the second blow Romanus exclaimed, ' Halt ! I am the Emperor of the Romans !' whereupon he was made prisoner.

[3] Alp Arslan placed his prisoner on a throne beside him, and treated him with the greatest respect. His son Melikshah subsequently married Romanus's daughter, and the wedding of the Turkish prince with the Christian princess was celebrated with great festivities.

[4] Vullers and Malcolm have been misled by erroneous Persian documents into spelling these names Kavert and Kadert. Alp Arslan adopted this roundabout route, to bring to order his brother Kurd, Viceroy of Kerman, who was said to have risen in rebellion.

[5] As the title of Khakan was never borne save by an independent prince, it may with safety be affirmed that Samarkand and the remainder of the eastern portion of Central Asia had not at that time passed into the actual possession of the Seldjukides.

[6] At the bride's entry into Nishabur, a thousand male and a thousand female slaves preceded the palanquin of the beautiful Samarkand princess, each carrying some costly present, and scattering in her path musk, ambergris, and aloes.

H

other sons and relations, he went in 458 (1065) to Khahrezm, to chastise a rebellious vassal; on a similar occasion, a few years later, he marched an army against Shems ul Mulk, the celebrated ruler of Bokhara, and, during the expedition, fell a victim to his own self-confidence, and to a soldier's insulted dignity,[1] on the banks of the Oxus on the 2 Moharrem, 465 (1072). He died in the forty-fourth year of his age, and the twelfth of a glorious reign. Alp Arslan was the second prince of the house of Seldjuk, who was alike distinguished as a soldier and as a statesman; and it is a unique instance in the annals of Islamite peoples, that the third in descent, Melik-shah, should have proved the same, and have been capable of continuing to raise the influence and power of his dynasty with equal ability and equal success.

Melikshah's reign was certainly the culminating point of the glory of the Seldjukides. It took him nearly five years to render the throne he had inherited safe against the designs of his uncle Kurd, and when he had overcome him, he marched in 470 (1077) to Samarkand, to attack, in the person of his own father-in-law, the most powerful opponent of his dynasty. The object Melikshah constantly kept in view was the consolidation of his power in the gigantic empire, and he was enabled in a great measure to accomplish this work through the wise counsels of his celebrated vizir Nizam ul Mulk; the peace, prosperity, and flourishing civilisation of the twenty years of his reign render them the brightest spot in the history of Islam. The science, poetry, industry, and architecture of Iran were more largely indebted to this great prince than to any of his successors. He is said to have travelled twelve

---

[1] In the country (or, more properly speaking, the province) of Zem, a small fortress near the spot where Alp Arslan designed to cross the Oxus arrested his onward progress for some time. When it was at length taken, the commandant, Yusuf Khahrezmi, was brought before the Sultan, who loaded him with abuse and ordered him to be crucified. Yusuf, determined to avenge himself on his murderer, fell on Alp Arslan with a dagger. The servants of the Sultan were about to cut him down, but the latter interposed, and, trusting to his own skill with the bow, sent an arrow flying at his aggressor. The arrow missed. Alp Arslan had scarcely time to fit a second one, before Yusuf again fell on him and inflicted a mortal wound.

times through his entire dominions from Yemen to the distant
Oxus. Princes vied with each other for the honour of entering his service, and the Khalif Muktadi, a creature of his own,
considered it a great privilege to be allowed to come forward
as a suitor for his daughter's hand.[1] Mindful of the oriental
adage, ' Perfection and decay go hand in hand,' he determined
as far as possible to provide, during his own lifetime, against
discord breaking out amongst those who should come after
him, by dividing the empire between his different relations.
Anatolia was given to Suleïman Shah, whose family had
hitherto governed Gazan ; Syria fell to his brother Tutush, the
adversary of the Crusaders ; Nushtekin Gartcha, who had
raised himself from slavery to the rank of generalissimo, and
who became later the founder of the dynasty of the Khah-
rezmides, was invested with Khahrezm ; Aksonghar[2] got
Aleppo, Tchekermish Mosul, Kobulmish Damascus, Kho-
martekin Fars, and his son Sandjar was entrusted with the
administration of Khorasan and Transoxania. These precau-
tions proved, however, ineffectual to preserve the dynasty of
the Seldjukides from the common fate of oriental sovereign
races, for after the death of Melikshah, which took place in
485 (1092), his son Berkyaruk (the Very Brilliant One) had
scarcely ascended the throne before the flames of discord
were kindled amongst the numerous members of the family,
and they speedily fell a prey to the generals and the other relations of the deceased prince. The events of the period between this time and the death of Sultan Sandjar in 552 (1060),
though embracing more than half a century, comprise little or

---

[1] The *trousseau* of Melikshah's daughter gives us some idea of the wealth and
magnificence of the Seldjukide prince. The princess was followed on her entry
into Bagdad by 130 strings of camels (a string consists of ten or fifteen camels),
laden with the richest silks of Rum, seventy-four mules with gold collars and gold
bells, laden with twelve silver trays full of precious stones and jewellery of all
kinds, and finally, thirty-three led camels with golden saddle-cloths and carrying
more jewellery of various kinds.

[2] Aksonghar, or more correctly Akshonghar (not Aksangar, as it is often called,
and as it has been misspelt by myself in my dictionary of *Tschagataische Sprachstudien*), is a Turkish word, also used as a proper name, and signifying ' White
Falcon.'

nothing of any interest as bearing directly on the history of
Bokhara, for this last-named Seldjukide was the only one
who during his unusually long reign of some forty years
exercised any influence on the destinies of Transoxania, as
he was also almost the only one of all his race who took to
heart the decay of their power in their old hereditary dominions, or made any earnest endeavour to arrest it.

It is certainly a matter of surprise that this family of
Turkish chieftains, who made their authority so long felt in all
portions of the Islamite East, and even in Africa itself, who
threw down so many ancient thrones, and founded so many
new dynasties, were yet never able to maintain themselves
successfully in their own old home beyond the Oxus.   From
the moment when the brave grandsons of Seldjuk, driven out
by their rivals, migrated with their flocks and herds to the
northern borders of Iran, their influence in Transoxania began
to wane exactly in proportion as their conquests spread over
Iran and Arabistan and carried them farther and farther westward.   The historians of the Seldjukides—mostly Persians
or Arabs—have tried to magnify the reigns of Alp Arslan
and Melikshah, by placing the eastern frontiers of their
dominions far beyond Khokand ; asserting even that the
coinage of Kashgar bore the name .of Melikshah.   These
statements do not appear, however, to be correct.

The special history of Bokhara (written by Narshaki) always
describes Shems ul Mulk, alluded to above, as the most high
and mighty Padishah, i.e. Sovereign Prince, whose dominions
extended beyond Khodjend, whose public buildings, karavanserais, schools, baths, &c., were still pointed out centuries
later, who died about 480 (1087), and whose shrine is still
visited by devout souls at Bokhara.   His successor Arslan
Khan, father-in-law to Sultan Sandjar, enjoyed equal honours,
bore the same titles, and also left a name gratefully remembered by the people of Bokhara.   He died in 525 (1130),
and was buried at Merv.   The authority of the Seldjukides
at Bokhara, Samarkand, and Fergana, was therefore un-

doubtedly no more than nominal, for the real power lay either in the hands of the native princes or in those of the Uigur princes, reigning in Eastern Turkestan.[1]

Tchakar Beg and Togrul Beg, the first Seldjukides who carried their victorious banners eastward to Belkh and westward to the centre of Armenia, never dreamt of turning their eyes on the countries beyond the Oxus; it was reserved for Alp Arslan, after subduing the Byzantine Empire, to endeavour at first by peaceable means to establish his rule in Transoxania, for which purpose he allied himself by marriage with Suleïman Khan of Samarkand. This attempt proved, however, abortive, for a few years later he found himself obliged to cross the Oxus with a large army, and the expedition cost him his life. Melikshah continued the campaign against his father-in-law, whom he finally overcame, but it is doubtful whether his authority ever extended as far as Fergana, much less farther; for if that had been the case, history would not have preserved to us the name of Khidr Khan, who is said to have been a

---

[1] The oriental historians describe the princes reigning at that time in Eastern Turkestan as belonging originally to *Kara Khitai*, the modern Chinese provinces of Shensi and Kansu, and comprise under this description all the Turks living in the far East. We cannot endorse this view, the more so as the monuments of the Uigur language, mentioned above, abundantly prove that the Turks living east of Fergana and extending into China were a perfectly distinct tribe, entirely different from their brethren in the west and the north. They had a common Turkish dialect, that of the *Kudatku Bilik*, which was equally understood in the east and west of the country of the Uigurs, and which only degenerated later, when, about the seventh century of the Hegira, the Uigurs began to mingle with the other Turkish tribes. The accounts given by oriental historians do not of course tally with our own. Djuveïnï, who has been followed by all later historians, describes under the name of Uigurs or Etrak—Uigur—'Uigur Turks,' the Turkish tribe principally located at Almalik and Bishbalik; he calls their chief 'Idi Kut' (Lord of Fortune) and their priests 'Kam.' Not only these two words, but all the others described as Uigur by Djuveïnï and his followers, will be found in my 'Monuments of the Uigur Language' (*Uigurische Sprachmonumente*), taken from a manuscript written 150 years earlier for the Uigurs of Kashgar, which strongly confirms my impression that the language of Bishbalik was identical with that of Kashgar. Djuveïnï's particular Uigurs differ only in so far from their western clansmen that in the eyes of the Mohammedans they were 'Kafir'—i.e. unbelievers who had embraced Christianity or Shamanism, whilst the latter were strictly orthodox Mohammedans, professing Islamism and refusing to hold intercourse with their heretic brethren. If therefore any portion of the Turks in the East are called 'Uigurs,' the designation must apply to the whole tribe which formed the ethnographical link between the Chinese and the Persians in Fergana.

contemporary of Melikshah, to have reigned in Turkestan, and to have emulated Melikshah in power and magnificence.[1] However proudly the banners of the Seldjukides may have waved over Western Asia, in the East the most strenuous exertions, such as those of Sultan Sandjar, produced little or no result. It is true that Bokhara and the western part of the khanate always acknowledged the suzerainty of the Seldjukides, but the eastern portion of Transoxania would not recognise the authority of those princes, the centre of whose power really lay in Persia; and no one was better aware of this fact than Sandjar, himself warmly attached to Khorasan and the eastern world of Islam. This unhappy prince marched in the year 524 (1129) against Mohammed the ruler of Samarkand,[2] a son of the above-mentioned Suleïman Khan, to force him to fulfil his duties as a vassal. Samarkand, a fortress of evil repute in those times, was surrounded, and driven at length by hunger and pestilence to surrender. Mohammed was carried prisoner to Khorasan, but was subsequently pardoned by Sandjar and reinstated in his former dignities. This was the first campaign against Transoxania. The second was only the more unfortunate. In the year 535 (1140), Samarkand again revolted; her rebellious chief, named Ahmed, lay crippled with gout, but his 12,000 slaves defended the place, and although Sandjar overcame them, and entrusted the administration of Samarkand to Nasr, the son of Ahmed, the final result of the campaign was to involve him in a disastrous war, and ultimately to destroy the influence of the Seldjukides in Transoxania almost entirely.

The Uigurs, who have already been alluded to in the preceding chapter, were at that time governed by a powerful

---

[1] The relative position of Khidr Khan and Melikshah has also struck Gibbon, who very naturally enquires how the latter, considering the gigantic power he is credited with in Western Asia, could suffer the existence of so distinguished a rival in the East.

[2] According to the Djihankusha, Bokhara had also rebelled against Sandjar under the leadership of a certain Tamgatch Khan, and it was not until he had suppressed the revolt there that he proceeded against Samarkand.

prince named Kurkhan.[1] According to the Djihankusha, whence later historians have chiefly derived their information, Kurkhan came from the interior of Khatai (the northern portion of China), and first settled with his numerous followers on the eastern borders of the Kirghis Steppes; but finding himself molested there by the nomads, withdrew farther south, and founded the city of Imil. But even there he could not remain in peace ; he at last settled at Belasaghun,[2] and fought with success the powerful tribes of Kangli, Kiptchak, and Karlik; and having extended his authority over a portion of the so-called Khatai and over the cities of Bishbalik and Almalik, he attacked the principalities of Kashgar and Khoten which were at war with each other, subdued both, and began to extend his conquests gradually westwards in the direction of Fergana and Transoxania. Sandjar, alarmed at the increasing power of his eastern neighbour, was anxious to check it, and Kurkhan on his side was no less anxious to pick a quarrel. The occasion was not far to seek.

The country north-east of Khokand, the home of the Kiptchaks and Kara-Kirghises, was tenanted by certain bodies of nomads from Kara-Khatai with their flocks, on whom Sandjar had levied heavy contributions in the shape of a tax. The greybeards of Kara-Khatai were anxious to satisfy the Sultan to the extent of 5,000 camels and 10,000 sheep, but as this was not thought enough, they invoked the assistance of Kurkhan, who soon afterwards invaded Transoxania with an army in the year 536 (1141), and so thoroughly routed Sultan Sandjar that the latter had to fly, leaving behind him his harem and all his baggage, and accompanied only by 300 men (who afterwards

---

[1] *Not* خان کور Kör Khan, as, following Djuveïnï, oriental historians have called him. Djuveïnï maintains that this word signifies in the language of Kara-Khatai 'Khan of the Khans,' which may be inferred from the Uigur meaning of 'Kurakan,' Protector, but cannot be positively asserted. Klaproth's view of the matter in his *Journal asiatique*, 1828, p. 293, does not rest on any more positive authority.

[2] Belasaghun was called by the Mongolians *Gubalik*—i.e. 'beautiful city,' as Mirkhond rightly names it. In the map of Asia in the fourteenth century, prefixed by Col. Yule to his excellent work, *Cathay and the Way Thither*, Belasaghun is placed north-east of the modern Urumtchi.

dwindled down to fifteen), and with the greatest difficulty got across the Oxus. The losses of the Seldjukides were estimated at 30,000 men, the military reputation of Sandjar, who had hitherto been reckoned a second Alexander, was gone for ever, and gone for ever was the authority of the Seldjukides in Transoxania. Sandjar, after his defeat, was pursued by one misfortune after another, and had to endure the degradation of seeing himself a prisoner of Turcoman nomads, in the neighbourhood of the modern Andkhoï, and spending three years of great wretchedness among them. He succeeded at last in escaping, but the weight of his sufferings had deprived him of reason, and he died on the 26 Rebiul evvel, 522 (1128). His nephew Mahmud Khan reigned for six years after him; he was related on his father's side to Boghra Khan of Kashgar, but the latter had his eyes put out by a rebel, and whilst Khorasan itself fell partly into the hands [1] of the Khahrez-mians, and partly into those of the lords of Gur (of the northern portion of modern Afghanistan), and was partly overrun by the robber hordes of the Guzz, Kurkhan asserted his authority over the greater part of Fergana and Transoxania.

Thus ended the rule of the first Turkish dynasty in Transoxania, which, strangely enough, had contributed absolutely nothing, either to increase the political importance of their old home, or to advance the civilisation of their countrymen. Although themselves Turks, the Seldjukides, whilst rejoicing in the splendour of their possessions in Western Asia, seem to have deemed the little country on the Oxus scarcely worthy of their attention. Their greatest princes reigned just at that period of civilisation when the Persian language was beginning to compete with Arabic as the language of literature, both in Iran and Turan; and, as the Seldjukides were great protectors of poetry and science, we find Togrul Beg, Melikshah, and Sandjar all intent on reviving the soft and beautiful tongue of Iran, whilst Turkish, which in another portion of

---

[1] In consequence of the devastations which ensued, the poet Enveri wrote his celebrated elegy *The Tears of Khorasan*, which has lately been so cleverly translated into English by E. H. Palmer and J. Cowell.

Asia [1] could boast of a flourishing literature, was only used by the ruling family as the language of common life. The same state of things existed among the Turkish princes of Khahrezm and the powerful vassals in the cities of Transoxania ; for although the government was almost exclusively in the hands of Turks, the numbers of the settled Turkish population were still comparatively very small.

---

[1] In Eastern Turkestan, where the ethical and political poem *Kudatku Bilik* was composed in the year 462 (1096), consequently nearly a hundred years before the death of Sandjar.

VII.

UIGURS AND KHAHREZMIAN PRINCES.

528 (1133)—615 (1218).

BOKHARA, that ancient seat of learning and peaceful arts, and
Samarkand, celebrated far and wide for its natural beauties,
had at all times been exposed to danger from the covetousness of their warlike and turbulent neighbours, both in the
east and in the west; during the fifty years that elapsed
between the decay of the Seldjukides' rule and the invasion
of the Mongolians, they were a special apple of discord
between two ambitious neighbours, the Uigur Kurkhan in
the east, and the Khahrezmians in the west. We have already
described the first apparition of the former, and will also give
some account of the latter so far as our limits will permit,
dwelling more especially on those portions of their history
bearing most directly on their policy towards Transoxania.
Khahrezm, the country forming the modern khanate of Khiva,
was in the time of the Seldjukides an appanage or fief belonging to the office of chief jug-bearer or Tashtdar,[1] and as
such was granted by Melikshah to the general Nushtekin
Gartcha.　His son Mohammed Kutbeddin succeeded him in
491 (1097), and governed Khahrezm for thirty years.　The
star of the Seldjukides was declining, and he, in common with
the other vassals of the gigantic empire, was only bound by a
nominal allegiance to the ruling house.　He assumed the title
of Khahrezm Shah (Prince of Khahrezm), but was no more
jug-bearer to the Seldjukides' Prince of Khorasan than the

---

[1] The servant who hands his master the ewer containing the water for the
ablutions prescribed by the Mohammedan ritual is still called Tashtdar.　The definition of *butler*, or cup-bearer, given by Malcolm in his *History of Persia*, is therefore wrong, the Persian word for the latter being Tshashneghir.

present Khan of Khiva is to the Sultan, although he holds the same title from him.[1] Kutbeddin was succeeded by his son Atsiz, a prince of great abilities and boundless ambition, who raised the reputation of his sovereign's house by his enlightened patronage of literature,[2] but, on the other hand, made use of his increasing power entirely to emancipate himself from the control of Sandjar, his suzerain and protector. As long as the latter was favoured by fortune, Atsiz showed as much faithfulness and devotion[3] as he afterwards did enmity and active hostility when misfortunes overtook Sandjar. He rebelled three times and invaded Khorasan, but Sandjar had always generously pardoned him, although the turbulent conduct of the Khahrezmians was the more reprehensible, as by their attacks they were really only promoting the objects of a third common enemy, Kurkhan, who, after his first success against Sandjar, had taken possession of all Transoxania, and had sent a division of his army under Otuz, one of his principal generals, to Khahrezm, where it had inflicted great sufferings, and had then retired laden with spoils to Samarkand. Atsiz did all he could to wipe out this disgrace. In 546 (1151), he went to Djend to join Kemaleddin,[4] the

---

[1] The present rulers of Khiva are titular cup-bearers of the Sultans of Constantinople. It is not a little remarkable that the descendants of the former servant of the Seldjukides should have been able to maintain so long, and in spite of a cessation of all intercourse during some centuries, the privileges of the family of their masters.

[2] Reshidedin Vatvat (swallow), the poet mentioned by Hammer-Purgstall in his *Geschichte der persischen Redekünste*, was held in high honour at his court, and had so much offended Sultan Sandjar by a satirical poem (see Hammer's above-mentioned book, p. 121) that he made a vow that if he should take him alive after the fall of Hezaresp, he would have him hewn in seven pieces. Hezaresp was taken and Vatvat remained in concealment, until it came into the head of Muntahab-eddin, Sandjar's secretary, to divert his master's wrath by the following joke. He begged him to consider that the poet Vatvat was a wretchedly lean little bird, and ought not to be cut up into seven pieces but only into *two* at most. The Sultan laughed, and pardoned the poet.

[3] When Sandjar was at Bokhara, putting down the rebellion of Tamgatch, a few conspirators determined to surprise him out hunting, and to kill him. Atsiz dreamed a dream about this plot, woke up suddenly, got on horseback, and arrived just in time to defeat the plan of the miscreants. Sandjar was as much astonished at the curious coincidence of the dream as touched at the devotion of Atsiz.

[4] Kemaleddin, a bosom friend of the poet Vatvat, afterwards shamefully

viceroy of the place, with whom he had a secret alliance in his campaign against the unbelieving [1] Uigurs, but his exertions were in vain; he had to submit to pay a yearly tribute of 30,000 pence (denars), and, in spite of his boundless ambition, to leave his heirs burdened with this obligation.

The death of Atsiz occurred at Kabushan in 551 (1156); his son Il Arslan succeeded to the government, and seems to have made another attempt to free the house of Khahrezm from the burden imposed on it, but to have failed as his father had done.

A mission from Transoxania is said to have invoked the assistance of Il Arslan in the year 553 (1158) against the encroachments of the ruler of Samarkand, a vassal of Kurkhan's. He hurried thither with a considerable force, but, although Bokhara opened her gates to him peaceably, he could obtain no advantage over the army assembled by his opponent before Samarkand, which contained within its ranks all the Turkomans dwelling between Karaköl and Djend, and had to retire without accomplishing anything. The Uigurs remained as before, in possession of the greater part of Transoxania, and Fergana and the Khahrezmians had to content themselves with the western border country of Bokhara.[2] There ensued a peace of six years' duration between the two border countries, during which time Il Arslan established his government on a firmer basis in Kho-

betrayed Atsiz, and the poet was suspected of being implicated in the treachery, and was for some time in disgrace.

[1] We have already remarked that the epithet of ' Unbelievers,' taking it even in the strictest Mohammedan sense, cannot be said to apply to all Uigurs. Most of them, including Kurkhan himself, were Mohammedans, and the others principally professed Christianity, and especially one Turkish tribe—that of Naiman—is said to have consisted entirely of Christians (tersa).

[2] Djuveini, who frequently betrays his partiality for the Khahrezmians, maintains that Ilik Turkoman, alarmed by the apparition of Il Arslan, at once submitted, and that the Samarkandians begged for mercy. This does not, however, appear to have been the case, for Samarkand and Bokhara only recognised the supremacy of the Khahrezmians as long as they were occupied by their troops. Under the government of Il Arslan and Tekish the Khahrezmians only retained the western portion of Bokhara, that is the towns of Amuye, Karaköl, and Djend, which lay in the north-west.

rasan, after driving Mahmud (the last of the Seldjukides in Khorasan) from his throne and putting out his eyes.

In the year 560 (1164) hostilities broke out again. The Uigurs were accused of having invaded the possessions of the Prince of the Khahrezmians, and Il Arslan sent off his general, Ayar Beg, to Amuye, intending himself to follow in person shortly after ; but before he could overtake him, Ayar Beg's army was routed by the Uigurs, he himself taken prisoner, and the ambitious Il Arslan forced to fly. He fell ill during his retreat, and died in the same year. He had named as his successor his youngest son, the learned and able Sultan Shah, but his elder son, Tekish,[1] refused to give up his birthright, and having secured the help of the Uigurs by promising them the punctual payment of the tribute exacted, he drove his brother from the throne after ten years of civil war, and mounted it himself to become the greatest prince of his race, and to add to the insignificant little country on the lower course of the Oxus dominions whose borders should stretch southwards to India and the Persian Gulf, westward to the Euphrates, and northwards to the Volga. Tekish began by initiating a policy of friendship towards the Uigurs in Transoxania, not so much to keep his promises as because he felt himself weak. He seemed anxious first to establish his throne on a firm basis, and next to extend his power in the west, so as to be able later to prosecute his designs on the East with greater freedom. As concerns his first object, he could only attain it at the price of eight years' continued warfare with his brother Sultan Shah ; but in his second he was materially assisted by the disorganised condition of affairs at the court of Togrul-bin-Arslan, the last of the Seldjukides in Persia. A rebellious vassal of the latter, Kutlug Inandj,[2] summoned him into the field to assist him,

---

[1] Not Takash, as it is spelt even by the learned Quatremère in a note to his remarkable translation of Rashideddin's *History of the Mongolians in Persia.* Tekish is an old Turkish word, signifying battle, encounter, fight. So also *tekishmek*, to fight, to meet in battle.

[2] Kutlug Inandj (the Fortunate Believer), son of the Ata begh Ildeköz (Overseer

and he not only succeeded by a bold stroke in possessing himself of the throne of Persia, but also attacked those dreaded fanatics, the Assassins, in their stronghold of Arslan Kusha (Lion-tamer), and even forced the Khalif Nasireddin, after beating him, to enter into a treaty of alliance which the proud Abbaside had a short time before scornfully rejected.

In this manner Sultan Tekish succeeded, in spite of the turbulent spirit reigning amongst his vassals, and even among his own children, in founding an empire but little inferior in extent to those of the first Seldjukides and of the Samanides. But he nevertheless continued to pay tribute to his eastern neighbours, for at his death, which took place at Khahrezm on the 10th Ramazan of the year 596 (1199), after a reign of twenty-eight years, he left directions for his heirs *to avoid all disputes with Kurkhan, and to consider him in the light of a strong bulwark against a mighty enemy beyond, ever on the watch to break loose.* Whether these prophetic words, pointing to the invasion of the Mongolians, really proceeded forth from the mighty Khahrezmian, or were put into his mouth by later historians, it is not easy to determine ; but his son and successor, Mohammed Kutbeddin, was certainly not in any case the man to carry out the wishes of his dying father. He was brave and resolute, but under the influence of boundless ambition, and unable to bear the degradation of

of the People), had behaved with the deepest ingratitude towards the unfortunate but noble-minded Sultan Togrul. He had been imprisoned for a criminal attack on the person of his sovereign, and generously pardoned by the latter ; this generosity he repaid by going at once to Khorasan to ask Tekish to assist him with arms against his benefactor. It is said that in the last battle Togrul mounted his horse in a state of drunkenness, and placed himself at the head of his troops, clad in shining armour, swinging his ponderous club in the air, and reciting with many gesticulations inflammatory verses from the *Shahnameh*, invoking ruin on the heads of his enemies. Whilst going through these evolutions, he unfortunately dropped his club ; his own horse was struck on the knee by it, fell and threw him. Kutlug Inandj perceiving this, hurried up ánd killed him. Tekish had his head cut off the dead body and sent it to Bagdad, to the Khalif, a bitter enemy of Togrul's. A poet, on seeing the headless corpse next day, wrote as follows :—

'How whimsical, O king ! are now the waves of fate ;
The clouds will soon the glory from the heavens take.
Thy head, which yesterday did reach unto the skies,
Lo ! sundered from thy body low to-day it lies.'

owing allegiance to a neighbour whom he regarded as a barbarian,[1] he was ever on the watch for an occasion to break with Kurkhan.

On first assuming the government, he was precluded by circumstances from revealing this feeling. His rival, Shehabeddin, Prince of Gur, had invaded and grievously devastated Tus and the neighbourhood. Mohammed took arms against him, and found himself involved in a protracted warfare in which the Uigurs came to his assistance, whilst Shehabeddin on his side was joined by the rebellious Prince of Samarkand, and crossed the Oxus in the year 600 (1203) with an army numbering upwards of 70,000 men. Mohammed was only able to collect in haste some 10,000 horsemen to oppose him ; but nevertheless, thanks to the bravery of his Uigur auxiliaries, obtained a decisive victory. Shehabeddin had to escape for bare life, leaving all his treasures behind him,[2] and was never able subsequently to recover from this blow ; he died in the year 602 (1205). Mohammed obtained possession of Herat and of the entire province of Gur ; and having, by the suppression of sundry other disturbances in Khorasan, consolidated his power over all Iran, he began to think the time had arrived for turning his attention towards Turania.

In place of remembering the gratitude due to Kurkhan for the assistance he had rendered him against Shehabeddin, he behaved to him with studied insolence, and when the Uigur envoys appeared at his court in the year 606 (1209) to claim the yearly tribute, the faithless Khahrezmian

---

[1] I repeat here the opinion expressed in the Introduction, that the inhabitants of Khahrezm were at that time exclusively Persian, and that the Khahrezmians, although themselves of Turkish origin, had so thoroughly imbibed Persian notions of culture and civilisation that they looked on the Turks in the light of barbarians.

[2] Shehabeddin, seeing the battle was going against him, had thrown himself hurriedly into a fortress, but the Uigurs surrounded it and soon made a breach ; the Prince of Samarkand, however, a partisan of Kurkhan's, inspired by religious zeal, sent a private message to Shehabeddin, recommending him not to delay, but to save his own life at least, even at the price of leaving his treasures to the unbelievers. The Uigurs who were entering the fortress were most probably Christians.

expressed himself unable to endure the degradation any
longer, and determined on refusing it. As he did not choose
to appear as acting personally in direct opposition to his
father's last injunctions, he left his capital on the arrival of the
Uigur envoys, having ostensibly entrusted the regency to
his mother, but in reality given his private instructions to
his own negotiator, Mohammed, May (?). Turkhan Khatun,
Mohammed's mother, following scrupulously the same policy
as her deceased husband, received Kurkhan's envoys and sent
them on their way again in the most courteous and friendly
manner ; but as soon as the Khahrezmian envoy reached the
court of the Uigur and explained the real intentions of his
master, Kurkhan, though much astonished, saw at once that
he must prepare for an open attack on Mohammed's part,
and in point of fact it was not long delayed. Mohammed
gave out that he had been invited to come to the assistance
of Transoxania, which was suffering grievously under the yoke
of the Uigurs, and invaded Bokhara in the same year. The
country sided with him, and the capital opened its gates to
him. At Samarkand things went equally well. The governor there at that time was Sultan Osman, a remarkably handsome man, much praised by all oriental historians, who was
at enmity with Kurkhan in consequence of the latter having
refused him the hand of his daughter. He was, therefore, all
the more ready to receive the friendly advances of Sultan
Mohammed, who gave him his daughter in marriage ; he
became his vassal, and accompanied him on his campaign in
the north, whither he proceeded after installing Tartaba, a
distinguished Khahrezmian general, as governor of Samarkand. Kurkhan, on being informed of these events, sent
orders to his generalissimo Tayankou, who was at Taraz, the
capital of Djadj, to prepare for a vigorous resistance ; but
fortune was against the Uigurs, their army was totally defeated, and Tayankou[1] himself was severely wounded and

---

[1] Whilst Tayankou (not Taniku, as spelt by D'Herbelot) was lying wounded on
the field of battle, one of his female slaves was tending him, when a soldier be-

taken prisoner. It may be imagined how much this decisive victory increased Sultan Mohammed's self-confidence and pride. He chose to be called Iskender-i-sani (Alexander the Second), and assumed the title of Zil Allahi fi'l arzi (the Shadow of God on Earth), and on his return to Khahrezm, flushed with victory after the taking of Otrar, was cruel enough to have his unhappy wounded prisoner, Tayankou, thrown into the water.

But, in spite of these successes, Sultan Mohammed was still far from having attained his object, the possession of all Turkestan. He had scarcely left the shores of the Yaxartes before Kurkhan himself, in spite of his advanced age, for he was now ninety years old, appeared in person before Otrar with an army, retook the places he had lost, and shortly after detached a body of troops to lay siege again to Samarkand. Sultan Mohammed hurried back to Transoxania. He had at the same time to put down a rebellion which had broken out at Djend, but the Uigurs on hearing of his approach raised the siege and retired to the north.[1] The Khahrezmians pursued them, and a battle ensued in the year 610 (1213) not far from Binaket, in which the two opponents each led their armies in person ; after many hours' hard fighting, the battle was drawn. So at least it is affirmed by the historical work the ' Djihankusha ;' but the circumstances that the two principal generals of the Khahrezmians, Tartaba and Ispfahabad, both went over to the enemy, and that Mohammed himself was missing from his camp for several days after the battle (having got entangled among

longing to the enemy came up and was about to cleave his head with his sword, but the slave shrieked and called out the name of the wounded man ; thereupon the soldier spared his life, but took him prisoner, and he was carried before the Sultan.

[1] Djuveinï ascribes the precipitate retreat of the Uigurs to the fact that Kurkhan, disturbed by the revolt of Kütshlük at Almarlik, found himself obliged to concentrate his forces. This assumption may be tolerably correct, but we cannot help observing that Djuveinï does not seem very clear concerning the understanding between Mohammed and Kütshlük. In one place he describes the alliance as having been concluded during Mohammed's first campaign, but in another place he fixes it for the period of the second campaign.

the enemy's troops, and only escaped owing to his habit of always assuming in battle the dress of his adversaries), would seem to point to a defeat of the Khahrezmians, though, on the other hand, the precipitate retreat of Kurkhan leads us to a different conclusion ; and this latter seems to be the more probable, especially when we take into consideration the fact that a third combatant had by this time appeared on the scene, who was the more formidable to the old prince of the Uigurs, as he zealously promoted Sultan Mohammed's objects. This was Kütshlük Khan,[1] the son of Tayang Khan, prince of the Turkish tribe of Naiman, who had retired before the increasing power of Djenghiz from the neighbourhood of Bishbalik westwards, had sought protection from Kurkhan, and even allied himself with him by marriage, but afterwards made common cause with his rebellious vassal, and broke out into open revolt.   For the sake of weakening Kurkhan by creating a diversion in the east, Kütshlük entered into an alliance with Sultan Mohammed, in which it was agreed that the latter should attack Kurkhan from the east, and the former from the west.   If Mohammed should overthrow his adversary, he was to incorporate Kashgar and Khoten with his own dominions ; but if Kütshlük should be beforehand with him, he on his part was to be at liberty to extend his frontiers to the shores of the Yaxartes.   Sultan Mohammed received Kütshlük's envoy at Samarkand, and then entered on his second campaign feeling confident of success.   As matters turned out, after the battle of Binaket, Sultan Mohammed would have been justified in continuing his course against Eastern Turkestan, but he contented himself with the former line of frontier at Otrar, and returned proud and satisfied to Khahrezm.   But the aged Kurkhan was in a very different frame of mind. He had been forced, by the formidable proportions assumed by the revolt of Kütshlük, to retrace his steps hurriedly, and had in addition met with the misfortune of seeing discord and mutiny amongst his own troops during the retreat, and his own subjects griev-

---

[1] Kütshlük is a Uiguric word, signifying the strong or powerful one.

ously molested by them. On arriving at Belasaghun [1] the inhabitants closed their gates against him, and defended themselves obstinately for sixteen days, hoping all the time that
Sultan Mohammed, to whom they looked for protection, would
pursue Kurkhan.   They were overcome at last, and 75,000
people fell in the ensuing massacre.   No wonder that such
events should have diminished the number of Kurkhan's
friends,[2] and when Kütshlük, taking advantage of what he
deemed a favourable opportunity, attacked him, he was utterly
routed and had to give way.   Placed under the protection
of his own former protégé,[3] Kurkhan solicited the favour of
a subordinate post for himself, but Kütshlük treated him with
distinction, and the last powerful Turkish prince in the East
died at the age of ninety-two years, having reigned eighty-one
years over the Turkish people inhabiting the region between
the interior of China and the Oxus.

  After the death of Kurkhan, Sultan Mohammed found himself left without a single opponent who could inspire him with
any alarm either in Turan or in Iran, but still he could not
remain at rest, for his own ambition was ceaselessly urging him
on in the further path of conquest. On his return to his capital
he was unfortunate enough while heated with wine to pronounce sentence of death on Medjid-eddin Bagdadi, a deeply
venerated ascetic, against whom his mind had been poisoned
by enemies,[4] and the sentence had been at once carried out.
When sober he was seized with the deepest remorse, and sent
to the convent where the sheïkh had usually resided a bowl
containing gold and precious stones to be distributed among

  [1] The circumstance that Kurkhan was able, on his retreat from the shores of
the Yaxartes, without entering the territory of his rebellious vassal Kütshlük,
to reach Belasaghun before his arrival at Kashgar, points clearly to the fact that
this city did not lie north of Komul, as assumed by Col. H. Yule, but much
further to the west beyond Almalik.

  [2] The word in the German text is ' Feinde ' (enemies), but the context makes me
think it must be a misprint for ' Freunde ' (friends), otherwise the sentence is
obscure.

  [3] Djuveïnï says he married the beautiful daughter of Kurkhan, who had acted
as his representative in the government during his absence.

  [4] Mirkhond says he was accused of being too intimate with the mother Sultana.

the brethren as a sin-offering; but Nedjmeddin Kubera,[1] the superior of the convent returned the gift saying, ' Neither gold nor precious stones, but the life of the Sultan, my own life, and the lives of many thousand true believers will have to be poured out as the blood-offering for our deceased saint.' Mirkhond looks on these words as a prophecy of the destruction to be wrought by the Mongols, and expressly remarks that this sin of the Sultan's was the primary cause of his fall ; he also mentions as his second unpardonable sin, the removal of the Khalif Nasireddin, a deed which has been severely blamed by all Mohammedan historians.

The relations between the Khahrezmian princes and the khalifs of Bagdad are well known to have been always uneasy; the former wished to play the same part as the Seldjukides towards the chief of the Islamite hierarchy, and, as the latter declined the proffered guardianship, there were frequently open quarrels as in the time of Tekish ; whilst at other times, again, all sorts of intrigues were set on foot in Bagdad, under the mask of simulated friendship. When, for instance, Shehabeddin, prince of Gur, died in the year 611 (1214) and Sultan Mohammed proceeded to Ghaznee with the intention of conquering this province, he found in the treasury there letters in which the Khalif had invited the deceased prince to go to war with the Khahrezmians, and had even gone so far as to send him a diploma, investing him with the dignity of Sultan. Furious at this, Mohammed proclaimed in a solemn assembly the deposition of the Khalif, appointed in his place the learned Mollah Ala el Mulk of Termez, and instantly set off for Bagdad, to instal his own creature in the place of the fallen Abbaside. He had advanced beyond Hamadan, when the severity of the winter, and the deep snow in the mountain-valleys hindered his further progress.[2] The elements seemed to con-

---

[1] Nedjmeddin Kubera, who was executed at Khahrezm during the invasion of the Mongols, is still held in high honour as a saint in Khiva, and his shrine in the ancient Urghendj is visited yearly by thousands of orthodox pilgrims.

[2] The road by Hamadan and Kermanshah is to this day in winter the terror of travellers, and during my residence in Persia I often heard of persons coming to grief there, and even being frozen to death.

spire against allowing a Mohammedan to interfere with the Buddhistic Holagu, and the proud Khahrezmian retraced his steps, profoundly disgusted at the failure of his enterprise, but he was met by a messenger from Kaïr Khan, his lieutenant at Otrar, with the intelligence that he had succeeded in capturing 400 spies of the Mongolian prince Djenghiz Khan, who had arrived in Otrar in the disguise of peaceable merchants,[1] and that he was only awaiting the Sultan's orders. Mohammed, who had been offended by a previous mission from Djenghiz [2] and was under the influence of temper, ordered the prisoners to be executed. The messenger returned to Otrar, and Kair Khan at once carried out his master's orders, although the victims were all Mohammedans, and had enjoyed the special protection of Djenghiz in consequence of their extensive commercial relations in his dominions. Djuveïnï is right in saying that 'their blood was shed, but every drop of it was expiated by a torrent ; their heads fell, but every hair of them was revenged at the cost of a hundred thousand lives.'

Only one escaped to carry the tale of horror to the Mongol prince, who did not at once give way to his indignation, but sent first an envoy to demand explanations. · When

---

[1] It need hardly be said that they really were peaceable merchants. Djuveïnï remarks that as the Mongols had no cities and did not practise agriculture they were dependent for everything on merchants, and greatly protected them. A society of merchants had been formed before at Khodjend, who proceeded with their caravans into Mongolia, carrying presents for the khan of brocades, linen and other suitable things. When these were presented to Djenghiz Khan he caused lists of them to be drawn up, and paid a fair price for everything in spite of the protestations of the merchants. He encouraged them to renew their visits and promised them all the protection in his power.

[2] Mirkhond tells us of an embassy composed of Mahmud Yalwadj (the latter word is erroneously used as a proper name ; it really means yolaudj, Uiguric for envoy), Ali Khodja of Bokhara, and Yusuf of Otrar, sent by Djenghiz Khan to Sultan Mohammed with many costly presents, such as silver vessels containing musk from Tartary and Thibet, agates, brocades, and rare stuffs woven in green and white wools (sof). They announced with the deepest expressions of devotion that Djenghiz Khan Lord of the East wished to live at peace and in unity with Sultan Mohammed the Lord of the West whom he loved as a son and whose welfare would always be dear to him. Although the proud Khahrezmian at first resented this paternal attitude, a friendly compact was made to which Djenghiz always remained faithful. This whole story of Mirkhond's appears to me, however, to be a myth.

this envoy likewise was thrown into prison and executed, Djenghiz could no longer contain himself, and determined that his sword, hitherto so triumphant in the east, should now also be directed against the west. Thus Sultan Mohammed Kutbeddin became the primary cause of the misfortunes and of the irreparable injury inflicted on Transoxania, the whole Islamite east, and even on a portion of Europe itself, by the invasion of the Mongols; for, as we shall presently see, from the moment of their first successes on the Yaxartes, hopes dawned on the Mongols which encouraged them, and led them on further and further in the distant paths of conquest stretched out before them.

VIII.

THE MONGOL INVASIONS.

615 (1218)—624 (1226).

THE districts inhabited by Turkish races at the present time comprise two distinct tracts of country, one stretching southwards from the icy shores of the Arctic Ocean, the other eastwards from the Adriatic, both merging into each other in the eastern portion of Asia, known as the desert of Gobi.[1] Here, from time immemorial, the Mongols, a people[2] nearly akin to the Turks in language and physiognomy, had made their home, leading a miserable nomadic life in the midst of a wild and barren country, unrecognised by their neighbours, and their very name unknown centuries after their kinsmen, the Turks, had been exercising an all-powerful influence over the destinies of Western Asia.

This race produced, however, in the year 549 (1154),[3] a hero

[1] *Gobi* is Mongolian for *barren, empty desert*, and is as little a proper name as another word we often use as such—*Sahara*, which is simply *Arabic* for an *open space*—a *common*.

[2] The ethnographical relationship of the Mongols to the Turks becomes more definite the further we get away eastward from the western Turks, i.e., the Osmanlis. There is so strong an intermixture of Iranian and Semitic elements among the Roumelians, Anatolians and Azerbaidjans that they have not retained in their personal features any traces of the primitive national type of the Turks. The Turkomans, Özbegs, Nogais and Kirghiz approach more nearly to the Mongolian type ; and, in the Buruts and Kiptchaks, the only variation from it is a slight difference in the complexion. As regards the Mongol language, there is but little affinity between its grammar and that of the Turkish language, but three-fourths of the words in common use are to be met with among the Turks.

[3] This was the year for which Mohammedan astrologers had predicted a fearful gale which should come.from the east. No storm came, and the soothsayers were derided, but the prediction was supposed to have been fulfilled later by the birth of Djenghiz, who was identified with the destructive tempest which was to break loose over the land.

named Temurdji,[1] who proved himself possessed of ambition, of an iron will, and a determination which exactly
fitted him to mould the hardy primitive natures of his countrymen into the fit instruments of that power by which he took
the world by storm far beyond the frontiers of his own pastures,
and may be said to have revolutionised all Asia. We have
no accounts of his early youth beyond a few mythical stories.
He does not appear at all on the stage of history until upwards of forty years old, when we first find his name mentioned in connection with hostilities carried on by him both
with his own kinsmen and with the neighbouring Turkish
princes ; he was victorious over them, and shortly assumed the
name of *Djenghiz*, or more properly Tshinghiz, i.e., the strong,
the powerful one.[2]

Ong[3] Khan, prince of the neighbouring tribe of Kerait,[4] was
the first adversary of any importance overcome by Djenghiz.
He defeated him in the year 599 (1202),and his fall was followed
by the speedy overthrow of Oyurats, Kungrats and Naimans,
scattered Turkish tribes living westwards of the Mongols,
and in closer proximity to Buddhist, Christian and Mohammedan influences, to which they owed a higher degree of general
culture probably than the Mongols had attained to, although
their military capacities were far inferior to those of the troops
trained by Djenghiz under a discipline of Draconian severity
The policy followed by the victorious Mongol was that

---

[1] I follow Djuveini, who calls him Temurdji—*not* Temudjin.

[2] Though I have followed other Orientalists in adopting the spelling of Djenghiz,
I cannot refrain from remarking that, from an etymological point of view, *Tshen-
ghis* or *Tshinghiz*, as the orientals, that is, the Turks and Persians spell it, is
undoubtedly more correct. The word is purely Uiguric, compounded of *tsheng* or
tshing — straight, upright, firm, strong ; and *kizz* or *ghiz*—*impetuous*, powerful.
The right meaning of the word is, therefore, the *very powerful*, or the man of
strong might.

[3] *Ong* is also a Uiguric word, and signifies *right* or *the just one.*

[4] According to Abulgazi, *kerait* means whirlwind, but the etymology is quite
unknown, and I rather incline to the opinion that it is a Persian corruption of
kirit-—grey dog. The names of most Turkish tribes and families are taken from
animals. Thus we have *mangit* (which Abulgazi turns into 'thick forest'), compounded of *mang* — sick, and *it* — dog ; and further, *oyurat* (spelt by some oirat)
— grey horse ; *kungrat*, or more correctly *konghur at*, chestnut horse, &c.

of never, after a success, embarking in any fresh enterprise until he had thoroughly incorporated the conquered tribes in his own army and disciplined them under the *Yasao* (Code of Laws) into fit instruments for carrying out his further plans. His progress was thus slow but sure, until by the year 603 (1206) he had succeeded in subduing nearly the whole of the nomads of the desert of Gobi, and had fixed his residence in the fortress of Karakorum. About this time he first came into contact with the Uigurs, and from the eastern branch of this people he borrowed a creed for his nomads and letters in which to reduce their language into writing ; the accountants, secretaries, and civil servants of both Djenghiz and his immediate successors were almost always taken from the same nationality. The prince of these eastern Uigurs, called in Uiguric Idikut, i.e., 'Lord of Fortune,' submitted of his own accord to the Mongols, with his whole people, the greater part of whom were not Mohammedans. Djenghiz loaded him with favours, and subsequently found him of great service as a most faithful ally both in his campaigns against China and Transoxania. The western Uigurs, however, especially the Mohammedan Turks of Kashgar and Khoten, behaved very differently. As long as they remained united under the powerful sceptre of Kurkhan, Djenghiz did not venture to attack them, but when Kütshlük succeeded to the throne, and drew upon himself the enmity of the whole Moslem population by his anti-Islamite sentiments,[1] it appeared to Djenghiz, then just returned from a successful campaign in China, that the moment was come to strike a blow in the west. A Mongolian army commanded by General Tshepe attacked Kütshlük, who, finding himself forsaken by his allies in the hour of danger, was driven back and fled to the mountains of Bedak'hshan, where he was subsequently taken prisoner and delivered up to

---

[1] Kütshlük's wife was a Christian ; whilst she was endeavouring to convert the Mohammedans of Kashgar and Khoten to her own faith, Kütshlük was seeking by violence to enforce his own (Buddhist ?) creed. The followers of Islam, however, resisted manfully, and the Imaum Djelaleddin of Khoten died a martyr's death, at the head of a band of faithful believers.

the Mongolians. Arslan Khan, Prince of Almalik in the north, had long been at enmity with Kütshlük, and the district of Almalik submitted peaceably to the Mongols. Djenghiz now found himself in possession of supreme authority from the eastern frontier of the desert of Gobi to the western slopes of the Thien-Shan mountains, absolute master of many towns of a large agricultural and peaceable population, and also of many wild warlike tribes; and it is scarcely probable that he would have paused here in his victorious career even if he had not had the legitimate pretext for hostilities against the Khahrezmian Prince, Sultan Mohammed, which we have already alluded to in the preceding chapter. He found himself at the gates of an empire of whose extent, riches and civilisation he had received the most marvellous accounts, and his opponent was a prince at the height of his reputation, in whom he recognised a rival in every respect his equal, and a foeman in every way worthy of his steel.

It was in the year 615 (1218) that the Mongol conqueror set off on his campaign against the Khahrezmian prince. He was accompanied by his sons Tchaghatai, Oktai and Djüdji,[1] and by his principal generals, with a strong force of picked troops, estimated at 600,000 men; the idikut of the Uigurs and Siginaktekin, lord of Almalik, joined this army. The route taken was through the valley of the Ili, and the northern portion of Fergana towards Otrar; the troops were concentrated before this fortress, and divisions sent out thence in the following directions :—One division, under the two sons of Djenghiz, Tchaghatai and Oktai, remained to reduce Otrar; the second corps d'armée, commanded by Djüdji, struck off to the right across the desert of Kizil Kum on the road to Djend; the third corps of 5,000 men, under the Generals Alak Noyan and Sintu [2] Boka, proceeded along the right bank of the Yaxartes towards Binaket, whilst Djenghiz himself, with the élite of his army,

---

[1] Not Djudji. Djüdji or Djüdjin is a Mongolian-Turkish word, and means guest.

[2] Also called Suday, Suntay, or Subutai.

undertook the chief operation of all, and marched direct on the heart of Central Asia, Bokhara. We must go somewhat carefully into the separate operations of these four divisions, who overran Central Asia in four distinct currents of destruction,·and will begin therefore with those of the first division at Otrar.

This strong frontier fortress was occupied by a garrison of 50,000 troopers, commanded by Kair Khan, who has already been mentioned; they were reinforced by an auxiliary corps of 10,000 men under Karadja, the vizir of Sultan Mohammed, and the entire defending force was therefore of considerable strength; nevertheless, the historian states that at the aspect of the Mongolians investing the place, a panic seized the Mohammedans. Considering this beginning, it is creditable to them to find that the garrison offered a gallant resistance for five months, and would probably have held out longer still if differences had not taken place between the two commanders. Kair Khan, conscious of being the chief culprit in the affair of the murder of Djenghiz's subjects, had elected to hold out or die; but Karadja, deeming resistance hopeless, had from the first shown a desire for negotiation, and he finally separated himself from his colleague and went over, on a dark night, with all his men to the Mongolians. The next morning he was taken before the sons of Djenghiz, who reproached him for deserting his post, saying, 'How can we expect to find thee faithful when thou hast so shamefully betrayed thine own master and benefactor,' and then caused him and his followers to be beheaded. Kair Khan, however, continued the defence with the courage of a lion. His men were all sacrificed in successive sorties of fifty at a time, in which they sold their lives dearly; and when literally the last two soldiers had fallen at Kair Khan's side, the latter is said to have retired from the walls of the fortress on to the roofs of the houses, and from this elevation to have defended himself single-handed with bricks, handed to him by his female slaves, against the infuriated enemy, who were determined at any price to take him alive. At length the bricks were exhausted, he was surrounded, taken prisoner, and carried as a trophy of war by Oktai to the *green palace* (Kökserai) of Samarkand, where he was subsequently put to death by means of molten silver dropped into his ears, in remembrance of his covetousness, to which the unhappy merchants had been sacrificed. Thus Otrar, the key of Turkestan on the north-western side, fell into the hands of the Mongols, who rased the place, and put the inhabitants to death, and then marched southwards on Samarkand.

Djüdji's operations against Djend were equally successful. He first attacked Signak, on the borders of the desert, and connected with Djend by a canal. The Mongols had previously sent an envoy, Hasan Hadji, to demand the surrender of the place, but the inhabitants of Signak fell upon and murdered him. Exasperated at this act of violence, Djüdji stormed the place, and in retaliation put every single soul to death. He left the son of the murdered Hasan Hadji in charge of the ruins of Signak, and pursued the march on Djend by way of Ozkend and Ashnas; the former of these places surrendered, but the latter had to be taken by force, and on the 4th Sefer of the year 616 (1219) he encamped before Djend, where the news of his approach had caused the wildest confusion and uncertainty. Kutluk Khan, governor of the place, retired in alarm on Khahrezm, leaving the town in a state of complete anarchy; and when Djintimour, Djüdji's herald, appeared at the gate of the town to warn the inhabitants of the danger impending and endeavour to dissuade them from a hopeless resistance, he narrowly escaped the fate of Hasan Hadji at Signak, and only succeeded by extreme caution in saving his life. He had scarcely withdrawn before the Mongolian army appeared under the walls armed with battering-rams and scaling-ladders, and prepared to storm the place. It is said that the garrison were so ignorant of the arts of war that, being curious to see how the Mongols would contrive to get over the perpendicular wall, they remained watching the operations of the enemy like unconcerned spectators, until the advancing legions upset their notions of security by plundering and sacking the town ; the inhabitants taken with arms were put to death, and the peaceable artisans were kept nine days in captivity outside of the town, and then sent back stripped of all but bare life.

The rich districts on the shores of the rivers, which were mostly inhabited by a peaceable population, were entirely cut off from all communication with the more warlike Khahrez-mians by Djüdji's occupation of the western portion of Trans-oxania ; at the same time, the two generals, Alak Noyan and Sintu Boka, made an attack with a small body of 5,000 men on Binaket and Khodjend.   In the first-named place, the com-mandant Ilerku (of the tribe of Kangli) surrendered uncon-ditionally with the whole garrison, and Binaket shared the fate of Djend ; that is, the armed inhabitants were either put to the sword or shot down with arrows, and the rest of the popu-lation either fell into slavery or were incorporated by violence into the Mongolian army.   The blow against Khodjend followed.   The fortress of this town was built at a point where the Yaxartes divides into two branches, and offered an unex-pected resistance to the Mongols, partly in consequence of the natural advantages of its situation, but still more owing to the heroic conduct of the commandant Timour Melik, of whom oriental historians say ' If Rustem were still alive, he might be his *page*.' [1]

Alanku, who directed the siege operations, found himself baffled in spite of the 50,000 slaves and 20,000 Mongols who invested the place for him, the slaves being employed in gangs of ten, each guarded by a Mongol overseer, in fetching stones from the mountains three leagues off.   Timour had but a weak garrison under his orders, but he had contrived to get twelve ships built, fitted with damp felt and a species of glue (?) made of vinegar and lime, by which they were ren-dered proof against the fire of the enemy, and enabled to ap-

---

[1] In the original text of the *Djihankusha* it is *Gashie dari*, i.e., the office of sabretash-bearer.

proach with safety so close in shore that the soldiers could pour
through the portholes of these vessels a hail of arrows on their
adversaries. Timour defended himself thus for a long time, and
when he at length became convinced of the uselessness of prolonged resistance he had seventy ships laden with all his portable treasures, and escaped down the river by Djend into the
desert and thence to Khahrezm. The Mongolians pursued him
along the banks during all this adventurous voyage. At
Binaket a chain was stretched across the river, which he is said
to have shivered to atoms at one blow. On landing at Barklik
Ket he had to face one more battle, the description of which
smacks of the marvellous, but nevertheless he finally escaped
safely to Khahrezm,[1] whilst the Mongol generals took possession of Khodjend, and then marched with their army on
Samarkand, where they were appointed to meet their commander-in-chief, and receive his further orders.

But Djenghiz Khan himself, with his son Tuli, had meanwhile been performing no less brilliant feats of arms. The
road taken by him in marching from Otrar southwards on
Bokhara is not distinctly traced; we only know that the first
place he appeared before was Sertak,[2] north of Bokhara. The
inhabitants of this pleasant little town were as much taken by
surprise at the apparition of the Mongols emerging from
the desert as if they had tumbled from the clouds ; they did
not realise the danger, however, and even prepared to resist

---

[1] Timour Melik, on seeing the impossibility of holding out longer at Khahrezm,
hurried thence to join the fugitive Sultan Mohammed, whom he soon overtook,
and to whom he rendered signal services. He at length parted from him, however,
and went, disguised as a dervish, to Damascus, but after a short time there became
home-sick, and commenced, in spite of many obstacles, his return journey to
Fergana. There he heard that his son, whom he had left as an infant
but who was now grown up, had been taken into favour by Batu and put into possession of his father's former property. He therefore went to him at Khodjend,
and addressed him thus : ' If thou shouldest see thy father, would'st thou know him
again ?' 'No,' was the answer, ' for I was but a baby when he left me ; but I
have a slave who would know him.' The slave was called, and recognised Timour,
but the news of his return could not long be kept secret, and he fell a victim to the
revenge of a Mongol.

[2] Not *Zernuk*, as Mirkhond spells it ; Djuveïnï calls it Zertuk, which is closer
to Sertak in Belkhi's geographical manuscript.

them, but when the herald sent on before as usual by the Mongolians explained to them the fire and sword which they would be inviting, they thought better of it and submitted. Those who were taken with arms in their hands had to join the army, and the fortress was rased to the ground; but the peaceable part of the population who had come out of the town with all their horses and mules were allowed to return unmolested to their homes. The name of Sertak was changed by the Mongolians to *Kutluk Balik,* 'Lucky City.' The second town takes by Djenghiz in the territory of Bokhara was *Nur.* The road along which he marched, led by Turkoman guides, was a new one, and was known long after as the 'Khan's road.' The advanced guard led by Tahir Bahadoor, a Mohammedan and probably a Turk, had spent the night in the beautiful wood outside Nur manufacturing scaling ladders, which they carried across their saddles as they rode up to the walls of Nur. The inhabitants had closed the gates, some doubted the truth of Djenghiz's approach, others still reckoned on help from Sultan Mohammed. When, however, Tahir sent them word that the mighty Mongol was indeed close at hand, but would not molest them further than by making a halt in their town, unless they resisted him by force, they opened the gates to him. The inhabitants were ordered to carry out of the town all stores and implements of agriculture, all wheat, sheep, beasts of burden, &c., and as soon as this had been done the Mongolians entered the town and plundered the houses, but without doing the slightest personal injury to any Nurian ; and a deputation sent to Djenghiz's camp was very courteously received. On being asked what amount of taxes they had been in the habit of paying, they replied 1,500 dinars. He desired them to pay this sum over to his advanced guard, and dismissed them well satisfied. From Nur, Djenghiz hurried on to Bokhara, and encamped before that city in the first days of the month Moharrem of the year 617 (1220), and began immediately to play against the outer works of the

fortress; Bokhara, having probably heard rumours of the
bloody preliminaries of the campaign, was not entirely unprepared to meet the terrible onslaught now made on her. There
were 20,000 men within the walls, headed by Kök Khan
(a Mongol or rather Uigur deserter), Sevindj Khan, and
Keshli Khan. It is difficult to imagine what they could
expect to do against the Mongols, who outnumbered them
by hundreds; however, they attacked first, but were almost
completely annihilated; only a few succeeded in escaping back
into the town, and the terrified inhabitants sent a deputation
of notables to Djenghiz to sue for mercy. They accompanied
him on his entry into Bokhara; the splendid ' Friday mosque
fitted out so magnificently by the great Samanide attracted
his attention, and he rode straight into it on horseback, and
took up his position in front of the great pulpit. His son Tuli,
who accompanied him, mounted the pulpit itself. Djenghiz
enquired if he was in the Sultan's palace, but on being told
it was the house of God, he dismounted, went up a few steps
of the pulpit, and called to the Mongols standing behind
him, " The hay is cut, give your horses fodder." It may be
supposed with what alacrity this permission to plunder was
received by the Mongols, and how these savages, intoxicated with the aspect of luxury of the capital of Central
Asia, fell on the unhappy city of Bokhara. They not only
rifled every house and every cupboard, and carried off all
treasures of every kind, but even the holy relics which had no
intrinsic value whatever were not spared. The Korans were
torn to pieces and used as litter for the beasts; the chests in
which the holy books were kept were turned into feeding-
troughs for the horses. Sheikhs of high rank and mollahs of
eminence as scholars, had to wait on the soldiers in their
drinking-bouts, or play before them, in Mongolian fashion, on
musical instruments, and the most respected priests were set
to groom the mules.' Such is the account given us by the
Mohammedan historian. The description of the intentional
outrages to the religious feelings of the people may be exag-

gerated, but there can be no doubt that Bokhara was most severely handled, and went through terrible experiences even during this first onslaught.

Djenghiz Khan remained but a few hours in the town, he then went to the *Mosalla* (open place of prayer), without the walls, where the whole population was assembled, and enquired who amongst them were the *nobles*—that is, the rich people. Two hundred and eighty people were presented to him, 190 natives and ninety strangers, mostly merchants. He turned towards them, and after severely criticising the tyranny of Sultan Mohammed, proceeded to address them thus : ' Know, oh people ! that ye have committed great sins, sins which your princes have chiefly to answer for. You ask who I am who speak thus to you ! Know then, that I am the scourge of God ; if you had not sinned, God would not have sent me hither to punish you ; and now,' he continued, ' we do not require any account of your goods and treasures above ground, but tell us what you have *under* ground, and bring everything to light.' He did not omit to provide a guard composed half of Mongols, half of Turks, for the protection of the chief men of the city, who were thus preserved from all insult or injury. Things remained in this state until Djenghiz, feeling disturbed at the presence of the soldiers of Sultan Mohammed still concealed in the town, required them to be delivered up to him ; but the Bokhariots, so far from fulfilling the conqueror's will, not only connived at but encouraged the nightly sorties and secret conspiracies of these men. Djenghiz, at length justly exasperated, gave orders to set the town on fire. Bokhara was built mostly of wood, and was in a very few days reduced to ashes. A few mosques and palaces of brick alone remained standing amongst the ruins. The flourishing city on the Zerefshan had become a heap of rubbish, but the garrison in the citadel, commanded by Kök Khan, continued to hold out with a bravery which deserves our admiration. The Mongols used every imaginable effort to reduce this last refuge of the enemy ; the Bokhariots themselves were forced on to the

scaling-ladders : but all in vain, and it was not until the moat
had been literally choked with corpses of men and animals
that the stronghold was taken and its brave defenders put to
death. The peaceable portion of the population was also
made to suffer for this heroic resistance. More than 30,000
men were executed, and the remainder were, with the exception of the very old people amongst them, reduced to slavery,
without any distinction of rank whatever ; and thus the inhabitants of Bokhara, lately so celebrated for their learning, their
love of art, and their general refinement, were brought down to
a dead level of misery and degradation, and scattered to all
quarters. But a few escaped the general ruin. One of these,
on arriving at Khorasan in his flight, was asked concerning
the fate of his native city, and replied in the following terse
Persian distich, which has since become celebrated :—

> Amedend u kendend [1] u sukhtend
> u kushtend u burdend, u reftend.
>
> They came, destroyed, burnt,
> Murdered, robbed, and went.

'It was a terrible day,' says the historian Ibn ul Athir ;
'nothing was to be heard but the sobs and lamentations of
husbands, wives, and children who were being parted for ever.
The barbarians dishonoured the women and girls before the
eyes of their relations, who had in their helplessness nothing
but their tears to give them. Many preferred death to the
revolting spectacle ; thus Kadi Bedr-eddin and the imam
Rukn-eddin, with his son, infuriated at the sight of their disgrace, rushed on to certain destruction in an unequal combat.'

After Bokhara came the turn of Samarkand, the largest,
and during the time of the Khahrezmians, the most important, city of Transoxania. The fugitive Khahrezmian
prince had left behind him for the defence 110,000 men—i.e.,
60,000 Turks and 50,000 Tadjiks—with twenty elephants.

---

[1] Hammer-Purgstall, in his *History of the Golden Horde*, p. 80, translates *kenden*
by the German *graben*, to *dig*, to *cut* ; also moat or ditch (?). This is correct in one
sense, but kenden also means to *throw down*, to *destroy*, and is used here in that
sense.

Djenghiz Khan was accurately informed of all this, and was aware even before leaving Otrar of the severe struggle it would probably cost him to obtain possession of his enemy's former capital. In consequence of this, he had designated Samarkand as the point towards which all the separate divisions of his army were to converge, and he had first completely subdued the surrounding country, so as to isolate and thus weaken his powerful antagonists. The results of this manœuvre were perfectly successful. He marched rapidly on, carrying with him the captive Bokhariots whom he intended to employ in the storm of Samarkand. Many of them, unable to keep up with his rapid advance, sunk down exhausted on the road, and were pitilessly murdered. When he arrived before the magnificent capital of the Khahrezmians, he found so large a portion of his own forces concentrated around him, that he was able to detach 30,000 under the Generals Tehepe and Suntai in pursuit of Sultan Mohammed, and yet the fortress which he had expected it would cost him years to subdue fell into his hands at the end of three days' fighting. The gallant garrison, led by their brave Generals Alp Khan and Sheïkh Khan Berbalas (?) Khan, had made a successful sortie and inflicted considerable loss on the Mongols. But, nevertheless, Djenghiz on the third day put himself at the head of his troops to storm the town, and the Mongols very soon succeeded in getting possession of the gates. The Khahrezmians went on fighting desperately the whole of the next day, until towards evening divisions broke out among their own counsellors. Some were for surrendering, and sent the Sheïkh ul Islam, with a numerous company of mollahs, to Djenghiz to plead for mercy; but others withdrew into the citadel and continued fighting the next day. The Mongols however penetrated into the town by the gate Namazghiah, and drove out the inhabitants, in order to be able to rob and plunder unmolested. The Sheïkh ul Islam and 50,000 citizens, who enjoyed his special protection, were alone spared in this first onslaught. The citadel still held out, and cost

the besiegers many an effort. Alp Khan, at length seeing
the end draw near, made a bold sortie with about 1,000
heroic followers, and cut his way through the entire Mongolian army. The only people who surrendered were the
Kanglis and some other Turks who had been persuaded
by the Mongols that as kinsmen they would be treated
mercifully. By way of reassuring them, their heads were
shaved according to the Mongolian custom ; but that very
evening they were made an end of : 30,000 of them, with their
princes, Uluk Barishmas, Baghan and Sarsig Khan,[1] and
twenty generals, were murdered in a single night. The
flourishing city of Samarkand and the fortress were laid even
with the ground ; and the inhabitants, stripped of all they
possessed, shared the fate of their brethren of Bokhara.
Those who had contrived to escape were lured back by false
promises ; all capable of bearing arms were compulsorily
enrolled in the Mongolian army ; the artistic gardeners of the
place were sent off to the far East, where they were wanted to
adorn the future Mongolo-Chinese capital with pleasure-
grounds, after the fashion of those of Samarkand, and the
celebrated artisans, especially the silk and cotton weavers,
were either distributed as clever and useful slaves amongst
the wives and relations of Djenghiz, or else carried with him
to Khorasan. A few were sent as slaves to his sons Tchagatai and Oktai, who were then marching on Khahrezm.
This was the end in the year 618 (1221) of Samarkand,
which Arabian geographers have described as the most
brilliant and most flourishing spot on the face of the earth.

Transoxania was thus completely subdued ; there remained
only a few places south of Samarkand, which Djenghiz went
on in person to occupy as soon as he had given his soldiers a
little rest and allowed their horses to recruit from their forced
marches in the rich pastures of the valley of the Zerefshan.

---

[1] These names have been preserved in history through the list of victims
enclosed by Djenghiz in the report of his victories forwarded to Rukn eddin, the
son of Sultan Mohammed and Viceroy of Irak, in order to frighten him beforehand
by the details of the successes of the Mongolian arms.

He first went to Nakh'sheb (Karshi), which opened its gates to him, and where he fixed his head-quarters for the summer. Thence he proceeded to Termez, where the ferry across the Oxus for travellers southward to Belkh and thence to India was then situated. Here there were considerable fortifications protected by the Oxus, and relying on these the place resisted, but was naturally unable to hold out long against the Mongols flushed with success and with their victories over more than one formidable stronghold. The town was stormed and a census taken of all the inhabitants, after which they were distributed amongst the soldiers to be put to death. Djuveinï relates that one woman begged for mercy, promising the man who was to kill her that he should have as the ransom for her life a pearl of great value which she had swallowed. The Mongol, instead, ripped open her body, and as the pearl really was found, an order was immediately given to open and examine all the dead bodies. After the fall of Termez there remained only the districts of Künkürt and Saman [1] to overrun with fire and sword, and then the countries bordering on the Oxus and Yaxartes, at that time looked on as the furthest outposts by which the Islamite civilisation of Asia was protected against the incursions of savages, might be said to have suffered complete annihilation. The savage, blood-thirsty, and rapacious enemy was able now to pursue his course of destruction unchecked. The horrible crimes committed by the Mongols at Belkh, the ancient Mecca of Parseeism (which contained 1,200 mosques and was called afterwards the 'dome' or 'pinnacle' of Islam); the state to which they reduced Talkan, Herat, the great commercial city of Merv-er-rud, Merv with its fine schools, and the proud town of Nishabur ; and their further excesses in the enormous city of Reï, in Shiraz and Isfahan, do not belong to the history of Bokhara proper ; we may therefore turn away from them to learn the end of the last Khahrezmian prince, and briefly

---

[1] The latter comprises the district of Shehri Sebz, or Kesh, which contained the fortress of Sam, once the scene of Mokanna's revolt.

to examine the consequences of Djenghiz's appearance and the principal causes of his success.

Sultan Kutbeddin Mohammed, after giving the fatal order for the execution of the merchants under Mongolian protec- tion, returned by easy stages to Khorasan. Intoxicated by the results of his long reign, proud and reckless, he gave him- self up to pleasure, spending his time in gay company and feasting, until he reached Bokhara on the 8th Sha'ban 612 (1215), and pitched his tent in the green fields, to give himself up entirely to the amusements of the season.

> Let not thy heart by any woe be pained,
> To leave the world thy soul is soon constrained ;
> Enjoy the spring and brightness till they're past,
> Till from thy dust the grass must spring at last.[1]

From Bokhara he went to Samarkand, where he received the first intelligence of the movements of the enemy, that is, of the advance of that division of the Mongolian army which was marching under Djüdji from Otrar on Djend. He was on his way towards Djend to make a reconnaissance, when he learnt that this division was being followed by the great Djenghiz Khan in person with a considerable force ; however, he determined to attack the first army at once, but very soon found that the reports of the enemy's irresistible bravery were only too true. Though superior to them in numbers, he only escaped a crushing defeat thanks to the heroism of his son Djelal eddin,[2] and had to retire on Samarkand.[3]

---

[1] From Hammer-Purgstall's *Portraits of Great Moslem Rulers*, vol. vi. p. 180.

[2] Also surnamed Mengbirdi, or Mengberdi = Heaven- (Meng) sent. Our Orientalists have been mistaken in spelling this word Mankberni, and Hammer Purgstall has even translated this mistake into *snub-nose*, on the authority of the Tchaghataian dictionary printed in India of Fazl Ullah Khan. He has read *mank burni*, but has not understood the Persian interpretation of the Turkish word. *Mank* for mank is interpreted in the same book by ' disease in the nose,' which is so far correct ; strictly speaking, mank means *glanders* (a disease affecting the nostrils in horses), and the surname of the celebrated Khahrezmian prince would thus, according to my predecessors, be converted into the unpoetical appellation of *sniveller*.

[3] Riding along the edge of the moat at Samarkand, he is said to have called out to the inhabitants at work on the fortifications, ' If the Tartars only throw their

Alarmed and confused by the impending danger, his former overweening self-confidence changed to discouragement and despair. He fled across the Oxus to Khorasan. He wished to rest a few days in his camp on the much-admired plain of Nishabur, in order to bid farewell to all the delights and pleasures to which he still unhappily clung even in the time of peril ; but hearing that Tchepe and Suntai were close at his heels, he started off, and though hardly pressed by them, succeeded in escaping by Rei and the pathless mountains of Mazendran to Abeskun, in the neighbourhood of the modern Astrabad, and thence to an island in the Caspian Sea [1] (probably Oghurtshali). But although he had saved himself from the vengeance of his savage enemy, he was broken-hearted at the fate of his family, who had all fallen into Mongolian captivity, and he died on the 22nd Zilhidje of the year 617 (1220), so poor and so utterly abandoned, that for want of a shroud it was necessary to bury him in the only suit of clothes he possessed. Eflak Shah, who was at that moment administering the government at Khahrezm, had been formerly designated as his heir, but he had since nominated his heroic son Djelal eddin to succeed him. The latter, however, found that, instead of the sceptre, there was nothing left for him but the sword, with which to carry on in self-defence a desperate resistance. He retreated by Khahrezm, Herat and Ghaznee, collected fresh forces, and succeeded in two successful actions in inflicting considerable losses on the Mongols, much to the exasperation of Djenghiz, who was detained at the moment by the siege of Talkan. He rushed across Bamian and Kabul towards Ghaznee with such impetuosity, that the Mongols were not even given time to cook their

whips into this moat, they will be able to fill it up.' Hammer Purgstall, *Portraits of Great Moslem Rulers*, p. 180.

[1] Although the island to which Sultan Mohammed escaped is supposed by many to have been near the left-hand shore of the Caspian Sea, I prefer following the authority of the old geographical manuscript—*Mesalik ud Memalik*. According to the map belonging to it, Abeskun was in the neighbourhood of the modern Astrabad, and the island in question could therefore have been no other than Oghurdjali, or the northern Tchereken.

victuals ; but, in spite of this haste, he only arrived there in
time to learn that Djelal eddin had marched onwards towards
the banks of the Indus a fortnight before. The Mongols
hurried on by forced marches till at length they overtook the
fugitive prince, and attacked him furiously. Djelal eddin
defended himself with his accustomed bravery. He rushed
with the fury of a lion, now on the right, now on the left
wing, and again on the centre of the Mongols, until he was
at last driven up into a corner ; two horses had already
been killed under him ; he sprang on to a third, on which he
plunged from the bank some thirty feet into the waters of the
Indus, and succeeded in reaching safely the opposite shore.
The Mongols, seeing this daring act, wanted to pursue him,
but Djenghiz, astonished and touched by Djelal eddin's
courage, forbad them, and turning to his sons, exclaimed :—
'Such a father' (Sultan Mohammed, for whom Djenghiz
always expressed much admiration) 'was worthy of such a
son.' The attendants of Djelal eddin were overpowered, his
treasures, which he had thrown into the Indus, were recovered
by divers ; and his family was brought before the cruel conqueror, who caused all the male members of it—down to the
baby in his nurse's arms—to be put to death. Thus ended,
in the year 618 (1221) the rule of the last of the Khahrezmians,[1] and, with it, a dynasty which had reigned nearly 140
years with splendour and power scarcely inferior to the house
of Seldjuk. Djenghiz returned to Transoxania, and thence,
after a short stay in Samarkand, to his own home, where he
held a kuriltai in the year 621 (1224), in which he divided his
gigantic empire amongst his sons as follows : China, and
Mongolia were given to Oktai, whom he nominated as his
successor ; Tchaghatai received a part of the Uiguric passes as

[1] That is, of the last of the Khahrezmians in *Transoxania* ; for Djelal eddin had
still a brilliant career before him in Iran. He conquered the whole of the
southern portion of Persia, Azerbaidjan, and wrested nearly all Syria from the
Seldjukides, but his wonderful bravery degenerated later in life, as had been the
case with his father, into sensuality and love of pleasure, and he fell a victim to
the lances of the Mongols sent under the command of General Tchermaghum
to reconquer Iran at the time of the accession of Mengku Khan.

far as Khahrezm, including Turkestan and Transoxania ; Djüdji had died in the meantime, so Batu was made lord of Khahrezm, Desht-i-Kiptchak of the pass of Derbend, and Tuli was placed over Khorasan, Persia, and India. Though already seventy years old, Djenghiz once more took the field against Tanghut, which had rebelled against him ; but he died during this campaign in the year 624 (1226), leaving behind him traces throughout all Asia of the fire and sword with which his love of war had devastated the whole continent ; but nowhere so deeply marked as in Transoxania, where the civilisation of centuries had been destroyed, and the people plunged into a depth of barbarism in which the remembrance of their former greatness and their whole future were alike engulfed. No part of all Asia suffered so severely from the incursions of the Mongolian hordes as the countries bordering on the Oxus and the Yaxartes. The first onslaught of the savage inhabitants of the desert was especially fatal to such towns as Binaket, Khodjend, Bokhara, and Samarkand, as it was there they first came in contact with the circumstances of commercial trading and agricultural prosperity which whetted their covetousness and offered a prize to their love of plunder. Transoxania was in addition the great outlet by which the later streams of Mongols poured themselves out towards the Volga, the Euphrates, the Indus, and the Persian Gulf. No wonder, then, that within five short years, the great high roads of Central Asia, by which the products of China and India were conveyed to Western Asia and to Europe, were deserted ; that the oases, well known for their fertility, lay barren and neglected ; or, finally, that the trade in arms and jewellery, in silks and enamels, so celebrated throughout Islam, decayed for ever. The towns were in ruins, the peasants either murdered or compulsorily enrolled in the Mongolian army, and the artisans sent off by thousands to the farthest East to adorn and beautify the home of the conqueror. No less crushing was the blow received by science in the devastation of Central Asia. There is an

Arab proverb of the middle ages which says, 'Science is
a tree whose roots are in Mecca, but whose fruit ripens in
Khorasan.' Judging by the present condition of these
countries, such an estimate may well surprise us ; but we must
not forget that, at the most brilliant epoch of civilisation in
Islamite Asia, which was precisely in the same century in
which the invasion of the Mongolian conqueror took place,
Transoxania played an important part. Samarkand, Bokhara, and Görghendj had long carried on a noble rivalry with
Nishabur (the favourite resort of the intellectual world of Iran)
and with Merv (whose colleges enjoyed a world-wide reputation), and had not unfrequently borne away the palm in
rhetoric, grammar, poetry, and the science of medicine.

The Mongolian invasion unhappily put an end to the
intellectual life of Central Asia ; for although Iran and the
West gradually recovered from their misfortunes, and even
attained to fresh culture under the protection of the Djenghizides, Bokhara and Samarkand never regained their former
mental activity, and their intellectual labours were henceforth
entirely devoted to casuistry, mysticism, and false religion.
The chief cause of this, no doubt, was the fact that the
Mongolians destroyed the original Iranian population of the
towns, and with them the principal promoters of civilisation
and peaceful industry disappeared, leaving the Turkish
element unchecked. In some thoroughly Turkish countries,
such as the modern Khiva and Khokand, the national language
in the time of the Seldjukides was still purely Persian, and
though the uncivilised Turks, advancing from the desert on
the cities, would in any case probably in time have gradually
succeeded in destroying the nationality of the people, there
can be no doubt that the Mongolian invasion greatly
accelerated this consummation, and was the principal cause
of the obliteration of all Iranian influences in Transoxania,
and this may be looked on as the greatest injury inflicted by
Djenghiz on the countries of the Oxus.

As regards the causes of the Mongolian conqueror's

successes, there is no doubt they were as much owing to the personal qualities of Djenghiz and to the social condition of his people as to the political and ethnographical circumstances of the time in Islamite Asia, and more especially in Transoxania. Concerning the former, in spite of all the accusations of needless cruelty and love of destruction brought against him by Mohammedan contemporaries, it cannot be denied that Djenghiz had all the attributes, not only of a great captain, but of a conqueror and legislator in the best sense of the word. He instituted by his Yasao (code of laws) a strong military constitution, such as had been unknown hitherto in Islamite Asia, and was an immense advantage over the loose state of affairs under the government of the Khahrezmian princes ; and declared the equality before the law of all religions and all ranks, a proceeding which undoubtedly gained him more friends than his historians are willing to allow. Djuveinī says that Djenghiz fixed 40,000 miskals of gold as the fine for taking a Mussulman's life, but only the price of a donkey for the life of a Chinese; but other accounts state directly the contrary, and say expressly that both he and several of his successors made it a rule to make *no difference* between Christians, Mohammedans, and Buddhists ; he appointed several Mohammedan governors in Transoxania and Khorasan, and had several Buddhist secretaries ; and we know that his grandson Kubilai sent the foreign Christian, Marco Polo, on a confidential mission from the interior of China to Kerman. .

As regards the social condition of the Mongols, the reader of Oriental histories will be struck by the repeated descriptions of the Mongols as hardy, savage, and warlike : ' A people who weep at their feasts, but laugh in their battles, who follow their leader blindly, are content with cold and hunger, do not know rest or pleasure, have not even words to express them in their language. They prepare and carry their own arms, are animated by one soul and one spirit, not dainty in food or clothes, unpitying, ready to tear the unborn child from its mother ; crossing deep rivers with bladders, or else holding on to the manes and tails of their horses as they swim,' &c. Though we may assume that the circumstances of Transoxania herself were not very far removed from those detailed above, yet it seems certain that, not only the Iranian population of the towns, but even the fighting portion of the people, were weak and effeminate as compared with the Mongolians, and utterly incapable of resisting them. Added to this, the Turks, who had never been able cordially to unite with the Iranians, and who formed the chief contingent of Sultan Mohammed's army, were partly dissatisfied with the tyrannical government of the last Khahrezmian, partly carried away by their natural tendency to plunder and rob, and partly also swayed by feelings of clanship—all these motives combined urged them to desert in many places to Djenghiz, and instead of fighting the invading enemy, to join him as his cordial allies. It cannot, therefore, be a cause of much astonishment if, under these circumstances, the triumphs of the great conqueror over the divided and distracted country of Transoxania were both brilliant and complete.

IX.

THE DJENGHIZIDES.

624 (1226)—765 (1363).

THE picture presented to the reader's eye by the history of the two hundred years during which the Djenghizides ruled in Transoxania is a horrible and bloody spectacle. It is a history of wild anarchy, the unrestrained excesses of savage tyrants, murders and devastations alternating with each other, though the accounts still extant even of these atrocities are but meagre;[1] for there exists no chronicle of the history of Transoxania,[2] and we are obliged to content ourselves for our information regarding this period with what we can glean from the annals of the Mongols in China and Persia.

Bokhara and Samarkand, those two 'pearls of great price' of the West Islamite world, had during the lifetime of Djenghiz been torn from their south-western neighbours, to whom they were akin by blood, culture and religion, to be violently incorporated with the portion of the Mongolian empire known as the 'khanate of Tchaghatai,' supposed by some to consist of all the Uiguric passes, by others of the country lying between the Altaï mountains and Amuye on the Oxus, and containing a mixed but uniformly uncivilised population. Tchaghatai,

---

[1] Abel Résumat says, with truth, in his *Observations sur l'Histoire des Mongoles orientaux de Sannang Setzen*, Paris, Imprim. roy. 1852, p. 12 :—' Il n'y a que la dynastie du Tshakhatai et des enfants de Djoutchi qu'il nous reste peu d'espoir de connaître, parce qu'autant que nous le pouvons savoir, elles n'ont pas eu d'historien particulier, et que les traditions qui les regardent en sont devenues plus décharnées et sujettes à plus de lacunes.'

[2] In enumerating the materials existing for a history of the Golden Horde, Hammer-Purgstall mentions a *Tarikhi Turkestan*, but I have never obtained a sight of it.

the second son of Djenghiz, whose family reigned with short interruptions over Transoxania until the appearance of Tamerlane, was a scrupulous observer of the laws laid down by his father, and appeared disposed to heal the wounds of the bleeding country. A regular service of couriers was organised between the newly-annexed province and his hunting seat at Almalik, to keep him informed of all the affairs of government; and in spite of the drunken habits to which he, in common with most of Djenghiz's descendants, was addicted, he is said to have attended personally to every detail. His rule was strict but just.[1] Following the fundamental principle of the equality of all religions and nationalities, he had entrusted the government of Transoxania to a Mohammedan, Mes'ud Beg, the son of Mahmud Yolaudj, who had already filled a similar office in China. A poll-tax, varying from one to seven talents,[2] according to property, was introduced, but the priests of all the different denominations were exempted.[3] The peasants and artisans, who had remained in hiding ever since the horrors of the war, were gradually coaxed back to their former employments, and although the appointment of Mongolian officials to preside over the different towns seemed scarcely calculated to give the people confidence, we are never-

[1] The opinion of several European *savants*, adopted by me likewise in my *Tchaghataian Studies*, that the inhabitants of Central Asia had given their country and their national dialect the name of ' Tchaghatai,' out of love and respect for the son of Djenghiz, appears to be erroneous. In the first place the Central Asiatics themselves never called either the country or the language ' Tchaghatai ; ' the name was only used by the Persians on this side of the Oxus, i.e., 'in Irania ; but the inhabitants of the country themselves invariably called it *Turkestan* and their language *Turki*. Secondly, Tchaghatai, in consequence of his stern adherence to the Yasao and his fanatic Buddhism, was anything but popular with Musulmen. In his time the latter were forbidden under penalty of death to kill a domestic animal or to bathe by daylight in running water, and these prohibitions were the more irksome as they were prevented by them from observing the ordinances of their own religion.

[2] I follow the statement of Hammer. According to Djuveini the tax introduced by Mahmud Yolaudj in Transoxania varied from one to ten ; according to D'Ohsson from one to fifteen.

[3] It is said that the Jews were excluded from this privilege, but this appears to me to be an invention of the Mohammedan authors, who notoriously hated the Jews beyond everything, for it seems amply proved that the Mongolian rulers of China and Persia practised *complete* toleration in all religious matters.

theless assured that matters soon resumed their usual aspect, at least in Bokhara.

The name of the first Mongolian governor of Bokhara was Buka Bosha, that of the governor of Samarkand Djong-san Taïfu. We are told that the ruins of Bokhara were speedily replaced by new buildings,and even that by the year 632 (1234), within fifteen years of the destruction of the place, the colleges founded by Mes'ud Beg and Serkuti Beg were filled by a thousand students of different branches of science. Tchaghatai gave his entire confidence to Mes'ud, who, although a Mohammedan, was a faithful servant of the Mongolian interests, and his vizir was a Turk named Hedjir. There cannot be a doubt that, even if not actually beneficent, his government was animated by the most benevolent intentions towards Transoxania. Under his successors there were nothing but wars succeeding wars ; in his time, however, peace was only once interrupted by the opposition of a religious enthusiast, of whom we must speak somewhat more at length.

In the year 630 (1232) a man named Mahmud, by trade a sieve-maker, and hitherto considered a half-witted, stupid fellow, suddenly appeared at Tarab, a village some three leagues from Bokhara, proclaiming himself inspired by Peris and other spirits, and possessed of supernatural attributes. Djuveinï tells us that from time immemorial women had been addicted to witchcraft in Turkestan and Transoxania ; witches were called in to sick people, and practised spells and incantations by which they pretended to drive away diseases. Mahmud gave himself out as a magician of the same order. He first imparted his secret to his sister, and she spread reports of his powers until sick persons were brought to him in shoals from far and wide, and our authority declares that he restored sight to the blind by blowing dust into their eyes. His reputation soon spread from Tarab to the capital. A mollah of some consideration there, named Shemseddin Mahmud, helped to increase it by stating that his own father (an eminent man of learning) had left behind him a paper

declaring that a deliverer of the world would come out of
Tarab, and this circumstance inflamed still further the imagination of the enthusiast.   The fanatical sieve-maker soon
saw himself at the head of a widespread party, only awaiting
his orders to rise against the Mongols.   The governor
of Bokhara and the other officials became alarmed 'at the
suppressed broodings of this spirit of revolt.   They sent to
consult Mes'ud Beg, who was at that time at Khodjend,
but meanwhile invited the false prophet with many flattering
words to Bokhara, in order, as they said, that the inhabitants
might be blessed by a sight of him.   Their intention was to
fall upon him at a certain point on the road, where he would
be separated from his own people, and murder him ; but they
had hardly reached the place agreed on when Mahmud,
informed probably beforehand of their intention, turned, and
facing his escort steadily, reproached them with their
treachery, and threatened to strike them all blind.   The
effect of this prophetic demeanour on the superstitious Mongols may easily be imagined.   He was now really received
with great honour at Bokhara, and lodged in the palace of
Sandjar, where the people flocked in crowds to see him,
and showed such abject devotion, that they stretched out
their tongues to be spit upon by him from above.   The
affair assumed very serious proportions.   The mollahs and
nobles of Bokhara persuaded the Mongols to get rid of
him, but as the crowd about his lodging made it difficult to
approach it, he contrived to escape to a hill in the neighbourhood.   The people followed him there.   He was said to have
flown thither through the air, and the enthusiasm knew no
bounds ; in the evening he gave orders to his followers to
take up arms, for the time had now come to put the unbelievers to death, and he found himself in a position to
re-enter the town at the head of a fanatic multitude as both
prophet and ruler.   He appointed Shemseddin Mahmud,
alluded to above, Sadr Djiham, the highest spiritual dignity,
incited the populace to plunder the rich, and gave his blindly-

devoted followers the most exaggerated assurances of his power and greatness. 'My army is a hidden one,' said he, 'and abides in the air. See, these men in green and those others in white garments, at a sign from me they will come to us.' One man in the crowd said he saw them, and every one else said the same. He also pretended to have received arms out of the air, although at the same moment he took possession by force of the goods of some merchants of Shiraz who were entering the town with four asses' loads of sword-blades. On the following Friday he caused the public prayers to be recited in his name; he confiscated arbitrarily the property of the rich, retained the greater part of the spoils for his personal use, and spent his time in orgies with the most beautiful women, with whom his house was filled. The nobles of Bokhara who had fled before him came together at length at Kermineh, were joined by a contingent of Mongolian troops, and marched on Bokhara. Mahmud went out to meet them accompanied by his former apprentice. Both were unarmed, and placed themselves at the head of the crowd of fanatics to show the invulnerability of their sacred persons. The attack was about to commence, when a storm of wind arose enveloping the sectarians in a cloud of dust so thick as to render them invisible to their enemies. This was enough to send the superstitious Mongolians flying. The Bokhariots pursued them and massacred large numbers of them; but on their way back from their victory they discovered to their dismay that their prophet had disappeared—he had fallen in the fight. His brothers took his place, but their supremacy only lasted a week; for the Mongolian commanders Ildir Noyan and Djenghin Kurdji reappeared with a considerable force and put the fanatics to flight on the first attack. The exasperated Mongolians wished a second time to wreak their vengeance on Bokhara, but Mes'ud succeeded in restraining them. He urged them to pause till they could receive the emperor's orders, and by his intercession Bokhara was spared this time.

This episode was the only occurrence that broke the mournful
stillness which had fallen on Transoxania after the Mongolian
conquest. But in the year 639 (1241), Oktai, the Great
Khan or Emperor of the Mongolian Empire, and his elder
brother Tchagatai having died within a short time of each other,
the successors of Djenghiz fell to squabbling amongst themselves about the succession to the throne, and the Tchagataides,
partly by their violent party spirit and partly by their savage
and warlike temper, brought great misery to the country confided to their care. Tchagatai had left a numerous family,
and the names of his sons Bisü, Büri, Baidar and. Besenbuka
have been handed down to us. They were all present at
the kuriltai on the occasion of the accession of Kuyuk, but
he does not seem to have been particularly devoted to any
one of them, for he nominated as his successor his grandson
Kara Hulagu,[1] a minor, and his widow Ebüskün assumed the
regency. Her first step was to order the execution of Medjid-
eddin, the physician, and Hedjir, the favourite vizir of her
husband. She accused them of having caused his death,
but her real motive in getting rid of them was that she feared
they would put obstacles in the way of her ambition. She
appointed Habesh Amid, an ambitious cruel man, her
vizir and chief adviser, but was only able to maintain herself
on the throne during the interregnum which followed the
death of Oktai. Kuyuk took possession by force of the
authority of the latter, removed all his adversaries, the principal one of all being Ebüskün herself; nominated Bisü[2] in
the year 645 (1247) chief of the family of Tchaghatai, and

---

[1] Hammer-Purgstall calls him Kara Oghlan ; the manuscript of the *Djihankusha*,
to which I have had access, gives the name as Kara Ulag. It is difficult to
determine which is the more correct spelling, as in the absence of any historical
documents written in Mongolian, we are forced to have recourse to Perso-Arabic
authors, who had in the first place considerable difficulty in transcribing the
Mongolian names with their Arabic characters ; and, in the second place, even
where the original transcription may have been satisfactory, it has been terribly
mutilated by the carelessness of later copyists.

[2] He is thus named by Djuveini in the manuscript I have borrowed from.
D'Ohsson calls him Yissu or Yissou. See also Defémery (*Histoire des Khans
mongols du Turkestan, Journal asiatique*, tome xx. p. 402).

spread disorder and disunion, not only in Almalik, but throughout the khanate. Even Mes'ud Beg had to fly before him and take refuge with Batu, khan of Kiptchak. Bisü was a drunkard and debauchee ; but fortunately for his Mohammedan subjects he took as his vizir and adviser the pious and learned Khodja Bahaeddin, of Mergulan, a man for whose memory Djuveini expresses the utmost reverence, but who soon met an untimely fate at the hands of his rival Habesh Amid, whom he had sought to disarm by kindness of all sorts ; for when at the end of Kuyuk's three years' reign Mengkü[1] became Great Khan, and Kara Hulagu and Ebüskün were reinstated in their former dignities, Habesh Amid was again appointed vizir, and his first step was to throw the gifted Bahaeddin into prison, and, in spite of the eloquent verses addressed by the latter to the princess, he caused him to be sewn up in a piece of felt and kicked and trampled on until all his bones were broken.[2] Bisü lost his throne for refusing to acknowledge the authority of Mengkü. The latter therefore restored his partisan Kara Hulagu to the throne bequeathed to him by his grandfather, ordering him at the same time instantly to kill his rival Bisü, which he would have done had he not himself died before he could carry out the order. The government of the khanate of Tchaghatai fell into the hands of his widow Organa, who had her husband's late rival executed, and reigned ten years happily.

Organa was one of the three Mongolian graces of whom Vassaf says that ' three such forms of beauty, loveliness, grace, and dignity had never been produced amongst the Mongolians by all the painters of creation, with the brushes of the liveliest imagination.'[3] They were the sisters, and at the

---

[1] *Mangu*, as Hammer, D'Ohsson, and other Orientalists spell it, is decidedly a mistake. It is an Uiguric word signifying ' the Immortal, Heavenly One,' from *meng* ▬ Heaven and the adjective *kü.* It has the same meaning as the Arabic name Baki.

[2] When he saw that all chance of escaping Amid's vengeance was at an end, he addressed to him some lines in which he overwhelmed him with curses.

[3] Hammer, *History of the Golden Horde*, p. 162, according to Vassaf.

same time the wives, of the Mongolian princes of Kiptchak, Persia, and Transoxania.

The weal or woe of Transoxania in the time of the Tchaghataides, as already stated, depended chiefly on the changes occasioned by the succession to the imperial throne of China. As long as Mengkü lived, the wise and energetic Organa was allowed to govern in peace ; but the instant he was dead, in the year 658 (1259), war broke out between Arik-Bugha and Kubilai, and the effects of it were, as usual, severely felt in Transoxania. Arik-Bugha had nominated *Algu* chief of the Tchaghataide family, but Kubilai appointed Apishka, the son of Büri. Algu however anticipated his rival, drove out Organa, and established himself at Almalik ; meantime Apishka was taken prisoner on his road through the province of Shen-Si by Arik-Bugha. Algu repaid the service thus rendered him by his patron with the blackest ingratitude ; for when Arik-Bugha, finding himself driven into a corner by Kubilai, applied to his vassal for help in his sore distress, he positively and flatly refused it, although the force at his disposal amounted to more than 150,000 men : and not content with this, he arrested the three commissioners sent by Arik-Bugha to collect the taxes, took the money they had collected from them, murdered them, and then openly espoused the cause of Kubilai. Arik-Bugha was naturally enough furious at this treachery on the part of his former protégé, and, regardless of the threatening aspect of affairs in the East, he took up arms against him. Whilst his attention was occupied in the West, Kubilai made a descent on Kara-korum, and took it from him ; but he indemnified himself for this loss by his victories over Algu, who had to fly from Almalik to Kashgar, then to Khoten, and finally to Samar-kand. Arik-Bugha spent the winter of 662 (1263) at Almalik, where he treated the followers of Algu with extreme severity, and devastated the whole neighbourhood to such an extent that a horrible famine ensued, and many thousand people perished. As it was entirely the consequence of Arik-Bugha's merciless conduct, his best officers now abandoned him in disgust ; and, conscious that his position was too much weakened thereby to allow him to withstand a serious attack on the part of Algu, he offered to make peace on condition of retaining the country belonging to the Tchaghataides. The negotiators appointed were the Princess Organa and Mes'ud Beg. Algu agreed to the proposition, and to make matters still smoother, married the dispossessed princess Organa. Peace was now restored for a time to Transoxania. The administrative abilities of Mes'ud Beg were again called in to fill the exhausted treasury, and, as usual, the industrial and active population of Bokhara and Samarkand had to bear the lion's share of the burden. Thanks to the more settled condition of affairs, Algu was soon able to dispose of his second adversary, Prince Kaidu, a grandson of Oktai's, who, with the assistance of Batu, endeavoured to assert his rights to the northern portion of Transoxania, the province of Turkestan. Algu died in the year 662 (1263), a short time after his beloved wife.[1] Kubilai thereupon appointed Mubarek Shah, the son of Kara Hulagu, chief of the Ulusses (or tribe) of the Tchaghatai. His name proves him to have been a Mohammedan, and he is represented as a gentle and just prince ; but the Great Khan, in spite of his proved liberality in religious matters, does not seem to have placed entire confidence in this prince, who had abjured the faith of his fathers ; for he named secretly as his vicegerent Prince Borak, a great-grandson of Tchaghatai's, who was no sooner installed at the court of Mubarek Shah than he began to intrigue against him, seduced his soldiers from their allegiance, drove him off the throne, and then proceeded to take energetic measures against Kaidu, who had reappeared on the lower courses of the Yaxartes. Kaidu, the father of forty sons, feeling confident in his own strength, was aiming, not only at

[1] Vassaf says that Algu was under the impression that Organa had sinned by her too great partiality for the Mussulmen of Transoxania, and that her death was the punishment for this sin. He wished in revenge to plunder Bokhara and Samarkand, but Mes'ud succeeded in persuading him to abandon this project.

the sovereignty of Turkestan and Transoxania, but at the imperial crown of Kubilai himself, and the object of the latter in confirming Borak on the throne of Almalik was to secure in him a faithful ally against Kaidu. But he found that he had grievously miscalculated; Borak from the very first showed a friendly disposition towards Kubilai's rival, and they divided the cleverest armourers of Bokhara and Samarkand between them.[1] A short time after war broke out between Kaidu and Mengkü Timour, the lord of the Golden Horde, and Borak sought to make good use of the opportunity and took up arms against the former; but Kaidu soon made up his quarrel with Mengkü Timour, and gave his faithless ally so thorough a beating in a furious battle on the banks of the Yaxartes, that the latter had to retire hurriedly from Turkestan to Transoxania. His troops, disappointed of their promised plunder and determined on booty at any price, could only be indemnified by the sacrifice of their own countrymen; and Borak, with heartless tyranny, ordered the inhabitants of Bokhara and Samarkand to abandon their property, and escape from the towns for bare life, as they must be given up to the soldiers to plunder. The tears and entreaties of the inhabitants, however, obtained a modification of this cruel ordinance, and they were let off at the price of a heavy contribution and the consent of the armourers to work day and night at fresh armaments for the prince. In a short time Borak was again ready to take the field; but Kaidu was anxious for peace, and sent Prince Kiptchak Ogul, a bosom friend of Borak's, to Transoxania to negotiate. Kiptchak was most cordially received by the latter; they drank together the usual cup of peace, in which blood and gold were mingled,

[1] According to Vassaf, Bokhara contained at that time, in the year 661 (1263), 16,000 inhabitants, who were portioned out like so many sheep to different Mongolian masters. Five thousand belonged to the tribe of Batu, 3,000 to the Princess Süyür Kükteni, the mother of Hulagu; and the rest were slaves of the Great Khan's. These unhappy people were the chief sufferers by the constant hostilities going on amongst the princes of the house of Djenghiz. Thus we learn that Hulagu, to revenge himself for a defeat he had suffered at the hands of Berke, lord of Kiptchak, caused several subjects of the latter at Bokhara to be murdered.

and became *Anda*[1]—i.e. allies. Concord was thus re-established between Borak and Kaidu in the spring of the year 667 (1269). The festival of peace was held during seven days in the plain north of the Yaxartes.[2] Borak was to receive two-thirds of Transoxania, and one-third, Khodjend and its neighbourhood as far as Samarkand, was assigned to Oktai's Ulusses. Borak was not satisfied with this arrangement, and complained that he had come off worse than any of the Djenghizides ; and as he insisted particularly on the absence of pasture for his flocks, it was determined that he should cross the Oxus into Khorasan and receive some compensation there, so that the exhausted and desolated country in Transoxania might have some leisure to recover herself, and at least be able to gather in her crops in peace. Mes'ud Beg was commissioned by both princes to go through the country and persuade the terrified and fugitive peasantry to return to their occupations. Borak, however, grew impatient for the laurels he hoped to gather in an attack on Abaka, then reigning in Persia ; and, in spite of the miserable condition of the neighbourhood of the Oxus, wished to take up arms again at once. Mes'ud remonstrated, and was punished by seven lashes ; Borak soon repented of having in his anger inflicted this punishment, but did not, nevertheless, abstain from carrying out his intention of at once recommencing hostilities.

He began by sending Mes'ud to the court of Abaka, who was then at his winter quarters at Mazendran. The ostensible purpose of this mission was to settle certain money questions, but its real object was to obtain information concerning the military affairs of the Mongolian prince of Persia. Abaka

---

[1] Anda is Mongolian for an ally—one who has bound himself by an oath (andagha) to friendship with another. It appears characteristic that, just as the old Mongolians mingled gold and blood in their cup of peace, the custom of the old Hungarians in their A'ldomás (alliance) was to open reciprocally a vein in each other's arms and drink the blood out of one cup. The Turks practised the same observance in their alliances with the Hungarian Christians, as is seen by Petchevi's history.

[2] D'Ohsson calls this plain by mistake the plain of Tala. Tala is not a proper name, but the old Turkish word for plain, and still used in this sense in the east of Central Asia.

found out after a time the secret aims of the vizir of the Tchaghataides ; he had him pursued, and Mes'ud only escaped capture by a fortunate accident. Soon afterwards Borak sent out a second mission charged to gain over the Tchaghataian prince Nighudar, then residing at the Mongolian court of Persia, to the cause of his countrymen; but this failed, for Nighudar was prevented by Abaka's vigilance from carrying out his intention of striking off from the Caucasus and the country north of the Caspian Sea towards the shores of the Oxus. Meanwhile Borak had got his army into fighting order, crossed the Oxus at Amuye, and pitched his camp at Merv, accompanied by several princes of the house of Oktai, whom Kaidu had ordered to join him. The first attack was directed against Abaka's brother and General, Butchin (also known as Tebshin, Tushin, and Tishin),who was commanding in Eastern Khorasan—i.e., at Herat, Badghis—and who retreated on ascertaining the superiority of his opponent. Borak pursued him, and subdued all Khorasan; but divisions broke out in his army, which caused him to lose half his forces,[1] and the result was that Abaka was able to carry out a trick by which the successful commencement of the campaign was changed to an unfortunate issue. Borak was drawn into a trap,[2] and in spite of the unparalleled devotion of his generals, Mergaul and Djelairti, so thoroughly beaten that he had great difficulty in escaping

[1] The first person who deserted was Kiptchak, Borak's old friend. He was offended by the insolent conduct of Djelairti, and in spite of Borak's promise that it should be severely punished, could not be brought back. The second deserter was Tjabat, a grandson of Kuyuk Khan's.   -

[2] The trick was as follows : Borak, ignorant of the strength and condition of the enemy's army, had sent three spies into Abaka's camp. They were brought before Abaka and tortured until they confessed their object, and then tied up in momentary expectation of death. At that instant a courier covered with dust rode up, and proclaimed ' My lord, numerous enemies have invaded the country from Derbend ; the western provinces are ravaged with fire and sword.' This scene, arranged by Abaka himself, caused the greatest confusion in the camp, and there was talk of marching westward that very night. The alert was sounded, and the execution of the three spies ordered ; but Abaka told the officer charged with it privately to allow one to escape. He did so ; the fugitive reached Borak's camp, spread the intelligence, Borak marched in pursuit of the enemy he believed to be retreating, and was surrounded and cut to pieces by Abaka's men lying in ambush for him.

across the Oxus, himself much hurt by a bad fall from his horse. Broken in mind and body, he entered Bokhara in a litter, spent the winter there in useless efforts to revenge himself on a faithless ally to whom he attributed all his misfortunes, and died in the spring of 669 (1270), believed by many to have been poisoned.

Transoxania was delivered from a turbulent and miserable tyrant and persecutor, but the measure of her troubles was not yet complete.; for the fratricidal warfare between the families of Oktai and Tchaghatai continued to rage until the horrors of war had been let loose over all the cities on the Zerefshan, and the returning progress of civilisation amongst the inhabitants once more entirely checked.[1] On the death of Borak, Kaidu once more became sole master of both Turkestan and Transoxania, and appointed Nikbai, the son of Sarban, chief of the tribe of Tchaghatai, much to the indignation of the sons of Borak, who joined with the sons of Algu in kindling the flames of revenge in the devoted towns of Transoxania. Nikbai himself soon rebelled against his patron, and was attacked and killed in the year 667 (1272). He was succeeded by Tokatimur, and he in turn by Dua,[2] the son of Borak, who made up the quarrel with Kaidu; and if a sincere alliance could have been established between the two, the unfortunate khanate might have hoped for some peace ; but unfortunately a third firebrand appeared on the scene. Abaka had never forgiven the invasion of Khorasan by the Tchaghataides, and his vizir, Shemseddin Djuveini,[3] brother of the historian Djuveini, from whom

---

[1] D'Ohsson says with truth in his *Histoire des Mongols*, vol. ii. p. 521 : ' La prospérité ne pouvait être que précaire dans les provinces exposées à la rapacité des nomades turcs et mongols, qui regardant les fruits de l'industrie comme leur proie, n'attendaient que l'occasion de les ravir à leurs paisibles possesseurs.'

[2] Also called Tua or Tava.

[3] Shemseddin was actuated chiefly by motives of personal vengeance. When Mes'ud was sent on a mission to the court of Abaka, by Borak, Shemseddin went to meet him, and although he showed him every mark of respect, kissing his stirrup and going through all usual ceremonies, Mes'ud addressed him thus : ' Art thou the Prime Minister ? Verily thy name is better than thy looks.' D'Ohsson, vol. iii. p. 423 ; taken from Rashid-eddin's *Hist. of the Mongols.*

we have largely quoted, had only to draw his attention to a favourable opportunity of revenge to induce him at once to enter Bokhara with his army in the year 671 (1273), plundering, burning, and murdering right and left. He made 50,000 prisoners, and amongst other acts of vandalism, laid the celebrated college of Mes'udie in ashes, and finally departed. He was pursued by the Generals Tchaba and Kayan, and a few prisoners were taken from him ; but these same commanders themselves devastated the whole neighbourhood three years later, so that the unhappy country was left at last a barren desert, until the able administration of Mes'ud Beg succeeded in infusing new life into it. Unfortunately Dua was by no means the man from whom Transoxania could hope for the peace so needful to her. His comparatively long reign—from 671 (1272) to 706 (1306)—was a period of constant and bloody wars, by which this most ambitious of all the Tchaghataides succeeded in putting an end to the rivalry with the family of Oktai, and in once more incorporating the northern territory of the Yaxartes with the possessions of the house of Tchaghatai ; but these advantages were bought at the price of the renewed calamities that visited Transoxania. The hostilities between Kaidu and Kubilai had been going on for twenty years on the banks of the Oxus and Yaxartes, when Kaidu resolved in conjunction with Dua to carry them farther into the country of the Great Khan, Timour, who had succeeded Kubilai. In the year 701 (1301), shortly after the return of Dua from a raid he had undertaken on Lahore, in India, the united armies of Kaidu and Dua, to which forty princes belonging to their two families were respectively attached, invaded the north of China. They met the Imperial army between Karakorum and the river Tamir, and Kaidu, having in his lifetime gained forty-one battles, was beaten in this forty-second one, and sickened and died on his way home.[1] His eldest son, Tchabar, was proclaimed chief of the family of Oktai,

---

[1] Vassaf declares Kaidu to have been victorious, and to have died a natural death on his way home, laden with spoils.

thanks to the influence of Dua. Dua and Tchaba now made peace with the Great Khan Timour, but they soon fell to quarrelling with each other, and fought a battle in the year 703 (1303) between Samarkand and Khodjend, in which Dua got the advantage. Tchaba afterwards in a measure retrieved his fortunes, but having again incurred the enmity of the Great Khan, he soon found that there was nothing left to him but to submit to Dua, who received him gladly, in order that Turkestan, which had been taken from the Oktaides by violence, might once more be incorporated in the khanate of Tchaghatai.

Dua died in the year 706 (1306), and was succeeded by his son Köndjük, who did not live long; and the reins of government then fell into the hands of Talikava, a Tchaghataide descended from Moatugan, who was killed at Bamian. He was the second Mongolian prince on the throne of Transoxania who became a convert to Islam; but he seems to have carried his proselytising zeal to excess, for the Mongolian officers of his court rose against him, and murdered him at a banquet, and put Kebek, the son of Dua, a brave and upright prince, in his place. Tchaba carried on towards the son the hostility he had shown to the father, with results disastrous to himself; and the consequence was that he was beaten again, and lost the last chance of preserving Turkestan to the descendants of Oktai. The Tchaghataians, then, for some unexplained reason, and with the consent of Kebek, placed his own elder brother, Esenbuka[1], on the throne. Esenbuka first came forward in the year 709 (1309), and from then to 716 (1316) appears as chief of the Ulusses of Tchaghatai, and seems as such to have carried on a war with Oldjaitu, the Mongolian prince of Persia, the results of which were very important to Transoxania. Esenbuka had carried on hostilities with Tokadji, a commander in the army of the Great Khan Bayantu, in which he was worsted, and, to indemnify himself for his losses in the East, he determined

---

[1] I read this name Esen, not *Isen*, as D'Ohsson has it. Esen is a Turkish word, signifying *strong, healthy*.

to get possession of Khorasan. His army, accompanied by several of the princes, crossed the Oxus in the year 715 (1315), defeated Emir Yasaol, the governor of Khorasan, at Murghab, and pursued him to the river of Herat. Esenbuka thus obtained possession of all this portion of Khorasan; his soldiers inflicted on the unfortunate inhabitants during four months all the horrors of a Mongolian occupation, and would probably have remained still longer, if the advance of the Great Khan on the Issikköl had not forced Esenbuka to retire from Khorasan. Unhappily Transoxania soon had to expiate this raid of her rulers. Just as Abaka had done after the invasion of Borak, Oldjaitu, the Mongolian prince of Persia (who afterwards assumed the name of Khudabende,[1] servant of God), could not rest till he had punished the author of this invasion. Yassaver, a brother of Esenbuka's, who had embraced Islamism and was on bad terms with his brother, had sought and obtained a refuge at the court of the Mongolian prince of Persia. He went to war with his brother: Oldjaitu gave him two *corps d'armée* to assist him; they crossed the Oxus in the year 716 (1316) and terminated the war in his favour. Esenbuka fled, and Transoxania was once more given over to the most terrible ravages. The inhabitants of Bokhara, Samarkand, and Termez were sent into exile in the depth of a very severe winter, and thousands perished by the way. Esenbuka now disappears from the scene; Kebek resumed his former place, chastised the rebel brother who had brought such misery on the people, and died in the year 721.

From this time the star of the Mongolians in Western Asia began rapidly to decline. It was in vain that Ebusaïd endeavoured to build up again a dynasty in Iran and Arabistan. *Those* Mongolians, in adopting Islamism, and the manners of West Asiatic civilisation, had sacrificed the brute strength

---

[1] Khudabende is the only Mongolian prince of Persia whose memory is still honoured as that of a just ruler by the Turkish population of Azerbaidjan. I gathered many anecdotes of him from the lips of the common people, while exploring the ruins of his once-splendid monument at Sultanye.

they had brought from their old home in the desert, and the power it gave them ; and, like lions deprived of their manes, no longer inspired terror. Just as in the days of the decadence of the Seldjukides, the emirs governing provinces had traded on the weakness of their sovereigns to further their own private ends, so now vassals of Arpa Khan's—successor of Ebusaïd—rose openly against their ruler, and began to cut up and dismember the empire founded by the arms of Tuli and Hulagu.

Military despotism had always found a congenial soil in Transoxania and Turkestan ; and there the Djenghizides—thanks to their barbarian origin, and the terror inspired by their first appearance—were able to maintain themselves .longest ; but even there the reigning family soon lost its earlier prestige, and the princes who successively occupied the throne from Kebek to Kabilshah,[1] the last of the Tchaghataides, all reigned a comparatively short time, or else were but puppets in the hands of ambitious viziers. The chronicle of events in Transoxania during this period is confined to the mention of a raid in Khorassan under Alaeddin Tarma Shirin, who was beaten at Ghaznee, in the year 726 (1325) and retreated hurriedly across the Oxus. Tarma Shirin is

---

[1] The complete list of the Tchaghataides on the throne of Transoxania, with the dates of their respective accessions, is thus given by D'Ohsson : 1. Tchaghatai (D'Ohsson omits the date, but he is known to have assumed the government in 1222). 2. Kara Hulagu, 1224. 3. Yissu Mangu (called by me Bisü), 1247. 4. Regency of Arguna or Organa, the widow of Kara Hulagu, 1252. 5. Algu, 1260. 6. Mubarek Shah, 1266. 7. Borak. 8. Nikbai, 1270. 9. Toka Timour, 1272. 10. Dua. 11. Gundjuk (Köndjük), 1306. 12. Talikava, 1308. 13. Esenbuka, 1309. 14. Gebek. 15. Iltchikdai, 1321. 16. Duva Timour. 17. Tarma Shirin. 18. Busan, 1330. 19. Djinkshi. 20. Yissun Timour. 21. Ali Sultan of the house of Oktai. 22. Fulad. 23. Mohammed. 24. Kasan, 1333. 25. Danishmendje, 1346. 26. Bayan Kuli. 27. Timour Shah. 28. Kutluk Timour. 29. Elias Khodja, 1362. 30. Kabilshah. The latter of these princes are not further mentioned here, as their shadowy rule is mixed up in the history of the deeds of Timour which will be fully gone into in the next chapter. Mirkhond, in his *History of the Tchaghataides*, makes out that members of the family reappeared later as chiefs amongst the Djetes and the other Mongolians who distinguished themselves north of Fergana under Yunis Khan; but this seems to be an error, for, as we shall see by-and-bye, the princes of the Djetes and the Mongolians in question were descendants of the family of Kaidu.

described by the Arabian traveller Ibn Batutah, who spent two
months in Bokhara as his guest, as an extremely devout
Mohammedan, whose religious zeal was so great that he
allowed a mollah to rebuke him personally in the strongest
language in a public sermon, and only shed tears of humility
and repentance. He sacrificed both his throne and his life
for his Mohammedan faith ; being murdered by order of his
successor Bozan,[1] in the neighbourhood of Samarkand.[2] The
latter was only nominally a Mussulman. His tyranny
weighed heavily on the inhabitants of Transoxania, and they
applied for help to the neighbouring Mohammedan princes,
and those campaigns commenced in which a principal part was
played by the celebrated Tadjik, Husein Kert, who wanted
to wrest Khorasan from Arpa Khan. Husein, emboldened
by repeated successes, invaded Andkhoi and Shiborgan,
districts inhabited by the Turkish tribes of Arlat and Ai-
berdi, tributaries of Bokhara. The Turks opposed Husein's
advance, but were beaten and applied for assistance to their
prince Kazan Khan—or rather to their vizir, Emir Kazghan—
who succeeded in subduing Husein Kert. This Emir Kazghan,
the powerful vassal and kingmaker in Transoxania, deserves
all the more to be mentioned as his actions are the best proof
of the powerlessness of the latter Tchaghataides. Kazan, the
son of Yassaver, ascended the throne in 733 (1332). He was
a bloodthirsty tyrant—'so much so,' says Mirkhond, 'that
his principal officials all made their wills before attending his
kuriltai. He terrorised over the country undisturbed, until
Kazghan became his vizir, and determined to get rid of him.
Kazghan gained over the army, and then broke into open

---

[1] According to Ibn Batutah, this Bozan (whom he calls Buzun) was defeated
and put to death by Khalil, the son of Yassaver. Khalil is even said to have
advanced as far as Almalik and to have entirely defeated the Mongolian army at
Taraz. After ascending the throne of Bokhara, he rebelled against Sultan Husein
Kert, who had assisted him in all his enterprises, but he was beaten and carried as
a prisoner to Herat, where the Arabian traveller met him at the end of the year
747 (1372). *Voyages d'Ibn Batoutah.* Paris, 1855, vol. iii. p. 48–51.

[2] According to the author of the *Matla es Saadein*, Tarma Shirin fell ill at
Nakhsheb in 727 (1326), and died in consequence a natural death.

rebellion. In the first battle, which took place in the year 744 (1343), or, according to Mirkhond, two years later, the victory was gained by Kazan. Emir Kazghan was wounded by an arrow which destroyed one eye. The Tchaghataide could not, however, pursue his advantage, and was obliged to retire on Karshi, where he spent the winter. The severe weather made great havoc amongst his horses and beasts of burden ; and when, in the following spring, he resumed the offensive, he was beaten and died, after a reign of fourteen years. Emir Kazghan had no intention of seizing the reins of government himself, for he preferred following the pleasures of the chase undisturbed. He therefore placed on the throne Prince Danishmendje Oghlan—whom he, however, made away with two years later, and put Bayankuli in his place. He would probably have gone on making and unmaking princes in this fashion perpetually, if his brother-in-law, Kutluk Timour, had not murdered him one day out hunting. His son Abdullah succeeded to his dignity but not to his influence, and could not protect either himself or his respective sovereigns against the vassals whose power was daily increasing. He was finally overthrown by Emir Hadji Seïfeddin Berlas. The latter fled before the Tchaghataide Tukluk Timour, who had hurried from Almalik to Khorasan in order to put an end to the state of anarchy. But he left on the other side of the Oxus his nephew Timour, to whom it was reserved to pull down not only the successors of Tchaghatai [1] from the throne of Transoxania, but the whole rotten edifice of the Mongolian government in Asia, unhappily not without once more deluging the country with the blood of thousands of victims.

Before concluding this mournful episode of the history of Transoxania, we cannot resist throwing a glance over the civilisation and social conditions by which this . epoch is characterised. Amidst the terrible ravages committed by

---

[1] I say expressly the successors of Tchaghatai; for though the power of the Djenghizides was completely destroyed in the rest of Asia, there exists to this day a collateral female branch of the descendants of this conqueror of Djüdji's family on the throne of Transoxania.

the Mongolians, the science of theology and its votaries alone continued to flourish. In the days of the earlier Tchaghataides the mollahs of Turkestan had enjoyed a certain amount of protection, thanks partly to the principle of religious toleration,[1] and partly to the superstitious awe in which every class of the priesthood was held ; and in almost every town there was some one or other holy man to whom the Moslems had recourse in the day of peril. The spiritual teachers thus became at the same time secular protectors, and from this time forward we find the sadr-i-sheriat (heads of the religious bodies) and chief magistrates, and in general all men of remarkable piety, attaining an influence in the towns of Transoxania unknown in the rest of Islam; an influence which maintains itself to this day, though the land has been for centuries governed by Musulman princes. The seats of spiritual authority were filled by regular dynasties of learned men of certain families, as though they had been thrones. The most distinguished of these families were that of Sitadji and that of Khavend. The founder of the first of these, Djemaleddin Sitadji, an exegetical teacher and author of Suffite poems, settled at Khodjend in 628 (1230), and died in 640 (1242), during Djenghiz's invasion. The second family inhabited Bokhara, and the principal members of it were— Mevlana Kemaleddin, son of the celebrated professor and mufti, Emir Shemseddin Khavend. He is known as the author of the ' Minhadj ul Muzekkerin,' a valuable biographical work, and also of several divans. He died in 671 (1272), on the first day of the sack of Bokhara by Abaka's troops, above alluded to. And further we must mention Khavend Shah Farkheddin, and Mollah Tadjeddin, the learned author of the ' Bostan-i-Muzekkerin,' who died in 730 (335). Later on, when the latter Tchaghataides embraced Islamism, wholesale

---

[1] The best evidence of this toleration is to be found in the respect with which certain holy places in Turkestan were treated by the covetous and plundering Mongolians. A proof of this is in the magnificence and costly details which Ibn Batutah found in perfect preservation about the grave of Kotham ibn Abbas near Samarkand.

conversions took place in the time of Tarma Shirin, and the zeal of the newly-converted princes led them to favour in all ways this spiritual movement. We have seen descendants of the Mongolian conqueror [1] submitting to be soundly rated by fanatical mollahs in a public mosque in the face of their people, blushing and doing penance in the sight of all, and we begin to comprehend the exclamation addressed in his splendid Mesnevi by the greatest mystical poet of the East, whose soul was disgusted at the formal and hollow outward observances, without the spirit of religion, to the enthusiastic Sufi, who was going to Bokhara in the vain hope of finding there consolation for his sick and weary heart and mind :—

> Bokhara mirevi divaneï
> Laik-i-zendjir-i-zindankhanei.

> To Bokhara thou goest ; art thou mad?
> Nought but chains and bondage there to be had.

---

[1] This is related by Batutah of Ala-ed-dowlch.

X.

EMIR TIMOUR.
765 (1363)—807 (1405).

THE invasion of Central Asia by the Turks caused various ethnographical revolutions, the most important result of which was the preponderance of the Turkish element in all parts of Transoxania. The Turks originally entered the country as friends and allies of the Mongols of the eastern valleys of the Thien-Shan and of the Altai mountains, and soon settled down on the banks of the Oxus, where they found kinsmen and brothers who had long made their home there (so far as a Turk could do so), and had shared in the honours and dignities bestowed by former dynasties on distinguished warriors. The Turks were not far behind the Mongols in their aptitude for pillage, murder, and general devastation, and consequently had no difficulty in keeping in favour with the Tchaghataides; these latter, hating even the ashes of ancient Iranian culture, inhabited by preference the eastern or northern extremities of Tchaghatai's hereditary dominions. The Turkish chiefs soon became known in Transoxania as their lieutenants and representatives, and were, as we shall see presently, often confounded with them; indeed the last of the Tchaghataides were so entirely under Turkish influence that they scarcely understood the Mongolian tongue, and Turkish had become the language of the court and of society. The successors of Djenghiz Khan had no more devoted servants than the Turks as long as they themselves retained any real power or influence; but, as their authority began to decay, these same Turks endeavoured everywhere to usurp the place of their former masters, the empire of the Tchaghataides fell to pieces; north of Samarkand, the tribes of Djelair and Solduz wrested the power to themselves; in the south, in Kesh and Nakh'sheb the house of Berlas planted the flag of independence on the ruins of the Mongolian dominion.

Timour Beg (better known in Europe under the name of Tamerlane or Tamerlenk) belonged to the *Köreken* branch[1] of the above-named house.[2] He first saw the light on Tuesday evening, the 5th Shaaban, in the year 736 (1333), in a suburb of Kesh, called, by reason of its luxuriant vegetation, Sheri Sebz ('the Green city'), by which name the whole town was afterwards known.[3] His father, Turghai[4] (Thrush), was head of the tribe of Berlas, and as such had been invested with the province of Kesh and Nakh'sheb by Emir Kazghan. He re-

[1] The relations between the original family and its collateral branches among the nomadic tribes of Central Asia, as explained by me in my book of travels, were of course still more clearly defined in earlier times. Timour's *tribe* was that of Berlas, but his *branch of the family* was that of *Köreken*—a word which means 'handsome.' Klaproth and several of my predecessors might have spared themselves the trouble of identifying the word with *Kurkan* or *Kurkhan*, and translating it, 'Great Khan.'

[2] The opinion entertained by Weil, Hammer and many other Orientalists, on the authority of Mirkhond and Sherefeddin, that Timour was of Mongolian origin, involves a double error. The history of Timour's descent from Karadja Noyan is a pure fable, for the *Djihankusha*, to which Rashideddin, Vassaf, Mirkhond and others were largely indebted for their information, contains no allusion to this supposed vizir of Tchaghatai. That Timour should ever have been taken for a Mongolian can only be explained by the circumstance that the Persians long regarded the khanate of Tchaghatai on the further side of the Oxus as an integral portion of the Mongolian Empire—a natural conclusion from the prevailing adoption of the Mongolian costume, and the fact that the Uiguric-Mongolian character was always used in writing Turkish at that time. Clavijo, ambassador of Henry III. of Castille at the court of Timour, states: 'The territory of the empire of Samarkand is called Mongolia, and the language of the country is Mongolian, which, however, is not understood on this bank (of the Oxus). The characters used on the Samarkand side of the river (that is, Uiguric letters) are not understood on this (the Persian) side. The Emperor (Timour) has several scribes who read and write these *Mongolian* characters.' (*Narrative of the Embassy of Ruy Gonzalez de Clavijo to the Court of Timour at Samarkand*, A.D. 1403-6, translated by Clements R. Markham, F.R.G.S. London, Hackluyt Society, 1859.

[3] Baber relates in his classical work known as the *Babernamch*, that in the spring the walls and terraces of the houses were almost hidden by the luxuriant creepers and other plants.

[4] Not *Targai*, as spelt by Weil (*Geschichte der Chalifen*, vol. ii. p. 21).

mained a devoted follower of the latter until his death, and
the young Timour, who early showed signs of a brave and
chivalrous disposition, was brought up by his father not only
in principles of strict Mohammedanism, but also in his own political sentiments, which aimed at the overthrow of the Mongolian empire. Even if we decline to place implicit faith in an
obvious flatterer, the historian Sherefeddin, it may still be
assumed with certainty that Timour, from his earliest youth,
was fired by ambition and animated by a consciousness
of future greatness. He says in his autobiography :[1] 'As
early as my twelfth year, I began to be aware of traces of
extraordinary wisdom and power in my own mind, and bore
myself with studied dignity and self-possession towards all
who approached me. In my eighteenth year I was not a
little proud of my skill in field sports and chivalrous amusements, and spent my time in reading the Koran, playing
chess, and in various knightly exercises.' No wonder therefore that, when in his twentieth year his father declared him
of age and gave him a separate court (*Aul*), he should have
at once attached himself to a leader under whose banner he
believed himself most likely to enter on the path of battle
and adventure for which his whole soul was longing. This
leader was the Emir Kazghan, mentioned above, to whom he
was sent on an embassy by his father, in the year 1356, and
who was so favourably impressed by the young man that he
gave him his grand-daughter, Oldjai Turkan Khatun, daughter
of his son Sela[2] Khan, to wife, and took him with him as

---

[1] This work is entitled *Tüsükat Timour*, i.e., Decrees of Timour (from the
Turkish : *Tüsük*—decree, or law, with the Arabic plural *at*), and would therefore
appear at first sight a code of laws, similar to the *Yasao Djenghiz*. But as Timour
also relates in it the particulars of his wonderful career, and occasionally explains
the motives of his most remarkable actions, it may with equal propriety be
described as an autobiography. The first copy brought from India to Europe by
Major Davy, consists of an octavo volume of 457 pp. written in the Persian
language, consequently a translation of the original. The original, written in the
Tchaghataian language, was found in the library of Djafar, governor of Yemen,
was first translated into Persian, and afterwards, in the year 1830, by Major C.
Stewart into English. (Note in Markham's above-mentioned book, p. xv.)

[2] Not *Muslah*, as Petit de la Croix and d'Herbelot, misled by erroneous

,Mingbashi' (i.e., commander of 1,000 men) in his second campaign against Huseïn Kert in Khorasan. The campaign proved successful for Kazghan, but he soon after fell a victim to assassination, and Timour, having lost his own father almost at the same moment, and being overwhelmed with his double sorrow, was only too ready to accept the offers of friendship of Emir Huseïn, the grandson of the murdered Kazghan, and in conjunction with him to seek revenge on the murderers of his benefactor. But the battles which were the result of this resolution only fanned the flame of anarchy more and more fiercely in Transoxania, and Tukluk[1] Timour, the temporary chief of the Uluss, deeming it high time to protect the interests of his dynasty from total destruction, marched an army composed principally of *Djetes*[2] from Almalik on Samarkand, determined to strengthen the throne of his fathers by driving out the rebellious vassals.

His appearance amongst them caused some of the rebels to return to their allegiance, but others, such as Hadji Seïfeddin Berlas (who had become chief of his tribe on the death of Turghai), fled into Khorasan ; meanwhile young Timour betook himself to the court of the Tchaghataides, was well received there and confirmed as prince of the province of Kesh. Outward tranquillity was maintained in Transoxania as long as Tukluk Timour stayed there, but he had no sooner withdrawn eastward than the turbulent chiefs rose again and compelled him a second time to interfere with force of arms. The future conqueror of Asia remained passive, and when Tukluk at the head of his army appeared in Samarkand and proclaimed his son Ilias Khodja, viceroy, Timour was

manuscripts, have spelt it. The right spelling of the word is مصال and means in Turkish, home, or native country.

[1] Not *Togluk*, as spelt by Weil, Hammer and others. *Tuk* is Turkish for flag or banner, and *Tukluk* means one provided with flags (standard-bearer).

[2] *Djetes* (not *Ghetes*, as mis-spelt by Weil) was the name by which the Turkish races living on the frontiers of Mongolia proper were known ; the sole existing remains of them at the present time are the Burutes. These Mongolians are called to this day in Central Asia *Tchete-Mogul* = Moguls of the border, from the Turkish *tchet*, border, and Mogul, Mongol.

chosen as his most trustworthy adherent, to remain there as adviser to his princely son. It might easily have been foreseen that Timour, whose whole conduct hitherto had been ruled simply by a policy of shaping all means to a still distant end, would not be particularly pleased with his position as tutor to a Mongolian prince. He began at once to quarrel with the minister of the latter, then secretly left the court of Samarkand and made his way with a few faithful followers to the desert which extends between the present khanate of Bokhara and Khiva, down to the Caspian Sea. This was the time when he had to face the severest trials of his adventurous career, and the dangers and discomforts to be endured by a wanderer in a desolate wilderness.

He relates, with touching simplicity, in his memoirs, how he and his devoted wife Oldjai, accompanied by Emir Husein, whom they met in the desert, wandered about for a whole month night and day, often without food or drink, and were at last taken prisoners by a Turkoman, who shut up his beloved consort in a cowshed swarming with vermin. This was doubtless severe training for the man under whose sceptre half Asia was one day to bow, but yet it was principally in this fire of adversity that Timour (i.e., *iron*) was tempered to the polished steel of his brilliant future. Having escaped with his friends from captivity, he went secretly to Kesh, gathered around him there some of his old comrades in arms and former companions, and with them first roamed awhile about the banks of the Oxus, and then undertook a raid on Sistan, in which he met with varying fortunes, now wresting a fortified position from the Beludjis ; then, again meeting with a repulse ; on one of these latter occasions he received a wound in the foot which lamed him for life and obtained him from the Persians the surname of Timourlenk—'lame Timour.'[1]

---

[1] The malicious invention of the Syrian scholar Ahmed bin Arabshah, that Timour was originally a shepherd, had been detected in the act of sheep-stealing and had then received the blow which lamed him for life, has found credence solely amongst the inveterate enemies of the Tartar conqueror.

Whilst he was laid up by this wound his companion Huseïn succeeded in gaining possession of Belkh. Timour followed him there; the number of his adherents increased to 1,500, and he soon found himself in a position to make a stand against the troops sent by Ilias Khodja in pursuit of him. The first encounter between them took-place in the year 765 (1363), on the left bank of the Oxus, near Kunduz, and resulted in the complete victory of Timour over a force five times as strong as his own, and the retreat of Ilias Khodja's men to the other side of the river. After this the Djetes were relentlessly pursued and the Tchaghataides completely driven out of Transoxania, an object which Timour was the more easily able to accomplish, as Tukluk Timour Khan had just died and his son had passed the Yaxartes and gone to Almalik to take possession of his father's throne. As soon as the last of the Mongols had left the territory of Transoxania, Timour made his entry into Samarkand and was most cordially welcomed by the inhabitants, and during the ensuing festivities he was joined by his wife, who had hitherto remained in concealment. Timour was now virtually, to all intents and purposes, lord of his native country, and might have at once taken possession of the throne of Samarkand, but he saw that there were still many obstacles to overcome and many enemies to be conciliated before he could attain his ultimate ends, and, in order to avoid increasing the jealousy of his detractors by assuming at once the sovereign title, he prudently determined to place another member of the same family on the throne of Tchaghatai, left vacant by Ilias Khodja. He summoned a kuriltai, caused Kabilshar to be proclaimed sovereign, and shortly after set to work, materially strengthened in power and influence, to prosecute still further his ambitious plans.

It might easily have been predicted that the Djetes would not submit peaceably to their expulsion from Transoxania, and, in point of fact, Timour had hardly concluded his winter holiday at Samarkand when he heard of an irruption of the

latter under Ilias Khodja.   He immediately communicated
the intelligence to his friend, Emir Husein, who joined him
with a considerable force, and whilst Timour pitched his
camp between Tchinas and Tashkend, Husein crossed the
Yaxartes and met the enemy face to face.   The right wing,
commanded by Timour, succeeded in driving back the enemy,
but the left, under Emir Husein, was nearly overpowered,
and Timour's military genius and activity alone prevented a
total defeat.   This occurrence led to a violent dispute between
the two commanders, and was the commencement of the
quarrel which ended, after many years of rivalry, in the fall
of Husein and the absolute sovereignty of Timour.   For
the moment the united armies contrived to escape with a loss
of 2,000 dead.   Husein retired on his capital, Sali Saray, on
the opposite bank of the Oxus, Timour returned to Karshi, and
the Djetes advanced unmolested southwards, besieged Samarkand, and would no doubt have plundered the city in Mon-·
golian fashion, but for the breaking out of a plague which
carried off all their horses and obliged them to retrace their
steps, carrying the baggage on their own backs.

Under these circumstances a united attack on them might
have broken the power of the Mongols for long, if not for
ever, but meantime the divisions between the former comrades
had assumed formidable proportions, and Timour found himself
obliged to proceed against Husein by force of arms, and at
the same time to keep a watchful eye on the movements of
the Djetes in the north.   Although Husein could dispose of
larger reserves, as his possessions were much greater than
Timour's and his partisans far more numerous, it was evident
that he considered his rival by no means insignificant, for he
began by attempting to circumvent him by underhand intrigues and plots, and then finding Timour was not so easily
to be caught in the snares laid for him, he finally sent a division of his army, under Emir Musa, to cross the Oxus and
openly attack him.   Emir Musa was, however, driven back ;
upon this, Husein himself marched from Sali Saray, crossed

the Oxus with his entire army, and encamped on the farther side of the river at a place named Betik Tchektchek. Timour, aware of the immense superiority in numbers of his opponent, retired first on Karshi, and next on Bokhara, in order to learn more distinctly the position of his allies there, whom he reckoned on for help. He soon, however, became convinced that the assistance they could give would be insufficient to justify him in assuming the offensive, and determined therefore for the moment to abandon the field in Transoxania to Huseïn, and to avoid pursuit by a feint of invading Western Khorasan. Huseïn marched at once on Bokhara; the inhabitants of the place were mostly Tadjiks, who had always had the reputation of being cowards; they advanced indeed to meet him, but, although they were well armed, Huseïn's cavalry soon surrounded and so entirely defeated them that no power on earth would induce them to venture on a second attack. Timour's rival thus obtained undisturbed possession of nearly the whole of Transoxania, but Timour himself spent the winter in active preparation for the ensuing campaign, and in the following spring we find him again beyond the Oxus and on his way to Tashkend with a marvellously small [1] but determined body of troops, who had, in a series of daring enterprises (in which his brave son Djihanghir particularly distinguished himself), cut their way through his rival's army at Karshi and Samarkand. His intention in going to Tashkend was to induce his ally there, Keikhosru, of the house of Djelair, to take up his cause more warmly; in this he succeeded, for Keikhosru gave his daughter in marriage to Timour's son and to Timour himself auxiliary troops, with which he defeated and drove back across the Oxus Huseïn's army that had pursued him as far as the Yaxartes.

This victory of Timour's was in itself enough to teach his

[1] Huseïn's army of 12,000 men, protected by the fortress of Karshi, was attacked by Timour with only 243 men. These brave fellows crossed the moat of the fortress, on a log of wood, one by one, in the dead of night. Timour at their head, they scaled the walls, killed the sentries, and succeeded in driving out the garrison.

enemy the wisdom of moderation, and his alliance with the House of Djelair, itself a vassal of the Djetes, filled Husein with well-grounded alarm. He therefore offered propositions for peace, which were all the more joyfully accepted by Timour as he himself was not overpleased at seeing the Djetes mixed up, by their forcible entry, in the internal affairs of Transoxania; or, because, as his panegyrists say, the internecine killing and robbery of the true believers by each other filled him with horror. However that might be, peace was not only concluded but Timour hurried over the Oxus to assist Husein in chastising his rebellious vassal at Bedak'hshan, and next, still further to cement the reconciliation, we find the two taking part together in an expedition against Kabul, which Husein wished to incorporate in his dominions. In spite of all this, the peaceable relations of the two were not of long duration. No sooner had Timour left Bedak'hshan for the purpose of repelling a threatened invasion of the Djetes on the upper courses of the Yaxartes (in which he succeeded) than Husein, persistently fanning the flame, provoked a fresh dispute and forced his rival once more to turn his arms against him. This time, however, Timour was joined in his march on Belkh by all the principal of Husein's former partisans, who flocked to his banners, either because, as Sherefeddin would persuade us, they were disgusted at the ceaseless intrigues of their former chief, or because, as is more likely, they were attracted by the increasing *prestige* of Timour's good fortune. Notwithstanding this, Husein made a most determined resistance, and only surrendered on the fall of his last refuge Belkh, from the walls of which he descended into his enemy's camp to entreat him to spare his life, protesting, according to Mirkhond, his intention of 'making a pilgrimage to the Kaaba, there with tears and prayers to blot out the long list of his sins.' Timour was magnanimous enough to pardon the brother of his beloved wife, but the chiefs who surrounded him were not so ready to forgive the many insults they had suffered at the hands of Husein. They were determined to have his life, and, although Timour long resisted, he seems at length to have given way to them, for he who had been the friend and comrade of his youth, and later his unsuccessful rival, was dragged from a tower to which he had fled at the last moment, and put to death in the year 771 (1369).

Timour was now without a rival. His foreign enemies, including the Djetes on the east of his dominions, had been ·driven back by him at the point of the sword, and he thought now with reason that the time was come to put an end to the shadowy rule of the puppet who was nominally sovereign, and to set the hardly-earned crown of Transoxania on his own head. But, just as some centuries later Nadir, whose fate was so similar to his own, only proceeded to the culminating act of assuming the crown after a display of a certain amount of Oriental prudery, so Timour would not take on himself the highest dignity without the sanction of the legal vote of a kuriltai. The diet convoked at Belkh for this purpose was attended by nearly all the nobles of the former empire of the Tchaghataides, by the comrades in arms and companions of his youth, as also by his former opponents. Amongst the principal names, the historian mentions: Emir Sheïkh Mohammed Bayan, of the house of Solduz; Emir Oldjaitu[1] and Emir Keikhosru, of the house of Khatlan ; Emir Daoud, of the tribe of Dughlat; Emir Sarbughai, of the house of Djelair ; Emir Djaku, of the tribe of Berlas ; Emir Zinde Hashm, and many other chiefs of renown. According to the old Turkish custom Timour was placed on a white felt, lifted up on high, and, after the blessing of God had been invoked on his behalf by his spiritual adviser, Seïd Berke, proclaimed Emir of Transoxania on the 10th Ramazan, 771 (April 8, 1369). He distributed rich presents among his followers, won over, by his kindness and indulgence, many who had hitherto kept aloof from him,[2] and having established his power on

---

[1] It is incomprehensible to me how Petit de la Croix could have read this well-known word Oladja Itu.

[2] One of these was Zinde Hashm, Lord of Shiborgan, who rebelled several times against Timour, but was put down and finally converted by kindly treatment to the most devoted of his followers.

that side of the Oxus, crossed the river to set up his capital at Samarkand. From that time forward to his death, this was the spot whither he always repaired for rest and relaxation after the fatigues of his various campaigns, and whither were conveyed the colossal spoils and rich treasures which fell into his hands in so many different countries of Asia. His first care on assuming the reins of government was to re-establish something like order in the chaos reigning in the country. In spite of his zeal for the Islamite religion, Timour was a great admirer of the Djenghiz Code of Laws, and this, being a product of Turanian statesmanship, was no doubt better fitted to the social and political conditions of the Turko-Tartaric peoples than the purely Semitic institutions which owed their origin to the Koran and the Sunna ; it is therefore easy to understand why he laid so much stress on strictly carrying out the Yasao and so persistently upheld it against the Mohammedan priesthood.[1] He also copied faithfully the Mongolian conqueror's ordinances in all relating to the military organisation of the country. The dignities of *Tümen Agasi* (Lord of ten thousand), of *Yüzbashi* (centurion), and *Onbashi* (decurion) were continued. The political administration remained as before, except that the system of taxation was brought somewhat more into accordance with the directions of the Koran, and that the rules by which the granting of distinctions and the etiquette of the court were governed were borrowed in some degree from the ceremonial observed by earlier dynasties, especially by the Seldjukides and Khahrezmians. From the latter was taken the rank of Beglerbeghi or Emir ul Umera, which answers to our generalissimo, and whose distinctive insignia consisted of a large red flag ; that of the Tümen Agasi being a *Tuk*, i.e., a long lance with a horse's tail at the end, and that of the Yüzbashi the kettledrums slung to the saddles of their out-

---

[1] Arabshah especially unjustly accuses him of valuing the *Yasao Djenghiz* more highly than the Koran. The Islamite institutions were from the beginning calculated for a hierarchy rather than for a military government, and could therefore for his purposes scarcely have competed with the Mongolian code of laws.

riders.[1] The political officials were admonished as to the duties of acting with justice and consideration to the inhabitants and protecting the interests of trade; the military authorities were required to attend diligently to the well-being of their soldiers. Every cavalry soldier was to be provided with two good horses, a bow and well-filled quiver, a sword, a saw, a battle-axe, thread, and ten sewing needles, and in camp a tent was assigned to every eighteen men. Every officer was expected to be acquainted with certain fundamental rules of military tactics, and this is up to the present day a postulate of the education of an Özbeg Spahi or a Turkoman Sirdar;[2] the common soldier was under strict discipline; he was expected to be dashing and impetuous in battle, but to act with gentleness towards the enemy who threw himself on his mercy, and was, in a word, very far from being the grim ogre he was represented as by the enemies of Timour. Judging from the *Tüzükut-i-Timour*, the civil administration of the country was no less perfectly organised. At the head of it stood the Divan-beghi (Lord High Chancellor), assisted by the Arz-beghi (Lord Chamberlain), and four vizirs, the first of whom attended to everything relating to taxes, customs' duties, and police; the second to the pay and provisioning of the troops; the third to the registers and statistics of the army and all matters relating to inheritance; the fourth to the expenses of the Imperial Court. The higher officials were enjoined to carry out the laws and collect the taxes with all possible leniency; the custom of flogging is even supposed to have been expressly forbidden, for Timour says : ' The governor, who is less respected than the whip he makes use of, is unworthy of governing at all.'

[1] This fashion still flourishes. No Özbeg of high rank appears in the field or on parade otherwise than preceded by his outrider with a flourish of his kettle-drums.

[2] Before the young nomad receives a tent of his own—or, in other words, is declared of age—he is usually called on to appear before an assembly of notables, and there, either in a catechism in the form of questions and answers or in a set speech, to explain existing opinions generally prevailing on the subjects of religion, morals, cattle breeding, and chivalry.

The work of the reorganisation of Transoxania after more than a century of anarchy was no slight one ; the changes could only be gradually brought about, but, nevertheless, Timour, from the beginning, yielded to his thirst for conquest and aimed at extending his frontiers as well as at consolidating the internal affairs of his empire. He was of course obliged in the first instance to protect himself from the most formidable of his enemies, the Djetes, whose influence was not extinguished in their old home and who might fairly be presumed to be meditating the re-conquest of Transoxania. Timour himself took the offensive, but on his appearance in 772 (1370) the Djetes submitted of their own accord, and he returned to Samarkand. Soon after, however, Kebek Timour, the new governor, rebelled, and although an army sent off from Samarkand soon quelled the rising, Timour, not satisfied with his general's proceedings, entered on a fresh campaign against his old enemies, penetrated into their country, plundering and burning right and left, and finally returned home laden with spoils and carrying with him a large number of prisoners.

At the expiration of four years Kamareddin, the Prince of the Djetes, again gathered a large army together in the neighbourhood of Köktepe, and brought Timour with an unusually large body of troops into the field against him. The Djetes had the worst of it ; Kamareddin fled for his life, but his treasures and his harem, with his beautiful daughter Dilshad Agha, fell into the hands of the conqueror. Although Timour took the latter as one of his lawful wives, hoping to subdue his enemy to himself by the ties of relationship, he could not succeed in his ultimate object, i.e., the incorporation of this eastern portion of the former empire of the Tchaghataides, until after a fifth campaign, in which Kamareddin was completely defeated and forced to fly the country for ever. This occurred towards the end of the year 778 (1376).

Whilst all this was going on, the attention of our hero was also claimed in another direction, at Khahrezm, where Timour pursued a directly aggressive policy, and wantonly provoked a war. He falsely[1] asserted that Ket and Khivuk,[2] and in fact all Khahrezm, had formerly constituted an integral portion of the hereditary dominions of the Tchaghataides, and that their ruler Huseïn Sufi, of the tribe of Kungrat, consequently owed him tribute. He first despatched the *Tavadji*[3] *Alkama* to assert these claims in his name, but Huseïn sent him word that he had won his country *with the sword*, and that it should only be taken from him *by the sword*; on receiving this answer the proud conqueror took up arms, and would have immediately invaded Khahrezm if Sheïkh Djelaleddin of Kesh had not interfered with one more attempt at bringing about an amicable settlement. The good man's mission failed, however, as a former one had done, and Timour marched on Khahrezm in the spring of the year 773 (1371) with a large army, having just before his departure received an embassy sent to do him homage in the name of the new ruler of Herat, and to present him, among other costly offerings, with the famous charger *Kungoglan* (brown fellow), whose praises have been celebrated by oriental authors. His route lay by Bokhara and across the desert by Ket (in the neighbourhood of Hezaresp), which was taken after a severe siege; on to Khahrezm, the abode of Huseïn Sufi, and in spite of the defection of Keïkhosru of Khatlan, the place was taken after a battle in the open, in which the Khahrezmians were beaten. Huseïn died during the siege; his brother Yusuf Sufi made peace, and seemed enchanted, when Timour, by way of cementing the alliance, demanded the hand of

---

[1] I say *falsely* because Timour's biographer and also Weil (in his *History of the Khalifate in Egypt*, vol. ii. p. 23) are both in error in affirming that Khahrezm belonged to the hereditary dominions of the Tchaghataides. The khanate of Khiva, during the time of the Mongolians, was an integral portion of the empire of Djüdji.

[2] *Khiva* was in olden times called Khivuk, a word of Turkish origin, unknown in the time of the Seldjukides.

[3] *Tavadji*, originally *tapadji* (not *tevedji*, as Hammer and others have read it), was the designation of the official charged with all matters relating to recruiting and raising (or *finding*) troops. It is derived from the Turkish verb *tapmak—to find*.

Yusuf's niece, the beautiful Princess *Sevin*[1] for his son Djihanghir. Yusuf joyfully consented, and Timour was able to turn his face homewards, well satisfied with the results obtained. But no sooner was his back turned, than Yusuf, encouraged by the traitor Keïkhosru, not only refused to carry out his promise concerning the marriage, but took up arms against Timour and thus forced him to a second campaign in 774 (1372), in which he was again successful, and the result of which was that the Princess was at last bestowed on his son, bringing with her a magnificent dowry. The festivities on the occasion of the wedding at Samarkand were splendid, but Prince Djihanghir only survived two years, and the peace itself lasted scarcely longer. Timour had to undertake a third and then a fourth campaign against Khahrezm. During the last of these, Yusuf conceived the extraordinary notion that instead of the bloody encounters of the two armies, he and Timour should meet in single combat. He wrote to his opponent as follows : 'How much longer is the whole world to be plunged in pain and misery for the sake of two individuals ? The good of humanity and the welfare of their respective countries demand that these two men should meet face to face alone, and take their chance as to the question :

> ' Whose sword-hilt shall with blood be stained ?
> Fortune's favour who shall have gained ? '

Timour was enchanted with the proposal, and in spite of the remonstrances of Seïfeddin Berlas[2] against thus exposing his precious life, was the first at the *rendezvous*, and called on his opponent with a loud voice to come forward. But no Yusuf Sefi appeared ; timidity and alarm caused him to regret his proposal, he preferred a pitched battle, in which he was beaten, and he died in the fortress of Khahrezm in the year 781 (1379), at the very time the siege laid to the place by Timour

---

[1] The modern pronunciation is *Süyün*—the word signifies *the charming* or *beautiful one.*

[2] Timour forgot himself so far as grossly to insult the aged Seïfeddin Berlas, reproaching him with daring to tempt him to cowardice.

was going on. Enormous treasures fell into the hands of the conqueror, and were taken by him to Kesh, whither he also carried away with him many artificers and clever craftsmen, as well as many men of learning. He built a palace there in commemoration of his victories, and spent the winter in his native city, resting from his labours and giving himself up to relaxation and amusement.

Although his rivalry with his brother-in-law Emir Huseïn, and the expulsion of the Djete on his north-eastern frontier had taxed Timour's energy and perseverance in the highest degree, the overthrow of his enemies in western Khahrezm proved a still more onerous task, as the two sufis, in addition to their own considerable resources, could rely for support on the khans of Kiptchak, especially on the rulers of '*the golden Horde*,' as the empire of Djüdji is usually termed. The chiefs of Khahrezm and Seray had long been secretly allied against Timour, and the fall of the former was the sure precursor of the ruin of the latter. Timour, on his victorious return from Khahrezm, finding the whole of central Asia united under his sceptre, could not fail to come to the conclusion that the countries bordering on the Oxus and Yaxartes offered, after all, but a narrow field for his ambition, and, that he might now easily follow in the footsteps of Djenghiz, whom he had long taken as his model as a warrior. Guided by the fortunate star of his career so far, the successful subduer of all Turan might well aspire to the *rôle* of a conqueror of the world. Even if the fame of his military glory had not raised up against him, beforehand, maligners and enemies, he was never at a loss for a cause to justify his aggressions, and according to his biographer, he was fond of quoting the poet's words : 'As there is but one God, so there should be but one sovereign ! What is the whole world in comparison to the ambition of a great prince ? ' Nevertheless, in his own memoirs, we find the following passage : 'In every country where tyranny and oppression have got the upper hand, it becomes the duty of every prince whatsoever, in the interests of public peace and security, to root out the authors of the troubles and to attack that country. Every victorious prince is bound to deliver all peoples from their oppressors, and this is the point of view which induced me to undertake the conquest of Khorasan, and to purge the kingdoms of Fars, Irak, and Sham (Damascus) of their disorders.' In sustaining the part of a world-conqueror, Timour could rely, not only on his own undeniable military talents, and other personal advantages, but also on a well-drilled, enduring, and blindly-devoted army led by the most able generals. The soldiers marching under his banners were, for the most part, the same men who had been his companions and comrades in arms during all the varying fortunes and the perilous adventures of his earlier career and their officers, such as Djihanghir Berlas, Seïfeddin Berlas, Akbugha, Osman Abbas, Mohammed Sultan Shah, Kumari, Taban Bahadur, Urus Bugha, Pir Huseïn Berlas, Hamza, son of Emir Musa, Mehemmed Kazgan, Sarik Etke, and Mozaffar Utchkara—men who had given proofs of their military capacity, either at his side or arrayed against him. But the two circumstances most favourable to his ends were: first, the state of anarchy Asia was plunged in; and secondly, the strong warlike spirit reigning in Turkestan. The last traces of national unity had disappeared with the fall of the Mongolian power; the whole country was split up into a multitude of oligarchies, which, so far from assisting each other fought amongst themselves with the utmost bitterness. In this state of affairs, a strong hand like Timour's, supported by a bold spirit, and favoured by fortune, might well hope to found an empire which should stretch from the Irtish to the Ganges, from the deserts of Gobi to the Sea of Marmora.

We have dwelt fully on Timour's deeds in his own native country, as bearing more immediately on our subject, but his foreign campaigns may be more briefly discussed, although they would, indeed, well deserve a detailed description, as forming the most glorious epoch in the history of Transoxania;

the narrow compass of our work bids us content ourselves, however, with simply enumerating the net results, omitting the various incidents of each, especially as the latter are almost all to be found in works which have already long been made accessible to the European public.[1]

Timour's first conquest beyond the frontiers of Central Asia was in the north, in the dominions of the successors of Djüdji, who may be said to have brought the sword of the invader on themselves by the blind fury with which they prosecuted their own internal wars. Tokhtamish,[2] driven from the throne of his fathers by the redoubtable Urus Khan, had applied to Timour for protection, in the year 777 (1375), while the latter was engaged in fighting the Djetes. The troubles of his neighbours exactly suited Timour's purposes ; he received Tokhtamish most graciously, took him to Samarkand, loaded him with presents, and made over to him Otrar and Sabran, two provinces of Modern Turkestan, which placed him in a position to defend himself against his rival, whose eldest son Tokhta Kaya had been sent with an army in pursuit of him. Fortune did not, however, favour Tokhtamish. After two unsuccessful attempts he was beaten, and fled a third time to Timour, wounded and half naked ; the

---

[1] The following may be mentioned amongst the biographies of Timour within reach of European readers:—1st. The French translation of Sherefeddin Ali Yezdi's Persian book, which, although the work of an obvious panegyrist of the Tartar conqueror, contains the most detailed account of his life and actions. Petis de la Croix, the French translator, published his translation, which is unhappily but slovenly, in the year 1772. 2ndly. The English translation of Mirkhond's version of the *Life of Timour*, published in the year 1821, by Major David Price, in his *Mohammedan History*. Mirkhond's work, is however, nothing more than a reproduction of Sherefeddin's. 3rdly. Hammer in his *History of the Ottoman Empire*. 4thly. Malcolm in his *History of Persia*. 5thly. Weil in the second volume of his *Khalifate of the Abbasides in Egypt* ; and 6thly and lastly, d'Herbelot in his *Bibliothèque orientale*.

[2] Not *Toktamisch* as many of my predecessors, following the erroneous Arabic Persian transcription, have spelt it. *Tokhtamish* is modern Tchaghatai in place of the ancient *mengkü*, and signifies the *immortal*, the *immovable*, the 'undying one.' Amongst my travelling companions in Central Asia was a Hadji of Khokand, who, from purely religious feeling had his son Tokhta rebaptized by the Arabic name Baki باقی in the middle of our journey.

latter thought that in the discharge of the sacred duties of hospitality he could now do no less than put himself at the head of an army and declare war against Urus Khan. But this campaign was also doomed to be unsuccessful. The cold and wet weather in the inhospitable desert made a battle impossible, and the two armies lay for months opposite each other in enforced idleness; however, when in the following spring, 778 (1376), Timour once more determined on action in the cause of his protégé, circumstances favoured him, for just at that time Urus Khan and his son Tokhta Kaya both died, and the only rival left to oppose Tokhtamish was Timour Melik, Urus's younger son. It was manifestly impossible for him to maintain himself single-handed against the united armies ; he was defeated by Timour in the neighbourhood of Karatal, taken prisoner, and beheaded. Tokhtamish, thoroughly reinstated in his former position, pursued his victorious career until he had got possession of the entire khanate of Kiptchak, and having subdued Mamaï pushed forward to the interior of Russia and reduced Moscow itself to ashes in the year 786 (1384). Intoxicated by his successes he soon forgot the gratitude due to his protector. He wanted to play the part of a world-conqueror too, and in the year 789 (1387) invaded the western coasts of the Caspian Sea to attack Timour, who was at that moment occupying Azerbaidjan.[1] Miranshah, son of the latter, hurried over the Kur to meet him ; Tokhtamish's advanced guard was repulsed, and, as Tokhtamish himself hereupon retired precipitately, Timour for the moment treated the whole matter lightly and agreed to make peace in accordance with the precept of the Koran : ' Disputes are slumbering, the curse of God rests on those who awaken them.' But all this was done merely to enable

[1] Hammer-Purgstall, in his *Geschichte der Goldenen Horde*, p. 340, suggests that the primary cause of the enmity between Tokhtamish and Timour was the execution of .Sultan Huseïn, the grandson of Emir *Kazghan* (not *Asghan*), a prince of the house of Tchaghatai. Hammer and his authority, Djenabi, both forget that Emir Kazghan was not a Tchaghataide at all, but a Turk, and an enemy of the Mongols.

him to watch a better opportunity for venting his just displeasure, and this opportunity he found two years later. In
the winter of 791 (1389), in a snow so deep as to cover the
flanks of the horses, Timour marched out of Samarkand to
meet Tokhtamish, who had invaded his northern frontier,
and routed him utterly on the banks of the Yaxartes ; he
inflicted a second defeat on him in the following spring, on
the further bank of the same river; but still his thirst for
vengeance would not let him rest, so that in the winter of
793 (1391) he once more set out at the head of a large and
perfectly-equipped army, to attack Tokhtamish in his own
dominions. During six weeks the horses were exhausted by
marches and counter-marches across the inhospitable steppes
of Southern Siberia, and this passage of an army over a perfectly flat country may compare for hardships and fatigues
with the most celebrated marches across high mountains.[1]
The exhausted and starving soldiers scoured the country in
search of the enemy until at length they came on him in the
month of May, on the green banks of the Yaik (Ural). A
brilliant series of cavalry encounters ensued. Both armies
fought bravely for three days, both displayed prodigies of
valour, till at length Tokhtamish, betrayed by his own relations, was defeated and forced to fly for his life. Timour
followed in rapid pursuit to the interior of Russia, he is even
said to have advanced as far as Moscow, whose inhabitants,
as Gibbon truly remarks, would probably have found the
protection of a miraculous image of a holy Virgin insufficient, had not prudence and foresight enjoined moderation on
the Transoxanian hero. He returned home to his capital
after an eleven months' campaign, carrying back with him not
only an enormous array of prisoners (including the family and

---

[1] His army had to encounter, not only a climate of extraordinary severity, but
hunger and other privations besides. The daily ration of the soldiers was reduced
to a cup of pea soup (Bulamadj), and the march had at last to be suspended, and a
hunting expedition organised on a gigantic scale, the results of which were sufficient
in some degree to allay the pangs of hunger and so allow the march to be
resumed.

harem of his opponent), and all the treasures and precious jewels of the north, but also the proud consciousness of having now united under his own sceptre two of the principal portions of the former empire of Djenghiz. The third portion, consisting of Iran, Arabistan, and a part of India, was alone wanting ; and feeling now pretty secure in the north the time seemed come to devote his attention more exclusively to the west.

Timour had indeed commenced the conquest of the Persian-speaking countries (as we may term Khorasan and Iran) long before the total subjugation of Tokhtamish Khan. As early as the year 782 (1380), he had sent his son Miranshah Mirza, accompanied by some of his ablest commanders, to occupy Khorasan, and had himself followed shortly afterwards along the road opened up to him by his valiant son. The great conqueror had here to confront two separate dynasties. The north was under the rule of the Serbedars ; [1] some amicable relations had already existed between them and Timour in the days of his adversity, and they now submitted without resistance to his authority ; but the south was governed by the family of Kert (mentioned above), the same against whom Timour had fought while still comparatively a youth, and here his progress was not so satisfactory, for Gayas-eddin Pir Ali, the head of the family, preferred trusting to his own sword rather than to the magnanimity of the Tartar conqueror. He therefore set to work energetically to defend his dominions, which extended from the Paropamisian moun-

[1] The dynasty of the Serbedars, who, on the fall of the Mongols, got possession of the government of north-eastern Khorasan, came from Irak and traced their descent from a certain Shehabeddin, who reckoned amongst his paternal ancestors Imam Husein and amongst his maternal ones Khalid, the Barmekide. Shehabeddin had five sons, Emireddin, Abdurrezak, Vasieteddin, Nasireddin, and Shemseddin. The Serbedars' rule only flourished in Khorasan for about thirty-five years, but during that time the following members of the family attained to special eminence : 1. Abdurrezak, reigned one year and two months ; 2. Mes'ud, reigned seven years ; 3. Shemseddin, Togan Timour ; 5. Kassab Haidar ; 6. Yahya Kerati ; 7. Hasan Damghani ; and lastly, Ali Mueyyed Abdurrezak, who submitted of his own accord to Timour.

tains in the east, and the Murghab in the north, to the desert
country about Shahrud ; but all his efforts were merely a
fruitless struggle against destruction.   His capital, Herat, fell
after an obstinate resistance, and the other towns, such as
Kabushan, Tuz, Nishabur, and Sebzevar, all celebrated seats
of science and art, opened their gates to the invaders, for they
preferred being converted into garrison towns of Timour's
army to being reduced to heaps of ruins ; and the conqueror,
having in addition to Khorasan, got possession of Afghanistan, Sistan, and Beloochistan, found himself at liberty in the
year 788 (1386) to continue his march on Arabia and Persia
Proper.   .

Two separate dynasties were then reigning in the above-
mentioned districts of Iran.   The southern division, Fars
with Isfahan, was occupied by the Mozafferides, whilst Irak
Arabi and Azerbaidjan were in the hands of the Ilkhanis.
Shah Shedja, head of the first-named family, was wise enough
to avoid encountering the well-seasoned Transoxanian soldiers
with the effeminate children of his southern dominions ; he
submitted of his own accord, and the bonds of peace were
drawn tighter by an alliance concluded between his daughter
and Prince Pir Mohammed, the son of the deceased Djihanghir Mirza.   Sultan Ahmed, son of Sheïkh Oveïs Djelair, did
not, however, take the same view ; he believed his mounted .
Kurds and the warriors of Azerbaidjan equal to withstand
the onslaught of Timour's legions, and accepted the chances
of war, but experienced, from the very beginning, disasters
which compelled him to abandon his strongly-fortified capital
Sultanie, and retire on Bagdad, whilst his victorious enemy
crossed the Araxes triumphantly, brought all Transcaucasia
to his feet at a single blow, and entered the towns of Nakht-
chivan, Erivan, Tiflis and Shirvan as conqueror.   Gilan,
which, in consequence of its deep morasses and dense primeval
forests had hitherto been deemed impregnable, was forced to
do homage, and the Prince of Armenia, Tahirten, on the fall
of his celebrated fortress Van, was only too thankful to be

allowed to exist as a vassal of the redoubtable Emperor of the far East.

During this campaign the only sufferers from the wrath of the Tartar conqueror, were the dynasty of Karakoyunlu (black sheep), and the rebellious town of Isfahan. The former lost their two strongest fortresses, Akhlat and Adil Djuvaz; the latter saw 70,000 of her inhabitants sacrificed for having killed 3,000 of Timour's soldiers in a treacherous attack.[1] It was a horrible butchery, and filled the son of Shah Shedja, Zin ul Abidin, with such terror that he abandoned the intention he had formed of throwing off the yoke accepted by his father; and Timour, having received the solemn homage of the Mozafferides at Shiraz, returned, in the year 791 (1389), home in triumph to Samarkand, where, as usual, he sought relaxation and rest from his fatigues, and renewed strength for fresh labours in a series of festivities, hunting parties, and orgies. The campaign against Tokhtamish, which we have already detailed, then intervened, but on his return from it he undertook the so-called 'five years war' in the west, for the purpose of putting down the disturbances which had meanwhile broken out there, or rather in fact to reap, by the complete subjugation of Iran and Arabia, all the legitimate fruits of his former campaign. In the year 794 (1392), having just recovered from a short illness, he crossed the Oxus at Amuye at the head of a numerous and well-drilled army, and proceeded along the northern border of Iran to Astrabad, in order to chastise the rebellious Mazendran. Amul, the principal place in the Iranian highlands, and the seat of those wild fanatics, the Assassins or Fedayis,[2] was only reduced after severe fighting, and its bold defenders suffered for their resistance so horrible a massacre that even

---

[1] In this case, it was again a young blacksmith who, like Kaveh of old, excited the citizens of Isfahan to rise and attack the unsuspicious garrison. The consequence was that a pyramid was piled up of 70,000 heads of the inhabitants of Isfahan as a monument of the revenge wreaked on them.

[2] The members of a secret conspiracy are to this day called Fedayis. *Feda* is Arabic for *Sacrifice*, and *Fedai* for *one who sacrifices himself*—a martyr.

the pen of an Oriental historian recoils from describing it. That the silence of death should have fallen on the place after such a visitation is only too easily explained. Timour carried his blood-stained arms on against Luristan and Kuzistan, overran Hamadan, Burudjird and Dizful, and, having reduced the proud mountain fastness Kale-i-Sefid, attacked the Mozafferide Shah Mansur with his accustomed violence. The latter, who had succeeded during Timour's absence in uniting the five principalities of the Mozafferides under his own sceptre, was able to oppose a considerable force to him, but nothing could withstand the Tartar, flushed with victory. A fierce battle took place at Patila in which Shah Mansur charged at the head of his cavalry with the impetuosity of a lion, fell on the serried ranks of the Turkestani's, and breaking through every obstacle rushed on Timour's own person. The latter, surrounded merely by a staff of some fourteen or fifteen individuals, was in a position of the greatest peril,[1] but his grandson Prince Shahrukh Mirza rapidly rallied round him some of his retreating soldiery, threw himself across the enemy's path, cut off Shah Mansur's head in single combat, and laid it at his grandfather's feet with the usual salutation, ' So may the heads of all thine enemies be trampled by thy horse's hoofs.' The enemy was entirely defeated and the dynasty of the Mozafferides completely annihilated with the exception of two princes who had been blinded before and who were carried to Samarkand. Timour took possession of the treasures of Shah Mansur, distributed the conquered provinces among his generals, and then, in the year 795 (1393), continued his progress to subdue once more the Arabian portion of Irak. The Ilkanide Ahmed Djelair was unable a second time to avoid destruction. Having retaken Azerbaidjan and subdued Kurdistan, Timour crossed the Tigris

---

[1] Sherefeddin relates that Shah Mansur had got close up to Timour and made two thrusts with his sword at the emperor's helmet. Timour, on seeing this rush made on him, tried to defend himself, but his lance-bearer was out of the way, and it was owing to the shield-bearer Adil Aktash and the body-guardsman Kumari alone, that he escaped without any serious wound.

in the Sultan's own galley. Bagdad submitted without striking a blow, and her fugitive sovereign owed his escape from the tragic plain of Kerbela solely to the lightning swiftness of his Arab courser, but his wives and his son fell into the hands of the conqueror. The proud seat of the khalifate thus fell for the third time into the hands of the Tartar conqueror after a comparatively slight struggle, and although the other strong places of Mesopotamia—Mardin, Diarbekir, and Tekrit—offered more resistance, his victorious banners were carried in triumph through all Armenia and Georgia. But the sounds of rejoicing over these successes had scarcely ceased to echo through the lovely valley of Ming Göl (thousand lakes), when news arrived that Tokhtamish, who had been crushed years before, was rising up like a new Antæus and threatening an invasion of Caucasia, in the neighbourhood of Derbend. The flowing bowls had to be once more relinquished for the blood-stained sword ; Timour, however, waited quietly for his enemy to advance and commence the attack, remarking that 'it is better for the game to run itself into the net than to have to go after it. An old fowl does not fear the bird of prey, and if the grasshopper is but big enough to get his wings stained with red, he can shake off the attacks of the sparrow, blow for blow.' The flag of Timour was as successful on the western as it had already been on the eastern shores of the Caspian sea ; Tokhtamish was beaten, and fled to the deserts of southern Siberia ; his opponent followed in pursuit far into Russia, plundered Moscow, and then, leaving Kowurdjuk, son of Urus Khan, to govern the country as his vassal, returned to Georgia to add another to the list of triumphs he was there celebrating.

Thus the former adventurer from the steppes of Turkestan had gradually obtained possession of Northern and Western Asia ; his diadem was adorned by many a country, rich, beautiful, and of classical celebrity ; his rough warriors from the banks of the Issikköl, the Oxus, and the Yaxartes, and the bold horsemen of the vast deserts had carried off to

Samarkand all the portable treasures and jewels of Western
Asia ; embassies from far and wide came to do homage and
lay costly offerings at the feet of the world-conqueror, and yet
Timour's ambition was not satisfied, his thirst for war was not
assuaged. He returned home in the year 799 (1396), after an
absence of five years. His reception was magnificent : his
wives, daughters, and grand-daughters, surrounded by a glittering suite, welcomed him on the banks of the Oxus ; according
to the national custom,[1] gold and precious stones were showered
upon him, and an offering of a thousand richly-caparisoned
horses and mules presented to him. He recited his thanks-
giving *fatiha* over the grave of his father at Kesh, visited the
works carried out there in his absence, and finally made his
entry into Samarkand with extraordinary pomp. In addition
to the beautiful bride he had won on the field of battle, the
old warrior, now upwards of sixty-three years, had taken to
himself a young wife, Princess Tökel Khanum, to whom he
gave the charming summer palace of *Dilkusha* (opener of
hearts). A certain period was now to be devoted to feasting
and rejoicing, but the turmoil of pleasure seemed only to
awaken again in Timour a longing for the excitement of real
war, for, having during his stay in his capital partitioned out
his new conquests amongst his sons, he once more mounted
his war-horse to lead his troops to still more distant regions.
India in the south and Rum in the extreme west were still
wanting to justify entirely his pretensions to the title of
' Conqueror of the world ' (Djihanghir). To the Mohammedan
Asiatic the former country has always been the symbol of
untold riches, the latter, of great power ; and how was it possible, under these circumstances, for Timour to rest contented
until he had added them to the long list of his conquests?
His first object was to get possession of the peninsular region
enclosed between the Indus and the Ganges. His grandson,

[1] Slight traces of this custom survive to this day amongst the Osmanlis. Silver
coins are scattered before the Sultan in the procession at the celebration of the
feast of Bairam, and the bridegroom on first entering the bride's chamber must
also scatter gold and silver money before the bride as she advances to meet him.

Pir Mohammed, had preceded him some time before along
the Herat road and had laid siege to Mooltan. Timour was
determined that the march itself under his own leadership
should be splendid and imposing. He advanced by Belkh
across the snowy heights of the Hindookush. After braving
the icy winds of those regions, he had to plunge into the heat
of battle with the bold mountaineers, but nothing could shake
the resolution of the conqueror. He and his troops let themselves with ropes down the face of the steep precipices, their
opponents were panic-stricken, and Timour penetrated by
Kabul into India, through the identical pass in which, 440
years later, the army of a great European power was defeated
by the descendants of these very men. The Indus was
crossed in the first days of the ninth century of the Hidjra,
and having been joined by his son on the banks of the Sutlej,
he advanced on Delhi, the residence of Sultan Mahmud.
Finding himself hampered in his rapid progress by the enormous number of prisoners, he caused a hundred thousand of
these unhappy creatures to be massacred. It was a cruel
order, and every individual in the army was called on to take
part in its execution; the historian describes the horror and
repugnance of the gentle scholar, Nasireddin, at having to
strangle fifteen of his Indian slaves. Timour, in order to
delude his enemy into taking the offensive, began by playing
the part of moderation and irresolution; this strategy succeeded, the Indians fell into the trap laid for them, were
completely beaten, and Delhj, the rich commercial city on the
Indus, with all its treasures, and its inhabitants versed in various
curious arts, fell into the hands of the Tartar conqueror. A
similar fate overtook the holy city of Metra, the unhappy
worshippers of Vishnu were seized with the wildest panic, but
nothing could save them. Their holiest pagodas were destroyed and their idols broken in pieces. Timour advanced
to the sources of the Ganges, murdering and destroying everything in his path; after this merciless sacrifice of human life
he further regaled himself by hunting tigers, panthers, and

rhinoceroses, and finally returned home to Samarkand in the month of April, 1399 (801), with a quantity of elephants, Indian artificers, and prisoners of all kinds.

Timour's expedition to India, like the earlier òne of his Mongolian predecessor and the later one of Nadir, was nothing more than a brilliant feat of arms, without ulterior objects, and a raid on treasures; it was reserved for the genial Baber Mirza a century later definitively to plant the standard of the Timourides on the banks of the Indus and the Ganges. The splendour of even this temporary success increased, however, the brilliancy of Timour's reputation, and his boundless ambition drove him on to measure himself with the Prince of the mighty West (Rum).

His absence from the scene of his former achievements in the west had been short; but, nevertheless, the edifice of power raised there in the flush of victory had already received some rude shocks. The profligate government of his son Miranshah[1] had given occasion to just remonstrances and rebellion at Azerbaidjan; the death of a great vassal and neighbour tempted him to further annexation on the frontiers of the already unwieldy empire; and in consequence of all this he allowed himself but a short period of rest in his capital before again taking the field against Western Asia. He spared his guilty son, but put his counsellors and favourites to death, and then hurried by Herat and Kazvin towards the Araxes to settle accounts with Melik Gurgin, the rebellious Prince of Georgia. The latter had sought refuge amongst inaccessible rocks and in fortresses, but all in vain: his army was driven back at all points, his fortresses and his capital Tiflis were taken, and Timour, after a short but severe campaign, was able once more to pitch his camp in the lovely valley of

---

[1] Clavijo relates that Miranshah once caused several houses, mosques, and other fine buildings to be pulled down, in order, as he said, 'as the son of the greatest man in the world, to be famous for *something*; to be at least remembered as having *destroyed* this or that.' This Tartar Herostratus probably suffered from *delirium tremens*; his biographers, however, try to make out that he lost his senses in consequence of a fall from his horse.

Karabeg.   The hardy soldiers from the steppes of Turkestan
deserved some rest after their arduous exertions, and it was
all the more needed as their great leader had now determined
to attack his Turkish brother sovereign Bayezid, Sultan of the
Osmans ; the power of this heir of the dominion of Rum was
a thorn in Timour's side, and in addition to this Bayezid had
allied himself with the Turkoman dynasty of the Karakoyunlus,
against whom Timour's wrath was the more violent, because,
as autocrat of all Turkish tribes, he believed himself especially
entitled to claim allegiance from these former vassals of the
Seldjukides.[1]

A horrible and savage war ensued between the Turkish
rulers of Eastern and Western Asia, a war of which both
Christian and Mohammedan historians have left us terrible
and sickening details,[2] but which in its results was favourable
to the Tartar conqueror. Timour then proceeded to call
Ferrudj, Sultan of Egypt, to account for his father's crime
in having caused the murder of Timour's envoy, the learned
scholar, Sheïkh Save ; the son had fearfully to expiate the
father's deed, for Syria was overrun by the Tartars, and
her most flourishing cities sacked and destroyed.   Having by
his successes in Syria destroyed all possibility of an alliance
between the Osmanlis and the Arabs, Timour turned against
Bayezid, who was scarcely inferior to himself in power and
reputation, and who, presuming on this equality and de-
spising his adversary, was deaf to all suggestions regarding an
amicable settlement.   Timour was not exactly a person to require much provocation in accepting a quarrel ; he proceeded in
the spring of 805 (1402) from Sivas by Karashehr to Engürü

[1] Not only in Timour's time but even to the present day the Turk in the
furthest East claims relationship with his brethren in the extreme West.   The
simplest Turkoman is aware of the existence of kinsmen about Diarbekir ; and in
the East traditions and legends are far more powerful and enduring than Clio's
fables.

[2] Amongst the crimes recorded are those at the taking of Sivas ; according to
Ducas and Chalcondylas, Timour ordered the Christian knights in the service of
Bayezid, who were among his prisoners, to be thrown in batches of ten into open
pits and buried alive ; and at the same time had the Mohammedan population of
the town beheaded wholesale, though quarter had been promised them.

(Angora), on the plains of which a bloody battle ensued between the two armies; the Osmanlis were totally defeated, Sultan Bayezid and his whole harem were taken prisoners. This splendid and decisive victory gave Timour possession of all Asia Minor, and he advanced as far as Smyrna; but for the sea, he might have descended on Europe itself; however, his plans in the far East would not allow of a longer stay in the west, so after his hordes had well scoured the conquered country and plundered and devastated everything, he turned homewards and made his *ninth* triumphal entry into Samarkand in the year 807 (1404). As usual there followed a succession of feasts, weddings, orgies, and debauches, which were attended not only by envoys from all the countries of Asia, but also by the ambassador of the Most Christian European King, the Knight Don Ruy Gonzalez de Clavijo, sent by Henry III., King of Spain, on a mission of friendship to Timour.

We shall see in the next chapter that the Tartars were as strong in their convivial powers as in their military capacity. Anybody seeing Timour presiding at these festivities, surrounded by his brilliant court, would have found it difficult to believe that he was indeed the turbulent warrior he had proved himself; and yet, even in his old age, his brief holidays were spent in elaborating places for further conquests, and making preparations for earning further laurels. At the public audience of the different embassies, Timour had shown marked coolness to the Chinese ambassador, and it is very probable that the glorious conqueror of half Asia could not conceal his indignation on being called on to pay his yearly tribute by the representative of the ruler of Kambalu. His wounded pride would not let him rest; war was determined on, and the aged soldier set off with a small but well equipped army, in the depth of winter, to attack the 'celestial flowery empire.' He left Samarkand on January 4, 1405 (807), already suffering from a cold caused by the severe weather, but he paid no attention to it, crossed the frozen Yaxartes, and pitched his camp, in the month of February, at Otrar. Here he became so much worse that his physician, Mevlana Fazlullah, soon pronounced his state hopeless, and Timour, who had faced death a hundred times, remained in his last moments true to his heroic nature.

The children, grandchildren, and old companions standing around his bed wept bitterly at the approaching departure of their chief, but he himself bid them be of good courage, exhorted them to unity amongst themselves and to obedience towards Pir Mohammed, whom he had designated as his successor. He was asked whether he would not desire Mirza Khalil Sultan and other great dignitaries to be sent for, but he declined, saying he had but a few minutes to live, and expressing his regret that he could not see once more his favourite child Shahrukh Mirza. His strength gave way rapidly; he made signs to desire the mollah Heibetullah to perform the rites of the dying and to read the Koran over his bed, and expired in the early evening of the 7th Sha'ban, 807 (February 17, 1405). His body was brought to Samarkand and buried in the same magnificent mausoleum he had erected for his beloved spiritual teacher, Seïd Berke. It was Seïd Berke who first, in his early youth, had predicted his future greatness, and now the two rest side by side in the same vault.[1] Timour was seventy-one years old when he died. During more than half that period he had been absolute sovereign of Transoxania and had made himself lord of the whole of the Mohammedan East. He may fitly be compared for ambition, military talent, and indomitable will, with a Cæsar, an Alexander, a Djenghiz, or a Napoleon ; the furious bloodshed which characterised his wars, however, created horror even amongst his Asiatic contemporaries, and his Arab biographer, Ahmed bin Arabshah, though an inveterate enemy of the Tartar conqueror, might yet plead some justification for the speech he puts into the mouth of the Spirit of Winter, whom he describes as arresting the veteran warrior

---

[1] For a description of this building, now called *Turbeti Timur* (Timour's monument), see my *Travels in Central Asia*, London, 1864, p. 209.

in his progress across the icy plains of Central Asia, with
these words : ' Hold in thy rapid course, thou savage tyrant!
How long wilt thou continue to desolate an unhappy world
with fire and sword l If thou art a spirit of evil, know that I
am one too. We are both old ; we both have one and the
same object, that is, to bring slaves under our yoke. Continue, if thou wilt, to exterminate the human race and make
the world barren and cold, but thou wilt learn at last that my
breath is even colder and more destructive. Thou boastest
thyself of thine innumerable armies which fly to fulfil thy
bidding, and with which thou wilt destroy and lay low all
things, but know that my wintry days, with the aid of the
breath of the Almighty, are still more potent destroyers, and
that in the sight of God ! I will yield to thee in nothing.
Tarry awhile ! vengeance shall overtake thee, and all thy fire
and all thy fury shall not preserve thee from the cold death
borne in on thee by my icy winds.'

Having now taken as detailed an historical survey as the
limits of our work will allow, of Timour's life and actions, we
will endeavour, in the next chapter, to give an imperfect
sketch of his court and capital ; for Timour's government w
evidently the culminating point of the glory of the little
country beyond the Oxus, and shed a radiance over the annals
of the Turkish races, vestiges of which still illuminate to this
day the traditions of many tribes. The countries beyond the
Oxus and Yaxartes ceased at Timour's death to play a part
in universal history, for he was the last general who led
hundreds of thousands of Turko-Tartaric warriors from the
officina Gentium of Central Asia to Western Asia.

O

XI.

TIMOUR'S INDIVIDUALITY—HIS COURT AND CAPITAL.[1]

THE great conqueror from 'the Green city' is described by
his friends as a model of manly beauty, and by his enemies
as an ugly insignificant-looking cripple.   According to
traditions still existing amongst his countrymen, he appears
to have been of middle height, but strongly built, with a robust
frame, which, notwithstanding the wear and tear of a life
spent in almost unbroken warfare, retained its full vigour to
an advanced age.   His figure was erect, and his lameness was
in consequence little perceptible ; his voice was that of a
stentor, and could be heard rising even above the din of battle,
and resounding far beyond his immediate surroundings ; his
eyesight alone failed him, for, when in his seventieth year, he
gave audience to the Spanish envoys at Samarkand, he was
unable to distinguish them till they were brought close up to
him.   Up to that time there had been scarcely any inter-
mingling of the Turkish race with Iranian elements,[2] and
Timour's features were of a purely Mongolian type, so that
his biographer was certainly wrong in taking the ideal of

---

[1] The details given here of Timour's court and capital are chiefly taken from
Clavijo's work, mentioned above ; Mr. Markham, the learned Secretary of the
English Geographical Society, has rendered good service by his translation of this
account from Spanish.   Clavijo was a quick observer and his notes may be
entirely relied on.

[2] In the first place the slave trade with Iran was not as much developed as it
is now, for it was not till fifty years after Timour's death that the purchase of
Shiite Persians was made legal by Mollah Shemseddin's Fetva, and the mixture of
races was consequently rarer.   In the second place the Turks in Transoxania
consorted and intermarried far more readily with their kinsfolk the Mongolians
and Uigurs than with the Tadjiks, who were already branded with the reputation of cowardice.

Iranian beauty for his model in his portrait of his hero, and describing the Tartar conqueror with a long beard, fresh colour, and fair skin, for the only thing about him really Iranian or West-Asiatic was his dress.

The ordinary dress in the Oxus countries at that time was, like their social condition generally, a strange mixture of Buddhist and Islamite habits and customs. We find Timour appearing on state occasions in the same loose, flowing silken robes in which the inhabitants of central Asia parade about to this day, and which were then the fashion throughout Islamite Asia. His head-dress, however, was copied from Chinese or Mongolian fashion, for he did not adopt the Mohammedan turban, as Sherefeddin would gladly have seen, but wore a tall conical beaver hat [1] surmounted by a pear-shaped ruby set with pearls and brilliants. His custom, too, of wearing long earrings was purely Mongolian. Altogether he was by no means averse to ornaments and rich attire, which is the more remarkable, as during his long campaigns he had to endure so many privations, and bore himself under them all as a model of Spartan simplicity. There is a similar inconsistency observable in all the most remarkable points of his character. The strict Islamite and Suffite principles instilled into him by his father and spiritual teachers in early youth, were perpetually at war with the tendencies of his own turbulent nature and boundless ambition.

According to all appearance the latter predominated, for he is said to have declared that 'a government could only be established sword in hand;' [2] still we must find it difficult to condemn as utterly savage and brutal, the man who at the sack of Isfahan commanded his soldiers to spare the quarter inhabited by learned men; the man who entered

---

[1] *Hat* here means really *kulh*—cap, for a *hat* as we understand it, that is with a brim, is strictly forbidden amongst Mohammedans as a mark of Christianity. The head-gear of the modern Kirghiz has a brim, but with a slit in the front, by which the mollahs believe the prohibition to be evaded.

[2] This sentiment is put into his mouth by his Persian biographer in the following sentence :—*Mulkra eger karar khahi kerd tigra, bikarar baved kerd.*

into theological discussions with the philosophers of Herat and Aleppo, and rewarded with princely gifts those who most differed from him; who, when the great scholars Shemseddin Feneri, Mohammed Djezeri, and the celebrated Sheïkh Bokhari were taken prisoners by him at the court of his enemy, spared no efforts to win them over to his cause by presents and flatteries, though knowing full well that they had been amongst his most bitter adversaries; the man, finally, who always considered the artists and clever craftsmen he could enlist in his service as the most valuable of all acquisitions in a conquered country, and who once caused a whole library to be transported on the backs of mules from Broussa to Samarkand.[1]

Those who would rank Timour side by side with a Djenghiz, as a mere savage, wilful tyrant, are doubly in error. He was preeminently an Asiatic soldier who used his victories after the fashion of his time and country; and even the cruelties and the ravages which his enemies denounce most bitterly, were all more or less reprisals—though no doubt unjustifiably severe ones—for some injury suffered. At Isfahan and Shiraz he had to avenge the blood of a soldier basely betrayed; the inhabitants of Damascus, old adherents of Moavia's, had to expiate the martyrdom of the family of Huseïn, whose tragic end had filled Timour with indignation; and how many more so-called massacres, may after all have been painted in too glaring colours by the brush of his enemies, or may have been due to some occurrence of which we are left in total ignorance? It cannot however be denied that Timour committed enormous ravages in Western Asia, and that many remains of the civilisation of Islam which even the destructive spirit of the Mongols had respected, were swept away by the rush of the new Turko-Tartaric hordes over-running the country. The bitterness of Arabshah may thus

---

[1] It is well known that after carrying on furious polemics with the learned Kadi Sherefeddin of Aleppo, he extended his protection to him and his dependents (numbering 2,000 souls), and loaded them with presents.

have had some justification, but if we wish to pass an impartial judgment we must allow that Timour is to be blamed, not as a wanton destroyer, but merely as an arbitrary enforcer of the rights of conquest, by which he violently uprooted and transplanted much that fell into his power. Like almost all the conquerors belonging to Turkish and Arab tribes, he had a strong affection for his own native country, and we cannot wonder at, though we may regret, his evident determination to transplant both the political strength of West Islam and the decaying branches of Islamite civilisation to the rotten soil of the steppes of Turkestan.

It need scarcely be said that Timour's splendid career, animated by such views, had a most important and enduring influence on the whole condition of Central Asia. The courts of Kambalu, Ghaznee, Bokhara, or those of any other former dynasties, had never boasted of such riches or displayed such pomp as his court at Samarkand. Sherefeddin's description of the luxury and extravagance of Timour's feasts and ceremonies is but feeble compared to the glowing colours in which the court of the Tartar Emperor is painted by the good Christian knight, Don Ruy Gonzalez de Clavijo. He had seen much, or rather everything, there ; and the favour with which Timour distinguished him, may be estimated from the fact that at the solemn state audience in which he was received, the Emperor thus proudly addressed the dignitaries standing round him : ' Behold the ambassador sent to me by my son the King of Spain, who lives at the furthest extremity of the earth and is the greatest of all the kings of the Franks. Truly, these Franks are a great nation, and I purpose sending my blessing to my son the King of Spain.'

We may therefore rely on the noble hidalgo as a trustworthy guide to the court of Samarkand, and follow his footsteps in describing the peculiarities, the customs, and the ceremonies prevalent there at that period.

The court of Timour afforded specimens of the different customs and observances of all the various countries and tribes on the ruins of which his throne had been established. The court costume of silken, satin, or velvet robes was borrowed from Arabian or Islamite fashions, but the dress of the ladies of the court in which the *sheökele* (a high head-dress) was prominent, recalled the attire of Khahrezm and ancient Iran. It consisted of a long red silk dress trimmed with gold lace, fitting close to the throat but without sleeves, and falling in loose heavy folds, with a long train which it often took fifteen trainbearers to carry. The face was covered with a veil, and in travelling was powdered with a sort of tin cosmetic to preserve the complexion from dust and exposure. The head was covered by a helmet-shaped hat of red cloth, studded with pearls, rubies and emeralds, finished off with a vandyked trimming round the top, from which depended long drooping white feathers. Some of these feathers drooped over the eyes,[1] and their nodding movement as the wearer walked along was supposed to lend a peculiar charm to the countenance. The numerous ladies of Timour's court were covered with the jewels of half Asia, and the masterpieces of. the jewellers of Mooltan, Isfahan, Ghendje, Damascus, Broussa and Venice, and the men were scarcely less gorgeous with their jewelled swords, rich girdles and studs. The wealth of gold and silver plate was also fabulous. Clavijo describes a large golden casket, which he had seen in a tent, with a flat lid surrounded by miniature towers in blue and green enamel, picked out with different precious stones and pearls. The opening of the casket was in the shape of a door, and within was a shelf with a row of cups, and above the cups hung six golden balls studded with pearls and precious stones.

Close to this casket, there was a table two hands high made of solid gold with a border of jewels, and on the table lay a clear emerald, four hands long (?), which covered the whole top. Opposite the table was a golden tree in the form of an oak, the stem of the thickness of a man's foot, and the branches of

---

[1] Some remains of this fashion may be traced in the modern head-gear, or rather ornament, of respectable Turkoman women.

golden oak-leaves spreading in every direction. In place of fruit this tree was covered with numerous rubies, emeralds, turquoises, sapphires, and marvellous pearls, and on the branches sat birds enamelled in different colours. The princes of the imperial blood were always served on massive silver tureens (kontchas), and the members of the Imperial family amongst themselves drank out of large golden cups ; and if we add that at the great feasts, in which several thousand guests took part, the wine was always poured in golden flagons with gold saucers, we may have some idea of the extraordinary magnificence and wealth of Timour's household and establishment.

Our authority, who visited Timour's court at the very zenith of his glory, cannot find words to describe all the marvels of the festivities celebrated in the camp of the lovely plain of Kanigul,[1] outside Samarkand. Turks have always, from time immemorial, had a preference for the airy habitation of a tent, and have found the opportunity of displaying their wealth and pomp in the luxurious fittings of these portable houses more perfectly than elsewhere ; so it may easily be imagined that Timour, the greatest and most magnificent of all the Turks that ever lived, surpassed all others in the arrangement of his camp. It is only after having seen the really beautiful situation of Timour's capital, that it becomes at all possible to picture to oneself the brilliant effect which must have been presented by a holiday camp within a couple of miles northeast of the town, on the plain watered by innumerable canals and by the Zerefshan. A camp of this description often consisted of some ten or fifteen thousand tents, in which not only the court and the nobility but all classes of the population took up their abode, all the guilds were represented, smart shops were opened, workmen plied their trades, even temporary hot baths were erected. The first tents pitched were

---

[1] Kanigul, and not Chanigaul, as Petis de la Croix writes. Kanigul is a Persian word meaning ' the mine of flowers.'

those for the use of the Imperial family, which were usually
the centre, whence the rest of the camp spread out fan-shaped ;
the other tents were ranged in subordination to this central
group.   Each family, each vizir, each Tümenaghasi knew
exactly his proper place, i.e., if he was to take up his position
to the right or the left, in the first, second, or third row ; there
was not a sign of confusion perceptible, and in a marvellously
short time the beautiful plain of Kanigul, with the many
coloured flags waving on the tops of the tents, shone like a
gay flower-bed gently stirred by the breeze.   As regards the
shape of the tents, the round bell-tents still in use in those
countries seem to have been the commonest ; but the long
Arabian tents of Abraham, and the luxurious Seraperde of Iran
(curtain palaces) were not wanting, and it seems to have been
one of the latter that more especially excited the admiration
of the good Castilian knight.[1]   It was square-shaped, a hundred
feet wide, and about three spears' lengths high.

The centre pavilion had a circular dome-shaped roof,
supported by twelve blue and gold poles of the thickness of a
man's wrist, and the silken coverings of the poles were draped
in the form of an arcade.   Besides these, there were porticoes
on each side of the pavilion, each portico having six columns,
and the whole structure held together by upwards of five
hundred scarlet ropes.   The outer hangings of the tent were
of silk in stripes of black, yellow, and white ; within was a rich
carpet of crimson worked in gold, and other ornaments in
various silks.   The richest embroidery was in the middle of
the side wing ; at the four corners were four large spread-
eagles. The poles at each of the four corners were ornamented
with the ball and crescent, the centre pole having a larger
ball and crescent than the other four, and finally the whole
pavilion, which at a distance looked like a castle, was enclosed
within a high party-coloured wall, ornamented with pinnacles
or little towers.   There were besides other no less gorgeous
tents for the use of the Empress and the first Princesses ;

[1] Clavijo calls this tent *Zalaparda.*

some covered with hangings of yellow or pink silk embroidered in gold and hung within with the most costly brocades. Almost all the entrances were sufficiently lofty to admit a man on horseback ; there were windows, with gauze blinds to draw across when the windows were opened, and silken verandahs to keep off the sun. The most luxurious things about the tents however were then, as now, the carpets used as *portières* and the tent ropes ; the former were covered with curious gold and silver embroideries (one of them, brought by Timour from Broussa, had portraits of the Apostles St. Peter and St. Paul worked on it), the latter were fastened with buckles of massive gold and silver, and ornamented with arabesques in precious stones.

These tents, the description of which reminds one of the Arabian Nights, were the scene of the great feasts and merry-makings. We are not in possession of any detailed Tartar bill of fare, but, according to the meagre reports we have on the subject, the favourite dishes appear to have been roast mutton and horse-flesh, *pilau* (prepared exactly as it is now), puddings, fruit tarts and sugar-plums. The great delicacy of all was supposed to be the hind quarters of a horse cut up and covered with gravy ; this was always served on a gold or silver dish ; other, more ordinary roasts, were carried in on leather tablecloths,[1] and cut up by experienced carvers, but not handed round until after the emperor had eaten the first slice. Next followed dishes of minced meat ; and, in summer, fruit, especially melons and grapes, formed the conclusion of the dinner. Then came the drinking bouts, usual in Eastern Asia, presided over by the prince in person, without whose permission no orgies, whether public or private, might be held. The favourite liquors were wine, ' boza ' and ' kimis,'[2] but the

---

[1] These leather tablecloths have, in modern times been replaced by bright coloured Russian calico ; or, amongst the richer classes, by silk with long fringes, and are called *Desturkhan*, from *Destur*, *ceremony*, and *Khan*, or *Khoun*, *table*.

[2] The use of spirituous liquors, always affected by the Mohammedans, reached the *maximum* of excess under the Mongolian rule. Under the Khahrezmians, drunkenness was already common amongst the most distinguished men, and under

former had the preference, and was at first handed round by
butlers, who, kneeling on one knee, offered the cup on a salver
with one hand, and with the other held a napkin or handker-
chief before the person drinking lest he should spill any drop
over his clothes.   After the wine had gone round a few times
in this ceremonious fashion, decorum gradually ceased ; the
guests clutched at the flagons, and he who drank to Timour's
health in a bumper was bound to empty it at a single draught.
The object in drinking was then, as now, complete intoxica-
tion, and the contemporaries and successors of Timour had
certainly brought the arts both of drunkenness and gluttony
to rare perfection.   Anybody who fell down dead drunk, or
committed any great absurdity, was supposed to have contributed greatly to the general hilarity, and strong drinkers, like
brave warriors, were distinguished with the title of ' Bator '
(hero).   The æsthetic spirit of the Tartars required everything
to be done on a colossal scale, and no dinner was therefore
reckoned perfect at which horses were not served up roasted
whole, and at which the wine-flagons were not both extremely
numerous and of an enormous size.

These flagons or bowls (each containing according to
Clavijo about three gallons) were ranged in rows, forming as
it were an avenue up to Timour's tents ; and in addition
to these, other similar vessels were placed at different points
of the city of tents, protected by umbrellas, and periodi-
cally filled either with wine or cream and sugar for the
benefit of the people at large.   It may be easily imagined
that on such occasions there was no lack of conjurors,
jugglers and rope-dancers, who for the most part came from
Cashmere and India ; but those familiar with the customs
of Islam and of Asia generally will be astonished to find
ladies taking part in these festivities not even veiled, and
princesses giving public entertainments to which men and

the Djenghizides and Timourides *delirium tremens* was an ordinary malady ;
Baber's memoirs give some idea of the prevalence of this vice, and the discovery of
tobacco proved a real boon for the bacchanalian Asiatics

even Christian envoys were invited. The Spaniard gives us an account of a festivity given by the Princess Kanzade, the wife of Miranshah, a corpulent lady of forty,[1] to a great number of guests, at which the Tartar beauties made a considerable onslaught on the wine, whilst ancient knights assisted by young pages enacted the part of Ganymedes. Another time the Khanîm *par excellence*, i. e., the principal wife of Timour, gave a great entertainment within a circle of tents fenced in with carpet hangings, embroidered with arabesques and mottoes in gold and silver. The etiquette observed in waiting on these ladies was extremely strict. One person held the gold flagon, another the cup and saucer. It was necessary to kneel three times before approaching them, the butler was obliged to wind a napkin round his hand to avoid the very slightest personal contact with the princesses, but this exquisite propriety did not prevent the fair sex at Timour's court, any more than the delicate ladies of Persia now-a-days,[2] usually leaving the table in a muddled condition.

There would be still much to relate of the jousts of the athletes, the games with elephants coloured green and red, the races and other sports which made up the programme of the festivities on the plain of Chanigul. Timour had collected here enormous treasures and wealth from all parts of Asia ; and we have the best proofs that he did not grudge spending them—first, in the descriptions we have of his luxurious establishment, and secondly, as evidenced by the colossal buildings with which he sought to ornament both his capital and his native city.

Timour sought to commemorate every brilliant feat of arms, every joyful event, by some architectural monument.

---

[1] She lived apart from her husband, giving as a reason that Miranshah had once attempted, in a drunken fit, to murder her. So Clavijo states. Timour seems however, to have made a great favourite of this daughter-in-law, who held a splendid court at Samarkand.

[2] The clever but superficial Count Gobineau has drawn on himself the displeasure of the present Shah of Persia through having, in his book on the *Religions of Central Asia*, ungallantly injured the reputation of Persian ladies in Europe.

Hundreds of the best stonemasons in India and the most celebrated architects of Shiraz, Isfahan and Damascus were brought across the Oxus to carry out works which proved conclusively both that Islamite Asia, though given up for 200 years to the incursions of Tartaric hordes, could still produce artists worthy of our admiration, and that the conqueror, so often described as a brutal barbarian, was no stranger to the sense of beauty and refinement in taste.

Timour caused many fine buildings to be erected in various parts of his empire; amongst others, a mosque at Tebriz, a palace at Shiraz, an academy at Bagdad, and a mausoleum over the grave of the celebrated sheïkh, Ahmed Yesevi, at Haszreti Turkestan; but the finest specimens of his liberal tastes were to be found at Kesh and Samarkand. The former, the original home of his race, contained his family burying-place; here he erected a mausoleum over the grave of his father and over that of his eldest son Djihanghir, and a mosque with an outer court tenanted by mollahs, who recited the Koran night and day for the benefit of the souls of the departed. Timour had, from the very commencement of his career, shown a marked preference for Kesh, and had made it practically the intellectual metropolis of Central Asia; it was known as *Kubbet ul ilm 'w'el' edeb* (Cupola, or dome, of Science and Morality!); the professors of the celebrated academies of Khahrezm and the scholars of Bokhara and Fergana were transferred thither, and, if further proofs were wanting, the building of the beautiful palace of Ak Saray there, is evidence enough that at one time he intended to make it his capital. This palace was ten years in progress, and was exclusively the work of Persian architects, who followed the national (or more properly speaking the West Islamite) style so closely that they put the arms of the Sun and Lion over the principal front, thus decorating the abode of the Turanian conqueror with the emblems of Iranian princes.[1] As in all buildings of that period, the portale (called

---

[1] Timour's own arms were three rings, thus : °o° with the motto *Rusti Rasti*,

in Persian *pish tak*, or verandah) was the most imposing feature of the palace ; it towered above the rest of the building in the shape of an alcove or half dome, filled with fantastic niches, and covered over with glazed tiles in a mosaic pattern of flowers and arabesques. These glazed tiles were all made in Kashan, and bear to this day the name of *Kashi* ;[1] they were also used to decorate the internal walls, and the lofty apartments thus lined with arabesques in blue and gold, and, with mosaic floors to match, must have been surpassingly beautiful. This palace contained whole suites of similar apartments ; the gynacœum was a marvel of magnificence and luxury, and the great hall opened into a large shady garden, with lovely rivulets meandering among the flower-beds.

In the course of time, however, the beautiful position of Samarkand carried the day against the attractions of Kesh ; the former town became Timour's capital, and increased rapidly in size, splendour, and importance. According to the Spanish ambassador, the whole place was not much larger than Seville ; this, however, applies only to the citadel (ark) and fortress (Kal'a), i.e., the part within the lines,[2] but the beauty and pomp of Samarkand lay all beyond the lines, in the splendid gardens, stretching out some five or six miles, or more, and dotted with villas and imperial palaces. A fine avenue led eastwards from the turquoise gate (Dervaze-i-Firuze) up to the summer-palace of Baghi Dilkusha (the Garden of Pleasantness), whose broad high portale of blue

i.e., *Justice is strength* ; they were supposed to be typical of his power, ' encircling three zones,' south, west, and north ; but it is more likely that they were borrowed from the heraldry of ancient Iran, for the rings as symbols of strength and unity are also to be seen on the tombs of the Sassanides.

[1] Kashan is still the place where the best works in clay in all Persia are manufactured, but the trade in glazed tiles has considerably diminished, the present condition of the East not being such as to encourage ornamental building.

[2] Even with this hypothesis, Clavijo's estimate strikes me as too small. Assuming that I mean by *the Ark* the inhabited portion of modern Samarkand, and not merely the palace, old Samarkand must, judging by the lines of fortification still in existence, have been decidedly larger than Seville. As far as I can remember, I had to drive a good distance from the Dervaze Bokhara (Gate of Bokhara) through gardens and cemeteries of the suburbs before reaching the inner town.

and gold tiles could be discerned from afar, glittering against the sky. The first court was filled with the imperial guard, richly attired and superbly armed; in the second court the visitor came on six elephants in a row, carrying gay howdahs; finally, in the third and innermost court, Timour himself, seated on an embroidered silken carpet, gave his audiences. In the centre of each court was a pond (as is still often the case in Persia) shaded by elms and poplar trees, with a fountain in which crimson and gilt balls danced among the jets.

To the south lay the palace of Baghi Bihisht (the Garden of Paradise), celebrated both for its architectural beauty and its lovely grounds. Sherefeddin states that it was built entirely of clear white Tebriz marble, and stood on an artificial mound surrounded by a deep moat, and connected by several bridges with the Park, on one side of which was a chase or menagerie. Timour had given this palace to one of his grand-daughters, the daughter of Miranshah, and a special favourite of his; it was his habit to spend much of his leisure with her there, and the place was in consequence also known as his 'Halvet,' or Hermitage. In the same part of the town stood the *Baghi Tchinaran* (Garden of Poplars), so called from the fine avenues of poplars surrounding it. This palace stood also on an artificial mound in the middle of the garden, was built in the shape of a cross, and decorated by the chisel of Syrian artists; the interior was covered with frescoes, and filled with massive silver furniture, beds, tables, &c., besides grotesque knicknacks and costly ornaments of all kinds. We also have descriptions of two more palaces, Baghi Shumal (North Garden), and Baghi No (New Garden), a quadrangular building, each side of which was 1,500 yards long, and which contained fine sculptures in marble, and a floor inlaid with mosaics of ebony and ivory. Judging by the few remains still existing of the splendour of Samarkand, the descriptions of these places do not appear to be exaggerated. The mosque, built a century earlier by Sultan

Khudabende at Sultanie, was not to be compared to Timour's *Mesdjidi Shah*, which still towers above the ruins of modern Samarkand, and of which Baber relates that a verse of the Koran was inscribed over the doorway in letters so gigantic that they could be read two kerves (or miles) off. Later buildings in the same style, such as the great mosque on the Place Meïdani Shah at Isfahan, and the mausoleums at Kum and at Meshed, are all inferior to the productions due to Timour's munificence. Though the art of architecture continued to flourish to some extent in Central Asia under his successors, Shahrukh and Mirza Huseïn Baïkara, as is proved by the ruins on the Mosallah at Herat and by the neat mosque of the Princess Gowher at Meshed, yet there can be no question that the culminating point of its perfection was obtained under Timour 'the wild barbarian.'

The same may be said of the industrial conditions of the country. Timour compelled all the best weavers of Damascus, the celebrated cotton manufacturers of Aleppo, the cloth-workers of Engürü, the goldsmiths of Turkey and Georgia, in short, the clever artisans of every description, to migrate to Samarkand. Every nationality and every creed of Asia was represented there, and Clavijo's estimate, that the number of inhabitants of Samarkand (many of whom were compelled for want of houseroom to camp in caverns and under trees) amounted to no less than 150,000 souls, is probably correct. It is not surprising that Samarkand should, under these circumstances, have become the great emporium of all Asiatic commerce. An inland trade of vast magnitude and extension flourished there. India furnished caravans laden with spices and delicate fabrics, China contributed silks, porcelain, musk, agates and precious stones; and the northern portion of the gigantic empire sent large cargoes of costly furs across the desert. All these products of various zones were repacked in the bazaar of Samarkand, and exported again, not only to the principal cities of Western

Asia, but to Europe itself in two different directions. The first great outlet for trade was by Khahrezm and Astrabad, Nishni Novgorod and Moscow, and so into the hands of the merchants of the Hanse Towns ; the second was by Herat, Kazvin, Tebriz and Trebizonde, and thence through the medium of the traders of Venice, Genoa and Pisa to Europe. Notwithstanding the warlike and turbulent times, these communications were kept perfectly free and open throughout the entire range of country subject to Timour's influence ; the Spanish embassy so often alluded to is a proof of this, for they travelled through the whole district between Trebizonde and Samarkand, and through parts of the enemy's territory, with scarcely any escort, carrying large treasures on mules, perfectly safe and unmolested, shortly after the battle of Engürü, at the very time when anarchy seemed to be at its height in Western Asia.

We propose to treat more fully in the ensuing chapter of the intellectual progress of Central Asia due to the appearance of Timour, as the fruits of this progress more properly belong to the history of his children and grandchildren, the dynasty of the *Timourides*, altogether. The merit of having given a distinctly national bias to the intellect and science of the country, and of having thereby brought the Turkish element into a pre-eminence it had never before enjoyed, belongs, however, to Timour personally. The history of the Turks in Central Asia begins, in fact, with him ; for the princes of Khahrezm and the Seldjukides, though originally Turks, were entirely devoted to the Iranian and West Islamite culture, and did as little to extend Turkish influence and Turkish ideas as is done now by the dynasty of Turkish Kadjars reigning in Persia. Timour represented in his own person the victory of the Turks over the Mongolian-Chinese order of things, and was always anxious to assert the well-deserved supremacy of the Turkish element. Though his court was filled with foreign scholars and artists, Turkish was maintained as the sole official language, and, in writing, the Mongolian-Uiguric character, although hated, by fanatic Moslems as a remnant of Christian and Buddhist heresy, was retained.

Timour wrote a fluent forcible Turkish style—as is proved by the 'Tüzükat'—to which allusion has already often been made. He was not fond of the pompous language and extravagant metaphors to which the literary geniuses and official writers of the period were alike addicted, and he, before whom half Asia trembled and who had seen so many dynasties humbled to the dust before his throne, was wont to commence his diplomatic notes with the simple sentence : *'Men tingri Kuli Timur,'* [1] 'I, the servant of God, Timour, say as follows!' What a contrast to the list of titles a yard long of the latter khans and beggar princes of Bokhara.

In spite of the constant wars and troubles, an unmistakeable intellectual awakening, both in the field of religion and of science, manifested itself in the eastern portion of the Empire before the close of the great conqueror's reign. History tells us of an Alide of the family of Zin ul Abidin, the mystic Seïd Ali Hamadani, who traversed the whole civilised earth three times over, preaching and converting, and at length died in Khatlan on this side of the Oxus, in the year 786 (1384), having published several works on æsthetic and mystical subjects. Another great mystic, Khodja Bahaeddin, the founder of the order of Nakishbendi, lived in Timour's reign, and died in the year 791 (1388). He is to this day the patron saint of Bokhara, and three pilgrimages to his tomb, distant but a mile from the city, are considered equivalent to one pilgrimage to the distant Kaaba. Amongst the secular authors who deserve to be remembered, we may mention the poet Lutfullah *Nishaburi*, poet laureate and

---

[1] I wish here to correct an error into which I have fallen in my *Uigurische Sprachmonumente*, p. 17, where I have ascribed to Emir Timour the Uiguric charter dated from the banks of the Dnieper 800 (1397). now in the Imperial Library at Vienna. This document was issued, not by Emir Timour, but by Timour Kutlug of the house of Djüdji ; for Uiguric was also the official language used in the Golden Horde.

panegyrist of Prince Miranshah, which was by no means an enviable post, for this prince was well known as a drunken debauchee; but the poet contrived, nevertheless, to scatter some of the finest pearls of his poetry before the swine he was called upon tò adore. He was highly esteemed by Timour, and died in the year 786 (1384). Sheïkh Kemaleddin Khodjendi, whose kasides are as celebrated as the gazels of his contemporary and namesake at Ispahan, *Kemaleddin Ispahni*. When his native city was taken by Tokhtamish Khan, the conqueror compelled the poet to migrate to his capital on the Volga, and, though pleased at first with his new quarters,[1] he accepted, four years afterwards, an invitation of the Ilkhanide Sultan Huseïn to Tebriz, where a fine khankah or *convent* was built expressly for him, in which he diĕd, in the year 793 (1380). A year later the great scholar *Ulama Teftazani* died at Samarkand. He was born at Irak in the year 722, and published a commentary on Rihani when only in his sixteenth year. He lived successively at Herat, at Djam, Sarakhs, Samarkand, Gidjdovan, Turkestan, and Khahrezm, and was equally great as a theologian, a lawyer, a grammarian, and an exegetical teacher. The number of his finished works and of his treatises is said to have been greater than the number of years of his life. The poet *Ahmed Kermani*, author of the ' Timur Nameh,' a history of Timour in verse, lived on a footing of familiar intimacy with the great conqueror, who even permitted him to make jokes at his expense which would be punished with instant death at the present day by more than one of the half-civilised princes of Asia.[2] Timour extended favour and protec-

---

[1] He says in a poem (quoted in the *Tarikhi Sëïd Rakëïn*, p. 29) :

> Eger serai dilberan serai
> Biyar bade, ki farig shevem zi her du serai.

i.e., If thou art a Palace, verily thou art the Palace of Beauty. Bring me wine that I may renounce both palaces (in this world and the next). For further details regarding Kemaleddin Khodjendi see Hammer's *Geschichte Persischer Redekünste*, p. 255.

[2] Timour was one day in the bath with Kermani and some other wits ; the conversation fell on the individual worth of men, and Timour asked the poet,

tion to a considerable number of foreign scholars and poets, and all those carried by him from the different parts of Asia to Transoxania were amply compensated for their forced migration. Men of the calibre of Djezeri, the author of the greatest Arabic dictionary, received high office at court, and the learned professors from Nishabur, Bagdad, Merv, and Khahrezm obtained more lucrative posts than those they had left in the colleges of Bokhara, Samarkand, and Kesh. The time of Timour's glory was especially rich in foundations and endowments of colleges, the remains of which excite the astonishment of the modern visitor to Bokhara. Timour himself set the example, and some of the members of his family and different viziers and nobles seem to have vied with each other in founding, furnishing, and endowing colleges, mosques, schools, and hospitals, so that the intellectual progress of Central Asia must at least indirectly be reckoned amongst the list of his services to the country.

'What price wouldst thou put on me if I were for sale?' 'About five-and-twenty *aspers*,' answered Kermani. ' Why, that is about the price of the sheet I have on,' rejoined Timour. ' Well, of course I meant the sheet,' returned Kermani, ' for thou alone art not worth a farthing.'

XII.

THE TIMOURIDES.

807 (1405)—906 (1500).

TIMOUR was not by any means so fortunate in his successors as his Mongolian predecessor in the path of conquest had been. The former ruler had merely laid the foundations of a gigantic power, and had left the completion and extension of the edifice to the strong arms of his sons and grandsons; but the latter prince had, with his own hand, built up his fabric of empire to the topmost pinnacle, and his children, so far from strengthening it, were the first to shake it by their quarrels and the furious civil wars which eventually led to its ruin. The Djenghizides had maintained their power in Central and Western Asia during two centuries, but the successors of Timour barely retained 100 years' possession of the dominions they had inherited, although there were amongst them several men of marked ability, whose talents for government and noble qualities deserve to be held in admiration by posterity.[1]

The remains of the deceased hero had scarcely been laid to rest at Samarkand, and the funeral solemnities were not over, before his heirs began fighting for the crown. With the exception of the wise and noble Shahrukh Mirza, who was governing in Khorasan, all Timour's sons had died

---

[1] These circumstances have been commented on by the learned M. Bélin, who, in his *Notice bibliographique et littéraire sur Mir-Ali-Chir-Nevâï*, makes the following remark (at p. 29) in speaking of the Timourides :—'Il y a lieu de s'étonner que le goût des lettres n'ait pu exercer sur ces princes, doués, pour la plupart d'une certaine philosophie religieuse, une influence salutaire sur leur rudesse et leur cruauté naturelles.'

before him,[1] and he had therefore named as his successor the grandson in whose abilities he had most confidence. This was Pir Mohammed Khan, lord of India and of Kabul, who had spent his youth in hard fighting, but in his maturer years gave himself up to luxury and debauchery, leaving the cares of government to his crafty and treacherous vizir, Pir Ali Taz. He was at Kabul plunged in sensual pleasures, when the news of his grandfather's death reached him. If he had had the energy to rouse himself at once, and, exchanging the wine-cup for the sword, had instantly marched to the Oxus, he would have had little difficulty in possessing himself of the crown, amidst the confusion and shiftlessness into which the court had been thrown.[2] But he delayed, and the consequence was that he found himself forestalled by Sultan Khalil Mirza, a youth of one-and-twenty, son of Miranshah, who, with the assistance of a few influential officers, ascended his grandfather's throne, and hurried from Tashkend, where he had been staying, to Samarkand, in order to buy off, with the help of the treasures accumulated there, the officials who were seeking to carry out the instructions in Timour's will, by putting Pir Mohammed at the head of the government. The partisans of the latter were both numerous and influential,[3] and Khalil Mirza had reason to congratulate himself when he succeeded in overthrowing their plans and establishing his power over the countries beyond the Oxus; but, in spite of this success, his gentleness and dreamy temperament marked him out as a poet rather than a ruler, and whilst

---

[1] Timour had eight legitimate wives, but only four sons: 1. Gayas-eddin Djihanghir; 2. Muiz-eddin Omar Sheikh; 3. Miranshah; 4. Shahrukh Mirza.

[2] There was the great diversity of opinion in the Council of Generals as to the first steps to be taken. Some wished to keep the Emperor's death secret, and continue to advance upon the terrified Mongolians and Chinese; but others advised an immediate retreat, and this latter counsel ultimately prevailed.

[3] Only a small minority in the army voted for altering the dispositions in Timour's will. Mirza Sultan Husein, a grandson of Timour's, and General Burunduk were at the head of those who were dissatisfied with the turn of events; but they were unable to do anything to arrest Khalil's progress, as they never could agree as to the course to be pursued, and when they did at last proceed to take active measures it was too late.

he gained over many to his cause by the lavish prodigality with which he dispensed his grandfather's enormous treasures on the one hand, on the other hand he alienated many by dismissing old servants, and thereby making for himself in a short time a large number of bitter enemies. Much dissatisfaction is also said to have been caused by Khalil's passionate love for a former slave of Hadji Seïfeddin, a lady named Shad-i-Mulk (the Joy of the Empire), whom he married immediately after his accession to the throne. Timour had tried to put an end to his grandson's misplaced affection by getting rid of the beautiful slave, but she escaped, and survived to be raised to the throne, there to lead her husband into conduct which induced his most devoted adherents to take up arms[1] against him. The Emirs Khudadad and Sheïkh Nureddin first rose and took possession of the province of Turkestan, and of part of Fergana. Soon afterwards, some of the free tribes of the desert asserted their independence. Khalil, who was busy at Samarkand composing sonnets in honour of his love,[2] would have remained passive if Pir Mohammed, determined to assert his right to his inheritance, had not marched a large army to the Oxus, and seriously threatened Khalil's position. The first division of the army sent to oppose him betrayed their own cause shamefully, and Khalil had actually to fight his own troops. Mirza Sultan Huseïn, Khalil's nephew, commanded them, and rebelled with the intention of forming an independent empire on the banks of the Oxus. Fortunately Khalil was

---

[1] This woman had occupied in Timour's lifetime a very subordinate position towards the other women in her master's harem, and had had to endure many indignities for which she revenged herself mercilessly in the days of her prosperity, and thereby offended desperately more than one of the great nobles and chief supporters of the government.

[2]. The following lines quoted from these ballads by Mir Ali Shir, show more skill in alliteration than actual poetic beauty :—

'Ey turk-i-peri peïkerimiz terk-i-djefa kil
Kam dilimiz Laal-i revan bakhsh-ireva kil.'

' O thou, my beauty, like unto a Peri, leave off tormenting me, and let the love of my heart expend itself in a kiss (or *ruby*) in which my soul shall be expressed.' See *Matlaa es Saadën*, property of the Imperial Library at Vienna, p. 19.

warned of his designs, advanced against him, and overthrew him in the battle of Djigdelik, in the district of Kesh. After an abortive conference between the two pretenders to the throne, the flames of civil war broke fairly out. Pir Mohammed crossed the Oxus, was attacked in the neighbourhood of Nesef, and driven back with loss of his baggage and all his camp equipage. He made a second fruitless attempt; but every spark of his former energy had by this time been choked by his drunkenness and excesses of all kinds, and his own vizir, a certain Pir Ali Taz,[1] whom he had raised from the position of a servant to the highest dignities, treacherously murdered him in his tent[2] near Shiborgan, in the year 809 (1406). Khalil was by this time tolerably secured against attacks from the south, but the state of affairs was all the more gloomy in the north, where the rebel emirs Khudadad and Sheïkh Nureddin had extended their operations, and, having been joined by several other nobles, were about to march with a considerable force on Samarkand. Khalil sent out an army commanded by the emirs Arghunshah and Allahdad to meet the rebels, but unfortunately both these commanders were secretly in league with the enemy, and when, shortly afterwards, the brave but unfortunate Timouride, accompanied by a few faithful followers, proceeded to join the army, they were the first to betray him. He was surprised by a small body of Khudadad's men in the ruins of the citadel of Shiraz, takèn prisoner, and carried before his former vassal. Khalil had to abdicate the crown, and received as a compensation from the hands of his rebel servant the government of Kashgar; but this strange mutation of fate affected him

[1] In the lithographed copy of the *Rausat es Sefa*, this name is spelt Mir Ali Yar. It is also spelt Ali Yar in the *Tarikhi Sad Rakein*, and also in the *Tarikhi Mekim K'hani*, but I am nevertheless more inclined to believe in the correctness of the ancient and beautiful manuscript of *Matlaa es Saadèin*.

[2] The treacherous vizir committed this deed with the object of making himself prince of Afghanistan and Northern India. A revolt of the great nobles however forced him to fly; he escaped to Herat where Shahrukh had him executed, and thereupon placed his nephew's dominions under his own sceptre.

comparatively little, his thoughts were engrossed by his
enforced separation from his beloved Shad-i-Mulk, and he
did nothing but pour out his grief in mournful verses.
The victorious rebel had meantime taken possession of
Samarkand with all its treasures, and had given up the
Princess Shad-i-Mulk to the popular scorn and contempt,
exposing her to the grossest insults ;[1] but he did not himself
long enjoy the fruits of his success. Shahrukh Mirza, the
oldest of the surviving Timourides, was then at the height of
power in Herat, and could not remain any longer a passive
spectator of the events in Transoxania. He was the most
eminent and able prince of his race, his court was the focus
of all the learning and cultivation of the age, and he had
hitherto found the refined atmosphere of the Iranian civilisation in Khorasan far too congenial to trouble himself much
about the government of the Oxus countries. The events
which took place there on his father's death affected him but
little, but when he saw the dynastic interests of his family
seriously compromised, he could no longer avoid plunging
into war, much as he disliked it. On hearing of his nephew's
misfortunes he set off in pursuit of Khudadad,[2] who, being
unprepared for resistance, made a feigned submission. But
Shahrukh did not allow himself to be deceived ; he advanced
on Samarkand, where he was received by the inhabitants
with great pomp, whilst the rebel Khudadad made a precipitate retreat on Tashkend, and solicited help from the
Mongolian Prince Mohammed Khan, but it might have been

---

[1] Mirkhond says that it was Shahrukh who, after capturing Samarkand, exposed
the princess to these indignities. But the opposite version of the story, which has
also been adopted by Malcolm in his *History of Persia*, appears to me the more
probable one. Shahrukh himself had a romantic passion for his wife Gowher
Shad, and, judging by the traditions still extant of him, it seems difficult to imagine
him capable of thus further torturing his lovesick nephew.

[2] Khudadad traced his descent from the Tchaghatides, and although this may
have been doubtful, yet it is certain that he was in his own person the champion of
the pretensions of the Djete chiefs whom Timour had subdued, and that all the
Mongolians and Kalmucks of the north-east of Transoxania flocked to his
standard.

foreseen that the latter would hesitate to embark in hostilities with the mighty Shahrukh. Instead of assisting the fugitive rebel, he ordered his brother Shema' Djihan to arrest him. He was soon afterwards beheaded, and his head sent as a token of Mongolian friendship to Shahrukh Mirza.

When Transoxania had become in some degree pacified, the unhappy prisoner Mirza Khalil was remembered. He had been conveyed by a brother of Khudadad's, shortly after the execution of the latter, to a fortress in the Alatau mountains, and Shahrukh in consequence despatched his General Shahmulk to subdue this fortress. Mirza Khalil seems to have dreaded his uncle and deliverer more than his rebel captor, for he would not stir without a strong escort, which was granted him. Thus protected, he proceeded to the left bank of the Yaxartes, where Shahrukh was encamped; the latter received him affectionately, and loaded him with kindness, even restoring to him his beloved Shad-i-Mulk. He was not however, allowed to re-ascend the throne, but, as some compensation, Shahrukh appointed him Viceroy of Irak; he died however on his way thither, in the year 812 (1409), and tradition says that Shad-i-Mulk (the 'Joy of the Empire,' who might with more reason have been called 'the curse of his reign'), killed herself from grief at the death of her devoted husband.[1]

In the course of the following year Shahrukh was forced to cross the Oxus once more with arms in his hands. The nobles in Transoxania, emboldened by Khalil's indulgence, had made the change of government an excuse for rebellion. Emir Sheïkh Nureddin headed the movement, intending to secure the throne for himself, and began hostilities, but was defeated by General Shahmulk, and retreated on Tashkend, leaving his partisans to suffer severe punishment for their offences.

---

[1] It is said that Shad-i-Mulk could not endure life after the death of her faithful husband; she stabbed herself to the heart with a dagger, and was buried in the same grave with him.

Shahrukh Mirza had now united the whole of his father's former dominions (with the exception of Syria and Arabistan) under his own sceptre ; he entrusted the government of Transoxania to his eldest son Ulug Beg, who proved himself not only a worthy son of his father but even surpassed him in his love of science, and of all liberal arts ; he is the only one of the Timourides whose name has been honourably remembered for centuries even in Western Christendom. Ulug Beg, or rather (to call him by his real name) Mohammed Turghai, was fifteen years old at the death of his grandfather, and only about twenty when the difficult task of governing Transoxania was first entrusted to him, but his long rule proved the golden age of the Timourides in the countries beyond the Oxus. In consequence of the high esteem in which his father was held, peace had been but little disturbed in Turan, and, although the Mongolians in the north-east several times forced him into hostilities, and even obliged him once to advance as far as Aksu, we have only one really important invasion to chronicle during his reign, that in the north, which however ended unhappily, and brought a vast amount of misery on Transoxania.

Kowurdjuk, whom Timour had invested with the khanate of Kiptchak, had a son, Borak Oghlan ; this son was driven out by his enemies, and took refuge, in the year 828 (1421), in Turkestan, in the neighbourhood of Siganak. He soon made a claim to be put in possession of this fortress ; the commandant however, in reply, merely sent in an energetic complaint of the devastations caused by the Kiptchak or Özbeg troopers (as they are called by Abdurrezak, the composer of 'The Rise of the Two Fortunate Stars'). Ulug Beg determined to look into the matter for himself ; his father having some misgivings as to the martial capabilities of his son, sent off his second son Mohammed Djögi to his brother's assistance with some auxiliary troops, but Ulug Beg did not wait for their arrival to commence the attack. He was repulsed by Borak's small but splendid body of cavalry, and completely defeated; Djögi on his arrival fared no better, and the victorious hordes of Kiptchak were enabled to extend their raids unmolested beyond Khodjend. After this interlude, however, the young prince enjoyed some years of peace and leisure in which to cultivate the society which was most congenial to him, that of learned and scientific men, and to enrich his capital with monuments, the ruins of which offer to this day speaking evidence of the artistic feeling and lavish generosity of their author. Baber has given us in his memoirs a tolerably authentic description of Samarkand at that time, and mentions the following amongst Ulug's buildings :—1. A khankah (convent) whose dome was supposed to be the highest in the world. 2. A college in which there was a bath lined with mosaics of the most perfect description. This college, supported by a princely endowment, was erected in the year 828 (1424), but for the last two hundred years it has been in ruins, and in the place of the diligent students of yore, screech-owls have since then been the only tenants of the once-splendid abode. 3. The Mesdjidi Mokattaa (the Parti-coloured Mosque), so called because the inner walls and ceilings were adorned with fantastic arabesques and ornaments in mosaics of coloured wood. 4. The palace of Tchihl Sutun, with a magnificent colonnade of alternately straight and twisted pillars, and flanked by four towers. 5. The throne-room (körünüshkhane)[1] all in marble. The platform on which the throne stood was formed by a single colossal block of stone fifteen yards long, eight yards wide and a yard deep, which had, however, been cracked in the process of conveying it.[2] The garden attached to this building contained the picture gallery (Tchinikhane) covered with frescoes painted by

---

[1] Körünüshkhane means literally in Turkish, *The house where people come together*, consequently what we should call a ' club' or ' salon de conversation.'

[2] This does not seem to have been the same as the celebrated köktash (blue stone) which I saw at Samarkand and have described in my book of *Travels* (p. 206). There is certainly also a crack in the stone I saw, but there is too great a difference between the measurements taken by me and those given by Baber for them to relate to the same thing.

artists brought from China for the purpose. 6. The celebrated observatory commenced in the year 832 on the side of
the ' Kohek ' hill, at the instigation, and with the assistance
of the learned Kazizade-i Rum Gayas-eddin Djemshid
Muayyin-eddin Kashani and the Israelite Selah-eddin, who
had been summoned from Kashan by the prince and rewarded
with princely munificence. The building took a long time, and
as all these men, according to the poet's expression, ' saw their
star of life eclipsed betimes,' not one of them lived to see it
completed. The learned scholar Ali Kushdji brought the
work to perfection, and the celebrated astronomical tables of
Ulug Beg (also called the tables of Köreken) were drawn
up in the year 841 (1437). Ulug Begh discovered that the
calendar of Ptolemy did not agree with his observations at
Samarkand, he therefore undertook, with the assistance of
several learned men, a revision of the latter, the result of which
was that Tartaric science confirmed all the previous discoveries
of Greek learning.[1]   Abdurrezak, author of the work quoted
above, ' The Rise of the Two Fortunate Stars,' speaks with
enthusiasm of the different instruments he had seen used for
mensuration, for determining heights and degrees of latitude
and longitude, and cannot find words to express his astonishment at the celestial globes on which the courses of the stars
and planets were marked accurately, and the maps which
showed the exact shapes of all the countries, hills, deserts and
seas. The observatory was looked upon rightly enough as a
marvel, and the mother of the sovereign, the highly-respected
Gowher Shad (Jewel of Delight), came in 823 (1420) from

---

[1] Ulug Beg's tables are divided into four parts, and treat : 1. Of different epochs
and æras. 2ndly. Of the measurement of time. 3rdly. Of the course of the
planets. 4thly. Of the position of the fixed stars.   These tables were first made
known to the western world by the learned Oxford Professor, John Greaves, a distinguished mathematician and Orientalist, in the year 1642-48.   Dr. Thomas
Hyde translated and published them with a biography of Ulug Beg in 1665,
under the title : *Tabulæ longæ lat. stellarum fixarum ex observatione Ulug Beïghi
Tamerlanii magni nepotis.*   This book was reprinted with Sharp's corrections in
1767, and afterwards translated into French by M. Sédillot.   See Markham's
Indian Surveys, p. 235.

Herat to Samarkand on purpose to see it. But in addition to his taste for astronomy and mathematics, Ulug Beg cultivated with equal assiduity other branches of knowledge ; his court was the rendezvous of poets [1] and learned men from all quarters ; he and his father competed with each other in their endeavours to attract artists and scholars to take up their abode with them, and never since the time of the great Samanide had refined and liberal arts enjoyed such patronage as was extended to them by the government of Ulug Beg. Unhappily, these halcyon days only lasted as long as Shahrukh Mirza's life, for immediately after his death, in the y8 50 (1448), the unwonted serenity which had reigned for so long on the horizon of Central Asia was disturbed, heavy clouds gathered in the clear sky, and the noble fruits of peace were trodden down and consumed once more by the thunder and flame of civil war. Ulug Beg, as the eldest son of Shahrukh, considered himself heir to the entire empire, and on hearing of his father's death, set out to go to Khorasan. On his way he was met, however, with the intelligence that his nephew Ala-ed-dowlet, the son of Baïsonkur Mirza had forestalled him, seized upon Herat and taken his son Abdul-latif prisoner. The tender-hearted father did not dare to declare war against the man who held his own child's life in his hands, and therefore came to terms with him on the understanding that Abdullatif should be set at liberty, and the men and the treasures which had been seized restored. Ala-ed-dowlet fulfilled the first of these conditions, but not the second, for he executed a large number of the captive soldiers, and positively refused to give up any part of the treasure. Under these circumstances Ulug Beg had no alternative left but to go to war. Both parties were prepared to fight it out to the end. Ala-eddin had got possession of great part of the treasure amassed by Shahrukh in the course

---

[1] In addition to his own poet laureate, Khodja Ismet Bokhari, the poets Khiali, Burunduk, Rustem Khuriani, and Tahir Abyurdi occupied distinguished positions at the court of Ulug Beg.

of fifty years, he was ready to risk it all in the contest, and he
had also recruited his army largely. He nevertheless made
one more attempt to come to an amicable settlement, but it
failed, and a battle ensued at Turnab, four leagues from Herat,
in which Ulug gained a brilliant victory, and his enemy lost
both his crown and his army, and was forced to fly to Meshed.
Herat now reverted with all its treasures to the rightful heir,
Ulug Beg, the eldest son of Shahrukh Mirza. He went in
pursuit of his rival to Western Khorasan, and there, with the
help of his brother Esbul Kasim Baber Mirza, subdued one city
after another. But, unfortunately for him, during his absence
the Turkoman chieftain Yar Ali Beg of the tribe of Karak-
ojunlu escaped from the prison into which Ulug Begh had
thrown him, and renewed his old family feud with the Timour ·
ides ; he fell upon Herat, plundered it, and destroyed many
of the fine buildings and works of art with which Shahrukh
had enriched it. Samarkand was subjected at the same time
to a similar disaster, for a troop of reckless Özbeg cavalry
pushed forward to the very gates of the town and gave vent
to all their barbarous fury in the suburbs. Abdurrezak says
that ' The beautiful mosaic pictures brought expressly from
China were shattered on the walls of the picture gallery
(Tchinikhane) by the clubs of the Özbegs, the rich gilding was
scraped off, and the works of art which had cost years of
labour were utterly destroyed in the course of a few hours.'

Afflicting as these disasters must have been to the artist-
soul of Ulug Beg, a far heavier grief was in store for him, for
his beloved child, for whose sake he had first entered on the
path of conquest, repaid his affection with the blackest ingratitude. Abdullatif had fought very bravely at the battle
of Turnab, but had taken offence directly after, because his
father had pointed out his brother Abdulaziz and not himself
as the chief instrument of the success of the day. Another
cause of offence was that Ulug Beg had confiscated the
treasures found in the citadel of Ikhtiar-eddin which Abdullatif pretended to claim as his own property. Having persuaded

his father with some difficulty to give him a command at Belkh, he instantly set up the standard of rebellion there, and crossed the Oxus with an army. The unhappy father was forced to accept his unnatural son's challenge; he was beaten in the first battle, and, a fugitive in his own country, had to retreat to Shahrukhie (formerly Binaket). He was taken prisoner there with his younger son Abdulaziz, and the re-bellious and inhuman son actually had the cruelty to order his own father to be executed by the hands of a Persian slave named Abbas.

Such was the end of Ulug Beg, one of the most enlightened of eastern princes, in the year 853 (1449), having reigned thirty-eight years as his father's representative, and two years and eight months as independent prince of Transoxania, and the countries north and south of it. The parricide Abdullatif did not reap the fruits he had expected from his crime. Ebu-saïd, a great-grandson of Miranshah's had seized on the power at Samarkand. He had been well received when a fugitive at the court of Ulug Beg, the great Timouride hav-ing given him his own daughter in marriage, but this did not prevent his taking up arms against his benefactor at the moment when he was setting out to chastise his rebellious son. Abdulaziz, whom Ulug had left as his deputy in his capital, retired before Ebusaïd's superior forces, the latter took pos-session of Samarkand, and the consequence was that Abdul-latif, after his disgraceful victory, found himself obliged to con-tinue the struggle with this remarkable man as his opponent. Fortune seemed for a time to favour the parricide. Ebu-saïd was beaten and taken prisoner, but he escaped to Bokhara, and soon afterwards Abdullatif, having only reigned six months, was murdered in the year 854 (1450) by Baber Huseïn, a former servant of Ulug Beg's who had sworn to avenge his master's blood. His head was cut off and fixed over the portico of the splendid college built by his father, and 'The parricide dare not pollute the throne,' was the opening line of a poem of the day. All the troubles which overwhelmed Transoxania were looked on as the judgments of the Almighty on the dreadful sin of the ruler. He was succeeded on the throne by Abdullah Mirza, a grandson of Shahrukh, who had also been kindly treated at Ulug Beg's court, and had married another of his daughters. Ebusaïd again came forward to dispute the succession, but was again repulsed, and retreated beyond the Yaxartes to join the Özbeg chieftain, Ebulkhaïr, who placed a considerable body of troops at his disposal with which he attacked Abdullah, and in a single bloody battle took away his crown and his life after a reign of barely twelve months, and thus towards the close of the year 855 (1452) obtained possession of Samarkand, the capital of the empire of the Timourides. It was a dearly-bought victory, for the rough sons of the desert for the second time committed enormous depredations in all the towns, and, even after they were fairly gorged with plunder, it was only partly by fraud and partly by force that they could be prevailed upon to return to their desert home.[1] Ebusaïd is represented as the most ambitious of all the successors of Timour, and is said to have been fond of repeating a saying of his great forefather's : ' The world is too small to contain two conquerors at once ; ' acting on this sentiment he found the frontiers of the Turanian dominion too narrow, and extended the scene of his warlike operations more towards Khorasan and Western Iran than in Transoxania. At a time when all the members of the Timouride family were divided against each other and all animated by the lust of conquest, Ebusaïd had no hope of establishing his empire until he had overcome several formidable rivals. The first war in which he became involved, in consequence of his capture of Samarkand, was

---

[1] Ebusaïd appeared alone at one of the gates of the besieged city of Samarkand, made himself known and demanded admittance. When the Özbegs perceived that he had gone away from them secretly they grew suspicious. Some feared an attack on their rear and made off, but others had to be ejected by force. This behaviour of Ebusaïd's certainly does not betoken any great gratitude, and seems to have been the chief reason that Ebulkhaïr responded but coolly to the request for assistance made to him some time later by the Timourides.

with Esbul Kasim Baber Mirza,[1] who came forward in Khorasan immediately after the death of Shahrukh, was supported
by Ulug Beg, and, after the execution of the Turkoman
prince, Yar Ali, got possession of the government of Herat.
His reign is said to have been tolerably prosperous, and he
seems really to have wished to heal the bleeding wounds of
Khorasan. He had always rightly esteemed Ebusaïd a dangerous enemy, but he came to terms with him after he had
laid siege to Samarkand for forty days in vain. Ebusaïd had
not much difficulty in dealing with the sons of Abdullatif,
Ahmed and Mehemmed Djüghi,[2] who endeavoured to regain
possession of their father's throne, and disputed his claim to
the government. He defeated these two princes in the
neighbourhood of Belkh in the year 859 (1455); Ahmed was
killed but Djüghi escaped and retired beyond the Yaxartes,
soliciting help from the Özbeg prince, Ebulkhair, precisely
as Ebusaïd himself had done in the day of his adversity. The
steppes of North Transoxania had been from time immemorial the nursery whence armies were drawn, and although
Ebulkhair, either out of consideration for his former protegé,
Ebusaïd, or for other reasons, declined to plead Djüghi's
cause with him, he nevertheless assisted the son of Abdullatif
in other ways. He summoned his neighbour Bürghe Sultan,
a hero of the desert (of whom, we are told by Abulgazi, that
instead of an ordinary breast-bone, his chest was covered by a
breast-plate of bone!), and addressed him thus :—

'There is no member of my family equal to the task I have
to propose to thee, but thou too, oh Bürghe, art unto me as a
son ; call thy people together, take with thee the men I will
give thee and go ! help this Timouride out of his troubles.'

Bürghe Sultan accepted the commission and went to

[1] Mirza Esbul Kasim Baber (not to be confounded with the founder of the
Mongolian dynasty in India) was a grandson ot Shahrukh's, through his son
Baïsonkur Mirza.

[2] I spell this name Djüghi because I look on it as a Turkish word ; if it is however assumed to be of Persian origin and to signify *guardian*, the spelling adopted
by others of Ljoghi would be more correct.

Q

Tashkend, where he was joined by the old partisans of the Özbegs and the discontented Tchaghatides, and he then took Shahrukhie,[1] crossed the Yaxartes and marched straight on Samarkand. Emir Mezid, who commanded in the latter place, met him and forced a battle on him. The right wing of Djüghi's army was led by Pishkend Oghlan, commander of Ebulkhaïr's auxiliaries, and the left by Bürghe with his Tchaghatides.

The Samarkandians got the worst of it, Mezid Khan retired hurriedly within the fortifications, and Djüghi by degrees occupied the whole of Mavera ul nehr.

Intelligence of these events reached Ebusaïd at the moment he was himself engaged in a bloody warfare in Khorasan with Mirza Huseïn Baïkara, a rival in every way worthy of him. He prepared immediately to cross the Oxus. Bürghe and Djüghi were encamped on the banks of that river, and were disputing concerning the choice of their lines of defence. The former, relying on the bravery of his Özbegs, proposed to defend the line of the Oxus ; but the latter, mistrusting the fidelity of the Tchaghatides, preferred leaning on the Yaxartes. Djüghi's judgment in the matter was sounder than that of the reckless son of the desert, and was justified by events, for Ebusaïd had scarcely reached Transoxania before the Tchaghatides deserted in shoals to the enemy, so that Djüghi had to throw himself with the handful of men remaining to him for shelter into the fortress of Shahrukhie, whilst Bürghe made the best of his way home to the desert, plundering and ravaging everything on his road. Ebusaïd lay four months before the fortress of Shahrukhie, and would have taken it had not a fresh invasion of Mirza Huseïn's compelled him to conclude an armistice ; he went to Djordjan, defeated his enemy, and then returned in the year 867 (1462) to spend ten

---

[1] Shahrukhie was the name given to the former town of Binaket on its being rebuilt after having been destroyed by the Mongolians. It was called Shahrukhie in honour of Shakrukh Mirza.

more months before the walls of Shahrukhie. Finally, Djüghi, seeing his last hopes waning, entered into negotiations.

Khodja Obeïdullah, a pious sheïkh equally esteemed by both sides, appeared within the fortress carrying a flag of truce from Ebusaïd, and Djüghi expressed his willingness to surrender as soon as the sheïkh had sworn on the Koran that he should have a safe conduct to depart freely. Ebusaïd, however, troubled himself little about this oath of his deputy's, for on entering Shahrukhie, he made Djüghi prisoner and shut him up in the citadel of Ikhtiar-eddin, where he subsequently died. Having thus rid himself of his formidable rival, Ebusaïd appointed his own son Sultan Ahmed regent in Samarkand, and then went back to Khorasan for the purpose of consolidating his power there, and of extending his conquests in the distant parts of Irak and Arabistan. After Mirza Huseïn had been driven out, Ebusaïd found himself absolute master not only in Transoxania and Fergana (which latter country was governed by his son Omar Sheïkh), but also in Khorasan, Afghanistan, Sistan, Kerman and Fars ; but still his insatiable ambition led him to cast longing eyes on the fertile plains of Azerbaïdjan, more especially as a fresh hero had lately made his appearance there in the person of Hasan Beg, chief of the Turkoman dynasty of the Akkoyunlu. This was in the year 870 (1465) ; Khorasan was enjoying the much-needed peace, and Ebusaïd had been occupied for five months with the festivities in celebration of the circumcision of his youngest son, on which occasion a series of tournaments, public games, feasts with music and dancing, and illuminations were given, when Hasan Ali, prince of the Turkoman dynasty of Karakoyunlu arrived at the court of Merv to crave assistance against his father's enemies. His father Shah Djiham had been killed fighting against Hasan Beg, or Uzun Hasan, as he is more frequently called. It did not require much persuasion under these circumstances to induce Ebusaïd to take up the quarrel. He marched in the year 872 (1467) with a large army from Merv straight on Azerbaïdjan. Uzun Hasan, whose hands were full in other directions,[1] sent envoys to meet him and make peace, but Ebusaïd, intoxicated by his previous successes rejected all their propositions. Uzun Hasan finding war thus forced upon him, defended himself, however, with a desperation which soon made Ebusaïd repent of his rashness, for his troops were harassed on their whole march to Karabag so incessantly as seriously to reduce their numbers, and finally, he was himself attacked, taken prisoner and executed.[2]

Such was the end, after a reign of eighteen years duration, of the last of the Timourides who succeeded in keeping the different people of Central Asia, from the mountains of the Thien-Shan to Bagdad, and from the steppes of the Kirghiz to the Indus and the Persian Gulf, united under one sceptre, and who by his great military talents and general abilities might under more favourable circumstances have accomplished greater deeds still.

It need scarcely be said that his son and successor, Sultan Ahmed Mirza, was of course unable to retain more of his father's dominions than the government of Transoxania. In the west, the rising dynasty of the Seffides were laying the foundations of their future greatness at the expense of the Timourides ; in the south, Mirza Huseïn Baïkara, reviving for the last time the glories of ancient Khorasan, was setting up a powerful throne in Herat, whence he ruled for nearly

[1] He had just been forced to take the offensive against Ghedik (Hammer is mistaken in spelling this name Keduk) Ahmed Pasha, whom Mohammed II. had sent into Anatolia with a large army. The conqueror of Constantinople owed a grudge to Uzun Hasan for his hospitable reception of Ishak Beg, an enemy of the Ottomans.

[2] Ebusaïd had, at the first capture of Herat, caused the Princess Gowher Shad, wife of Shahrukh Mirza, to be executed, and in consequence of this Uzun Hasan now delivered up his prisoner to Yadikiar Mirza, the son of the latter, who in fulfilment of the duty of requiring blood for blood instantly had him executed. This is related by the historian of Mirza Huseïn Baïkara. Contarini, Venetian ambassador at the court of Uzun Hasan, mentions having seen in one of the rooms in the palace at Isfahan a picture of Ebusaïd (whom he calls Buzekh) being brought before Ughurlu Mohammed, the son of Uzun Hasan, bound with rope , and in another room a picture of the beheading of the once powerful Timouride.

a quarter of a century over Northern Iran, Afghanistan and Sistan; in the extreme east, Omar Sheïkh had proclaimed his independence, whilst in the northern territories of the Yaxartes, Yunis Beg, a supposed Djenghizide of the branch of Tchaghatai, supported by Mongolian auxiliaries, had openly renounced his allegiance. Sultan Ahmed, a mild, good-tempered, but by no means able man, could do little under such circumstances. He was not devoid of personal bravery, as is proved by the nickname given him by the Mongolians, Aladja, or 'Slayer;' but the influences of his superstitious training had been unfavourable to any display of spirit or daring. He had been educated in a strict observance of forms, showing such respect to his spiritual teacher, Khodja Obeïdullah, as always to remain kneeling in his presence with bowed head; on one occasion he continued immovable in this posture although suffering tortures from having accidentally knelt on a sharp piece of bone. He never omitted the prayers five times a day at the stated hours enjoined by his faith, even when tipsy; for, in contradiction to all these pious outward observances, we find him spending twenty and thirty days at a time in drinking and feasting.[1] Considering all things, we may well be surprised to find that he accomplished as much as he did, for he fought Yunis Beg, and re-conquered Tashkend, Sirem and the whole province of Turkestan; he also endeavoured to bring back his brother Omar Sheïkh to his allegiance: the two brothers fought more than once with each other, but the celebrated ascetic Khodja Ahrar undertook to bring about a reconciliation, and soon restored peace between them. On the whole, Transoxania enjoyed a tolerably long peace under the reign of Sultan Ahmed, and the enlightened influence of the intellectual activity flourishing at the court of Mirza Huseïn Baïkara at Herat, could not fail to make

---

[1] Mohammed had given as his principal reason for forbidding the use of spirituous liquors, that the faithful would be unable, if addicted to drink, to observe the five stated hours of prayer daily; the Mohammedans therefore imagine that they do not infringe the spirit of their prophet's rule by drinking so long as they remain able to observe the proper terms of prayer.

itself felt on the shores of the Zerefshan, although assuming
there somewhat different shapes. The example set by
Sultan Ahmed in promoting the building of houses of
prayer, palaces, colleges, and public baths, was followed by
the rich nobles with great alacrity. Amongst other buildings
dating from this period we may mention the summer palace
of Mahommed Tarkhan at Samarkand, which Baber has
described as wonderfully beautiful, rising up upon a series
of terraces, and overlooking rich and luxuriant meadows.
The strong government of Sultan Husein Mirza effectually
checked any serious disturbances during this period in
Khorasan, and the inhabitants of Transoxania enjoyed on
the whole, throughout the reign of Ahmed, a time of repose
and prosperity which they only learnt fully to appreciate
when this good, though but moderately-gifted prince, died in
899 (1493),[1] in the twenty-seventh year of his reign, and his
brother Sultan Mahmud seized on the reins of government.
This brother had gone through many vicissitudes after his
father's death, but had finally found a friendly reception at
the court of Ahmed, and had lived with him during some
years in the closest intimacy, until he one day left Samarkand, ostensibly on a hunting expedition, crossed the Oxus
and took possession of Bedakh'shan. It was from thence that
he came forward to ascend the throne. The first thing he
did was to seize the four young sons of his deceased brother
in the palace of Kökserai and have them executed. This
atrocious deed roused general indignation against him, and
the ill-feeling was increased by the tyranny and arbitrary
conduct of his officials. Trade and movement of all kinds
soon came to a standstill at Samarkand, and the better-
most class of the inhabitants, long accustomed to unbroken
peace and tranquillity, scarcely dared now show themselves
in the streets. Mahmud was not without some education,

---

[1] Seïd Rakim says 896, on the authority of several chronograms written on the
death of Sultan Ahmed. It appears to me, however, that the date given by Baber
is more likely to be correct, as he was himself a contemporary of Sultan Ahmed's.

and wrote bad poetry, but he gave himself up to debauchery, neglected prayer, and having no respect for religion had treated with contempt the highly-venerated Khodja Obeïd-ullah. As may be imagined his reign was not of long duration, for he died within six months of his accession, most probably a violent death : his crafty and influential vizir, Khosru shah, however, kept the event secret for several days, during which he gained time to clear out the national treasury ; but when at length the sovereign's death became known among the people a revolution broke out, before which Khosru shah had to fly, and escaped with great difficulty.[1]

The Timourides of Transoxania now fell into hopeless disruption and anarchy amongst each other, and it required no great skill to foresee that the complete decay of their power was at hand. Three out of the five sons left by Sultan Mahmud, Mesu'd, Baïsonkur, and Sultanali fell to fighting with each other about the succession. The first, the eldest of them, made common cause with Khosru shah, his father's powerful vizir, took possession of Hissar, Kunduz and Bedakh'shan, on the near side of the Oxus, and would have had the best chance of obtaining the crown but for the opposition of Sultan Huseïn Mirza, who turned against him and his ally, not so much from lust of conquest as in order to protect more securely his own northern frontier ; and with this opposition to contend with, Mahmud of course lost all chances of succeeding.

Baïsonkur Mirza, who had during his father's lifetime been governor of Bokhara, was summoned thence by a powerful

---

[1] Khosru shah was a Turk of the tribe of Kiptchak ; his early youth was spent in the service of the Tarkhans ; he afterwards got into favour with Sultan Mahmud, even in the lifetime of the latter had a troop of 5,000 or 6,000 men at his own disposal, and held in fief the province of Bedakh'shan, from the Oxus to the Hindukush. On the death of his master he proclaimed himself independent in these territories, and kept up an army of 20,000 men. Intoxicated by ambition and arrogance he turned against the sons of his benefactor, put out the eyes of one and killed another· (Baber, original text, p. 36.)

party, and raised to the throne in Samarkand with all the usual
ceremonial. Baïsonkur was a youth of eighteen, with a
thoroughly Turkoman type of countenance; he was not
without ability, but, in spite of his most strenuous endeavours,[1]
found himself quite unable to keep his unruly nobles or the
influential priestly party in order. Each party wished to
make him the instrument of its own selfish plans; the result
was that each was dissatisfied with him, and in the end all
united in endeavouring to drive him from the throne. The
rebels maintained that during his government at Hissar he
had shown himself far more genial and sympathetic, and that
his present coldness had in consequence disgusted them.
They invited his younger brother Sultanali to come from
Karshi to Samarkand, and did homage to him in the same
summer palace of Baghi-No, in which Baïsonkur, separated
from his own people, was kept under a sort of arrest. Both
princes were jealously guarded in this palace until, towards
evening, Baïsonkur managed, by a pretext, to get down to
the lower court, whence he escaped by the sewer or kennel
into the open country, and took refuge in the house of the
highly-esteemed Khodjeke Khodja. When the news of his
flight became known, the people congregated before the house
of the Khodja, but no one dared to force the doors, and the
end of it was that, after a few days had elapsed, several
friends of the Sultan, headed by the influential Khodja
Ebulmekarim, brought him forth from his hiding-place,
restored him to the throne, and took the most energetic
measures for suppressing the rebellion. Sultanali and his
principal supporter, the Dervish Mahommed Tarkhan were
seized, and, after an ineffectual attempt to escape, brought
before Baïsonkur, who sentenced the former to have his eyes
put out, and the latter to be put to death. The sentence on
the rebel Tarkhan was carried out on the spot, and in spite

---

[1] He has written some good poetry, which has, however, never been collected in
any volume. Baber says he was also distinguished for his skill in caligraphy and
in painting.

of the desperation with which he clung in his mortal struggle to the columns of the portico, he was hewn in pieces there and then. Sultanali was more fortunate. The barber-surgeon entrusted with the operation of ' lancing ' [1] (the technical expression used by orientals for blinding or putting out the eyes), had intentionally performed his task so unskilfully as to leave the rebel prince's eyes uninjured ; and the only person blinded in the affair was Baïsonkur himself, who believed himself safely rid of all his enemies at the very moment when Sultanali was escaping to Bokhara, where he planned a more furious attack than ever on his brother. Soldiers were sent in pursuit of him, but his party proved too strong at Bokhara, and as soon as it came to fighting, Baïsonkur was hopelessly beaten, and had to retreat hurriedly behind the walls of Samarkand. After this disaster he found himself surrounded and menaced on three sides at once. Sultanali was rushing in on him from the west, that is from Bokhara, and Mes'ud Mirza was advancing from the south ; whilst in the east, in Endidjan or Khokand (as we now call it), Baber Mirza, the intelligent son of Omar Sheïkh, though still a youth, had set up a claim to his grandfather's throne. This man may with truth be described as one of the most remarkable of all the princes, whether in the eastern or western world, whose names have been handed down to us in history ; and his memoirs have been described by a learned Orientalist of modern times as the 'Commentaries of the Cæsar of the East.' His own penetration had shown him very soon that the edifice of the power of the Timourides in Transoxania was crumbling to pieces, and he came forward in the hope of averting this calamity by strenuous exertions, which proved however, as we shall see, fruitless. Samarkand then found itself, in the beginning of the year 903 (1496), menaced on

---

[1] In Persian, Mil keshiden. *Mil* is the name of a sharp lancet-shaped surgical instrument, which is run red-hot into the eyes of the offender. The small lance used by orientals for dyeing their eyelashes with *kohl* (the dust of black ironstone) also known by the name of *Mil*.

three sides at once. Fortunately for Baïsonkur the winter proved to be one of unusual severity. Baber and Sultanali had concluded an alliance on the basis of dividing Transoxania between them, but they suspended active operations on account of the severe cold; and Mes'ud Mirza followed their example on account of the fire of his love for his newly-married wife, the daughter of the Sheïkh Abdullah Berlas, to whom he was passionately devoted, and he was only anxious to spend his honeymoon undisturbed by the cares of ambition. Baïsonkur's difficulties were only staved off and not averted, for as soon as the thaw set in the allies from east and west closed in and besieged Samarkand for seven months. Baïsonkur sought for assistance right and left, but the only response he met with was from the Özbegs of the lower courses of the Yaxártes, who, always ready for anything which promised them chances of plunder, advanced to the neighbourhood of Samarkand, but at the last moment found they could not venture on fighting the united forces of Baber and Sultanali, and returned again. Baïsonkur, finding further resistance hopeless, secretly left his capital in the year 903 (1497), and, crossing the Oxus at Termez, took refuge with his brother Mes'ud Mirza. He was not twenty-two years old when he lost his throne after a long series of adventures, and hardly-fought battles; even his enemy Baber Mirza describes him as a just and highly-cultivated man, and the only accusation brought against him is that of belonging secretly to the sect of the Shiites, though he is said to have become converted afterwards to the true faith. He died in the year 905 (1499).[1] After the escape of Baïsonkur the sovereignty of Transoxania passed into the hands of the allies, Sultanali took charge of Bokhara and the district of Miyankal, and Baber of the town of Samarkand and the eastern portion of the country, but neither was able to main-

[1] Baïsonkur, the second son of Sultan Mahmud, was born in 882 (1477), and is described by Baber as having large eyes and a dark skin, but in other respects a purely Türkoman type of countenance.

tain himself very long: the former had to fly before the violence of his unruly vassal, and take refuge with Sultan Huseïn at Herat ; whilst the latter, finding it impossible to obtain food for his soldiers in the devastated and famished neighbourhood of Samarkand, and being further pressed by the earnest entreaties of his mother to return home, abandoned the attempt and retraced his steps homewards.[1] There is no question but that neither of them ever wielded more than a nominal authority; the real power was possessed in Bokhara by Abdul Ali Tarkhan, and in Samarkand by Khodja Ebulmekarim ; but the great object was, as Baber avows, not to allow a throne which had been occupied by the same dynasty for a space of 140 years to fall into the hands of strangers. But all was in vain. The star of the house of Timour was declining, and the youthful Baber Mirza was unable to arrest its sinking course anywhere, least of all in Transoxania. Sheïbani Mohammed Khan, a Djenghizide of the house of Djüdji, who had won his spurs in the disastrous fratricidal wars of the Timourides, had by this time occupied all the principal positions in the country with his brave Özbeg troopers, and followed up his successes by taking possession of the throne of Samarkand, and thus terminating completely once for all the rule of the Timourides.

The events consequent on this change of dynasty will be duly related in the next chapter, but before entering on them we must throw a glance over the intellectual movement called forth and fostered throughout the eastern half of the Mohammedan world by the influence of the race of the lame conqueror from the 'green city,' an influence which has gained the Timourides a well-deserved title of honour in the annals of Asia. The objects to which the culture of the countries

---

[1] Nothing can be conceived more tender than the relations between Baber and his mother, an intellectual woman, well versed in all the affairs of state. Her love for her child had led her to disapprove and oppose his dangerous ambition, and her real reason for so earnestly pressing his return was that she foresaw the revolution then silently brewing in Endidjan, which eventually cost the adventurous Timouride his inheritance.

beyond the Oxus were chiefly directed, were somewhat different from the studies pursued at the court of Shahrukh Mirza, or of Sultan Husein Mirza Baïkara at Herat : in the latter, poetry, history, medicine, jurisprudence, and other so-called secular sciences were pursued hand in hand with theology ; but in the former, with the exception of a short period, in the reigns of Ulug Beg and Ebusaïd, a dreamy religion, speculative theology and monasticism prevailed, to the exclusion of all else. It is difficult to determine precisely the amount of literary activity in either country, for although the first impulse undoubtedly originated in Iranian sources, it was taken up by Tchaghatian-Turkish scholars, and Tartar princes not only liberally assisted authors and artists, but themselves entered the lists with them, not disdaining even to occupy inferior positions in their ranks. Mir Ali Shir, has left in his book of 'Precious Collections,'[1] a list of the princes of the house of Timour who occupied themselves with litera-ture. Shahrukh Mirza wrote both Persian and Turkish poetry ; the following quatrain of his is still preserved to us : ' The hero must burn and glow in war, when wounded his horse's mane should be his couch ; the coward who calls him-self a man and stoops to sue for the enemy's mercy shall die the death of a dog.' He also left some attempts at love sonnets, and the expressions of his devotion to his beloved wife Gowher Shad (Jewel of Delight) still survive in the ballad lore of the people of Herat. Sultan Iskender Shirazi, the son of Omar Sheïkh, and Khalil Mirza both wrote poetry in Turkish and Persian, and the latter has left a whole collection of Turkish poems which are very highly spoken of by the celebrated poet Khodja Ismes Bokhari. We have already mentioned Ulug Beg's proficiency in astronomy and mathe-matics ; in addition to these exact sciences he cultivated literature, painting, and music, and in proof of his extraordi-nary memory it is stated that he could repeat seven different

---

Medjalis en nefais. The passage here referred to is taken from the extract already published by M. Bélin in his work above quoted, p. 65-82.

versions of the Koran by heart. Baïsonkur, son of Shahrukh Mirza, who died in his father's lifetime,[1] was always surrounded by poets, painters, musicians, and scribes; his son, Baber Mirza, who died of drinking at an early age,[2] has left several poetic fancies in the Turkish language. Sidi Ahmed Mirza, the son of Miranshah, also left a collection of works (a *divan* and a mesnevi) entitled ' Letafet-nameh ' (Book of Grace or Beauty); and finally, the list may be completed by the name of Baber Mirza, the founder of the Mogul dynasty in India, whose memoirs, already alluded to, bring him before us as a poet, statesman, and philosopher of the antique type and of extraordinary distinction.[3]

Taking all these facts into consideration, and bearing in mind the Eastern proverb, ' The people follow the faith of their princes,' we can scarcely be surprised to find that the age of the Timourides was distinguished by a civilisation such as is to be found nowhere and at no other time amongst any of the people of Islam, excepting possibly, the most flourishing period of the Ommeyyads in Spain and that of the first Abbasides in Arabistan. Doubtless the culture of the Timourides was mainly the consequence of the intellectual awakening in Iran under the rule of the latter Mongolian princes, but still science and art never flourished at the courts of Meraga, Tebriz and Sultanie in anything like the the same proportion or in as many various forms as at Herat and Samarkand. We will content ourselves with enumerating the following amongst the poets of the age :—Mevlana Abdur-rahman Djami, called the God-like, the great master of prose and verse, who excelled in different sciences such as theology,

---

[1] He died on the 6 Djemazi ul evvel 836 (1432), according to the date discovered by M. N. Chanikoff on a tombstone in the Mosallah at Herat.

[2] He was warned by a dangerous illness to abstain from excessive drinking, and retired overwhelmed with shame and penitence for a short time to Meshed, spending whole days in the mosque of Imam Riza. But his passion for drink proved stronger than his self-control ; he soon relapsed into his former habits and died in 861 (1458).

[3] There is scarcely another book in the whole range of the literature of Turkey and Persia containing so much information written in so simple and agreeable a sty'e, as the *Baber-namch*.

exegesis, ethics, philosophy, grammar, as well as in poetry; Suheïli or Sheïkhum Suheïli, the masterly translator of Bidpai's Indian fables, who lived first at the court of Ebusaïd and afterwards for twenty years at that of Mirza Huseïn Baïkara; Kasim ul envar (Dispenser of Light), also called Muayyin-eddin Ali, the greatest mystic poet of the age, who lived first at the court of Shahrukh, but being dismissed by him retired to Samarkand, and died in 837 (1433); Khodja Abdullah Hatifi, also Mesnevi Ghuy (mesnevi poet), author of the 'Timour Nameh,' or biography of Timour in verse; Khodja Ismet Bokhari, poet laureate to both Sultan Khalil and Ulug Beg, and instructor of the latter in poetry, who died in 845 (1441). Mevlana Huseïn Kuberaï, a descendant of the celebrated Nedjmeddin Kubera (a pupil of the learned Ebulvefa Khahrezmi), executed by the Mongolians at Urghendj. Mevlana Huseïn was distinguished as a mystic poet, and wrote a commentary on the 'Mesnevi' of Djelaliddin Rumi. Khodja Abdullah Murvarid (the Pearl) wrote under the name of Beyani a *divan* or collection of sonnets and odes, entitled, 'Munis ul ehbab' (Confidant of Friends), a work on epistolary writings. Mollah Binaï, son of an architect at Herat, who was in high favour at the court of Mirza Huseïn in his native city, until he quarrelled with Mir Ali Shir; he then went to Transoxania, was in favour there with Sultan Mahmud, and later named poet laureate to Sheïbani Mohammed Khan; he died in 922 (1516). Mohammed Salih, author of the epic 'Shebani Nameh,' who wrote besides graceful sonnets and composed a Turkish mesnevi in the same measure as the Medjnun and Leïla. Baber will not allow these compositions any merit, but that seems only to be because Mohammed Salik was a protegé of Sheïbani's and lived at the court of the Özbeg prince. Helali, author of the popular mesnevi, 'Shah and Dervish' (or King and Beggar) the indecency of which is rightly blamed by Baber. His memory was so remarkable that he knew between 20,000 and 30,000 distiches by heart. Last, but by no means least, we must name Mir Ali Shir, who is celebrated as a statesman and general as well as a fertile and imaginative writer. Though not, as is generally supposed, the founder of East Turkish literature,[1] he yet fully deserves the honour in which he was held[2] both in his lifetime and after his death, not only on account of his numerous Turkish compositions, but also on account of his zeal in defending the Turkish nationality from the prejudice and ridicule of Iranian scholars. Four centuries and a half have elapsed since his death, yet his works are still amongst the household treasures of every well-to-do Özbeg, though often very imperfectly understood. Theology, exegesis and mysticism generally were diligently studied by a whole band of attentive scholars, who, attaching themselves to this or that 'great star of science,' were active both with speech and pen. Setting aside the fact that every literary man invariably took up some one or other branch of science, and that many were endowed both with the poet's gifts and with the mantle of heavenly science, we may mention the following as distinguished in various technical learning; Mevlana Husami, a Khivan by birth, long a pupil and companion of the celebrated Khodja Ahrar at Karaköl. Khodja Oberdullah, a disciple and energetic promoter of the doctrines of Bahaeddin Nakishbend, who was a mystic and scholar of such great renown that the princes of his time fought with

[1] Turkish literature has gone through many phases since the Turkish people first became known, but has invariably presented a true reflex of their social, political and religious condition; according to the most ancient evidence in our possession, it seems to have been flourishing as early as the ninth century of the Christian era. The date of the *Kudatku Bilik* (some portions of which were edited by me in 1871) is 463 (1070), and although the author describes it as the first book ever written in Turkish, the language shows distinct marks of literary facility and previous literary activity.

[2] The opinion already existed that the Iranian element was intellectually far superior to the Turkish one in the population. Mir Ali Shir undertook to prove, from the literary productions of his countrymen, that the Turks could also boast of able authors; but finding he could not pretend to bring forward any equals to the lights then shining in Persian literature, he shifted his ground from the question of literary ability to that of moral worth, painting in vivid colours the bravery, honesty and faithfulness of the Turks. This interesting controversy is to be found in his *Muhakemet el lugetein*.

each other for his favour. In spite of this he scrupulously
adhered to Mohammed's principle, ' El fakru fakhri,' ' Poverty
is my pride' and lived in the neighbourhood of Karaköl,
tilling his fields with his own hands ; he died in 895 (1489) in
the village of Kumaghiran. His book, ' Tohfeï Ahrar,' on
morality and religion is still much read, and pilgrims from
far and wide still visit his shrine at Samarkand. Further,
Mevlana Fasih-eddin, who lived at the court of Mirza Huseïn
Baïkara and enjoyed the special favour of Mir Ali Shir. His
commentaries on the principal doctrinal works of his time are
still studied in the colleges of Central Asia ; he died in 919
(1513). The commentaries of Mollah Abdul Gaffur are less
known, but no less highly esteemed ; he was a scholar of
Djami's and a lawyer, and died in 916. Three other celebrated lawyers were Mevlana Muayyin of Ferrah, well known
for his biography of Mohammed and of the pillars of Islam ;
Mevlana Kemaleddin Huseïn, known by his numerous
writings on the exegesis of the Koran, and independent
studies on ethics ; and Mevlana Mohammed Kazi known by
his book ' Silsileï arifeïn ' (Series of Learned Men). The most
distinguished historians were Sherefeddin, celebrated for his
biography of Timour; and Abdurrezak, for his eloquently written and instructive history of the Timourides. The *Debistan*
(School of Religion) which treats of twelve different religions
in the East, and which the learned Orientalist, Sir W. Jones,
describes as one of the most intelligent and instructive of
Eastern books, was written about this time. Mathematics,
arithmetic and geography [1] were also by no means neglected ;
and who can tell how many more of the works of the most
remarkable intellects of that remarkable age may have been
lost entirely, or are only very imperfectly known to us ?

We cannot here enter into detailed literary and historical
researches, and must therefore content ourselves with passing

---

[1] Pre-eminent amongst the latter are Djami's treatise in the form of a catechism
on India, and Vasif's *Bilad-i-Tshin* (Chinese towns), a description of China probably compiled from the reports of the mission sent by Shahrukh Mirza to Pekin.

over in silence the list of grammarians and lawyers, merely
remarking that many of the grammars and syntaxes in use
to this day amongst the Moslim youth in all countries, date
from this time, and that many ceremonials and dogmas peculiar to the Central Asiatics may be traced back to the
teachings of the learned men of that day.

Every notion a Mohammedan in Asia or elsewhere pos-
sesses of culture, refinement, high civilisation—in short, of all
those qualities now only known to him by name—is derived
from the conditions which then flourished at the courts of
Herat and Samarkand. Amongst the arts most assiduously
fostered were those of caligraphy and of painting, the former
was practised by Sultan Ali (whom Ali Shir employed to
transcribe his works) and the latter by Behzad and Shah
Mozaffar ; for although the Timourides were zealous Sunnites,
they nevertheless ornamented their books with coloured illus-
trations, and their magnificent buildings with fresco paintings [1]
representing not only arabesques and inanimate objects, but
also celebrated princes and warriors, and occasionally even
saints. Many fine architectural works were produced during
the reigns of Shahrukh, Ulug Beg, Ebusaid and Mirza
Husein, and it is said that the architects Usta Mohammed
Sebz and Usta Kavameddin executed between them several
thousand public works. According to the historian Sam
Mirza, Mir Ali Shir erected in Khorasan alone no less than
three hundred and seventy mosques, colleges, karavanserais,
hospitals, reading-halls and bridges. What might not therefore be expected of the great sovereigns and rulers of such an
age ? Constant wars have obliterated in the countries beyond
the Oxus, in most cases, even the traces of ruins, but about
Herat there is more than one point where signs of former
flourishing civilisation are to be found. The refined tastes of
the Timourides have left their impression not only in the town
of Herat, in the Mosalla and the Khodja Abdullah Ansari,

[1] According to Baber, Ebusaid had the palace of Baber Mirza ornamented with
sculpture and the walls covered with pictures of battles.

but along the romantic banks of the Murghab, where several jutting rocks are crowned by the ruins of former summer-houses, and these ruins afford positive evidence of the extent to which fine art and poetry were employed by them to grace and ornament the surroundings of every-day life.

In spite of the presence of so many grave and learned men, theologians and sheīkhs, it was the custom of the courts of Herat and Samarkand to have feasts and drinking bouts, lasting often days together ; songs and music were a prominent feature of these entertainments, and musicians and composers were consequently held in high honour. According to Baber the most distinguished amongst them were Khodja Abdullah Murvarid (whom we have already mentioned), Kul Mohammed Udi, Sheīkh Neyi, and Huseīn Udi, who excelled on the harp, psalter and guitar (or dulcimer) ; others again, such as Mir Shadi, Gulam, and Mir Gazu, were known as musical composers. Those who are acquainted with the present state of Moham-medan Asia cannot fail to be struck by the fact that the court of the Timourides also boasted of *dancers*, and, according to Baber, even a Seīd (of the family of the prophet) named Bedr was enrolled amongst the most distinguished votaries of the Terpsichorean art, and had himself invented several new dances. What would be the horror of a modern Moslem at the notion of a Seīd, with his thick and ponderous turban, executing a *pas de deux*, or taking part in one of the dances still popular in Iran under the name of Herati ![1]

Time changes all ! and thus it has come about that Central Asia declined after the fall of the Timourides from the height of civilisation and true enthusiasm for all that is refined and beautiful, into the slough of ignorance and barbarism from

---

[1] I saw the dance called Herati danced at Shiraz in the year 1862. The dancer got upon a chair, and, keeping time to the music in all his movements, wrapped himself up in a linen sheet, and thus draped, went through a series of evolutions more clever than graceful, after which he gradually unrolled himself. There are other dances called Khorasani which date from this period ; they resemble quadrilles, and the dancers execute a series of figures, mimicking the process of courtship in a not very æsthetic manner.

which it has never as yet recovered itself. With its civilisation its political importance rapidly decayed; the princes of Bokhara and Samarkand had for centuries ruled over the finest portions of Mohammedan Asia, but their part on the stage of history was now played out, and that which was formerly the splendid empire of Transoxania has sunk in modern times into the miserable khanate of Bokhara.

XIII.

THE ÖZBEGS AND SHEÏBANI MEHEMMED KHAN.
906 (1500)—916 (1510).

ONE of the most pleasing traits in the character of the Turkish people has always been their custom of adopting the names of those princes whose glorious reigns or whose exertions for the public weal had given them special claims on the gratitude of their posterity as surnames, thus raising each one as it were to the dignity of a founder of a race, and marking in the most definite manner the part played by each in the regeneration of his country and on the stage of general history. We thus see the Turks penetrating first into Western Asia, as the outposts of the mighty empire of the Seldjukides, and there establishing on the ruins of Byzantium a new empire in which to this day they bear the name of Osmanlis, in remembrance of their leader Osman ; and thus we find the Turko-Mongolian[1] tribes, inhabiting the eastern territories of the blue horde, i.e., the country lying between the Volga and the sea of Aral, assuming[2] in honour of Özbeg, the ninth ruler of the

---

[1] In order that no exception may be taken to the expression Turko-Mongolian, I must here remark that I look upon the Özbegs as a people of a mixed Turkish-Mongolian, and not of purely Turkish, origin ; such fusions are not only not improbable in the case of Turks and Mongolians all professing the Mohammedan religion and all living together, but did in fact take place, the best proof of which is afforded by the list of names borne by the thirty-two Özbeg tribes, many of which are undoubtedly of Mongolian origin and identical with many still in use amongst the nomads of the desert of Gobi. Thus, for instance, Khitay mong : Kitat (for the alteration of the final *g* into *t* see *Uigurische Sprachmonumente*, p. 23) = Chinese, Nöks mong ; nokoson, wool (the letter *n* is hardly ever to be met with in Turkish as an *aspirate*) ; Tas mong : tass, a sort of grey eagle ; Dörmen mong : dörben = four ; miten mong : mite, cowardice, &c., &c.

[2] The oriental historians of Central Asia describe the old home of the Özbegs by the vague designation of Deshti Kiptchak = the steppe of Kiptchak, by which

house of Djüdji, the political designation of Özbegs.[1] 'Özbeg Khan,' says Abulgazi in his history of the Tartars,[2] 'honoured and rewarded every one according to his merits. He invited the people to embrace Islamism, and by means of him many were admitted within the fold of the Mohammedan faith. Therefore the people of Djüdji's race assumed the name of Özbeg, which they will retain unto the world's end.' Özbeg converted his people, and was besides, as Hammer truly remarks,[3] the third of the four great rulers who adorned the throne of Kiptchak; but nevertheless the Özbegs do not appear to have played any remarkable part as a race either in his time or in that of his immediate successors, although their name appears occasionally in the annals of the Timourides and is even incidentally mentioned by the Arabian traveller Ibn Batutah.

A hundred and fifty years later, however, when the once powerful golden horde of Kiptchak had been broken up into four parts, and Ivan Wassiliewitsch, the deliverer of Russia from the Tartar yoke, was menacing the power of Djüdji's descendants on the upper course of the Volga, we find the name of Ebulkhaïr, prince of the Özbegs, in the list of chiefs and vassals who renounced their allegiance to the ruler at Seraï and exercised the rights of sovereignty as 'grey-beards,'

they mean that portion of the Turanian highlands, stretching in a length of 600 fersakhs and a width of 300 fersakhs from the Caspian Sea eastward. The assumption is however erroneous, for although the Özbegs may have roamed with their flocks southwards into Khahrezm, yet in the north-east they did not penetrate as far as the lower courses of the Yaxartes until the decay of the Timourides. Their original home was more probably on the banks of the rivers of the Ural and the Emba, or in other words, the country now known as the territory of the 'little horde.'

[1] The word Özbeg means his own master, independent. Curiously enough, the same word was in use amongst the ancient Hungarians as the title of a dignity or of a certain rank, and is still to be seen in documents dated 1150. The celebrated Sheïkh Khudadad, who died in 939 (1592) made a pun when he found his pupil Arif Sofi, bewailing, as an Özbeg, Baber's first victory over Sheïbani, saying in Turkish: 'Sanga·ösbeg in Kirek mu'—Thou wilt have thine own master—alias Özbeg.

[2] Abulgazi's *Shadjrei Turki* (Turkish genealogy).

[3] *History of the Golden Horde*, p. 281. The other three were Batu, Berke, and Tokhtamish.

or independent khans.   Ebulkha'ir had gradually retired,
with the tents and herds of his nomads, before the storm
which was gathering in the. north of Christendom against the
Moslem power, and had sought refuge in the eastern steppes.
There he had risen to so great a reputation that, even during-
the reign of Kitchik Mohammed,[1] the last prince of the blue
horde, with whose fall Djüdji's throne in Kiptchak crumbled
to pieces, the Timourides Ebusa'id, Mohammed Djüghi and
Huse'in Ba'ikara applied to him for help and protection, as we
have seen in the previous chapter.   The Özbegs, far removed
from the influences of the Mohammedan civilisation of the
western Serai and the southern Transoxania, and by nature
a rude barbarian people, retained the rough character of
the old Turanian warriors much longer than their brethren
who had settled down in fixed habitations, and been subjected
to the refining influences of the Timourides.   They only
nominally professed the religion of the Arab Prophet ; their
habits and customs were, like themselves, a strange mixture of
Turkish-Mongolian elements, and whilst the Turks on the banks
of the Oxus and Yaxartes were gradually becoming familiarised
with the language, literature and general refinement of Iran,
the Özbegs still went about wrapped in sheepskins and horse-
skins, and the only trace of spiritual life to be found about
them was a certain amount of deference paid to the supposed
miraculous powers of their national saint, the ascetic Khodja
Ahmed Yesevi.[2]   Later on they settled down by degrees into
fixed habitations, and gradually threw off their barbarous
customs ; in former days the name of Tchaghataian was used
to designate the. settled, comparatively civilised Turk of
Transoxania, in contradistinction to that of Özbeg, which

---

[1] Hammer always spells the name Kütchük, forgetting that this means in
Eastern Turkish, a *young dog*, and that *little*, the epithet of the Khan in question,
is *kitchik*. Such mistakes are pardonable enough when we consider how scanty our
knowledge of Eastern Turkish then was.

[2] Khodja Ahmed Yesevi is to this day the patron saint of the wandering nomads
in the steppes of Central Asia. His moral and religious poems, of which some
examples will be found in my *Tchaghataian Studies of Language*, are as highly
venerated by the Kirghizes and O:begs as the Koran itself.

meant the wild inhabitant of the north-western steppe,[1] but now-a-days the meaning has become inverted: the modern meaning of the word Özbeg is identical with that formerly expressed by Tchaghataian, and the uncivilised barbarous Turk is now known by the name of Kirghiz or Kazak (which signifies wanderers, vagabonds).

Ebulkhaïr seems to have had a perfectly just appreciation of the times in which his lot was cast. He indulged no thought of conquest, which would have been impossible under the circumstances then existing in Central Asia, and contented himself with merely coming forward when the successors of Timour invoked his help in the course of their furious civil wars. He assisted the cause of Ebusaïd, as also that of Minutchehr Mirza, and that of Sultan Huseïn Baïkara, and his Özbegs invariably returned home laden with spoil, which obtained for his reign of forty years the credit of being more glorious than that of any other prince of the desert. The Turkomans have a proverb, 'The sand of the desert is lightly blown away by a breath; still more lightly is the fortune of man destroyed.' Ebulkhaïr's power and reputation had raised him up enemies and rivals; the grey-beards of the neighbouring steppe united against him, and his own nearest relations, including Bürghe Sultan, mentioned above, turned against him, mindful of the Tartar proverb, 'If the enemy attacks thy father's tent join him and share the plunder.'[2] The consequence was that he was soon overcome; he lost his life in battle, and his numerous were family scattered over the

---

[1] This is proved by a distich which the author of the *Sheibani Nameh* puts into the mouth of his hero and which runs thus:

'Tchaghatai ili meni Özbeg diymesun
Bihude fikr kilib gam yimesum.'

I.e., 'the Tchaghataian people shall not call me an Özbeg, and shall not be afflicted with useless thoughts.' The name, which was then a term of reproach, became in course of time a title of honour; for the *settled civilised* Turks of all tribes are known at the present day as 'Özbegs.'

[2] In the original of Abulgazi, p. 106, the proverb is quoted thus: 'Atang yort'n jau tchapsa, ailandura birghe tchap.' Surely few languages possess any similar proverb breathing so emphatically the spirit of murder and plunder.

desert in all directions. The fifth of the eleven sons [1] whom he left behind him, Sheïkh Haïdar Sultan, nominally succeeded him, but his authority was very limited, and the eyes of the Özbegs were already turned to a grandson of Ebulkhaïr's, Prince Mehemmed Sheïbani, also called Shahbakht (or 'King's Fortune'), on whom all their hopes were centred, and who, in spite of his youth, had already given signs of unmistakeable promise.[2] Sheïbani (as we shall in future invariably call him) had lost his father Budag Sultan ('Blossom of Kings'), and his mother Kuzi Begum [3] (Mrs. Lamb), while very young,[4] and with his brother Sultan Mahmud was brought up under the guardianship of Karadja Beg, a faithful servant of their grandfather's, who took the warmest interest in the welfare of the orphan princes. Upon the death of Sheïkh Haïdar, Karadja and his charges, who were by this time grown up, were forced to retire before the enmity of Ebulkhaïr's family to the lower courses of the Yaxartes, where Sheïbani gathered about him the scattered 'Auls' (groups of tents) of his grandfather's hordes, and began quietly to make preparations for raising the diminished reputation of his house by fulfilling the sacred duty of requiring blood for blood ; his immediate object was to

---

[1] Their names were : Budagh Sultan, Khodja Mehemmed Sultan, Ahmed Sultan, Mehemmed Sultan, Sheïkh Haïdar Sultan, Sandjar Sultan, Ibrahim Sultan, Kötchküendji Sultan, Süyündj Khodja Sultan (whose mother was a daughter of Ulug Beg) Ak Burk Sultan and Seïd Baba Sultan. The descendants of the two first-named princes alone played any part in the history of Central Asia, and their genealogy has in consequence been accurately preserved. Nothing is known of the descendants of the other sons of Ebulkhaïr.

[2] He is sometimes called Shahi Beg by Persian historians, which has been transformed by Deguignes into Shaïbek. The Iranian historians are also mistaken as to the year of his birth ; the *Rauzat es Sefa* fixes it for 905, but that, as we shall presently see, was the year of his accession. Sheïbani was really born in the year 855.

[3] Not Nuri Begum, as it is spelt in the lithographed edition of the *Rauzat es Sefa*.

[4] Just before the taking of Samarkand in 906, Sheïbani told his poet-friend Mehemmed Salih that he had lost his father forty years before. The latter must therefore have died in the year 876 (1471), when Sheïbani, who was born in 855 (1451), would have been about twenty-one years old.

chastise Bürghe Sultan, who had taken up his abode on the borders of a wood in the upper courses of the same river, for his shameful betrayal of Ebulkhaïr. So long as he felt himself weak Sheïbani feigned conciliation, but he was only waiting for his opportunity, which came before long. In one of those long icy winter nights in which the steppes, at all times monotonous and melancholy, become perfectly appalling in their darkness and bleakness, he attacked the premises of his opponent with a handful of followers, and killed many of his servants. Bürghe himself lost his life in spite of a touching act of fidelity towards him by one of his own people.[1] Having thus succeeded in his first adventure, the young hero soon saw himself at the head of a considerable body of Özbeg troopers, with whom he felt himself equal to greater deeds of arms, the opportunity for which very soon presented itself. A collision with the Timourides in Transoxania was inevitable. The throne of Samarkand was at that time occupied by Sultan Ahmed, the son of Ebusaïd, and the northern frontiers of the empire were confided to the care of the viceroy Mezid Tarkhan, a son of Kishlik Khan. Sheïbani had at first offered his services to the latter, and was really for a short time in his pay, but Mezid soon found out that his Özbeg chieftains were going to ride roughshod over him, and determined to get rid of them at any price : he sent them off to Abdul Ali Tarkhan, the powerful vassal

---

[1] At daybreak, search was made everywhere for Bürghe, who was known to have been wounded ; some of Sheïbani's people discovered marks of blood on the snow, which they tracked farther and farther into the wood until they came upon a soldier lying severely wounded. They took him prisoner, and on asking him his name, he declared himself to be Bürghe Sultan. When brought before Sheïbani he recognised him at once as being, not Bürghe himself, but his servant Münghe Bi, and he asked him, 'Why didst thou give thyself out to be Bürghe Sultan?' 'My Lord,' answered the faithful servant, 'I was brought up with Bürghe, and have eaten of his bread and his salt many a time. When I saw that his life was sought after, I was willing enough to sacrifice my own for him, and receive in my own breast the arrow intended to kill him. That was my desire; it lies now with thee to fulfil it or not as thou willest.' Sheïbani was generous enough to reward the honest servant and set him at liberty, but Bürghe was nevertheless subsequently found and executed.

of Bokhara, whose court, as regarded its size, splendour and luxury, vied with that of his imperial master. He received the young warriors with open arms, and made good use of them in repelling the invasions of the Mongolians in the north-west. The grandsons of Ebulkhaïr were also employed against the rebellious vassals of the northern province of Turkestan; they felt themselves at home in these regions, and the security this feeling gave them, possibly still more the consciousness of their growing power, inclined them to declare themselves dissatisfied with the ordinary pay for their services; they were pacified at length by being put in possession of the towns of Otrar, Sabran, and Siganak, which in fact formed the nucleus from which the gigantic empire of Sheïbani was afterwards developed. Sheïbani was secretly supported by numerous partisans and adventurous nomads, and permanent cordiality between him, with his increasing power, and the decaying Timourides was impossible : a cause of quarrel soon arose, and before the death of Ahmed, Sheïbani had declared himself independent on the Yaxartes, forced the viceroy Mezid Tarkhan to enter into alliance with him, and exchanged the part of a mercenary in their service for that of the most dangerous rival of the house of Timour.

The impetuous warlike tempers of the young nomad chiefs were in themselves cause enough for endless wrangles and disputes, and on the other hand the state of anarchy and violence reigning amongst the vassals of Transoxania, contributed not a little to encourage Sheïbani Mehemmed Khan, who had began life simply as a harmless adventurer, to enter on larger plans of conquest. His first great enterprise was directed against Samarkand in the year 905 (1499).

The writer of the 'Sheïbaniade' informs us that Sultan Mahmud, Sheïbani's brother, had invaded the country as far back as in the time of Baïsonkur Mirza, and penetrated as far as Dizzak,[1] but had there been repulsed. On his return home

---

[1] The modern Djizzak.

Sheïbani reproached him for not having communicated his intentions to him beforehand, but he nevertheless determined to revenge his brother's defeat, and crossed the Yaxartes with an auxiliary force composed of 1,000 Djetes. The latter, however, betrayed him and obliged him to retreat hurriedly. Determined, as we are told in the words of his spiritual teacher,[1] to begin his conquest of the country 'not in the centre but from the very border,' he sent out an address to all the Turkish chieftains of the neighbourhood, drawing their attention to the favourable condition of affairs, and summoning them to assist in the overthrow of the Timouride rule. Though the edifice of power of the Timouride in Transoxania was become thoroughly rotten and tottering, there were, nevertheless, still many Turks who remained faithful to their masters in Samarkand ; Sheïbani found he could do nothing until these were won over, and it was not until he had induced the principal of them, Kütchüm Sultan, Süyündj Khodja Sultan,[2] Hamza Sultan, and Mehdi Sultan to embrace his cause, that he ventured on setting forth with a well-equipped army on his march on Samarkand.

There Sultanali had nominally reigned since the retreat of Baber to Endidjan, but the real direction of affairs was in the hands of the chief kadi, Khodja Ebulmekarim,[3] whom we

---

[1] Like all the Turkish warriors of that day Sheïbani had a spiritual teacher whom he consulted on all occasions, and whose advice he always blindly followed. His name was Sheïkh Manzur. Sheïbani, whilst still in the service of Abdul Ali, feeling the promptings of ambition strongly within him, one day expressed himself thus : ' Why should Abdul Ali, who is but of common birth, possess sovereign authority (Ahmed's vassals were at that time practically sovereigns) ; whilst I, who am born of princes, am but his servant ? ' This remark was repeated to Sheïkh Manzur, and when Sheïbani next visited him he had the cloth laid for supper. When supper was over and the cloth removed, the Sheïkh turned to the Özbeg prince saying : 'Dost thou see that this table-cloth is taken off, not by snatching it up in the centre, but by folding up each corner ? and so the country must be taken, not by seizing the capital, but by securing the frontiers.' About this time, says Seïd Rakim (from whom this anecdote is taken), Sheïbani went to Khiva, borrowed some auxiliaries of the tribe of Mangit, and began his conquests in good earnest.

[2] These two were his uncles. It would appear therefore that *all* the members of the house of Ebulkhaïr did not at once unanimously embrace Sheïbani's cause.

[3] Ebulmekarim, i.e. the 'most honourable,' was merely a title ; the proper name of this ambitious prelate was Khodja Yahya.

have already alluded to. We learn from the ' Sheïbani Nameh ' that his ancestors had held the post of Sheïkh ul Islame of Samarkand for 400 years. He proved, however, as unfit to govern as his nominal sovereign, and still more unequal to cope with the danger threatening the country from the advancing enemy. It is, therefore, not surprising that Sheïbani, after besieging the town for ten days and repelling a sortie from the gate of Sheïkhzade, entered the town by the gate of Tshihar-rah, penetrated unresisted up to the summer palace of Baghi-No,[1] and at length had himself to attack the garrison within the town. The conflict began at noon-day. Sheïbani took part in it, displaying reckless courage ; the butchery lasted all night ; the next morning a report was spread that Baki Tarkhan, a son of Abdul Ali Tarkhan, under whom Sheïbani had commenced his career, was coming from Bokhara to the help of the Samarkandians, and was already encamped outside the fortress of Debusi. At this news the Özbegs saw themselves forced to give up the advantages they had gained, and after investing Samarkand they hurried on towards Bokhara. That city, deprived of all auxiliary forces, had nothing for it but to capïtulate. Sheïbani set up his head-quarters there, installed his mother and her family in the palace, and then pursued his march towards Karaköl. The inhabitants of that place rose against the garrison and traitorously murdered them, which forced the Özbegs to recapture the place, and it was not until Karaköl had been visited with all the severity of Tartar martial law that the siege of Samarkand was undertaken. The well-fortified capital held out nine months, and would possibly have withstood the Özbeg onslaught still longer but for a famine which set in, and but for the discords between the ambitious Khodja Ebulmekarim and the Prince Sultanali culminating in open enmity. Sheïbani, aware of this state of

---

[1] It appears by this that Baghi-No and the other summer palaces, with their extensive grounds, were all in the interior of the city of Samarkand. If that is so, the space between the wall of the town and the fortress (within which was the citadel or ark) must have been greater than the present condition of the would lead us to believe.

things, wrote to the princely puppet, enquiring whether ' he
was not tired of the guardianship of the Khodja,' and advising
him to ' do homage to the star of the house of Ebulkhaïr, now
once more by God's grace in the ascendant, and thus secure
his own fortune by a friendly alliance.' By way of demon-
· strating still more strongly his friendly dispositions, he proposed for the hand of Sultanali's mother, who accepted him.[1]
All these transactions took place privately, in strict secresy ;
and at last one fine day, on a certain Friday, Sheïbani quietly
entered the besieged city on one side, while Khodja Ebulmekarim, totally ignorant of all that was going on, was at prayer
in a mosque on the other side. This took place in the
beginning of the year 906 (1500). The city, thunderstruck,
had to submit quietly to its fate. The marriage of Sheïbani
with Zohra Begum, the widow of Sultan Ahmed, was celebrated at once, but Baber says, the poor Begum was treated
by her new husband no better than a drudge, and Sultanali
died soon after,[2] apparently a violent death.

The yoke of the savage and covetous sons of the steppes
weighed heavily on Samarkand and the surrounding country ;
the inhabitants sought on all sides for help to shake it off, and
finally invited the brave and generous Baber Mirza to come
forward and deliver the home of his ancestors from slavery.[3]
We have already mentioned how much Baber had the interests
of his family at heart ; he was at that moment wandering

---

[1] The *Sheïbani Nameh* (Mehemmed Salih) says that Sultanali's mother took the
initiative, and had herself sent a messenger with a proposal of marriage to the
victorious Özbeg. The statement however sounds incredible.

[2] Baber says Sultanali was murdered, but the author of the *Sheïbaniade* declares
he was accidentally drowned whilst riding along the banks of the Koheks
(Zerefshan).

[3] The bitter enmity between the different members of the house of Timour is best
proved by the total indifference with which Sultan Huseïn Mirza, then in the
prime of life, witnessed the occurrences in Transoxania. He was no doubt
effectually hindered from any action in favour of Samarkand, on the one hand by
the revolt of his son Bediuzzeman, and on the other hand by the audacious conduct of Khosru shah at Hissar ; but if, instead of quarrelling with each other, these
three had united in action, Sheïbani could have accomplished absolutely nothing in
the face of their united power.

about the upper courses of the Zerefshan with a few followers, including Khodja Ebulmekarim. The Khokhandians drew near to Samarkand, under cover of the darkness one night in the autumn of 906 (1500), the inhabitants welcomed them gladly, and Sheïbani lost the town in the same way as he had gained it. His Özbegs were mostly encamped on the plain of Kani-gul, so that a regular defence was impossible. About 4co men were killed in the first surprise, and next morning Sheïbani promptly recognised the hopelessness of his situation, and saw that there was nothing left for him but to retire as quickly as possible, with what still remained to him, to Bokhara.

Baber remained in possession of Samarkand, but his prosperity only lasted till the following spring, that is, until the undaunted Özbeg chieftain felt himself again strong enough to venture on a fresh attack. The campaign began by a series of reciprocal surprises, in which wonders of bravery were displayed, which culminated in the great battle of Serpul on the banks of the Zerefshan, between Bokhara and Samarkand, in which Baber, notwithstanding his heroic exertions, was hopelessly beaten, and with difficulty escaped into the fortress of Samarkand. Baber ascribes his defeat to the plundering propensities of his Mongolian auxiliaries, but this does not appear to have been entirely the case. The courage and presence of mind displayed by the founder of the Mongolian Empire in India, and his principal officers, on that memorable day, are no doubt worthy of all praise, but the warriors of Transoxania and Endidjan, refined and accustomed to the courtesies of life, although numbering nearly 40,000 men, found themselves quite unable to stand against the impetuous savageness and bellicose roughness of the Özbegs. Baber's losses were very great ; in spite of his great intellectual cultivation, he was not free from superstition, and the fact that out of the number of his generals three *Ibrahims* [1] had fallen on that day struck his

---

[1] These were : Ibrahim Tarkhan, Ibrahim Saru, and Ibrahim Djani.

imagination as a bad omen. He endeavoured with his usual energy to take measures at Samarkand for renewing the fight, but soon came to the melancholy conclusion that the cause of his dynasty was hopelessly lost in Transoxania. Sheïbani had made good use of his victory, closely pursued the fugitives and shut them up in Samarkand. A siege of four months ensued, the hardest recorded in the annals of the former capital of Timour. Whilst the besiegers were feasting profusely on the produce of the fertile country around, the Tchaghataians shut up within the city were forced to have recourse to horse's and donkey's flesh, a fearful abomination in the eyes of a Mohammedan, and even to the bark of trees, whilst their horses were given wood-shavings in place of fodder. Anarchy and social disorganisation followed, and Baber, seeing himself already half abandoned in his deserted fortifications, escaped himself at midnight through the gate of Sheïkhzade, and saved his life by a perilous flight, in the course of which his elder sister Khanzade Begum was taken prisoner. She afterwards became the wife of Sheïbani.[1]

Thus fell Samarkand, and with it the Empire of the Timourides. The Özbegs, breathing only revenge, fell to plundering the city, but the inhabitants, justly dreading the rage of the conqueror, had already all taken to flight ; amongst the fugitives was Sheïbani's mortal enemy, the temporary chief Khodja Yahya. To avoid recognition, the pious man . had committed that which is a crime in the eyes of a Mohammedan and shaved off his beard. But he was nevertheless discovered, and taken prisoner. When asked by Sheïbani how

---

[1] 'It was a pitch dark night in the territory of Great-Sogd, which is cut up by canals and brooks. About daybreak I perceived that I had left my companions far behind ; my saddle-girths gave way, the saddle turned, I fell head over heels, and although I got on horseback again, I did not recover my senses till late at night. Life and late events seemed to pass before me as in a dream. It was nearly mid-day when we encamped near Ilanoti, killed a horse, and gave our beasts some rest . . . . . It was not till we reached Dizzak that we were able to refresh ourselves with fat meat, good bread, and the delicious flavour of melons and sweet grapes.' Such is Baber's account of this flight in his memoirs. Original text, p. 117.

he came to have conceived the horrible idea of shaving off his
beard, he replied by a Persian stanza, signifying 'He who
seeks to quench the flames sent by God will only burn his
own beard.'[1] The 'heavenly flame,' Sheïbani, was not however moved by this witty compliment, and Khodja Yahya's
ambitious career was cut short by the hand of the executioner.
The conqueror treated all the adherents of the fallen dynasty
with equal severity, and thereby caused a panic which paralysed all further resistance; and Sheïbani, after reconciling
himself with his brother who had threatened him with a revolt
at Oratepe, found his position so secure that he might easily
have undertaken an expedition across the Oxus, with his
comparatively small army. But the moderation and prudence
of the Özbeg conqueror were no less remarkable than his
bravery and perseverance. He had no sooner taken possession of the throne of Samarkand than his mouth began to
water for the fertile district of Khorasan, but the throne of
Herat was then still occupied by the mighty and magnificent
Mirza Huseïn Baïkara, and Sheïbani was too well acquainted
with the strength and the resources of such an opponent to
venture on direct hostilities; his attacks were confined to those
parts of Khorasan where Mirza Huseïn's authority was but
weak. One of these was Belkh, where Prince Bediëzzeman
had unfurled the standard of rebellion; another was the
territory of Khosru shah,[2] the former vizir of Sultan Ahmed,
who, after treacherously ridding himself of his benefactor, had
seized upon Hissar, Khatlan, Kunduz and Bedak'hshan, and
whom Sheïbani felt himself obliged to declare war against.
Before taking this step, the Özbeg conqueror had to make
himself secure in the rear by subduing Khaneke Sultan and
Aladja Sultan, Mongolian relations on the mother's side of
Baber, who could dispose of a considerable force of Mongolians

---

[1] The original stanza runs thus :—

Tchiraghira ki Yzd ber furuzed
Her ankes tuff kuned rishesh besuzed.

[2] See note in preceding chapter, p. 231.

and Kalmucks on the right bank of the Yaxartes, in the neighbourhood of Shahrukhie and Tashkend, and who, partly out of envy, partly from the desire to avenge their unfortunate nephew, were thwarting and obstructing the Özbegs in every way. The first campaign had to be undertaken before the year in which Samarkand fell was out. In the middle of an unusually severe winter Sheïbani marched northwards with his army wrapped in furs; his brother, Sultan Mahmud, and Timour Sultan led the advanced guard, composed of 6,000 of the bravest Özbegs; they had, however, to turn back and retrace their steps without accomplishing anything, in consequence of the extreme cold, and also probably because the more hardy Mongolians prevented their obtaining any kind of advantage. Sheïbani himself found the flame of his martial ardour considerably cooled in the icy atmosphere of the steppe, and returned to Samarkand. The Mongolians followed as far as Oratepe, and though this place was retaken and peace made with Khaneke in the following spring, it was nothing more than an armistice, for Sheïbani had scarcely entered the territory of Khosru shah before the Mongolians again challenged him, and this time instead of attacking his own frontiers, fell on Tembel Sultan, his viceroy at Khokhand.

Tembel's revolt had been the immediate cause of Baber's overthrow, and of the easy triumph of the Özbeg arms, and he had, in consequence, the strongest possible claim on Sheïbani's protection. But there were not wanting other reasons to induce the adventurous Özbeg prince to abandon for the moment his further conquests, and bring all his strength to bear on his enemies in the interior of Turan. Khaneke, no less brave and ambitious than Sheïbani himself, relied on all the Mongolians and Kalmucks between the Yaxartes and the desert of Gobi, and nothing more was needed than an understanding between the former and the Timourides in Khorasan to destroy once for all the future plans of the Özbegs. Conscious of this, Sheïbani, in 911

S

(1505), marched his entire army on Shahrukhie, which he invested, and then proceeded up the Yaxartes as far as Akhsi, five miles from where the Mongolian army was drawn up in order of battle. The picture drawn by the author of the 'Sheïbani Nameh' of the composition and equipment of the two armies is interesting and unique of its kind ; but the account of the battle, which lasted two days, and was one of the greatest ever fought between Mongolians and Turks, is no less remarkable : the result was in the end favourable to the Özbegs. Khaneke and his brother were taken prisoners, and when brought before Sheïbani were prepared for certain death, but the conqueror surprised them by an unexpected display of extreme magnanimity, comforting them in their trouble with appropriate parables, and swearing a solemn oath that not a hair of their own or of their belongings' heads should be injured. He only required the surrender of the fortress of Shahrukhie, in which the mother of the Mongolian princes was commanding. Touched by the generosity with which her children had been treated, she at once agreed to these conditions, peace was restored, and Sheïbani was thus enabled to turn his arms against his enemies on the left bank of the Oxus without fear of mischief in his rear. Meanwhile circumstances had of course considerably altered there. A bitter party warfare had raged between Khosru shah, lord of Hissar, Kunduz, Khatlan and Bedak'hshan, and the other vassals of Sultan Huseïn Mirza, who were striving for independence ; but nevertheless, on becoming aware of their common danger, they entered into an alliance against Sheïbani, and set every conceivable lever to work against him, but their exertions were in vain, and they could never obtain the slightest advantage over him. The Özbeg prince, after his other conquests, was prosecuting his campaign against Khosru shah, when he learnt that Tembel, in whose interests he had just brought an obstinate struggle to a close, had rebelled against him, and he was forced to embark on another campaign on the north-eastern frontier of his empire. Tembel and his seven brothers and sisters paid for their ingratitude with their lives. Sheïbani then hurried back across the Oxus, and his mere presence proved sufficient to disperse the armies of his opponents united at Khatlan, where Baber held the most prominent position. His brother Sultan Mahmud had in the meantime taken Kunduz, where he fell ill, and died. Hostilities were now commenced against Tchin Sofi, lord of Khahrezm, a devoted adherent of the cause of Sultan Huseïn Mirza; Sheïbani himself led his advanced guard. He was followed by Prince Obeïdullah, who had only been married a fortnight when he left his young wife at the call to arms. As usual, the march was commenced in the depth of winter, to facilitate the passage of the Oxus at any point which might be deemed most favourable. Özbegs were now opposed to Turkomans, who formed the chief portion of Tchin Sofi's army, but they were well matched: the siege of Khahrezm, the chief fortress, lying between the modern Khiva and Hezaresp, was prolonged with extraordinary obstinacy, until it became evident that the most pressing necessity was that of effecting the total destruction of Khosru shah, so as to deprive Tchin Sofi of all chances of assistance from that quarter. Khosru shah, so powerful of yore in all the territory of the upper Oxus, now saw himself beaten on all sides by Sheïbani's generals, until, finally, he was taken on his retreat and put to death with 700 of his most faithful followers.[1] His head was cut off and sent to Tchin Sofi, then surrounded by ruined fortifications and a famished soldiery, but he did not nevertheless allow himself to be thereby in the least intimidated; he had courageously resisted the attacks of the Özbegs during six months, and he held out three more, until at length the citadel was taken by storm, and he met his death on the ruins by the arrows of his own people. Hardly five years had elapsed since

---

[1] Mirkhond relates that he fell alive into Sheïbani's hands, was first dragged through the streets of Kunduz tied to a donkey's tail, and then executed. Mirkhond says further, in speaking of Khosru shah's character, that 'he was severe and just as a ruler, pious as a Mohammedan, but cruel and ungrateful as a man.'

the taking of Samarkand, and now Sheïbani found himself, as the result of this last success, in possession of the whole of Turan, Endidjan in the east, Shahrukhie and Tashkend in the north, the mountainous Hissar, Belkh and Bedak'hshan in the south, and now, finally, Khahrezm in the west; all had submitted to his victorious arms: the poverty-stricken Özbegs, who previous to the capture of Samarkand were wrapped in sheepskins, now saw themselves steeped in the riches and luxuries of Transoxania, and the fame of the successors of Ebulkhaïr had spread far and wide.

Sheïbani now felt himself for the first time equal to attack the aged Sultan Huseïn Miŕza, and the decisive action between the house of Timour and the Özbegs was now to be fought; it need scarcely be said that both parties entered the lists fully equipped and perfectly armed. Sheïbani's former deeds of arms had attracted to his standard all the warlike spirits of the Oxus and Yaxartes countries, and in addition to this all the principal spiritual authorities were active in promoting his cause. The Iranian people had long ceased to play any part in the affairs of the countries of the Oxus, but the different Turkish tribes were all the more filled with enthusiasm for this new Timour, who would lead them to fresh plunder and fresh spoils, and joyfully swelled the ranks of his followers. Sultan Huseïn Mirza, conscious of the impending danger, had summoned his sons and other relatives to rally round his throne with their troops and march against the invading Özbeg army. A large contingent drawn from Afghanistan, Sistan, Khorasan, Fars and Djordjan was gathered together in the north of Herat, but it lacked the chief element of strength, unity; and the Timourides were still wasting their time in petty squabbles with each other when Sheïbani crossed the Oxus near Kerki, in the year 911 (1505), and totally defeated the vanguard of their army near Meïmene. Meantime Sultan Huseïn Mirza died, fortunately for himself, as he escaped being a witness of the ruin of his family; but most unfortunately for his sons, who were all at sixes and sevens with each other, and who lost with him the last shadow of resolution and authority, and consequently their last hope of salvation. His successor Bediuzzeman Mirza summoned a family council in which Baber Mirza, already lord of Kabul, and his vizir Djihanghir took part; but this forced unity availed nothing, for Sheïbani, who had advanced as far as the right bank of the Murghab, reckoned so confidently on a complete victory, that he, without further preliminary, despatched an envoy to Herat to invite Bediuzzeman to do him homage, pointing out at the same time the great respect which the old Sultan Huseïn Mirza had always paid to his grandfather Ebulkhaïr. The proud Timouride gave the envoy a curt answer, upon which the Özbeg army advanced from Merv and offered the army of the Timourides battle on the plain of Mervitchak.[1] There was immense emulation amongst the Özbegs to serve in the advanced guard, and the distinguished names of Timour Sultan, Abdullah Khan, Mahmud Sultan and other near relations of Sheïbani are enrolled amongst those in the front ranks of the combatants. The only Timouride on the other hand who showed any signs of courage was the aged general Zulnun, who attacked the enemy, but was overpowered directly and fell. This was enough to cause a general panic; Seïd Abdullah Mirza escaped and joined Kebek at Meshed, Abdulbaki and Emir Mohammed Burunduk fled to Sebzevar, whilst Bediuzzeman himself got away to Herat with Muzaffar Huseïn Köreken; but they were only able to stop there a few hours, for the Özbeg army was close at their heels, and the successor of the powerful Sultan Huseïn Mirza saw himself forced to abandon his family and his treasures, and wander forth a homeless fugitive. Herat opened its gates to the enemy, and Sheïbani made his entry there on the 11th

---

[1] Now called *Martchah*, on the lower courses of the Murghab, one of the haunts of the Sarik and Salor Turkomans. A few years ago both Martchah and ·Pendjdeh paid tribute to Herat, and were inhabited by Djemshidi nomads, who related to me whilst I was living amongst them marvellous stories of the many ruins existing there.

Moharrem of the year 913 (May 24, 1507). More generous than the former conquerors of the city, he contented himself with levying a contribution of 100,000 *tenghes*, and spared this celebrated seat of science and art the infliction of a visit from his plundering Özbegs. He took up his abode outside the city ; the members of his fugitive adversary's family were presented to him, and although himself at that time fifty-eight years old, he fell so violently in love at first sight with the bride of Muzaffar Husein Mirza that, in spite of all representations and the assurance that she was already the legal wife of the above-named Timouride, he determined to marry her. The treasures of the family, including an enormous quantity of gold and silver plate, and valuable rubies, onyxes, pearls and diamonds were brought out to the camp. The family of Bediuzzeman were treated with every mark of respect and consideration, and all the people, who, from fear of the Özbegs,[1] had hidden among the rocky defiles of the Badgiz hills, gradually returned and resumed their ordinary occupations.

Sheïbani had conquered the throne of Transoxania on the battlefield of Serpul, and the battle of Mervitchak now put him in possession of the whole of Khorasan. It was in vain that the few Timourides who had escaped alive from that great slaughter collected their forces for a last desperate resistance ; the Özbegs, like the Mongolians of old, overran the whole of western Khorasan with lightning rapidity, and one fortress after another fell into their hands. Prince Ebul Mushin Mirza, on hearing of the catastrophe of Mervitchak, collected together a considerable body of troops from Irak at Meshed, but the Özbegs, headed by Mehemmed Timour Sultan and Obeïdullah Khan (the former a son, and the latter a nephew of Sheïbani's), surprised the Timouride army

---

[1] Outside the town of Herat the Özbegs appear, from the accounts of Per-sian historians, to have acted pretty much after the fashion of their kinsmen the Mongolians. They tortured the poor defenceless people to make them give up their hidden treasures, and made prisoners of as many as they could carry with them.

one morning before Djam, whilst their officers were all still sleeping off the effects of the previous night's orgies. Ebul Mushin Mirza and his immediate attendants were cut down, and the whole army fled in disorder. The Özbeg arms were no less fortunate at Sebxevar, on the western frontier of Khorasan, whither Ibn Huseïn Mirza, the former commandant of Kain, had retired with the remnant of the Timouride army. The town was taken, Ibn Huseïn succeeded in escaping, but the two princes Abdul Baki and Burunduk, lost their lives in the defence. Twelve princes of the house of Timour had now fallen by the sword of the Özbeg, but Sheïbani's ambition was not yet satisfied. After the taking of Herat he hurried across the Oxus, leaving his sons behind him in Khorasan; he was received with great pomp at Bokhara, but merely passed through and pressed onwards on his march to the northern territories of the Yaxartes, to punish the Mongolian Mahmud Khan, a son of Yunis Khan, who had rebelled in his absence.[1] As soon as peace had been restored there he returned to Khorasan to complete the work of conquest. In the year 914 (1508) the province of Djordjan also fell into his power. He had now brought nearly all the countries possessed by the successor of Timour under his sceptre, and the administration of them was entrusted as a reward of merit to his most distinguished warriors. Herat was confided to Djan Vefa Baï, Merv to Kobuz Naïman, Belkh to Khahrezm Sultan Shah, Hissar and country round about to Mehdi Sultan and Hamza Sultan, Kunduz to Ahmed Sultan, Tashkend to Süyündj Khodja Khan, Akhsi to Djani Beg, Endidjan to Mahmud Shah Sultan, Khahrezm to

---

[1] Mahmud Khan, a son of the same Yunis Beg who had rebelled against the Timourides in Transoxania in the time of Sultan Ahmed, took the opportunity of Sheïbani's absence to advance with his five sons against Endidjan on one side, and against Samarkand on the other, with the intention of getting possession of the government of Transoxania. He was encamped with a considerable force near Khodjend, on this side of the Yaxartes, when confronted by Sheïbani. A fierce battle ensued, in the course of which all his five sons and a great portion of his army met their death in the waters of that river. It was in 914 (1508). (*Tarikhi Seïd Rakeïn*, p. 118.)

Kushtchi Köpek, and Turkestan to Kütchkündji Khan; he had before given the viceroyalty of Bokhara and Karaköl to his brother, Sultan Mahmud, and on his death transferred it with the pearl of the whole empire, Samarkand, Kesh, and the district of Mirjankal to his own eldest son and presumptive heir, Mehemmed Timour Sultan.

In imitation of Djenghiz and Timour, the grandson of Ebulkhaïr retained for himself the post of commander-in-chief of the army. By force of arms he had raised himself from the position of a wanderer in the desert to that of ruler of many countries ; by force of arms he hoped to pursue still further the path of conquest, and who can say whether his career might not have been a repetition of Timour's, if a second combatant had not now appeared on the scene of action, no less ambitious, no less brave and resolute than himself, and as determined to extend the frontiers of his empire on the east as he had been to extend his own in the west ?

This was Shah Ismail of the house of Sheïkh Sefi[1] of Erdebil, who in consequence of his holy life was venerated as a saint by the Turks of Iran, and whose shrine is still held in high honour by the Persians of the present day. Shah Ismail had placed himself at the head of his followers and dispersed his enemies when but a youth of fourteen years old, and he succeeded, by the light of religious enthusiasm, in transforming the humble dervish's carpet of his family into the brilliant throne of all Iran.

Ismail was of Turkish origin (for it is only professed flatterers who, to exalt still further Sefi's sanctity, have striven to trace his pedigree to Musa, the seventh Imam) and was idolised by the seven Turkish hordes [2] living westward of the Caspian Sea.

---

[1] Malcolm, in his *History of Persia*, is mistaken in considering the name of Sheïkh Sefi as identical with the name of the well-known sect of Sufi. The order of which Sheïkh Sefi was the head held totally different doctrines, and had totally different objects from those forming the groundwork of Sufiism. It is only the Osmanlis who read this word Safevi, the Persians always pronounce it Sefevi.

[2] The Turkish 'hordes,' or more properly speaking, tribes, which abode in

His victorious arms led him to the acquisition of the greater
portion of Iran and Arabistan, and the zeal with which in
pursuance of the traditions of his race he took up the cause
of the sect of the Shiites, and encouraged as a national
sentiment the strong party reverence for the fourth Khalif
Ali and his posterity which had been repressed for centuries, is reckoned amongst his most shining merits. Shiism
was as old as Islamism itself, and had always numbered more
disciples among the people of Iran than in any other part of
the Mohammedan world. The sectarian bitterness which
lay at its root was mixed up with the expression of the anger
and resentment of the persecuted and insulted nationality of
Iran against the tyranny of the Semitic conqueror; and
though a few native Shiites were to be found here and there
both beyond the Euphrates and across the Oxus, as is proved
by the example of Baïsonkur Mirza, and by the revolt of
Sherik bin Sheïkh ul Mehdi during the Arab occupation of
Bokhara, yet Persia proper was always the spot most
suspected and most persecuted by the Sunnites, i.e., the
orthodox followers of the old tradition, for its obstinate adherence to this sect. As long as these sectarians remained in
obscurity their enemies contented themselves with fighting
them with the weapons of controversy and contempt; but
when the Sefides inscribed their doctrines on their banners
and espoused them openly to the great detriment of the Sunnite
princes, the latter took up the quarrel, and both parties saw
their religious differences inflaming their political objects.
In Western Asia the sectarian feeling added great bitterness
to the war between Uzun Hasan and the conqueror of
Constantinople, and the war-cry of the Turks of Iran was
already Ya Ali! (Oh! Ali!). In the east the flame smouldered
longer, and only leapt up in the regions of intellectual con-

Transcaucasia, on the southern shore of the Caspian Sea and in the west of Khorasan, and are still to be found in parts there, first migrated from Central Asia
under the leadership of the Seldjukides. The names of these tribes were:—
Ustadjlu, Shamlu, Nikallu, Baharlu, Zilkadar, Kadjar and Efshar.

troversy; a contemporary sketch of the court of Sultan Huseïn Mirza shows us the Perso-Sunnite writers of Herat and Transoxania labouring to prove that Iranian culture and learning were not the exclusive attributes of the sect of the Shiites. Later, in the time of Uzun Hasan, who is known to have lived on friendly terms with the Timourides in Khorasan, this question began to agitate the minds of men in Central Asia, especially in Bokhara, the more so as the death of Ebusaïd was regarded by many as that of a martyr to the righteous cause of the Sunnites. In proportion as the disciples of Shiism increased in Iran, so did the hatred and bitterness of the Central Asiatics wax stronger and stronger against these heretics; and even before the death of Sultan Huseïn Mirza, the philosophers of Herat, in conjunction with the ulemas of Bokhara and Samarkand, had branded the Shiites as beyond the pale of Mohammedanism, sanctioned the public sale of them as slaves,[1] and declared marriage with them to be mekruh, i.e., abominable.[2]

Such was the attitude of the two sects towards each other when Sheïbani Mehemmed Khan, after his successes in Khorasan, appeared in the prosecution of further conquests on the frontiers of Iran, and found a collision with Shah Ismail inevitable. The Turks have a proverb, 'He who has once grasped the sword-hilt needs no further pretext,' and Sheïbani might have followed it, but he hoped to excite greater enthusiasm by engaging in a religious war; and therefore first

---

[1] According to the principle 'Kulli Islam hurre'—Every Mohammedan is free, the Shiites could not be legally admitted to the slave-markets of Central Asia until the mollahs had cast them out of the pale of Islam. This occured at the time in question, and the celebrated lawyer Mollah Shems-eddin Herati is said to have been the chief promoter of this Fetwa, so pregnant with consequences for the future of Iran.

[2] Mekruh = contemptible, abominable, is a compromise between haram—prohibited, and helal—allowed. According to the principles of Islam there is no sin in marrying a non-Mohammedan, for even some of the Sultans of Turkey married Greek and Servian princesses. This was not, however, the custom in the Eastern Islamite world, and the learned doctors there, always more fanatical than their western colleagues, declared such a deed to be mekruh.

assumed the part of a teacher towards the brave Sefide, and wrote to him in the year 914 (1508), as follows :—

'Oh! king of Iran! It has become known to me that thou art encouraging the infamous sect of Shia, thus following only blind passion and devilish suggestions; be therefore warned! Renounce this criminal sect and return to the assembly of the Sunnites, or else verily the flame of rebellion and wickedness thou hast kindled will devour thee. I tell thee once more thou art pursuing the path of error, return unto the straight ways of faith, lest thou shouldest fall for ever into the hands of the devil. But if thou refusest to listen to these my words, know that I am entering Iran with innumerable armies, and that with my naked sword I will seize thy fortress Ispahan, high though her battlements may be, and lay her even with the ground. Yea! my punishments shall be terrible, and the inhabitants of Iran shall keep them in remembrance, even to the last day.'[1] Shah Ismail appears to have left this letter unanswered, and Sheïbani, interpreting this as an evidence of weakness, hereupon applied himself more eagerly than ever to extend the frontiers of his already large empire. Some plundering hordes of Özbegs had advanced in the south of Khorasan beyond Kandahar, and a similar expedition was being organised against Kerman, when at length an envoy from Shah Ismail made his appearance to warn the conqueror against proceeding further. Sheïbani replied by fresh threats, and sent the Sefide a keshkul or beggar's scrip and beggar's staff,[2] with the following message :—'Receive these presents which represent to thee thine own heritage. As regards myself, I have inherited the sword and the kingdom from Djenghiz, my renowned ancestor. If thou art not contented with thy beggar's staff, thou must take the responsibility of the consequences on thyself.' Khondemir relates that Shah Ismail replied thus : 'Very well ; if I am a dervish, I will

---

[1] From *Tarikhi Seïd Rakeïn*, p. 110.

[2] Keshkul, the half of a cocoa-nut shell, in which alms are gathered, and Asa, the pilgrim's staff, are part of the insignia of a dervish.

make a pilgrimage to the shrine of the holy Imam Riza, at Meshed, and we will meet there.' Shah Ismail was at all events prepared for war. Sheĭbani was prevented continuing his march southwards by the revolt of the Firuzkuhi,[1] a people haunting the peaks of steep rocks, and was making vain efforts to subdue them, when he received the intelligence that Shah Ismail was actually advancing on Meshed with a large army. To his great disgust and alarm news arrived at the same time from Transoxania that his son, Mehemmed Timour, had been surprised on his march against the Kirghiz on the Yaxartes by Boyunsiz Hasan and terribly defeated.

Thus the brave arm and searching eye of Sheĭbani seemed equally needed in three places at once. In addition to this his own troops were exhausted and worn out with long marches. Whilst he was at Merv endeavouring to decide whether he should cross the Oxus, or await the enemy on the borders of the desert, the latter had driven out the Özbeg garrisons of Damghan, Sebsevar and Nĭshabur, had already reached Meshed by forced marches, and was advancing nearer and nearer with his threatening columns. It was impossible for Sheĭbani to get up any reinforcements under the circumstances, so that there was nothing left for him but to protect himself as best he could behind the walls of Merv in the hope that some help might still come to his relief. But Shah Ismail was not a Roman cunctator. Perceiving that the application of force would only enable the besieged to gain time, he had recourse to fraud, and sent Sheĭbani the following letter : ' Thou promisedst me formerly to visit me at Azerbaĭdjan, but as thou hast never kept thy word, I have now come to visit thee myself in Khorasan. Nevertheless thou deignest not to receive me, and hast shut thy doors in the face of thy guest. As thou seemest to choose to remain hidden, and as I am forced by certain events to return to Iran and Azerbaĭdjan, I have now determined to break up my

---

[1] The Iranian tribe of the Firuzkuhi is described in my *Sketches of Central Asia*, p. 327. They always remained true to their old character as a people of robbers.

camp, and leave our meeting to the future chances of fate.'
The announcement thus made was at once carried out, and
the army of the crafty Persian had no sooner marched off
than the diminished and exhausted Özbeg troops, led by
Sheïbani in person, fell upon their rear, pursued them across
the Murghab, and only perceived that they were themselves
the victims of a fraud when they found the bridge broken
down behind them and a circle of 17,000 Persians closing in
round them near Mahmudabad. A horrible massacre ensued.
Even their enemies confess that the Özbegs, notwithstanding
their desperate situation, defended themselves heroically.
When more than half their number had been killed, Sheïbani,
with a few faithful followers, broke through the serried ranks
of the Persians, and got into a deserted farmyard, hoping
under shelter of the walls to prolong the mortal struggle. He
was soon surrounded and killed with all his men, and his body
was afterwards found covered with wounds beneath a heap of
other corpses buried amongst the ruins.

Sheïbani was sixty-one years old when he thus died a
hero's death.[1] Shah Ismail had his enemy's skull mounted in
gold and used it as a drinking cup ; according to another
account he sent it to Sultan Bayazid at Constantinople, who
had had a political understanding with the ruler of Transoxania.[2] The right hand of the corpse was also cut off and
sent to Aka Rustem, lord of Mazendran, and a zealous

---

[1] According to a chronogram in the *Tarikhi Seïd Rakein*, it was on a Friday
that he thus died a martyr's death, but we have no precise indication of the day or
month.

[2] Hammer maintains in the 32nd book of his *History of the Ottoman Empire*,
that diplomatic relations were first established between the Porte and Transoxania
towards the end of the reign of Sultan Suleïman, the legislator, but this is
obviously an error ; for if Sheïbani had not coquetted with Sultan Bayazid, the
sovereign of Constantinople, Shah Ismail would certainly not have sent the latter
the skull of his enemy, which he only did to annoy the Sunnite chief of Western
Asia. An understanding seems to have already existed even between Ebusaïd
and Mohammed the Conqueror. Both Hammer, in the above-mentioned chapter,
and Senkowsky, in his *Table généalogique*, give us erroneous and confused dates, but
this cannot be wondered at if we take into consideration the very defective and
scanty historical authorities then at their disposal.

partisan of the Özbegs, with the ironical message : 'Thou hast always declared thy intention of clinging to Sheïbani, and as that was not possible in his lifetime, Shah Ismail now sends thee the hand of thy patron that thy wish of holding fast by it may be fulfilled.' This story is related by Persian historians. According to the version current in Central Asia, his mortal remains were buried in the same year that he died, 916 (1510), in the splendid college he had built in Samarkand, and his grave there is held in universal reverence down to the present day as that of a shehid (martyr).

Sheïbani Mehemmed Khan was undoubtedly a remarkable man, whose extraordinary career deserves all the more to be attentively studied as it formed the turning-point which converted the historically celebrated state of Transoxania into the politically insignificant khanate of Bokhara.

In considering the events just recorded three considerations are forced upon us. In the first place, Sheïbani was the last of the world-conquerors who came forward supported by the rude strength of the inhabitants of the steppes of Central Asia and founded an empire extending far beyond the Oxus ; after his time, fortune no longer favoured any warrior, whatever his ambition or his talents might have been, to the same extent, and the consolidation of affairs in Iran opposed. an insurmountable barrier to the extension of the influence of Bokhara and Samarkand in the west. Secondly, the ethnographical revolutions in Central and Western Asia entirely disappear from this time forward, for the Özbegs were the last tribe who descended from the *officina gentium* of the Turanian highlands into the south-west. Thirdly, the fall and total extinction of the Timourides destroyed the last though feeble link still binding the Mohammedans beyond the Oxus and Yaxartes to their brethren in Western Asia. This rupture was naturally hastened by the Shiite zeal of the Sefides, who drove as it were a wedge into the centre of Islamism. This hierarchical-social revolution was just accomplished when Sheïbani descended with his nomads from the northern steppes into the country; the separation of Transoxania was thus rendered more complete, and the river of the Oxus gradually became again, as it had been in ancient times, the frontier-line dividing Iranian and Turanian life from each other.

As regards the individuality of Sheïbani, he most assuredly was not the wild barbarian he is represented by his Iranian enemies. He showed great respect, and even childlike submission to the religious teachers of his time, was himself addicted to the muses, and always carried a small pocket library about with him in all his campaigns; just as Timour had held theological discussions with the philosophers of Damascus and Aleppo the Özbeg conqueror disputed over certain verses of the Koran with Kazi Ikhtiar and Mohammed Yusuf, the first exegetical scholars in Herat. Baber says ironically that Sheïbani wrote stupid tasteless poetry and had it read publicly; but even this statement proves that this man of the sword, following the notions of culture prevailing in his day, busied himself also with his pen, and he distinguished himself in this way above most of his compeers, for in spite of the sarcastic remarks of his deadly enemy, his compositions bear evidence of remarkable poetic talent and of a thorough acquaintance with the Turkish, Persian and Arabic languages.[1] He took into his service many learned men who were left homeless and destitute by the death of Sultan Huseïn Mirza and gave them liberal salaries; he built mosques and colleges at Bokhara, Samarkand and Tashkend, and was always accompanied, even in his campaigns, by different learned men, who exercised the greatest influence over him;[2] and, although,

---

[1] The author of the *Sheïbani-nameh* gives us some of Sheïbani's poems, which may be reckoned, both for ideas and language, amongst the best productions of East Turkish literature.

[2] When Mollah Binai, the poet laureate of Sheïbani, handed to the philosophers of Herat the summons for the surrender of the town, the latter proceeded to the camp of the Özbegs to enter into negotiations, and it was solely due to their influence that the conqueror contented himself with imposing a money contribution, and entered into an agreement with them regarding the sum.

when he first appeared on the scene of history, the name of Özbeg was thought synonymous with rudeness and barbarism, and later, even down to the present day, has still been considered so by the Iranians, this definition does not apply to Sheïbani personally, who was himself quite as civilised and as highly cultivated as many princes of the house of Timour.

XIV.

THE SHEÏBANIDES.

916 (1510)—1006 (1597).

WHEN the terrible news of the catastrophe of Merv reached Transoxania, the members of the house of Sheïbani, realising on the one hand their own inability to assume immediately a defensive position, and on the other the threatening attitude of the dispossessed Timourides, felt that nothing was left for them but to make peace as quickly as possible with Shah Ismail, whose victorious soldiers were marching on the Oxus. The Özbegs had to give up the left bank of the river, and it was agreed that the Oxus should become again, as it was in the olden times, the line of demarkation between Iran and Turan. The peace was, however, but of very short duration. Baber Mirza, though in possession of the lovely region of Kabul, was impelled by his intense patriotism still to hanker after his old home on the banks of the Oxus and Yaxartes, and had no sooner received intelligence of the end of his former opponent, than he allied himself to Shah Ismail, and soon received assistance from him in his endeavours to reconquer the throne of his ancestors. He crossed the Oxus in the year 917 (1511) with an army composed of Persians, fugitives from Central Asia, Bedak'hshanians, and Afghans, and took possession of Samarkand, after meeting with hardly any resistance.[1] This unexpected success was, however,

---

[1] It is to be regretted that no account exists in Baber's own memoirs of this his last attempt to re-conquer Samarkand. The chapters of Baber's book are headed with the date of the different years, but there is a blank from 914 (1508) to 925 (1519), so that we are obliged to take our account of this campaign from other less direct authorities.

scarcely due so much to Baber's own intrepidity as to the
dissensions existing in Sheïbani's family. On the death of
the latter, a fraction of the Özbegs did homage to Mehemmed Timour Sultan, the son of the conqueror; but another,
and by far the larger majority, following the old Turanian
custom of paying respect to age alone, wished to put at their
head Ebulkhaïr's son, Kötchkündji Sultan.[1]   The former
only occupied his father's throne a few days[2] before he was
got rid of—apparently by a violent death—and the military
commanders then rallied round the grey-headed Kötchkündji
on the lower courses of the Yaxartes to decide on the next
steps to be taken.   Kötchkündji was unanimously elected as
Sheïbani's successor, but, as his years prevented him from
taking any active part in the field, he was represented there
by another member of his family, who proved but little inferior to the founder of the dynasty himself in military talent,
ambition, and bravery.   This was Obeïdullah Khan, the son
of Mahmud Sultan,[3] the conqueror of Western Khorasan, who
had been trained to arms in his uncle's campaigns and who
was undoubtedly the most able of all the Özbeg princes.
Obeïdullah had to begin over again the task of Sheïbani, with
the disadvantage that the spirit of unity among the Özbegs
was destroyed.   Fortified by the fatiha granted him by the
holy Sheïkh Ahmed to bring a blessing on the expedition, he
set forth with 5,000 horsemen, crossed the Yaxartes, and
taking the desert road on the left bank of that river, invaded
the north of the khanate of Bokhara before Baber had got
even an inkling of his enemy's movements.   The Özbegs'
camp was pitched on the banks of the lake of Melik, in the

---

[1] The literal meaning of Kötchkündji is nomad, vagrant; and Kodjüm seems an
abbreviation of it.

[2] Sheïbani had two more sons besides, Khurrem Sultan, and Süyündj
Mehemmed Sultan; there is no explanation as to why these two were passed
over in the succession.

[3] Mahmud Sultan, was, as we know, the younger brother of Sheïbani, and
his death, shortly after the taking of Kunduz, has been already mentioned.

district of Khaïrabad[1] but the outposts were pushed far beyond Bokhara. However, it is said that when Baber advanced with his army of 70,000 men,[2] Obeïdullah recalled these outposts for the sake of concentrating his forces. This was interpreted by the Bokhariots as signifying a retreat; the welcome intelligence was communicated to Baber, who pressed on and offered his enemy battle on the banks of the lake. Obeïdullah accepted the challenge. Emir Sehedja-eddin and Urus Mirza, with 1,000 men each, attacked the centre of Baber's army; the other Özbegs followed with their usual impetuosity and recklessness; and although the small body of troops was almost surrounded, such a confusion had nevertheless been created in the ranks of the enemy that a panic, and soon a general flight ensued. Baber is said personally to have exposed himself to the greatest danger during the battle, and only retreated when the banners of Obeïdullah were actually waving over his head. He seemed to feel that he had now dealt the last blow in defence of his father's throne, for when he had returned from the field of battle he only remained in Samarkand long enough to pack up his treasures and collect his family and attendants, and then took refuge in the fortress of Hissar. His reign had only lasted six months, and he was never destined to see again the beloved home of his ancestors. Obeïdullah entered Samarkand unopposed in the year 918 (1512) and placed his uncle Kötchkündji Sultan on the throne there, but retained for himself the government of Bokhara in order to complete there his military preparations; for the defeat of Baber had by no means secured the stability of the Özbegs' position, as their most powerful opponent was armed and equipped on the other shore of the Oxus, and jealously

---

[1] Khairabad is a short stage north of Bokhara. I did not myself see the lake of Melik during my travels in Bokhara, but I passed over one extremity of the desert of Melik. (See my book of *Travels*, p. 198.)

[2] I follow here the authority of Seïd Rakeïn, but the numbers appear to me nevertheless to be exaggerated, when we consider the smallness of the force with which Obeïdullah ventured to attack this army.

watching thence every movement of the successors of Sherbani.

As soon as Shah Ismail had received intelligence of the defeat of Baber, he became anxious to prevent a fresh invasion of Khorasan by the Özbegs, and at once sent orders to Nedjm Sani,[1] the governor of that province, to assist Baber by every means in his power, and without loss of time to march into Transoxania. The Persian army joined Baber at Termez, and their united forces attacked and took Karshi. Nedjm Sani, inflamed by Shiite party spirit, had the cruelty to put the whole garrison and all the inhabitants, including the celebrated poet Mollah Binai, to the sword; which so disgusted[2] the chivalrous, generous-minded Baber, that, sacrificing his last chance of reconquering Transoxania, he broke off his alliance with Persia, and let the reckless Sefide general pursue his road to Bokhara alone. His well-merited punishment soon overtook him. The Özbegs allowed him to advance unmolested into the interior of the country; one fortress after another fell into his hands, and when he at length reached Gidjdovan with his tired and famished soldiery, a handful of cavalry proved sufficient to inflict a crushing defeat on the proud vizir of the Persian king, in a battle in which he himself and most of his general officers lost their lives. The Persian historian, describing this man's wealth and luxury, informs us that the daily consumption in his kitchen included 100 sheep, an innumerable quantity of chickens, ducks and geese, and forty hundred weight of cinnamon, saffron, and other spices, and that the dishes were all either of gold or the rarest Chinese porcelain.

The victory of the Özbegs was complete, and Shah Ismail's intention of covering Khorasan by undertaking this campaign had only produced a directly contrary result, for

[1] Nedjm Sani is Arabic for the *Second Star*. This man's real name was Mir Yar Mehemmed.

[2] Although the commandant of Karshi was a cousin of Obeïdullah's, Baber's generous soul revolted from the sight of the cruelty of the Persians to his deadly enemy's near relation.

Obeïdullah crossed the Oxus near Tchardjui with his great uncle Djani Beg, a son of Khodja Sultan,[1] in the year 919 (1513), was joined at Murghab by Timour Sultan, who had advanced from Samarkand by Kerki, and together they proceeded to attack Meshed. Detachments of the Özbeg army penetrated by Termez as far as Belkh, spreading ruin and destruction around them, and within a few months of the victory of Gidjdovan the Özbegs under Obeïdullah saw themselves again in possession of the countries originally gained to them by the sword of Sheïbani.

Shah Ismail, seeing the fruits of his previous victories thus suddenly scattered to the winds, had once more to turn his arms against Khorasan, although he was aware of Sultan Selim's attack, and his attention was fixed with anxiety on the western frontier of his dominions. The Özbegs did indeed retire across the Oxus on hearing of his approach, but the manner in which these light skirmishers of the desert, who undertook more raids than regularly planned expeditions, kept hovering nearer and nearer to the frontiers of Persia was a terrible plague, and entailed great misery on the north-eastern borders of the unhappy Iranian country. Though we have no positive evidence of the fact, there can be little doubt that an understanding existed at this time between the Özbegs and Osmanlis, for the rulers of Constantinople had no sooner unfurled their banners against the growing power of the Sefides, and thus drawn away the forces intended for the protection of the northern borders of Iran, than the Özbegs flew to arms, and, crossing the yellow waters of the Oxus, entered the sorely-tried territory of Khorasan. We find that Oberdullah alone invaded Irania six different times, with no further results than the devastation and ruin of his unfortunate neighbour's country. The history

---

[1] Khodja Sultan, the second son of Ebulkhaïr Khan, had two sons, Djani Beg, and Boyali Sultan ; none of the children of the latter succeeded to the government, but the last of the Sheïbanide rulers of Transoxania were the descendants of the former.

of these invasions is a melancholy and tiresome one, but we
cannot avoid giving a sketch of it. The *first* invasion was, as
we have already stated, immediately repulsed. The *second*
undertaken by the Ozbegs at a more favourable moment,
that is at the time Shah Ismail had just been beaten and
weakened in the battle of Tchaldirïm, is stated by Persian
historians to have been on a much larger scale. Obeïdullah
had received his uncle's permission to cross the Oxus with
30,000 Özbegs, but did not reap any success commensurate
with the scale of his preparations, for he had to retire after
laying siege for ten days in vain to Herat. The impetuosity
of the Özbegs proved unavailing against the energy and
determination of Sam Mirza and Duermish Mirza, the two
commanders in Khorasan, and they had to content themselves with venting their fury on the crops, which they completely destroyed. The *third* invasion took place after the
death of Shah Ismail, in the year 931 (1524). The reckless
warlike Sheïbanide passed through Tchardjui, and threw
himself on Merv, whilst Ebusaïd, son of Kötchkündji, advanced by way of Kerki, and appeared before Herat. He
accomplished, however, very little, but Obeïdullah not only
got possession of Merv and Meshed, but extended his raid
as far as Astrabad, which he took and confided to the administration of his son Abdulaziz. The latter was of course
unable to maintain himself long there, and Obeïdullah had
only got as far as Damghan, on his road to Belkh, when
Shah Tamasp, the son and successor of Shah Ismail, arrived
to the rescue of the threatened province, and drove back the
Özbegs to their own country. The Transoxanians had
reckoned without their host, in regarding the death of Shah
Ismail, and the consequent internal troubles of Iran, in the
light of troubled waters in which it would be easy for them to
fish. Tamasp, though but a youth when he ascended the
throne, was determined to put down the nuisance of the
Özbeg invasions. Obeïdullah, aware of this, gave his people a
most alarming description of the enormous forces with which

the young Persian king intended to cross the Oxus. We can hardly believe Tamasp to have had any such intention, but Kötchkündji Khan feigned anxiety to be beforehand with his enemy, and thus the *fourth* invasion of Khorasan was undertaken in the year 935 (1528) by Obeïdullah, with an army collected together out of all the different tribes and families inhabiting the Turanian highlands, and numbering in its ranks all the principal Özbeg princes, including Borak Sultan from Tashkend, Kötchkündji and his son Ebusaïd from Samarkand, Hamza Sultan from Hissar, and Kisten Kara Sultan from Belkh. The Persian historians, who are given to exaggeration, state that no such enormous body of Tartars[1] had ever before crossed the Oxus at once : but they forgot to add that the roar of cannon and sound of firearms had never before been heard in those regions. Tamasp had brought out with him about 6,000 guns, and the celebrated archers of Turan were now for the first time brought face to face with the western scientific discovery by which mere brute force was to be paralysed. There can be no question that two very remarkable armies were now face to face, and the bitterness of the struggle was increased by the coincidence that the principal action commenced between Djam and Zorabad[2] on the ninth Moharrem, the vigil[3] of the day on which the Shiites keep the anniversary of the tragic end of Huseïn, near Kerbela, with every demonstration of woe. The first rays of the rising sun had tinged the rows of

---

[1] The Persian authority, the *Rauzat es Sefa*, gives their number at 200,000, and names every imaginable country and people as taking part in this expedition.

[2] This is the large plain ,which now forms the line of demarkation between Afghanistan and Iran, and between Herat and Khorasan respectively. Djam, the first place one enters on Persian territory in coming from Herat, is now a miserable village, the inhabitants of which live in mortal terror of the Turkomans. According to the accounts received in India by Baber, this battle was not fought between Djam and Zorabad, but between Djam and Kharghird. Baber puts the Özbeg army at 300,000 men, and the Persians, whom he calls Turkomans, only at from 40,000 to 50,000.

[3] This evening is regarded by the Shiites as the holiest of the whole year. They fast and mortify their bodies in every way, the better to prepare their minds for the mourning of the following day, the sad *rusi ashura*.

arrows poised by the archers—the scene might have recalled the struggles of old between Efrasiab and Rustem—when, under the cover of thick clouds of dust, Tamasp was at first nearly surrounded by the Özbegs, on whose side victory seemed to incline. The Persian army, imitating Turkish tactics, had entrenched themselves behind their chariots, and placed their archers in the front row. The Özbegs rushed on the two wings and succeeded in breaking through their lines, but the bulk of the Persian army turned their flank, fell on their rear and drove them back in cônfusion. Fifty thousand Özbegs and twenty thousand Iranians are said to have fallen.[1] But the blood of Sheïbani was not yet considered sufficiently avenged.

In 938 (1531), when Tamasp was fully occupied in the West with Sultan Suleïman, Obeïdullah for the *fifth* time invaded Iran with an army in different detachments. He marched himself on Herat, his son Abdul Aziz on Meshed ; Kamishoghlan (the Boy of the Rushes), whose bravery is highly extolled, advanced on Astrabad ; and Khankeldi Batur on Sebsevar. Khorasan, Sistan and a part of Iran were exposed to their depredations for a whole year and a half; but as soon as peace had been re-established between the Persian king and the emperor of the Ottomans, and the former found himself at leisure to turn his attention to the devastated territory of Khorasan, the Özbegs as usual decamped laden with slaves and spoils of all kinds.

Soon after this, in the year 940 (1533) Obeïdullah at length ascended the throne of Transoxania. The aged Kötchkündji, after a life spent mostly in the society of ascetics and dervishes, had died in the year 937 (1530), and been

---

[1] According to Baber's account, nine Özbeg Sultans, including Kötchkündji himself, with his son Ebusaïd, and Obed Khan, were said to have fallen into the hands of the Persians, but of the latter Ebusaïd alone was alive. This statement is, however, entirely untrue, for we shall see in the course of this chapter that all three successively occupied the throne of Transoxania for several years subsequently ; and the oldest of them, Kötchkündji, did not die for two years after this catastrophe.

succeeded by his son Ebusaïd Khan. The latter died suddenly at the end of three years, and it is very doubtful whether he was not secretly got rid of by Obeïdullah. After ascending the throne Obeïdullah continued, as before, to harass his neighbours by constant attacks. In 942 (1535) he undertook the *sixth* invasion of Khorasan, on which occasion he is said by native authorities to have at length wrested the fortress of Herat from Sam Mirza, without however succeeding in keeping it any time.[1] This proved his last campaign in Khorasan, for after a fruitless attempt to bring baok Khahrezm to its allegiance to Bokhara, he died in the year 946 (1539), in the fifty-sixth year of his age and the sixth of his reign, and was buried in the chapel of a college built by himself. The government of Trans-oxania had hitherto been more or less divided amongst the children of Kötchkündji and Sheïbani, and the result was general confusion amongst the Özbegs after the death of Obeïdullah. The partisans of the former family set Ab-dullah, the son of Kötchkündji on the throne, and upon his death, six months afterwards, elected his brother Abdullatif[2] Khan, but the other and more powerful party did homage in the year 948 (1541) to Obeïdullah's son, Abdulaziz. We are not informed whether any rivalry existed between these two, or whether they shared the government peaceably between them; the only fact we gather from the scanty and confused records of the time is that Abdulaziz remained on the throne up to the year 958 (1551), and continued at that time at peace with Persia, only undertaking one single campaign against Belkh, and displaying a character exactly opposite to his father's. He fostered the influence of the mollahs in reviving a stricter religious tone, and expended far

---

[1] The *Rauzat es Sefa* asserts the contrary ; according to it, the Özbegs had to retire before the vigorous resistance opposed to them by Sam Mirza.

[2] Deguignes, in his *History of the Huns and the Turks*, vol iii. p. 472 (of the German translation), confuses this Abdullah with the later and greater Abdullah. He makes Abdulmunin immediately succeed this first Abdullah, thus leaping entirely over about half a century in the history of Bokhara.

more care on building mosques and convents, and on other pious works than on secular objects; this was on the one hand most beneficial to the country, exhausted by constant wars, but on the other hand its northern regions were left more exposed than ever to the depredations of the unoccupied nomads.   Upon his death Mehemmed Yar Sultan,[1] a son of Mehemmed Süyündj Sultan, then staying at Tashkend, was appointed to succeed him, but as he died on his road to Bokhara—or, according to another account, was murdered at Samarkand in the year 961 (1553)—Burhan Khan, a grandson of Obeïdullah, was raised to the khanate in spite of many objections: his debauchery and wild life—being often not sober for days together—soon drew upon him universal contempt and hatred.   In the midst of the disorder caused by this disgraceful *régime*, Borak Khan,[2] a son of the same Mahmud Khan who had been defeated by Sheïbani, suddenly appeared from the north-eastern steppes of Central Asia, and overran with his savage mercenaries the most flourishing parts of Transoxania.   Everything was ruined and devastated from Otrar to Bokhara, and it is impossible to describe the misery inflicted on the country by the cruelty and barbarity of this tyrant.   It was at that moment of terror that Abdullah Khan, the son of Iskender Khan [3] and great-grandson of Ebulkhaïr, a man who well deserves the title of the greatest of the Sheïbanides, first appeared on the scene.   He was born in 940 (1533); his paternal ancestors do not appear to have been distinguished by much intelligence, for his great-grandfather went by the nickname of *tintek*—goose; his

---

[1] According to another account his name was Mehemmed Rehim; but this is incorrect, for Mehemmed Rehim, a son of Obeïdullah Khan, and father of Burhan Khan, was dead before this.

[2] His real name was Noruz Ahmed.

[3] His father, Djani Beg, had twelve sons: Dost Mohammed Sultan, Kisten Kara Sultan, who reigned.long in Belkh, Payende Mehemmed Sultan, Rusten Sultan, Iskender Khan, Isfendiar Sultan, Suleiman Sultan, Pir Mohammed Sultan, Shah Mehemmed Sultan, Yar Mehemmed Sultan, Djan Mehemmed Sultan, and Nur Mehemmed Sultan.

grandfather Djani Beg was an idiot;[1] and his father, finally, does not appear to have been a shining intellectual light, for the chief things we learn of him are that he performed his devotions punctually five times a day,[2] and that he was a skilful falconer. In spite of this parentage, the venerable Khodja Kasani is said to have predicted the future greatness of the infant Abdullah; when Iskender Khan presented his child to him for his blessing, he exclaimed, joyously: ' This child is born under a fortunate star, and will some day be a very great ruler.' To make his blessing more efficacious, the holy man took off his own girdle of camel's hair and bound it about the child's loins. The Khodja even foretold particular events in his future career, and his education was in consequence confided to the best teachers of the time, of whom there were many in the reign of Obeïdullah, as is especially noted by Seïd Rakeïn.

At the age of 22, full of eagerness to defend the rights of his family, Abdullah came forward with a handful of men to resist the atrocities of Borak Khan, who had just taken possession of Bokhara. He was obliged in the first instance to retreat to the little fortress of Tarab, near Bokhara, the native city of the prophetic sieve-maker of the time of Tchaghatai; the inhabitants received him but coldly, he reproached them for their apathy and promised them many privileges in the event of his success. The result was that about 300 infantry joined him. Whilst he was thus preparing himself for the struggle he received intelligence of Borak's death, which occurred in 963 (1555). Abdullah hereupon

---

[1] Abulgazi relates that he allowed his wives before their confinements to pour grease on to the fire, to guess from the splutterings of the flame whether they would have boys or girls. This superstition is still practised in Central Asia, and finds its counterpart in the melting of wax or lead by European girls on New Year's Eve, to see from the shapes into which it runs whether they will be married in the course of the year.

[2] He also diligently performed the rite of *Nafile*. Nafile are the prayers or Rikaat (genuflections) gone through by devout Mohammedans, in addition to the canonical rites, as works of perfection with which they seek to propitiate the Almighty.

hurried to Bokhara, took possession of the town and neighbourhood, and saw himself suddenly in a position to attack
Burhan Khan, whom he defeated and put to death,[1] and
having thus driven out the invaders he firmly re-established
once more the authority of the Sheïbanides in Transoxania.
In imitation of Sheïbani and Obeïdullah, who, although practically sovereigns of the country, had left the actual seat of the
khanate to others, the more freely to pursue their military
career, Abdullah placed his father Iskender on the throne
of Samarkand and put himself at the head of his army to
reconquer the original frontiers of Sheïbani's empire. The
greater part of his life was spent in this enterprise, but he
was more fortunate in his conquests than any of his predecessors, and also contributed more to the restoration of
prosperity to the countries of the Oxus and Yaxartes, so that
he well deserved, as we shall presently see, the title given to
him of 'Benefactor of his people.'

Under him the frontiers of the khanate of Bokhara were
pushed forward in the north far beyond the inhabited parts of
the province of Turkestan. Peace was seldom disturbed in
this neighbourhood after the death of Borak, except in the
year 975 (1567), when Baber Khan, son of the latter, again invaded Transoxania and advanced as far as Samarkand,
where he seized Khosru Sultan, the reigning prince, and
carried him and many noblemen of the city and all their
treasures off. Abdullah, being then with his army in
Khorasan, had to grin and bear it for the moment, but a few
years later, in 983 (1577), Baber was called to account and
driven with his army in confusion across the Yaxartes ; a
peace ensued, which was, however, of short duration, for three
years afterwards Baber attempted a fresh invasion, and
Abdullah had again to take the field against him. A decisive
battle ensued near Ak Kötel (the White Hill) in the district of
Zamin (consequently near Samarkand) in which Baber Khan

---

[1] He was treacherously murdered by a certain Mirzaki Kushdji (Bird-catcher).

was completely defeated and pursued by Abdullah far on to
the steppes as far as the Ulugtag (Great Hill), where the latter
erected a monument opposite to the one put by Timour in
remembrance of his campaign against Tokhtamish. In imitation of the great conqueror's habit of recording his victories in
stone, Abdullah intended by this column to immortalise
his various successes. In the *East* not only all Fergana, but
also Kashgar and Khoten were subdued by the Sheïbanides ;
in the *south* an aggressive policy had been pursued on the one
hand by the family of Baber [1] and on the other by the Sefides,
who both coveted the possession of Belkh ; but the power of
the Özbegs was even greater than in the time of the first
Sheïbanides. Belkh was fortified, Tokharistan and Bedak'hshan
were incorporated with Transoxania, and once more the bright
green waters of the Murghab became the frontier of Turania.
In the *West* the arms of Abdullah were again victorious, in
spite of the united opposition of the Iranians and Khahrezmians. Astrabad was surprised and taken ; the prince of
Ghilan, an ally of the Sultan Murad III., had to take refuge
at Constantinople, and the frontiers of the empire of the Sheïbanides were extended in this direction further than they had
ever been before. In the beginning Abdullah's expeditions
against Iran were mere raids, or 'Alamans' as the Turkomans call them ; for Tamasp, after having, to the great disgust
of the Özbegs, made peace with Sultan Suleïman in the

---

[1] Baber Khan, son of Borak Khan, was the last of that Mongolian dynasty
whose chiefs from the time of Kaidu onwards, consequently from 665 (1266) to
986 (1578), had seized the opportunity of each period of anarchy in Transoxania
to interfere there in defence of the rights of a certain branch of the family against
the rulers of the house of Tchaghatai, and of the cause of the Djenghizides in
general. Their power was crushed for a time by Timour's wars against the
Djetes, but they recovered themselves in the days of his successors, and gained over
to their cause the Kalmucks and Kirghizes. In the time of Ebusaïd they had
gained such a reputation in the neighbourhood of Tashkend, that a son of the
latter Omar Sheïkh married a daughter of their chief Yunis Beg, and from this
union sprang the celebrated Baber. During the troubles of the Sheïbanide time,
they took possession of Khokand, and Sheïbani had, as stated, to go to war with
Mahmud Khan, a son of Yunis Beg. After Mahmud's defeat by Sheïbani, his
son Borak, and after him *his* son Baba Khan, attempted in vain to restore the failing
fortunes of the family.

year 969 (1561), was at leisure efficiently to protect his own eastern provinces, and a larger undertaking against them was out of the question. But after the death of Tamasp, Iran, and more especially Khorasan, fell into the wildest anarchy under the disorderly rule of his sons, and the bands of Özbeg troopers poured over the northern borders. In 974 (1566) Mohammed Mirza, the son of Tamasp, himself narrowly escaped falling into the hands of a plundering horde of Özbegs on his way to Herat with a body of 15,000 men ; he threw himself with difficulty into the fortress of Turbet-i-Haideri, and only avoided being taken prisoner by a severe struggle. Later on the bitter wars of succession and the rivalry among the great Persian nobles, still further cleared away the obstacles in the path of Abdullah's ambition, and during the struggle between Shah Abbas, surnamed the Great, and his rival Mohammed Khudabende, the fortress of Herat fell into the hands of the Özbegs after a nine months' siege. Ali Kuli Khan_ Shamlu, the Persian viceroy of Khorasan, and many other nobles were executed, a large number of the inhabitants were carried prisoners to Bokhara, and the north-eastern part of the province of Khorasan given up to the most dreadful devastations.

This was the occasion on which the guardians of the tomb of Imam Riza [1] who were at the same time wardens of the numerous benefices, fields, gardens, vineyards and other possessions of the venerable Alide, addressed a letter to Abdullah, enquiring how he made it accord with his religious feelings to destroy the goods of Imam Riza, and thus to waste the substance by which so many thousand pious

[1] Imam Riza is the richest saint in Persia, for he is not only proprietor of whole bazaars and streets in the celebrated commercial city of Meshed, but owns outside the town, and in other parts of Khorasan besides, fields, vineyards and caravanserais. These provide first for the kitchen of His Highness, in which every pilgrim is entitled to receive gratis for three days rations of Pillau (rice), with meat and bread. The Imam is always called ' His Highness,' and spoken of as though he were still living. He owns a free public bath, a soap manufactory, a hundred cells, and other commodities for the use of pilgrims. The wealthy only are expected to make a free-will offering at his shrine. He dispenses hospitality gratis to the poor, and is entitled ' Sultan-el-gureba '—Prince of Strangers.

pilgrims, including many Sunnites, were supported? The Transoxanian mollahs present in Abdullah's camp replied by a long controversy on Shiism in general, alleging that according to their principles and their faith, the disciples of Shia were worse than the unbelievers, whose destruction was ordained by God himself. If it was the duty of every Moslem to wage war on unbelievers, how much more was it his duty to fight against those who had wandered from the right path, and, in spite of their connection with the saint whose bones rested in the midst of them, had fallen into grievous sin. As regarded the reproach cast on them for destroying Imam Riza's fields and gardens, they were well aware that they were devoted to pious uses, connected with the shrine of Imam Riza. But it was an open question who had most right to the enjoyment of them—the warriors fighting for the cause of God and right, and deprived of all means of subsistence, or those who had sinned against Allah and treated with contempt the most exalted guardians of the faith.[1] The Shiite mollahs were of course ready enough with a rejoinder. They had the tact to begin by proposing a sort of general council of an equal number of Sunnite and Shiite philosophers, who were to decide whether the Shiites were traitors to the faith for declaring the three first khalifs usurpers, and asserting the hereditary rights of Ali. Shiism was as old as Islamism itself, and if the adherents of this sect were really so abhorred, how came Imam Riza to settle down in the midst of them? why did he not rather go to Transoxania? etc., etc. These discussions had no more definite results than the council of Sunnite and Shiite philosophers, convoked 150 years later by Nadir Shah at Bagdad.[2]

[1] The three first khalifs, Ebubekr, Omar and Osman, are declared by the Shiites to have been unscrupulous usurpers, and their names are only mentioned with curses.

[2] Nadir is supposed by modern Persians to have been himself a Sunnite at heart. He was clear-sighted enough to perceive the danger threatening all Islam from this schism, and wished to bring about a settlement. He summoned a sort of council at Bagdad, but it came to no result, in consequence of the bitterness on both sides.

Whilst the two parties were thus striving to settle by the pen
a schism which the sword had for centuries failed to quell,
young Shah Abbas advanced with an army from Kasvin,
and Abdullah retired by Merv to Bokhara. Abbas, as is
rightly observed by Malcolm in his 'History of Persia,'
effected this diversion rather with the object of increasing his
own prestige than with any definite intention of driving
out or conquering the Özbegs, for he only remained a short
time at Meshed, and then hurried to Georgia, where the
Osmans threatened him with hostilities, and soon after
defeated him. As had often before been the case, the echo
of the Ottoman victory in the west resounded in the east,
for Abdullah had no sooner received the intelligence than he
made a second attempt to conquer Meshed, and entrusted
the vanguard of his army to his son Abdulmumin Khan, the
Viceroy of Belkh.

Abdulmumin, a savage warrior, and a cruel and ambitious
man, hurried forwards with his uncle Din Mehemmed, and
a large force, to which Kul Baba Kökeltash, the faithful
servant of Abdullah and governor of Herat, had attached
himself. Their first attack was directed against Nishabur.
A few Özbegs were taken prisoners in an affair of outposts,
and set at liberty again in order that they might let their
young commander know that Nishabur was simply a part of
Meshed, and that if the latter were taken the former would
be sure to submit. In consequence of this information
Abdulmumin now directed all his efforts against Meshed,
sparing no sacrifices and no pains to subdue it. The commandant of the fortress, Ummet Khan Ustadjlu, had done all
in his power to repel the attack, but the panic became
general; many of the people from the surrounding country
took refuge in the city, which was but imperfectly pro-
visioned, and the consequence was that famine came to the
assistance of the Özbegs, and finally, at the first assault,
caused the surrender of this holy city of the Shiites into their
hands, with all its treasures, monuments and wealthy bazaars.

When Abdulmúmin's troops entered the town, they found that the inhabitants of both sexes, and the numerous holy and learned men, had all congregated in the outer court of the shrine of Imam Riza, in the hope that they might be protected there by the sanctity of the spot; but the Özbegs, in their blind fury, cut down and destroyed everything that came in their way; even the supposed descendants of Imam Riza, who were clinging to the holy shrine of their ancestor, were there pitilessly massacred. It is said that Abdulmumin himself looked on from the court of Mir Ali Shir, whilst his soldiers were murdering children and old men, common people and learned philosophers indiscriminately, and that even the shrieks of a thousand victims and their dying groans were unavailing to move his pity. Not only the public streets but the holiest precincts of the mosque and the shrine itself were deluged with blood, and in the general sack of the town the grave of the Alide suffered more than most parts, costly offerings of pious pilgrims which had been accumulating there for three centuries, falling into the hands of the conquerors.[1] Amongst them were enormous massive gold and silver candelabra, whole suits of armour in precious metals, splendid single stones, buttons, studs and other articles of jewellery richly ornamented, and, most valuable of all, the magnificent library with its celebrated copies of the Koran, marvels of the art of caligraphy, the gifts of the former sultans: all these were dragged away, torn up and completely destroyed. The vengeance of the Sunnite conquerors did not even spare the very dead, for the ashes of Tamasp were torn from their grave by the side of Imam Riza's and scattered to the winds with curses and execrations. In order to gratify another Sunnite enemy of the Sefides by the report of this deed, Abdulmumin despatched his chamberlain

[1] The reader is referred to page 142 of my ' *Wanderings and Adventures in Persia* ' (Pesth, 1867), for an imperfect sketch of the riches and treasures accumulated there. Kum is very far behind Meshed in importance, and it should not be forgotten that much was done by the Timourides to add to the magnificence of Imam Riza's monument.

U

Mehemmed Kuli to Constantinople to Sultan Murad III. with a letter, in which, after describing in the most bombastic style his victories in Khorasan, he gives an account of scattering the ashes of Tamasp, and goes on to say that, in order completely to annihilate the godless set of Shiite heretics, he should soon march upon Irak, and solicits the assistance of the Sultan in this enterprise. This plan came to nothing for two reasons. In the first place the Ottomans not only declined to help their co-religionists in the extreme east, but did precisely the contrary, promising assistance to the Persians, as they began to be uneasy at Abdullah's victories, and to think that his further successes might prove inconvenient to themselves. In the second place, Shah Abbas, who had been detained at Teheran by illness during the sack of Meshed, had now recovered, and was taking the most energetic measures of defence. For the moment, however, Abdullah was completely victorious, and had got possession of a great part of Khorasan, including the towns of Herat, Meshed, Sarakhs, Merv, Khaf, Djam, Fusheng and Ghurian, all which he retained very nearly till his death.

Abdullah Khan's reign had reached the culminating point of its glory with the conquest of Khorasan, but it is, no doubt, remarkable that, in spite of his long military career and uninterrupted chain of victories beyond Transoxania, he did not become independent at home until about this time. We have already stated that immediately after his first bold proceedings he had entrusted the reins of government to his father Iskender Khan, but the latter does not seem to have retained them long, for, although he survived till the year 991 (1583), we find records of several other rulers in the interval occupying the throne of Samarkand, and exercising the sovereign rights of Khutbe u Sikke (public prayer and coinage of money), which proved their independence. Amongst these was Khosru Sultan, who was beaten in battle when Baber Khan invaded Transoxania from Tashkend in 975 (1567), taken prisoner and murdered. He was succeeded by

Sultan Saïd, a son of Ebusaïd's and grandson of Kötchkündji, who reigned five years, protected learning, and did much towards the beautifying of Samarkand. He died in 980 (1572), and his brother Djuvanmerd Ali Bahadoor took his place. In his reign Abdullah Khan first began to interfere with the internal government of Samarkand in consequence of the following circumstances: Djuvanmerd had two sons, Ebulkhaïr Sultan and Muzaffar Sultan, who were at constant war with each other; the former called Baber Khan into the country to assist him against the latter, who had attached himself to Abdullah, but was nevertheless beaten. The father of these amiable children took part with the vanquished one, and Abdullah perceived that the only way to put an end to the whole affair was to get rid both of the old father and of his two children altogether. Djuvanmerd and Muzaffar were taken prisoners and executed at Samarkand; a similar fate overtook Ebulkhaïr shortly after, and in the year 986 (1578) Abdullah, having thus put an end to the dual system of government in Transoxania, received the homage of his subjects at Bokhara as independent sovereign of all Turan.[1] It is difficult to understand why he had not taken this step long before. He had been victorious in the north, east and west of Transoxania, he was master of nearly all Khorasan and Tabaristan, so that he could most certainly have taken possession long before of the isolated little country of Samarkand. It could not have been weakness, but rather regard for his near relations and a dislike to family quarrels which had made Abdullah, in spite of his habitual cruelty and severity, pursue so moderate a policy. We find him acting with the same forbearance towards his brother Pir Mehemmed Khan. The latter had succeeded Kisten Kara

---

[1] He had only one rival now left to contend with, namely, Abdul Sultan, a son of Abdullatif's, who had raised the standard of rebellion at Zamin. Abdullah defeated him in a battle in the open; he retreated to the hill country of Hissar, but continued thence to harass his opponent until he was finally taken prisoner and executed in the year 588 (1580).

Sultan, son of Djani Begh in the government of Belkh, and reigned there as an independent prince until his death in the year 974 (1566). Abdullah would then have been ready enough to recognise his son Din Mehemmed Khan as the lawful heir of his father, but his own son Abdulmumin, whose savage and cruel disposition has been already noticed, insisted on having all the provinces on the hither side of the Oxus made over to him. Din Mehemmed resisted this claim, and Abdulmumin, on taking possession of his new government, seized him and all his superior officers and had them put to death, to the great indignation of his father. Abdulmumin's conduct was indeed the one dark cloud which constantly overshadowed the bright horizon of the otherwise fortunate Sheïbanide's life. Abdullah adored him as his only son, and to gratify his boundless ambition had allowed him, as heir to the throne, to assume the title of Khan, which was in general only borne by Turkish sovereigns themselves.[1] The father was called Ulug Khan (the Great Khan) and the son Kitchik Khan (Little Khan). This did not, however, satisfy the latter, and we soon find him again roaming about with his savage plundering bands of horsemen, scouring hill and plain, north, south, and west. The constant warfare in which his son was engaged was favourable to Abdullah's own policy in Khorasan, and he did not therefore restrain him. Besides, he felt flattered at the heroic bravery of his son ; but Abdulmumin, soon becoming intoxicated with the success of his own arms, began to dispute his father's supremacy, and in a short time openly arrayed himself against him. The first cause of quarrel was Abdulmumin's claim to unite all the Cis-Oxonian territories of the Sheïbanide empire under his own sceptre ; to effect this object he wished to turn the grey-headed Kul Baba Kökeltash, the faithful servant and old companion to whom Abdullah owed so much, out of Herat.

---

[1] I say expressly *Turkish sovereigns*, for in Persia the title of Khan is also borne by noblemen. In Turkey it belongs to the Sultan alone.

Abdullah of course refused to listen to this, and when Abdulmumin, who had just defeated the Khahrezmian prince Nur Mehemmed Khan,[1] and had 20,000 horsemen at his orders, took up arms against Kul Baba Kökeltash, sent orders to the latter to lay aside all scruples and resist the attacks of the rebel prince as he would those of any foreign enemy. This was enough to irritate the headstrong son to revolt openly against his own father. Abdullah was amusing himself hunting on the upper courses of the Oxus in the year 1004 (1595) when Shah Mehemmed, one of the nobles in the service of Abdulmumin, arrived with the intelligence that his master and a body of skirmishers were advancing with hostile intentions. Abdullah, almost beside himself between indignation and fear, hurried back to Bokhara ; Abdulmumin, however, appears to have repented of his intention, and retired to Belkh. Subsequently, however, some bloody encounters took place between the two, and the mighty Sheïbanide, deeply hurt at the ingratitude of his own child, had the additional mortification of perceiving that his long and arduous wars in the north of his empire had not led to the desired results, for he received at the same time the news, first, that one of his best generals had been totally defeated by a horde of Kalmucks, and secondly, that his old enemies the Persians, whom he had so often beaten, were destroying all the fruits of his years of struggle in the west of the empire. We have already spoken of the alliance existing between the Princes of Khahrezm and the Kings of Iran. It was a natural result of the aggressive policy pursued by the Sheïbanides towards Khahrezm, for though the ruling classes of both countries were alike Özbegs, the little country on the lower courses of the Oxus suffered much at the hands

---

[1] Nur Mehemmed, a bastard son of Ebu-Sultan, Prince of Kharezm, had, regained possession of his paternal inheritance at Merv, after the death of Obeïdullah, and through fear of the Özbegs had entered into an alliance with Shah Abbas. He was, however, in spite of this, overcome by Abdulmumin ; he took refuge with Shah Abbas, but afterwards quarrelled with him, was taken prisoner, and died in the fortress of Istakhr.

of the larger, stronger and more powerful Bokhara. The khans of the house of Sheïbani were bent on incorporating it by force with their dominions; and took every opportunity of surprising and occupying the towns of Hezaresp, Khivuk (now Khiva) Ket, Vezir and Urghendj. Their dominion of course only lasted as long as they remained in the country, and when at length Abdullah, by his cruelties and unheard-of reprisals, had actually himself forced the reigning prince Hadjim Khan into the arms of Shah Abbas, the rule of Bokhara over Khorasan drew to its close, for Shah Abbas had found amongst the Turkoman subjects of Khahrezm auxiliaries fully equal to cope with the Özbegs of Transoxania, with whose assistance he contrived even before the death of Abdullah, as early as 1004 (1595), to reconquer not only the strong places Meshed, Merv and Herat, but nearly the whole of Transoxania besides. This destruction of all his hopes, added to his grief as a father, threw Abdullah into deep despondency, and he died at Bokhara after a short illness, on the 2nd Redjeb 1006 (Feb. 6, 1597), in the sixty-eighth year of his age, having reigned upwards of forty years in Transoxania, first as regent, and afterwards as independent sovereign, and leaving behind him a name which has become a household word on the lips of every Bokhariot down to the present day.

Just as modern Persians are in the habit of ascribing to Shah Abbas the Great all the fine karavanserais, bridges, cisterns, artificial roads cut through rocks, and other works of public utility bequeathed to them by their ancestors, whether entire or in ruins, so does the modern Bokhariot regard every movement of former centuries as an evidence of the generosity and liberal tastes of Abdullah Khan. Tradition says that the architect of Abdullah Khan being once asked how many works he had carried out for his employer, replied that there were altogether 1001 mosques, colleges, baths, hospitals, karavanserais, bridges and cisterns—and this was before half the years of his reign had expired. It seems really marvellous, how, considering the constant wars in which he was engaged, Abdullah found it possible to devote so much time to the internal affairs of his government, for, however exaggerated the praises lavished on him by the inhabitants of Bokhara and Samarkand may be, so much remains certain, that trade, agriculture and science found in him a powerful and enlightened patron, and that no other Sheïbanide ever equalled him in earnest endeavours for the increase of culture and the prosperity of his people. Many of his richly-endowed colleges are still frequented by students; and the shady alleys of the pleasure-grounds (Tchiharbag) laid out by him at Bokhara, Samarkand, Kermineh and Meshed[1] are still the favourite resorts of the people during the hot season. The best preserved part of the bazaar of Bokhara is that built by him in 990 (1582); the fine bridge flanked by four towers over the Zerefshan at Kermineh is now almost the only permanent communication between the two shores, for the other bridges built by him have all been destroyed, either wilfully or by natural causes. He caused mile-stones (tash) to be placed along all the Transoxanian roads, organised regular communication between the different parts of the country by a good posting system (Yam), and placed the whole traffic and daily life of all classes of the people on a footing of security never before known.[2] No wonder, therefore, that the fame of his reputation should have spread far and wide. Ambassadors came to him from China[3] with costly presents and friendly assurances; Sultan Murad III. sent from Constantinople to solicit his alliance, and the

---

[1] The Özbegs appear to have felt quite at home at Meshed, for Abdullah Khan laid out public pleasure grounds there, which were completed in the year 1004 (1595). He also built a karavanserai, which is called to this day *Karavanserai Özbeg*.

[2] The greatest misfortune which visited Transoxania during Abdullah's reign was a plague, in the year 999 (1590), which first attacked human beings and afterwards carried off a vast quantity of domestic animals.

[3] *Tarikhi Mekim Khani*, whence this statement is taken, says the Prince of Mongut, but this seems a mis-spelling of Tangut, the name given at that time to China and Tibet by Central Asiatics.

Khan of the Krimea deputed special embassies to congratulate him on his victories. His reign may with truth be called the last ray of the glory which had at various times surrounded the throne of Transoxania.

All that has been said of Abdulmumin's character leads us readily to believe the alacrity with which that unworthy son took possession of his deceased father's throne, and the kind of actions by which his government was inaugurated. His first step was to wreak his vengeance on the venerable Kul Baba Kökeltash, a faithful servant of his family, universally honoured for his many virtues, whom he took prisoner at Herat and dragged about after him on foot heavily laden with chains. He entered Bokhara in this fashion; many did homage to him from terror, few from any real regard, and having taken possession of all his father's treasures both there and at Samarkand, he set off to visit personally all the places where any of his father's old servants were filling posts in the government, to reward their services by death under the hand of the executioner. This he did at Oratepe, Khodjend and Tashkend, in which latter place the venerable Kökeltash was put to death with his nearest relations. Thence Abdulmumin proceeded to Endidjan and Akhsi, to get hold of his cousin Özbeg Khan,[1] who had been acting as governor there for some time. Özbeg resisted, but died himself a few days after the commencement of the siege, so that Abdulmumin soon accomplished his object, and turned back. As he did not make the slightest mystery of his murderous intentions a report soon spread that he would never rest till he had killed off all his father's old servants and friends. The latter soon realised the danger they were in, and to avoid it determined to get rid of the bloodthirsty tyrant himself. The conspiracy was headed by an old soldier of Kazakian origin, named Abdulvasi Bi; he proposed the murder of Abdulmumin in the following oracular language :—'Words are useless; we must have deeds.' He

---

[1] Özbeg Khan was son of a brother of Abdullah Khan's.

then tested the courage of his companions by laying his hand on the heart of each, in a secret meeting; and lots were drawn to decide who should do the deed. It was the month of July, and to avoid the heat Abdulmumin travelled generally at night; the conspirators lay in ambush for him on his return to Samarkand in the dark, in a pass between Oratepe and Zamin. A great part of the army had already passed by, and when the Khan with his own torchbearers reached the narrow part of the path where there was only room for two horsemen abreast, a shower of arrows met him and he fell motionless to the ground. The man on whom the lot had fallen then sprang forward and cut off his head, and then killed the councillor who was immediately following him. All this passed so rapidly that the fact was not even discovered till day-break, when, some of the stragglers in the rear of the army coming up, stumbled over the bodies, and recognised the headless corpse of their chief by his clothes.

Thus ended the six months reign of the able but savage, obstinate, and tyrannical ruler Abdulmumin Khan;[1] as he was the only surviving male offspring of Abdullah, the dynasty of the Sheïbanides, which had occupied the throne of Transoxania exactly a hundred years, became extinct with him. The confusion that ensued may easily be imagined. It was reported that Abdullah's widow had brought forward a second son whom she had always kept in girl's clothes, and that one party was disposed to recognise him as prince; but the country was split up into too many fractions for any practical result to follow. Some wished to proclaim a child of Abdulmumin's only two years old; others wanted old

---

[1] He had done some good in forwarding the rebuilding of Belkh. His predecessor as governor there, Kisten Kara Sultan, appears to have contented himself with restoring the citadel, originally built in the time of Ebusaïd, destroyed two-and-twenty times, and finally restored by Kisten Kara. Abdulmumin bestowed much attention on the town, which was half in ruins when he took possession of it, but in six months it was already in great part rebuilt. The beautiful domes covered with Kashi (enamelled tiles), the fine portale of the palace, the bazaar Babadjanbaz, and the tomb of Ali are all attributed to him. (*Tarikhi Mekim Khani.*)

Pir Mohammed Khan, Abdullah's only surviving brother
who was half stupefied with opium ; others again a brother-
in-law of Abdullah's. All these different parties were influenced with the bitterest animosity; and whilst they were
mutually seeking to destroy each other, their enemies on
the frontier were watching an opportunity to reconquer
the territories wrested from them by Abdullah. Shah
Abbas was the first to move ; encouraged by the favourable prognostications of his astrologer, and assisted by
the arms of 40,000 Shiites, thirsting for revenge, he took
Sebzevar and Meshed at the first assault ; and later, Herat,
after totally defeating in a bloody battle the Özbegs concentrated there. In the north, Tökel Khan, prince of the
Kazaks,[1] entered the country from Tashkend, and advanced
on Samarkand with a horde of Kalmucks, Kirghizes and
Mongolians. Ishim Bi, the commandant of Samarkand,
succeeded in repelling the invader, but not until he had put to
death four princes of the house of Sherbani,[2] and many adherents of the dynasty ; but peace, which had been so cruelly
disturbed by the extinction of the Sherbani family, was still
far from being restored.

Before entering on the history of the next, that is the ninth,
dynasty ruling in Transoxania, it will be well to give the
reader some idea of the state of civilisation existing in the
busy period of the Sherbanides, an epoch during which the

---

[1] The Kazaks (erroneously called Kirghiz by us) first appeared in Transoxania as
an independent tribe under the leadership of Tökel Sultan. Lewchine, in his
Description des Hordes et des Steppes Kirghiz-Kazaks, p. 141., calls him Tevkel
Sultan. The Kazaks seem to have assumed a threatening attitude in the
steppes north of the Yaxartes some time before this, for as early as 941 (1534)
Ivan the Terrible received the following report from his envoy Danila Gubine :
' Et les Kazaks, Sire, sont très-forts, dit-on, et l'on dit, Sire, qu'ils ont fait la guerre
à Techkène (Tachkend), et les fils du roi de Teehkène, dit-on, se sont battus avec
eux deux fois, et les Kazaks les ont battus.' (Lewchine, p. 140.) Tökel sent
several embassies to Czar Fedor at Moscow, and appears to have been one of
the most powerful of the Sultans of the Kazaks.

[2] These were Hezare Sultan, and Pir Mohammed Sultan, sons of Özbeg
Khan; also Mehemmed Kuli Sultan, son of Suleïman Sultan and grandson of
Djani Beg ; and lastly, a son of Payende Mohammed Sultan.

process of separation of the east Islamite world from western Islam was completed and Mohammedanism assumed the character in which it is met with up to the present day between the eastern frontier of Iran and China. There was naturally nothing like the amount of culture existing under the Timourides to be found under the Sheïbanides. These rough warriors, who believed in the powers of their *Yada tashi* [1] (magic stone) to control the elements, cure diseases, and ensure victory in battle, were sincerely devoted to their religion and to its priests. In the time of the Mongolian occupation, a few remarkable mollahs, in virtue of their spiritual powers, had been practically rulers of the land, controlling by their veto the will of the most imperious despots, and this experience was repeated under the Sheïbanides. The teachers of godly wisdom not only enjoyed the complete devotion of the people, but the princes vied with each other for their favour, and, whether we ascribe it to superstition or to fear of popular opinion, it remains equally a most remarkable manifestation, how the mightiest princes of this dynasty invariably bore themselves towards the mollahs, not only with respect but with all the marks of the most abject humility. Two of these mollahs were most especially honoured, and invested in their lifetime with the odour of sanctity.

Makhdum Aazam, more usually called Mowlana Khodjhaki Kasani, a pupil, under the Timourides, of the celebrated ascetic Khodja Ahrar, is said to have distinguished himself by a most holy life, to have been endued with miraculous power, and to have been treated by all the princes of his time with a respect bordering on fear. He died at Samarkand on the 21st

---

[1] This was especially the case in the battle of Djam. Baber, in his memoirs, p. 450, describes how at sunrise, the magicians set to work with their magic stone to create confusion amongst the Persians. In spite of three centuries of Mohammedan teaching, this stone still keeps up its reputation among the nomads of Central Asia. The Serdar (chief) of a Razzia of Turkomans, or the leader of a Kirghiz Baranti, to this day carries it carefully with him, and in case of the deadly bite of a viper or a scorpion its efficiency is valued as highly as that of a *fatiha* (blessing) from the Koran. Further details of the Yada tashi are to be found in Quatremère's *History of the Mongolians*.

Moharrem 949 (1542), and his tomb, a league off at Dehbid,[1] is to this day a much-frequented place of pilgrimage. Kasim Sheïkh Azizan, a pupil of Khudadad's, celebrated like the former for sanctity of life rather than for any profound learning, was held in high respect, as is best illustrated by the following anecdote :—Sheïkh Azizan was living at Kermineh and heard that Abdullah Khan, then at war with Djuvanmerd Ali of Samarkand, intended to pay him a visit. The sheïk was friendly disposed to the prince, and went a little way out of the town to meet him. He soon saw a long train approaching headed by a man walking bareheaded, with a cord round his neck, the other end of which was held by a horseman. To his great astonishment he recognised in this abject creature the mighty Abdullah, the ruler of so many countries. He asked why he appeared thus in the garb of a penitent ; and Abdullah replied, ' I have imposed on myself as a penance to go in this fashion from the Kham Rabat to the khankah (convent) of the Sheïkh.' Sheïkh Azizan was deeply affected by this, himself placed the prince on horseback and put his own mantle on him, and the two returned thus together to Kermineh. Abdullah of course desired by this act of humility to implore the help of the Sheïkh in his enterprise against Samarkand ; he obtained it and got possession of the place. Sheïkh Azizan died about three years afterwards, in 989 (1581).

Theological studies were alone pursued at this time with any ardour. Amongst the most distinguished scholars were Mevlana Isam-eddin the son of Arabshah, who first lived at the court of Sultan Huseïn Mirza at Herat, and afterwards went to Bokhara ; he was much in favour with Obeïdullah Khan. This prince, notwithstanding his warlike propensities, was not averse to poetry and tried himself to make verses. Being doubtful as to the right interpretation of an Arabic quatrain, he one day asked Isam-eddin to explain it to him,

---

[1] For further accounts of Dehbid, see my *Travels in Central Asia*, p. 214.

and received from him in the course of a few hours 656 different readings of each line of the quatrain in question. This story is told by his panegyrist Seïd Rakim. He died in 943 (1536) at Samarkand ; his best known works are : marginal annotations on Tefsir-i-Kazi, and on Djami's exegetical works. Mevlana Sadik, a learned exegetical scholar of Samarkand, who made two pilgrimages to Mecca and wrote valuable commentaries on theological works and glossaries of some abstruse poetical compositions. In his later years he lived in Kabul at the court of Hekim Shah, where he died in the year 1007 (1597). Amongst other equally distinguished men we may further mention : Mollah Zia-eddin, a learned theologian who died in 973 (1565) ; and Khodja Djelal Djuibari, a pupil of Makhdum Aazam's, who was held in high honour both as an ascetic and as a learned theologian and exegetical teacher. Turkish had now become the popular language, so that the poets from this time forward were all exclusively Turks ; the most distinguished of them seems to have been the Özbeg prince Mehemmed Salih, whose father was deprived of the government of Khahrezm by the Timourides, and who entered whilst very young into the service of Sheïbani. He is the author of the ' Sheïbani Nameh' (Sheïbaniade), a masterly epos which raises him even above Newai.[1] The other poets of this period were mostly mere rhymesters and concocters of chronograms, but history has preserved the names of Emir Ali Kiatib and Molla Mirek, poets laureate to the first Sheïbanides. Also that of Mollah. Mushfiki, who wrote chronograms on the various buildings of Abdullah, and also a few sonnets, *kassides*, and epigrams. He died in 994 (1585). Kazi Payende of Zamin, a perfect master of language, left a work especially deserving of notice, a poem of eighteen strophes in praise of the Vizir Kul Baba Kókeltash, in which there is not a single dotted letter. This

---

[1] I hope shortly to publish this fine poem, both in the original and in a translation. Flügel mentions it in his catalogue of the manuscripts in the Imperial Library at Vienna, but was unaware of the author's name.

is equivalent to a poem written in a European language without using the letters b, kh, f, j, k, n, p, sh, t, tch, or z.[1]
Finally, Shirin Khodja, a poet of the time of Obeïdullah and
Khair Hafiz, a popular singer and musician at the court of
Abdullah, who died in 981 (1573). The architectural monu-
ments of the time of the Sheïbanide owe their origin in
addition to the public spirit of Abdullah Khan, chiefly to the
theological and Suffite tendencies of the spirit of the times.
Numerous mosques, convents, colleges, halls, and mausoleums
were built in memory of deceased saints. Amongst them
may be mentioned : a mosque built at Samarkand by the
Vizir Aleïke Kökeltash in 934 (1527) to which Kötchkündji
Khan gave a pulpit of white marble. The college of Abdullah
Khan, which is in good preservation to this day, has a high
portico, and over it a text of the Koran inlaid in enamelled
tiles with letters more than two feet long, so that it can be
read at an enormous distance. Abdulaziz Khan restored the
Mesdjidi Mogak, formerly a Parsee temple, and built the
convent at the tomb of Khodja Bahaeddin, a short league
from Bokhara. Finally, Ebusaïd built a college at Samarkand,
and the millionaire Mir Arab another at Bokhara, which is to
this day the most richly-endowed school in all Central Asia.

The above sketch represents after all a very petty and
miserable state compared with the luxury, the wealth and
civilisation reigning at that very time amongst the Sefides in
Persia, or with the noble objects pursued at that moment in
India by another prince of Turanian origin, Timouride Ekber
Shah, who founded the great empire on the Indus and the
Ganges in which he reigned gloriously and splendidly for a
space of fifty years, studying and investigating both Christianity and the doctrines of Bramah, and devoting himself to
the welfare of his people.[2]

---

[1] The poem is called *Bi-nokat*, undotted ; the curious thing is that orientals
have time and patience to write whole books in this way.

[2] Ekber Shah, a grandson of Baber, ascended the throne in 1556 at the age of
fourteen, and (as is abundantly proved by Colonel H. Yule, in his excellent

work, *Cathay and the Way Thither*, vol ii. p. 531) early expressed a desire to become acquainted with Christianity. In 1578 he received the Portugese envoy, Cabral, from Goa, and hearing that an excellent priest was then living in Bengal, he sent for him to hold a public disputation with the Mohammedan mollahs. The accounts given by the Jesuits of an order issued by him in 1590 for the destruction of all mosques and minarets, appears apocryphal, but it seems established beyond doubt that a party of Christian missionaries visited the country at his own express invitation.

XV.

/ *THE FIRST ASHTARKHANIDES.*
1006 (1597)—1099 (1680).

A RETROSPECTIVE survey of more than three centuries will give us some information with regard to the origin of the dynasty of the Ashtarkhanides, which succeeded the family of Sheïbani in the dominion of Transoxania, and maintained their rule for nearly 200 years. Emir Timour had scarcely driven the posterity of Tchagatai from the throne of Samarkand, and put an end to the Mongol occupation, when he was summoned by a scion of the house of Djüdji to perform similar service in the Mongol's dominions on the banks of the Volga. In the heat of contest against his rivals Urus Khan and his sons, Tokhtamish had certainly not reflected on the dangerous consequences of the assistance he had invoked. The weapons of Timour fought first for him and then against him. In the end Tokhtamish, after many ups and downs of fortune, was murdered; [1] the descendants of Urus Khan were deprived of power and consideration, and the members of the princely house of Djüdji, the band of union, at the best but slack, having been quite broken by the intervention of Timour, were dispersed in every direction. One of the princes, who in consequence of these revolutions played at the head of their hordes an important part in history, was Kutluk Timour,[2] who, as ally of the emperor of

---

[1] According to the Russian Chronicles, Tokhtamish was murdered not far from Sumen in Siberia, by order of Shadi Beg, the successor of Kutluk Timour. (Hammer, *Geschichte der goldenen Horde*, p. 366.)

[2] With regard to his origin the accounts given by the authorities to which I have been able to refer, vary as follows:—According to the author of the *Tarikhi*

Samarkand, acquired renown by his victory near Kiev 802 (1399), over Tokhtamish and the Polish army, allies of the latter. The successors of Kutluk Timour were, however, afterwards obliged to retire to the khanate of Astrakhan or Ashtarehan [1] on the lower course of the Volga. At first unknown, they were in course of time elected chiefs by the nomads of that region. This branch of the descendants of Djenghiz, named from their place of residence Ashtarkhanides, lived for two centuries in obscurity, till at last disunion, or more probably the growing power of the Russian grand dukes, forced them to seek a new home ; and Yar Mehemmed Khan,[2] accompanied by his son Djani Khan, migrated to Transoxania. The Sheïbanide Iskender Khan, who at that time ruled in Samarkand, received the fugitives in a very friendly manner. The Sheïbanides were always proud of their descent from Djenghiz, and, by way of showing the fullest measure of hospitality toward their foreign relatives, Iskender Khan gave his daughter Zehra Khanīm, a sister of the celebrated Abdullah Khan, in marriage to Djani Khan. Yar Mehemmed, called on account of his advanced age *Kari* ('the Grey'), died soon after his settlement in Transoxania. Djani Khan, however, for a long period took part in the wars of Abdul-

Mekim Khani, his genealogy was Djenghiz, Djüdji, Urus, Buga Sultan and Kutluk Timour. In Abulgazi, p. 100, we read Tchenghiz, Djüdji, Tokai Timour, Uz Timour, Abay, Tumgan and Kutluk Timour. Hammer again, in his *Genealogy of the Descendants of the Fourteen Sons of Ulus Djüdji*, differs from both these authorities to such an extent that it is impossible to make out what he considers the origin of Kutluk Timour.

[1] According to the present orthography of this word, we might derive Astrakhan from Ashdar (اژدر) Khan, which would point to a Persian origin. But the correctness of the old derivation from Hadji Tarkhan appears all the clearer when we remark that in the MSS. of Central Asia this word is always written with a Shin and Te.

[2] In the genealogy of Yar Mehemmed Khan we again find a material discrepancy between the author of the *Tarikhi Mekim Khani* and Abulgazi. The first writes, Kutluk Timour, Bahadir Khan, Mehemmed Khan, Havak, Nagishlan (instead of Mangishlak), and Yar Mehemmed. The latter, on the other hand, and his account is probably the correct one, writes Kutluk Timour, Ali Timour, Timour Kutluk, Timour Sultan, Mehemmed Khan, Djurak, Mangishlak, Mehemmed Sultan and Djan, more correctly Djani Sultan, where Yar Mehemmed Khan should be inserted between the two last names.

lah, who on his part recognised the merits of his brother-in-law, and entrusted the governorship of Nishabur to the eldest of his nephews, who had especially distinguished himself in the wars of Abdulmumin against the Persians. Djani Khan had, it should be observed, three sons, Din Mehemmed, Veli Mehemmed, and Baki Mehemmed.

When Adulmumin was murdered at Zamin, and the country became a prey to anarchy, certain of the most influential men of the land offered the crown to the old Djani Khan. He, however, declined the honour, and said: ‘It is true I am a descendant of Djenghiz, but it would be most seemly that the dominion of Transoxania should be committed to one who is at the same time a kinsman of the Sheïbanides.’ As with these words he pointed out his sons, the eldest of them, Din Mehemmed, was proclaimed khan, and his return from Khorasan was awaited with impatience. But we have already shown in the preceding chapter that just then such events were taking place in that province as prevented Din Mehemmed Khan from quitting that field of his activity, however desirous he might be to do so. Shah Abbas, who saw himself freed from his most formidable opponent by the deaths of Abdullah and Abdulmumin, had driven the Özbegs from all the strong places of Khorasan, and had inflicted on them a crushing defeat. Din Mehemmed Khan [1] fell in the battle, or, according to another account, in flight. His whole camp and all its treasures became the booty of the conqueror. So extreme was the general confusion of the Özbegs, that even the wife of Din Mehemmed Khan could escape only through the self-sacrificing courage of a faithful servant, Khaki Yasaul by name. He had placed

---

[1] While the *Rauzat es Sefa* describes his death in the battle before Herat with such detail that the whole story can scarcely be doubted, the *Tarikhi Mekim Khani* tells us how Din Mehemmed, wandering, after the unfortunate conclusion of the battle, among the Karai nomads near Andkhoï, was recognised through his royal dress and slain. The true state of the case is the more difficult to make out, because this murder on the part of the Karai is stated to be the motive for the expedition of vengeance undertaken against them by Baki Mehemmed Khan.

the lady in hot haste upon a horse, and had hidden the princes Imamkuli and Nezr Mehemmed in bags on either side of his saddle, and then galloped wildly away. A bullet, however, struck one of the saddle bags in which Nezr Mehemmed was concealed. It wounded him in the foot, so that he was all his life lame. Bokhara had thus lost her newly-elected prince, but as his two brothers had succeeded in making their escape over the Oxus, the eldest of them, Baki Mehemmed Khan, was in 1007 (1598) placed on the throne of Transoxania, while the younger one, Veli Mehemmed Khan, received as a fief Belkh and the territory this side the Oxus. The unity which prevailed between the brothers could alone have succeeded in settling the affairs of the countries on the Oxus so much sooner than might have been expected, and averted the danger of dismemberment by which they were threatened, not only by Shah Abbas but also by rebellious nobles. In Transoxania the public peace was soon restored by the expulsion of the Kazak prince, Tökel Khan, but in the territory this side of the Oxus the founders of the new dynasty encountered a much more formidable opponent in the great Sefide king. Belkh, together with the province of Tokharistan and the adjoining Bedak'hshan, which had formed since the days of the Samanides an integral portion of Bokhara, had by this time all the more value in the eyes of the Özbegs, as in the first place many of their race had settled on this side of the river, i.e., in Kunduz, Aktche, Shiborgan and Andakhud,[1] and in the second place the supposed sepulchre of Ali,[2] the honoured

---

[1] This is the Andkhoï or Andkhuy of the present day. According to the laws which determine the change of sounds in the Turkish language, the change of *y* into *t* when it occurs at the end of a word is very frequent. Andakhud or Andakhut is a Mongolian word meaning 'united happiness.'

[2] With regard to this apocryphal tomb of Ali, the *Tarikhi Säïd Rakéïn* tells the following story :—In the time of Sultan Huseïn Mirza Baïkara, a man learned in history made the discovery that, during the reign of Sandjar the Seldjukian, the tomb of Ali Ibn Ebu Talib had been discovered in the village of Khodja Khaïran, not far from Belkh. Excavations were at once commenced, and a building was found on which was found a flat stone bearing the inscription : ' This is the tomb of the Lion of God, the Brother of the Prophet, namely Ali, the Darling of God.' When

saint of the warriors of Islam, had to be defended against
Shiite conquest.　As the attention of Abbas was at that time
directed not only to the interior of his realm but also to its
north-western frontier, the capture of Herat by the Persians
exercised for the present only an indirect influence upon
Belkh.　Mehemmed Ibrahim, a Shebanide by birth, and a
favourite of Shah Abbas, had by means of Persian assistance
got possession of Belkh.　But his profligate life excited the
indignation of the people of Belkh to such a degree, that, in
spite of their leanings towards Iran and their dislike of
Özbeg rule, they gave their right hands to Veli Mehemmed
on his approach, and assisted him to conquer the ‘Mother of·
Cities,' as Belkh was called.　After Veli Mehemmed had
made himself master of the citadel, the abandoned favourite
was put to death, and only his principal officers succeeded in
making their escape to Isfahan.　To propitiate the Persian
king they took with them the precious diamond which
Abdulmumin had formerly taken from ·the monument of
Imam Riza.　The jewel was replaced with solemn ceremony
in the shrine of the saint of Khorasan, the Özbegs were
confined within the limits of Kasvin, and Belkh gave no
further occasion for any more disputes.　Much more serious
was the encounter with the Persians in the year 1011 (1602),
when Baki Mehemmed Khan took the field for the purpose
of avenging the death of his brother, who was said to have
been murdered by the tribe of Karai, who dwelt in Kunduz.
The Karai or Kara-Turkomans[1] inhabit even now that part
of Central Asia, and, what is equally remarkable, still
live in constant hostility with the neighbouring Özbegs and
Turkomans.　Although the murder of Din Mehemmed can-

this intelligence was communicated to the Timouride prince above mentioned he
set out accompanied by a large escort and performed the first pilgrimage prayer to
the newly-discovered tomb in the year 885 (1480).　In course of time splendid
buildings were raised on the spot, of which, however, but few traces are to be
found in Mezari Sherif at the present day.　The correctness of the discovery is
not in the least doubted by the inhabitants of Central Asia.

[1] On these Kara-Turkomans, who in respect of physiognomy and stature most
resemble the Yomuts, see my *Travels in Central Asia*, pp. 237 and 304.

not be laid unconditionally to their charge, their undoubted friendship with the Shiite Persians was a sufficient reason for Baki Mehemmed Khan in concert with his brother attacking them, and mercilessly cutting down all who fell into their hands. A number of those who bore arms threw themselves into the fortress of Kunduz, which they defended to the utmost. It was not till large portions of the walls had been undermined and blown into the air, together with hundreds of the garrison, that the fortress could be taken by storm. None of the prisoners were left alive. The power of the Kara tribe of the Turkomans was broken in this war, and it has never since recovered itself.

By this terrible act of vengeance on the part of the ruler of Bokhara, Shah Abbas, as was to be expected, was especially moved. He set out from Merv with an army against Aktche for the purpose of relieving his allies, intending first to chastise the Ashtarkhanides in Belkh, and then to advance across the Oxus against Bokhara. But the warlike host of Özbegs did not keep their enemies long waiting for them. The Persians had already advanced as far as the tomb of Baber Abdul, in the vicinity of Belkh, when an epidemic disease invalided more than half their number. In this condition they were attacked on both sides. A terrible defeat was the result, and Shah Abbas himself escaped with difficulty, accompanied by a few thousand of his followers.[1] This was the only war of importance waged by Baki Mehemmed Khan during his reign. The rebellion of his nephew Bediuzzeman, who in 1011 (1602) retired into the mountainous Karategin, was put an end to by the capture of the strong place, Mesdja. In like manner the revolt of Mehemmed Zeman, the governor of Bedak'hshan, whose father had had the rebellious Bediuzzeman executed, was nipped in the bud. Thus, under the circumstances, the reign of Baki Mehemmed Khan may be con-

---

[1] Even the Persian chronicles do not attempt to conceal the disastrous termination of this campaign. The *Rauzat es Sefa* says that the extraordinary heat and thirst had severely tried the Persian troops, and that it was difficult to resist the nomads who burst suddenly upon them from all parts of the desert.

sidered a tranquil one.   After he had sat but seven years on
the throne, in 1014, he fell ill.   No sooner was that known than
the Kazaks began to ravage the land.   In the general consternation all eyes were turned towards the highly-honoured
saint, Sheïkh Alem Azizan, whose miraculous powers were
expected to restore the prince to health.   In such mines of
divine erudition the Bokhariots then, as now, sought for
secular knowledge.   As the Sheïkh prescribed the fresh breezes
of the Oxus, Baki Mehemmed Khan was carried in a litter
on board ship, in which he floated for several days on the
river.   The pious man had, however, failed in his diagnosis,
for the patient died soon after, towards the end of Redjeb
1014 (1605).

Veli Mehemmed Khan, who had come from Belkh to visit
his sick brother, succeeded him in the government after he
had defeated at Termez the two sons of the deceased who had
risen against him.   Veli Mehemmed Khan's character was
that of a good-natured prince ; but, as he was too much addicted to sensuality and wine, the unrestrained tyranny of
his officials alienated from him all hearts even in the beginning
of his reign.   Of his vizir Shahbeg Kökeltash, whom he
left behind as governor in Belkh, we are told that he had
the heads of criminals pulled off their shoulders by oxen
harnessed to them.   Others he had boiled in oil.   From
others, again, he had the skin scraped off with wool cards.
These cruelties, combined with the unjust execution of the
three vizirs [1] of the late sovereign, called into existence a
powerful opposition party.   At its head stood the two princes
mentioned above.   They chose Imamkuli Khan to be their
chief, and declared Veli Mehemmed Khan, at that time enjoying the pleasure of the chase in the neighbourhood of Karshi,
to have forfeited the throne.   Without soldiers, without re-

---

[1] Dostum Argun, Shah Kitchik and Hadji Naiman (such were the names of
these vizirs) were of great reputation in the time of Abdullah Khan.   During
the government of Baki Mehemmed Khan they were raised to the rank of Emir
ul umera, the Ottoman Beglerbeg in its former signification.   See the *Tarikhi
Seïd Rakein.*

sources, the dethroned sovereign had to abandon all thoughts of returning to Bokhara, where his rival was already placed on the throne, while his vizir had expired under the ingenious tortures he had so often inflicted upon others. No other course now remained open to him but to make his escape to Persia, and take refuge with Shah Abbas, the old enemy of his house. It hardly need be said that the great Sefide endeavoured as much as possible to turn to account this quarrel of kinsmen, and received with the utmost cordiality the fugitive Ashtarkhanide. Shah Abbas went three hours' journey from Isfahan to Dowletabad to meet his guest, and saluted him with a paternal embrace. About twenty thousand musketeers formed the lane through which the refugee entered the city. All the houses and shops in the bazaar which he passed were adorned with costly carpets. Poets celebrated his entry in kasides. We cannot be surprised that the sight of all this magnificence inspired the Özbeg prince with the hope of being again restored to sovereignty. We can hardly believe that Abbas thought seriously of conquering and annexing Transoxania. He rather reckoned on protecting the sorely-harassed northern frontier of Iran by establishing a good understanding with the ruler of Bokhara. Not long after he sent Veli Mehemmed, escorted by 80,000 Persians, towards the Oxus. Here again our attention is called to the boundless influence possessed by the higher clergy in Bokhara. Just as in sore sickness they were resorted to for medical advice, so on the approach of an enemy strategical council was required of them. Imamkuli was beside himself with fear when he heard of the vast numbers of the enemy, and betook himself for counsel to a descendant of Makhdum Aazam, the Khodja Mehemmed Emin. This pious man was not in the least disturbed though the number of warriors at the disposal of Imamkuli was small. In his religious enthusiasm he himself took part in the struggle, hung bow and quiver on his clerical robe, shot off the first arrow, and after he had thrown a handful of dust against the enemy, which had the effect of

enveloping them in darkness, gave the signal for the general
assault. A fierce combat began, and my authority relates
with all seriousness that the darkness defended the Özbegs as
it were with a wall, while it rendered the hostile camp, pitched
beside the Lake of Maghian, indefensible. As regards the historical course of this war, be it observed that at first Imamkuli
abandoned his capital from fear of the enemy, but in the subsequent battle by the Lake of Maghian,[1] in the beginning of
Redjeb 1020 (1611), the advantage was on his side. Veli
Mehemmed fell alive into his hands, and, after he had reigned
six years, was beheaded by order of his enthusiastic sheïkh.

After these events there followed a long period of rest and
peaceful relations between Persia and Transoxania. Shah
Abbas had, by his successes against the Porte, inspired with
such respect all his neighbours, including the Özbegs, that
even the usual predatory forays into Persian territory were
discontinued. The Turkomans, who even at that time formed
a cordon all along the north of Iran, from the desert country
around Andkhoï, to the eastern shores of the Caspian, were
subsidised by the Shah or his allies. Imamkuli, however,
undertook a campaign on a small scale againt the predatory
Kazaks and Kalmucks, in the north of Turkestan, which we
mention on account of a circumstance which conspicuously
illustrates the hypocrisy of Islamism. A numerous horde of
the above-mentioned nomads had advanced, plundering and
burning, as far as Samarkand, for which they were chastised
by Imamkuli. In order to prevent the repetition of such
calamities, he entrusted the frontier town of Tashkend, which
it seems had had a hand in the robbery, to his own son
Iskender. The latter, however, had not been long there
when he was killed in a tumult by the rebellious inhabitants.
On the news of the death of his son, Imamkuli, inflamed with

---

[1] The *Rauzat es Sefa* speaks of the bank of a river (rud) on which the Persian
army encamped. No mention is made of any great decisive battle. With regard
to the time, too, there is an important discrepancy, as the Persian chronicle states
that the fighting began on the eleventh day of Moharrem.

rage, at once set out for Tashkend, swearing that his wrath should not be stilled until the blood of the insurgents reached to his stirrups. Tashkend was, however, a strong place, which could not be reduced without a long siege. When at last the fortress was taken, a terrible massacre ensued, in which only the aged and the children were spared. But Imamkuli, remembering his vow, observed that the stream of blood only reached to his horse's fetlocks. Wishing not to incur the guilt of perjury, he determined to slaughter the aged and the children, when the ulemas bethought them of a means of averting the massacre and yet save the king's vow. A trench was dug into which the blood of the slain was drained. Into this trench rode Imamkuli, the blood was found to reach to his stirrups, and the conscientious prince ordered the carnage to cease.

At the same time, in spite of these confused notions of morality, religion, and humanity, Imamkuli was the only sovereign of Transoxiana who, without war and without conquest, made his country rich, prosperous, and happy. He is depicted as the genuine prototype of Islamite princes, who procured for the laws of religion the largest measure of respect, during whose long reign of thirty-eight years the highways enjoyed perfect security, who by preference spent his time in the society of the pious and poetical *beaux-esprits*. Often exchanging the robe of the prince for the mantle of a dervish, he wandered about the city accompanied by his vizir, Nezr Divanbeghi, and his favourite Abdulvasi, so that he might learn how things were going on. Of the learned men of the time he chiefly associated with the Mollah Yusuf Karabaghi, and especially patronised the poets Mollah Turabi and Mollah Nakhli. He once rewarded a kaside, composed by the latter, with its weight in gold. Several successful poems of his own have been preserved. The following anecdote regarding his adventures when incognito is worth relating :—The young mollah of a college was madly in love with a beautiful creature, but he was poor, and the object of his affections

required a decisive proof of his passion in the form of a new
dress for an approaching festival. The mollah's sorrow and
melancholy knew no bounds, and in his desperation he called
to mind the Mohammedan principle, ' The property of the
unbelievers belongs to the believers.'[1] He determined to
break into the shop of an Indian jeweller by night and so
procure the money which he so urgently needed. *Dictum
factum.* The mollah went to the bazaar accompanied by two
trustworthy servants and forced his way in through the
door, imperfectly secured on account of the much-vaunted
security of property. He had regained the street with a.
casket of jewels in his hand, when the Hindu, awakened by
the noise, raised an alarm, and caught the mollah by the
collar just as the watchman came up with a torch in his
hand. The mollah hastily knocked the torch out of his
hand, and then, concealed by the darkness, exclaimed, ' Ah !
Nezr Divanbeghi, thou hast made a foolish joke.' To this came
the answer, 'Your Majesty, it was not me but Abdulvasi
Kurdji.' As it was well known that Imamkuli wandered
incognito with persons bearing these names, the terrified
watchman, supposing that he had spoiled some jest of his
prince, ran off as fast as he could. What followed is easily
told. The injured Hindu appealed to the justice of the Prince
and complained of neglect of duty on the part of the watchman.
The latter when summoned supposed he was going to be ·
punished for too much zeal. The whole affair came to light.
The mollah called on to return the stolen property, did so,
and, on his appearance before the Prince, was not only pardoned his offence, but withal received a present.

In the absence of political events, the historiographer of the
Ashtarkhanides has adorned the reign of Imamkuli with such
like episodes and stories, a few of which we present to the
reader, as they reflect as in a mirror the spirit of the age as

---

[1] ' Mal-i-kiafirin hest ber m'uminin helal ' is the Persian version of this proverb,
which is often acted on, although the Koran declares the property of unbelievers
who pay taxes to be inviolable.

manifested in the Central Asia of that day. A good deal of interest is told us about the diplomatic relations between the Mogul empire in India and the khanate of Bokhara. After his return from Tashkend, Imamkuli sent an embassy to Djihanghir, the Emperor of India, to make an official announcement to the latter of his accession to the throne. The descendant of Baber, who had by that time united the whole of the northen half of the Indian peninsula under his sceptre, received the ambassadors of his brother sovereign in a friendly manner, and even condescended to make jocose observations. Djihanghir—' Conqueror of the world,' is the signification of his name—was at that time languishing in the chains thrown around him by his charming spouse, Nurdjihan ('Light of the World'), and thought only of love. He consequently did not scruple to enquire after the fair ones of Imamkuli. Such indiscretion,[1] than which nothing is a greater breach of Mohammedan good manners, gave offence to the ambassadors of Imamkuli, one of whom answered : ' My sovereign is freed earthly passions ; he has never concerned himself for the things of this world.' At this Djihanghir smiled and observed : ' When then has thy prince seen the world, that it has inspired him with so much disgust ? ' When this speech was reported to Imamkuli on the return of his ambassadors, the Özbeg prince felt himself insulted by it. Soon after Djihanghir, by way of returning the compliment, sent a particularly skilful physician envoy to Bokhara. Among the many costly presents which the latter brought with him was a scarlet tent, adorned with precious stones and diamonds, which was valued to be worth one year's tribute of Hindostan. But Imamkuli, mindful of the insulting speech, let the Indian envoy wait six months for his reception. In vain did Divanbeghi plead for the envoy. Imamkuli always answered : ' If I receive him and his

---

[1] Nothing is considered by a Mohammedan more insulting than for a man with whom he is not on an especially friendly footing to enquire after his wife's health. Even in such cases of peculiar intimacy as allow of the enquiry being made, the words 'wife' or 'woman' must be avoided, the indirect expressions 'thy household,' 'thy family,' and the like being used instead.

presents, I lay myself under an obligation ; if I receive him
and decline his presents, I commit a breach of etiquette ; it
is therefore best not to receive him at all.'   But as Divanbeghi
still urged the reception of the envoy on his reluctant master,
the latter at last agreed to give the long-delayed audience at
some accidental or informal meeting, e.g., during the chase.
The cunning physician at once had the splendid tent set up,
with the other costly presents inside, in such a position that
the prince must pass by it in hunting.   None the less did
Imamkuli turn his head away and seem to be engaged in conversation with one of his retinue.   ' O Turning-point of the
World,'[1] said the physician, ' look once in this direction.'
With that Imamkuli cast a hasty glance at the objects displayed, and turning to Rehim Pervanedji, said ' Take them,
all these have I given to thee.'   The ambassador was astonished, but as there was a very fine sword still left behind,
he asked next day for an audience in order to present it.
This being granted, he said, ' Two remarkable swords have
been left behind by Ekber Shah ; one my Emperor hath
kept for himself, the other he sendeth thee, his brother, as a
token of his friendship.'   The Özbeg prince could not well
refuse this present.   When, however, he attempted to draw the
sword from its sheath, and found it somewhat difficult to
do so, he remarked, with a reference to Djihanghir's former
project of conquering Bedak'hshan, which was never carried
into execution : ' Ah, your swords are too difficult to draw.'
' Only this one,' answered the envoy, with ready wit, ' because
it is a sword of peace ; were it a weapon of war it would leap
readily from its scabbard.'   History has preserved another
witty remark of this ambassodor, who afterwards gained the
favour of Imamkuli, and was by him graciously dismissed.
On one occasion the two poets Nakhli (the Palmy) and

---

[1] The present king of Persia allows himself to be addressed by his subjects as
Kible-i-Alem, ' Turning-point of the World.'   The princes of. Bokhara were
still more sublime, for they were called ' Turning-point of Humanity,' ' Kible-i
Alemian.'

Turabi (the Earthy) competed with one another in poetical composition at the court of the prince of Bokhara. The prudent physician was asked to which of them he gave the preference. 'O prince,' he answered, 'out of the earth grows the palm.' In consequence of this decision, the last-named poet was treated with greater distinction. Djihanghir's embassy returned home in 1036 (1626). A year later he died, and was succeeded by his son Shahdjihan, who would satiate his lust of conquest by the capture of Belkh. As however Imamkuli came out to meet him with a well appointed army, he soon repented of his rash undertaking, and assured the Dadkhah[1] Hadji Mansur, who had been sent from Bokhara to settle the question amicably, that he never intended war, but only a hunting expedition on a large scale.

Thus Imamkuli was enabled to preserve the peace which he so anxiously maintained. For his friendly relations with Persia, which were only disturbed for a short time after the death of Abbas the Great,[2] he had to thank his brother Nezr Mehemmed Khan, the governor of Belkh; who, in consequence of his relationship with the principal saint of Khorasan, took up a friendly position towards Iran and Shah Abbas, exchanged amicable embassies with the latter, and in 1031 (1621) presented him through his envoy Payende Mirza, among other presents, with fifty horses of Turkestan. How Nezr Mehemmed was related to Imam Riza is explained in the following manner:—When Abdulmumin took Meshed and had all the inhabitants massacred, Abutalib, the head of the descendants of Imam Riza, seized the bridle of Din

---

[1] Dadkha means 'one from whom men seek justice,' hence a 'judge.' It was the title of the earlier viceroys of Central Asia. At present we find this title used only in Khokand, and in Eastern Turkestan.

[2] This happened during the government of Shah Sefi. In consequence of the numerous executions, disturbances broke out in Merv, and the authority of Persia was weakened in that time. Imamkuli is said to have sent 15,000 men from Bokhara, and Nezr Mehemmed Khan 20,000 from Belkh, under the leadership of his son Abdulaziz, against Merv. These esieged the place for a long time, but on the approach of a larger Persian army the Özbegs retired.

Mehemmed as he rode through the city, and implored him to spare his family and accept his hospitality. Din Mehemmed took up his quarters in the sheikh's house, and married his daughter Zehra Banu Begum.[1] From this marriage sprang Nezr Mehemmed, who was thus by birth not only a Seïd but also an Alide. This nobility of birth, in the eyes of the religious inhabitants of Central Asia no small advantage, had, however, never disturbed the concord of the brothers. Nothing showed more clearly their mutual respect as the reception given by Nezr Mehemmed to Imamkuli, when the latter came to Belkh at the head of his army to repel the invasion threatened by Shahdjihan. Nezr Mehemmed went to meet him more than two English miles out of the town, accompanied by his twelve sons, and on foot. Although Imamkuli remonstrated, 'Thou art a Seïd, and art held in great honour, it doth not beseem thee to go on foot,' the other still set no bounds to his loyal submission. Arrived in Belkh, where all the great men of Transoxania were at that time assembled, he presented the customary 'nine gifts,' and with the eight slaves he ranged himself as the ninth.[2] After his return to Bokhara, Imamkuli lived several years of undisturbed felicity and peace, so that the people of Central Asia can only compare his reign to that of Sultan Huseïn Mirza

[1] This lady, of whom it was related that she was saved from the unfortunate battle together with her two sons, appears after the death of her husband to have returned from Bokhara to Persia. We know that later on she became, at the command of Shah Abbas, the wife of the Kadjar chief Mihrab Khan, and from their marriage sprang Murteza Kuli Khan, the governor of Meshed. At the time of the siege mentioned in the preceding note, he made a daring attempt to relieve Merv, but was captured by the Özbeg and sent to Bokhara. Imamkuli received him as his step-brother with peculiar respect, and gave him back his freedom. This relationship between the Ashtarkhanides and the Turkish house of the Kadjars is still recognised by the reigning family of Bokhara, although the latter are connected with the Ashtarkhanides only by the mother's side.

[2] He did this with the usual form 'Bu sikez kul Nezr Mehemmed bile tokuz'— 'Here are eight slaves, with Nezr Mehemmed nine.' This expression of politeness had been used among the Turanian people from time immemorial, and was therefore no invention of Ibrahim Sultan of Georgia, who held similar language to Timour, as we are told by Sheref eddin Ali Yezdi in his biography of the lame conqueror of the world.

Baïkara in Herat. In 1050 (1640) he at last fell ill, and as he wished in his character of pious Moslem to spend his last hours 'in the neighbourhood of the Prophet,'[1] he called his brother to him from Belkh, gave him the sceptre, in the place of which he himself assumed the pilgrim's staff. He remained over the following Friday in Bokhara. In his presence in the great mosque the 'Khutbe' was read for the first time for Nezr Mehemmed Khan, when the whole congregation burst into sobs and bitter tears. Soon after he left his capital, his country, and the people whom he loved and had so long made happy, and took his way across Iran to Mecca. On his journey he was received by the king of Persia with royal honours. He died in the sixty-second year of his life in Medina, where, among other benefactions founded by his pious munificence, a public garden and bath still exist.

This remarkable prince was still alive, and occupied with the duties of religion, when the edifice of peace, which his reign had been spent in erecting, collapsed, and was replaced by revolution, war, and fraternal discord. Nezr Mehemmed Khan, who mounted the throne in 1052 (1642), soon perceived that he had succeeded to his brother's dominion, but not to the respect with which he had been regarded. He sought to gain men's minds by his liberality, for he had immense treasures at his disposal, and has indeed been reckoned the richest prince of the houses of the Sheïbanides and Ashtar-khanides. We are told that it required six hundred string[2] of camels to transport his treasures. Eight thousand horses were to be found in his stables, without counting his numerous brood-mares. He had eighty thousand sheep of the breed

---

[1] To die Mudjavir bolmak, 'in the neighbourhood (of the prophet),' is still regarded by the inhabitants of Central Asia as an act most pleasing to God. Happy is he who can carry it out.

[2] By Katar, a Turkish word, which is also used by the Persians to denote a train of beasts of burden, is understood in Central Asia, from six to ten camels tied one behind the other. The English expression 'a string of camels,' best expresses the sense of the word.

that produce the blue (kebud ?) lambs, and four hundred chests full of the orange-coloured Frengish satin. All this wealth, however, contributed but little to the consolidation of his power. He himself first broke the long peace of the lands about the Oxus by sending an army to conquer Kharezm, after the death of Isfendiyar Khan, the ruler of that country. Immediately a certain Baki Yüz (?) set up the standard of revolt in the northern part of his dominions. When he sent his own son Abdulaziz to reduce the rebellious province to submission, his child not only made common cause with the rebels, but allowed himself to be by them proclaimed prince in his father's stead. Nezr Mehemmed Khan was in Karshi when this news was brought to him, with the addition that his son was marching straight on Bokhara. Knowing the energy of his unnatural rival, his only thought was to secure at any rate that part of his dominions which lay on this side of the Oxus. After a reign of barely five years he fled to Belkh, where he was well received by the inhabitants, and divided his dominions with the sons who still remained faithful to him. Khosru Sultan received Gur, and his son Kasim Sultan Meïmene and Andkhoï; Behram Sultan was established in Gulab; Subhankuli in Salu Tchihardjui, the ford over the Oxus now known as Khodja Salu; and Kutluk Sultan in Kunduz. In the meantime Abdulaziz Khan had mounted the throne in Bokhara. Not content with his crime he would gain over the ablest of his brothers to be his accomplice. He wrote a penitent letter [1] to his father, imploring his forgiveness; and requested that his brother Kutluk Sultan might be sent to Bokhara to receive his further explanations. Nezr Mehemmed Khan complied with the request. Kutluk had no sooner arrived in Bokhara than he was persuaded by Abdulaziz to revolt. Against him was now despatched Subhankuli,

---

[1] The author of the *Tarikhi Mekim Khani* naively attempts to persuade his readers that Abdulaziz was only brought by force to turn against his father. We are told that in case of his refusal he was threatened with death.

with the promise that if he succeeded in recalling his brother
to his duty he himself should receive the title of Kale khani
(commander of a fortress). As Kutluk was not prepared for
open hostilities, he had to shut himself up in the fortress of
Kunduz. Subhankuli pressed the siege with all possible
despatch, and, having reduced the fortress, had his brother
executed, by way of most effectually recalling him to his duty.
This conduct naturally incensed the father's heart, and he
reproved Subhankuli, saying : ' I sent thee to correct thy
brother, and not to kill him.' So he delayed the promised pro-
motion, and Subhankuli also rose in revolt. The unfortunate
Nezr Mehemmed Khan, weary of struggling against his
rebellious children, and doubtful of the fidelity of his
Özbegs, invoked the assistance of Shahdjihan, the Emperor
of India, without reflecting that the ambitious son of
Djihangir, whose greedy glances had been already directed
towards Belkh, would, instead of saving him, bring about his
utter ruin. And so indeed it came to pass. Aurengzib and
Murad Bakhshi, the two sons of Shahdjihan, appeared in the
field with a powerful army. Khosru Sultan, who attempted
to resist them, was defeated, taken prisoner, and sent to
India. Nezr Mehemmed Khan, who did not become aware
of the hostile intentions of his allies until they had arrived
in the vicinity of Belkh, with difficulty made his escape from
his own Özbegs, and fled by way of Shiborgan and Merv
to Iran, where he hoped for a friendly reception from
Abbas II., a great grandson of Abbas the Great.

Nor were these expectations of Nezr Mehemmed Khan
disappointed. When his situation was known in Isfahan,
Abbas II. invited him to his capital, and at the same time
sent him a thousand ducats to defray the expenses of his
journey. Orders were given that he was to be treated with
princely honour in all places through which he passed. A
guard of honour was sent to receive him twelve miles from
Isfahan, and the Shah himself, surrounded by the grand
dignitaries of the kingdom, advanced two hours' journey from

Y

the capital to meet him.   After Abbas had bestowed on him
a paternal embrace,[1] he was transferred from his own worn-
out beast to a noble charger, and his entry into the city was
celebrated by festivities and illuminations.   After the King
of Persia had entertained him as his guest for two years and
a half, he was sent back to his own land accompanied by an
army, with whose assistance he reconquered Belkh.   But the
devastation of the Indian army and the war waged by Abdulaziz against those intruders, had destroyed the prosperity
of the country to such an extent that Nezr Mehemmed Khan
sat rather on thorns than on a throne.   In Belkh itself famine
prevailed to such an extent that a thousand florins[2] were
given for an ass-load of corn.   At the same time, the winter
of the year 1060 (1650) was more intensely cold than had
ever been known before.   The Indian army in its retreat,
pursued by the Özbegs troops, suffered severely from the
cold.   Thousands were frozen in the passes of the mountains,
and the author of the 'Tarikhi Mekim Khani' relates that
when he was sent the following year to India as diplomatic
agent[3] he saw piles of human bones along the highways.
Besides all these sources of human misery, hostilities prevailed
more than ever between Nezr Mehemmed Khan and his sons.
For some time the people of Belkh were on his side, but at
last, weary of the endless feud, they went over to Abdulaziz,
the ruler of Bokhara, who had sent his brother Subhankuli
with a large detachment against their father.   Nezr Mehemmed Khan finally determined to abandon the contest, and in
order that he might spend his last days in peace to go to
Medina.   He wished to be reconciled to his sons, and to give

---

[1] According to the historians of Central Asia, Abbas II. had disguised himself
in the dress of a common soldier, and, by way of showing especial honour to his
guest, walked a long way by the stirrup of Nezr Mehemmed Khan.   It was
only when the latter's attention was called to the fact that he recognised his royal
brother and embraced him.

[2] In the text *rubia*, the Indian rupee.

[3] *Vakaanigar*, 'one who surveys what has happened.'   It is the title of a
secret agent, in contradistinction to *vakaanuvis*, 'one who describes what has
happened,' a reporter.

them his blessing, but Subhankuli declined to receive this last manifestation of paternal feeling. Broken-hearted Nezr Mehemmed set out on his pilgrimage. Fate was not so favourable to him as to his brother. He died on the way in Simnan, and only as a corpse was allowed to touch the hallowed soil of Arabia.

When the news of his death arrived in Transoxania his sons put on public mourning, pious gifts were distributed, and readers of the Koran recited the holy book day and night for the health of his soul. It was as if a dearly-beloved father had died, and not a rival with whom they had long contended. But the spirit of discord in the family of Nezr Mehemmed Khan did not disappear with his death. The period for mourning appointed by law had hardly come to an end when Abdulaziz, afraid of the rivalry of Subhankuli, would deprive him of Belkh, and for this purpose sent out his brother Kasim Mehemmed Sultan at the head of an army over the Oxus. But Subhankuli was not a man to be easily got rid of, nor was the poet-prince Kasim Mehemmed equal to the task of contending with him. After a long but fruitless struggle, Kasim Mehemmed was forced to retire to Hissar, and peace was concluded on the terms that Subhankuli should be recognised as heir-presumptive. Many friendly messages were exchanged between the brothers, until several of Subhankuli's party came one day to Kasim Mehemmed, and under pretence of a secret message the latter was drawn aside into a chamber and there murdered. The historian of the Ashtarkhanides relates that in him the most accomplished prince of that house died an untimely death. He left behind him a divan of more than a thousand pair of verses in the Turkish and Persian languages, and was besides a master of prose composition. After Subhankuli had thus rid himself of a dangerous rival, he established friendly relations with Abdulaziz, and even rendered him assistance in the war waged by the latter against Khahrezm, during which the western part of Bokhara

was threatened with serious danger from the Özbegs who
dwelt along the lower course of the Oxus.

For at that time there ruled in Khahrezm, Abulgazi
Bahadur Khan, a man whose career of varied adventure
reminds us of that of Baber. To him the khanate of Khiva
is indebted for its independence of Bokhara, the world for an
historical work entitled 'The Genealogy of Princes.' Inspired
by the deepest hatred againgst the sovereigns of Transoxania,
especially against Abdullah Khan, who had treated his
ancestors in a tyrannical manner, this man had even in early
youth set before him as the great object of his life the ruin of
the foreign rulers. To him alone is to be attributed the expulsion of the Bokhariots from the lower course of the Oxus.
He may be said to have made his first appearance in the
year 1054 (1646), when, after the recall of Kasim Mehemmed
Sultan from the post of governor of Khiva, he made himself
master of that place. His first wars were waged either
against the Turkomans in the interior of Khahrezm or against
the plundering bands of the Kalmücks. He did not assume
the offensive against Bokhara until his assistance was sought
by Subhankuli in his war with Abdulaziz Khan. Peace, it is
true, was soon re-established between the two brothers, but
by that time Abulgazi, already in Kökürtlik,[1] which belonged to the territory of Bokhara, was not disposed to
abandon his long-cherished plans of vengeance, and extended
his ravages as far as the town of Karaköl, which he laid in
ashes. In the following year he made a second incursion,
and on this occasion pressed forward as far as Kermineh.
Abdulaziz attacked him with an army of 60,000 men, and,
cut off from his own forces and surrounded by the overwhelming numbers of the enemy, Abulgazi would have lost
his life were it not for the heroic conduct of his son Anusha
Khan, only fourteen years old, who succeeded in rescuing
him from danger. The Bokhariots sustained a decisive

---

[1] Kökürtlik is the name of that place in the desert on the right hand of the
Oxus, which is regarded as the frontier point between Bokhara and Khiva.

defeat. Abdulaziz was wounded, and only escaped by swimming across the river; while Abulgazi, laden with prisoners and treasures, returned to Khiva. But his lust for vengeance was not yet satiated. Repeatedly renewing his incursions, he at one time extended his ravages as far as Vardanzi, at another up to the very gates of Bokhara. It was not until his sixtieth year that this continual shedding of blood between two sovereigns of the same religion and the same race aroused in his breast feelings of moderation and pity. He became reconciled to Abdulaziz, and died soon after in the year 1074 (1663). Our readers have often had occasion to observe that in the case of Tartar warriors the voice of humanity is not listened to until the approach of old age is felt. So it was now. His warlike son and successor Anusha Khan[1] paid but little regard to the treaty of peace concluded by his father. In 1076 (1665) he made an inroad into Bokhara, advanced as far as the residence of the Khodja Djuibar, and abandoned that holy place to plunder. Abdulaziz happened to be in Kermineh when this took place. He hurried back at once, and at midnight arrived before the city gate, which was in the hands of the Kharezmians. Accompanied by only forty faithful followers, he succeeded in cutting down the guard, and forced his way, fighting as he went, into the citadel. From this place a summons went forth inciting the population to murder the Khivans that very night. All who could bear arms, whether Özbegs, Tadjiks, Rayas or foreign merchants, fell upon the enemy, surprised in his nightly rest. The massacre was terrible, and but a small part of the army of Anusha escaped to Khiva. This catastrophe for a long time discouraged the Kharezmians from disturbing the peace of Bokhara.

In the meantime, however, Abdulaziz, worn out with constant feuds with his enemies and sick of the cares of government, owing to the quarrels with his brothers, determined to

---

[1] The author of the *Tarikhi Mekim Khani* ascribes this expedition to Abulgazi. Evidently an error, as Abulgazi was by that time no longer among the living.

follow the example of his two predecessors. He resolved to
abdicate in favour of Subhankuli, to take up the pilgrim staff
and go to Mecca. When Subhankuli was summoned to come
to Bokhara and assume ·the sovereignty, he sent the Atalik
Imamkuli and the Pervanedji Tangriberdi to say that he would
willingly comply with the request when Abdulaziz had himself
left the capital. This message did not produce a good impression upon Abdulaziz, and the men of Bokhara took
advantage of it to dissuade their sovereign from carrying out
his intention of resigning. But Tangriberdi, who saw that
the interests of his master were in danger, went to Abdulaziz
Khan and spoke as follows : ' Lord, with thy permission I
will relate a story of which I am now reminded. When
Sultan Ibrahim from Belkh passed through Nishabur on his
way to Mecca, he visited Ferid-eddin Attar,[1] the wisest man
of his times, and stayed with him to supper. But the highly
honoured was, as is well known, very poor. So when evening
was come he prayed to God, and O wonder! a dish full of
good food was suddenly placed upon the table from which
both his guest and himself eat and were satisfied. The
Sultan invited the holy man to return the visit on the following day, when he also prayed, and in answer to his prayer
several dishes full of dainty meats were served before them.
Ferid-eddin, marvelling at the diversity of the heavenly
blessing, exclaimed : "O God, why have I obtained but one
dish, but the Sultan several ?" Thereupon a voice answered,
"Ye are verily both My servants, but Ibrahim hath given up
for My way sceptre and throne, but thou only a shop; as
his merit is greater, so is also his reward." And so too is it
with thee,' continued the crafty Tangriberdi ; ' thy pilgrimage
is really worth all the trouble it will cost thee, for it has a

---

[1] Ferid-eddin Attar (the spice merchant), born 613 (1216), was the author of
works much read in the Mohammedan East, the *Mantik et teïr* (Logic of Birds) the
Pendnameh (Book of Counsels) and the *Djevahirnameh* (Book of Jewels). He is
said to have lived to be more than a hundred and fourteen years old, and to have
given up his business in order the better to apply himself to the contemplative
life.

thousand times more merits than that of another.' Abdulaziz, moved to tears by this parable, was confirmed in his previous resolution. He at once began to prepare for his journey, on which he started in the year 1091 (1680) accompanied by more than three thousand pilgrims, who had attached themselves to his caravan. Like his predecessors, he enjoyed on his way through Persia the hospitality of Iran. Shah Suleïman, the son of Abbas II. treated him with royal honours. In Isfahan he was lodged in the charming palace of Tchil Sutun. As the festival of Noruz was at that time being celebrated with all the festivities customary on that occasion in Iran, the Özbeg prince could take his farewell of the pomps and glories of the world amid the delightful gardens of Isfahan, then in the full bloom of spring, and amid all the magnificent splendour of the Persian court. Thence he took his way by Hamadan and Bagdad through the desert, where he had the misfortune to be attacked by a large band of Beduin robbers. They demanded forty thousand ducats as his ransom, threatening in case of refusal to proceed to extremities. Not wishing to defile his hands with blood on his pious journey, Abdulaziz promised them the half of the sum, but as the Arabs would not abate their demands he at last became enraged. 'Have I reigned for forty years and am I now to be dictated to by robbers?' he exclaimed. 'Up to battle ; if I fall it is in the service of God.' Fortunately the struggle terminated in favour of the pilgrim prince. He reached in safety the goal of his wishes, and died soon after in the seventy-fourth year of his life. He was buried at Medina near his father and his uncle.

Abdulaziz was a man of remarkable corpulence, and indeed is said to have been the stoutest man of his time. One of his historians avows that a child of four years old could find room in one of the legs of his boots. A poet was daring enough to make this corpulence the butt of his wit. Abdulaziz heard of it, and sent for the satirist, who appeared before him trembling for his life. The prince addressed him in the

following terms : ' O Mollah, I am told that thou hast
composed a poem in ridicule of me ; do not the like to others
or thou may'st see reason to repent such conduct.'   With
that he presented him with ten thousand dinars, and a
robe of honour.   The poet replied : ' Lord, better had'st thou
had me hewn into ten thousand pieces, than thus disgrace me
by thy magnanimity.'   And indeed he left Bokhara, and
emigrated to India.   Abdulaziz, who had proved so heartless
in his conduct toward his father, displayed similar magnanimity on several other occasions.   He himself was by no
means wanting in culture ; he wrote good verses, and during
his pilgrimage is said to have written some beautiful hymns.
He is also said to have been remarkably familiar with the celebrated work ' Bokhari.'   Learned men had always free access
to him, and caligraphers he so greatly esteemed that he
supported for seven years the celebrated caligrapher Mollah
Hadji, whom he employed to make a single copy of ' Hafiz.'
The artist only wrote a couplet a day, and when on his journey
Abdulaziz presented this copy of ' Hafiz ' to Shah Suleïman,
the latter was more delighted with this one present than with
all the jewels and costly stuffs given him by the ex-prince of
Transoxania.   Daring in battle, calm in danger, Abdulaziz
was often inaccessible for days to the impressions of the
outer world.   This was attributed by many to his practice of
continued meditation ; for the princes of Bokhara, who took
part in bloody battles, and strove with their fathers and
brothers for objects of worldly ambition, were obliged, by way
of propitiating popular favour, to spend hours in the society of
holy men, meditating on the greatness of God, and reflecting
that all earthly activity is but mere trifling.

XVI.

SUBHANKULI KHAN AND THE END OF THE ASHTARKHANIDES.

1091 (1680)—1150 (1737).

BY this time we have advanced some two centuries since the fall of the Timourides and the commencement of the decay of Transoxania. It is therefore not to be wondered at that the picture presented by the political and social circumstances of the small states on the Oxus should become even more and more meagre and obscure; that internal dissensions, the strife of brothers, and petty squabbles take the place of more important events in the roll of their history. Subhankuli Khan, who after the departure of his brother for the holy cities of Arabia assumed the government in Bokhara in the first days of Moharrem 1091 (1680), had to contend against the very difficulties with which he himself had formerly troubled his brother. He had to turn his arm now against his restless neighbours in the west, now against his rebellious vassals, nay even against his own children. As usual, Belkh, the Dauphiné of the Ashtarkhanides, was the original source of troubles. Subhankuli had placed there as governor his son Iskender Khan, who had hardly filled that post for two years when his brother Ebulmansur, who had secured the support of a powerful party, contrived to poison him, and seize on his office. Subhankuli, however, refused to confirm his violent and passionate son in that post, which he conferred on another younger son, Ibadullah. But who obeyed the words of the prince unless they were emphasised by the use of weapons? Ebulmansur succeeded in maintaining himself for four months at the head of affairs in Belkh, but forfeited

the favour of his adherents by the execution of Ibadullah
from a feeling of rivalry.   A conspiracy was formed against
him, and as he went one day to visit his aunt, they fell upon
him and murdered him.   He was succeeded by a third son of
Subhankuli, named Siddik Mehemmed Khan, a debauchee
like his murdered brother.   By way of taking revenge for
the latter he had his murderers flayed alive, and torn limb
from limb.   At the same time he refused obedience to his
father, and did not go to his assistance when Anusha Khan,
from Khiva, wasted Transoxania with fire and sword.   After
Subhankuli had succeeded in putting a stop to those incursions he felt inclined to pardon his son for his neglect of
duty, but afterwards learnt, to his great sorrow, that his non-
appearance was due to a rebellious purpose.   When he
crossed the Oxus to call his child to account, Siddik Mehemmed assumed an attitude of open hostility, and shut himself up in Belkh.   But the father's heart still recoiled from
forcible measures.   He first of all reproached him for his
ingratitude in a letter, and promised him forgiveness if he
would return to his obedience.   This plan succeeded, for
Siddik Mehemmed appeared before his father as a penitent,
and died soon after, in the year 1096 (1684).   By this time
Subhankuli was convinced of the danger of entrusting important posts to his children.   The governorship of Belkh was
therefore conferred on a loyal noble, Khadim Bi Atalik.[1]
On his death in 1099 (1687) it was conferred on the devoted
and valiant Mahmud Bi Atalik, of the tribe of Kungrad.
This governor justified the choice made of him by keeping the
Özbegs and Turkomans of the neighbourhood in check, and the
prosperity of Belkh increased to such a degree, that an ass-load

---

[1] The literal meaning of Atalik is ' one who fills the place of a father.'   It
was in the earliest times among the Turko-Tartars the title of those nobles of the
country who acted as counsellors of the princes.   It has also the meaning of
guardian, tutor, and instructor, and it is only in modern times that it is found
in the sense of vizir or minister.   The Sheïbanides and Ashtarkhanides had
several ataliks, one forming part of the suite of each prince.   The present khan
of Khiva has a definite number of ataliks, the rulers of Bokhara and Khokand
confer it as a title of distinction.

of corn (two and a-half centner) cost forty tenghes, or one pound sterling.[1] Fruit and other provisions could not be sold at all.

Of course the number of devoted vassals such as Mahmud Bi was insignificant in comparison with the rebellious chiefs of the several Özbeg tribes, who, for want of a foreign enemy, satisfied their desire for war in the interior of the country, either by fighting against one another, or by rebelling against their sovereign. Of the latter class Bayat Kara, the chief of the Özbeg tribe Bayat, was especially conspicuous. He maintained himself in the mountainous country of Hissar, and revolted seven years running. Mahmud Bi repeatedly took the field against him, but as he could not easily reduce his place of refuge, the strong fortress of Naiman, it was necessary to come to terms with him. When he was in difficulties Bayat Kara promised to appear wrapt in a shroud, with bow and sword hanging from his neck, i.e., as a penitent sinner. But he never kept his word, but employed the time given him to collect fresh forces for a new revolt. Eight times was he defeated, till at last he himself was slain; his head was struck off and sent to Bokhara. No less tedious were the wars between the Özbeg tribes of Ming and Kipt-chak; the first of whom dwelt in Meimene and Andkhoï, the latter in the neighbourhood of Belkh. These internal struggles were all the more injurious as the western neighbour of Bokhara, namely, Khiva, took advantage of them to carry out its plundering forays. Anusha Khan, the warlike son of Abulgazi, had, as we have seen in the previous chapter, extended his incursions as far as Bokhara during the reign of Abdulaziz, and in consequence of his boldness suffered a severe defeat. After the accession of Subhankuli he renewed his predatory expeditions, and is even said to have surprised Samarkand in 1095 (1683). Subhankuli was in the greatest straits, the Urgendjer devastated the whole country, whilst his insolent vassals refused him assistance. Mahmud Bi alone stood with his accustomed loyalty

[1] According to the present value of the tenghe in Bokhara, twenty-four make an English pound, but in Khiva, forty.

by his master's side, defeated Anusha Khan in a pitched battle near Gidjdovan, and pursued him as far as Kharezm. This, however, did not prevent the restless Anusha from invading Bokhara the following year, while Subhankuli was in Belkh ; but as he was again unsuccessful, he was, on his return home, seized by his own people and put to death. The Urgendjer raised his son Irnak [1] on the white felt. He seems at first to have enjoyed the favour, nay, even the protection of Subhankuli. But this did not prevent him from treading in his father's footsteps and invading Bokhara ; nay, on one occasion, in 1098 (1688), he advanced as far as the gates of the capital. It was therefore high time to take measures against this evil. Mahmud Bi collected a powerful army, attacked Kharezm itself, and destroyed the army of his opponent. Certain of the nobles of Kharezm passed over into the camp of the victor ; Irnak Khan was sent out of the world by poison, and Khiva passed again under the supremacy of Bokhara—a state of things which, however, at the most lasted only two years.

Even at this time, in the midst of all these political calamities, and in spite of all the unmistakeable signs of ruin and decay, Bokhara enjoyed in a high degree the respect and esteem of the Mohammedan princes of the Sunnite sect. Blinded by the glories of the past, none of them would recognise the rottenness of the present. Thus we find that embassies of honour came with costly presents to the court of Subhankuli from distant Khoten and Kashgar, from the Crimea, and even from India. From the last named country the proud Aurengzib sent, in 1096 (1684), one of his grandees, Zeberdest Khan, with elephants and other presents to Bokhara, in order to gain in the ruler of Transoxania an ally against the Shiites of Persia. The ambitious emperor of India suspected that Persian intrigues were the cause of the continual restlessness of the Afghan tribes on the further side

---

[1] Irnak, or Ernak, is an old Turanian name, for as far as we know a son of Attila was so named.

of the Suleiman range of mountains. As he did not wish ⸘
openly to attack Shah Suleïman, a son of Abbas II., at that ·
time ruler of Persia, he thought that he might quiet his
adversary by means of an Özbeg invasion of Khorasan, ⸜
of old times the hostage of Iran.[1] Similar motives led Sultan
Ahmed II.[2] to send an embassy in answer to one of congratulations previously despatched to Constantinople from
Bokhara. This last was certainly sent by Subhankuli, and
not, as the Ottoman historians assert, by Mohammed Bahadir.
At its head was a certain Mustafa Tchaush. The last named
arrived in Transoxania in 1102 (1690); he brought with him a
diplomatic document, which is a true expression of the self-
deceiving and false language used by the officials of the
Porte of that time. Although Ahmed II., as is well known,
sustained crushing defeats everywhere—in Hungary, Poland,
Dalmatia, Syria, and on the Mediterranean—he sends an
account to his brother. prince on the Oxus of brilliant feats of
arms, and glorious victories over swarthy infidels, in which he
urges him to take a part, which suggests the thought that
the secretary of the Porte had copied, and sent to Subhankuli, out of the ' Correspondence of Sultans'[3] by Feridun Bey,
the report of some victory of Mohammed the Conqueror, or
of Selim II. This interesting letter, which the 'Tarikhi
Mekim Khani' communicates, in the Ottoman original runs as
follows :—

' In the name of the merciful and gracious God.

' He who hath inherited the throne of the Sultanate and a
fortune, who hath spread out the carpet of quiet and security,
who from the time of his ancestors hath been partaker of

[1] The war, was, however, fortunately avoided through the mediation of the
Princess Djihanara (Ornament of the World), a lady of unusual talents and
address, who contrived a *rapprochement* between the two courts.

[2] Ahmed II. ascended the throne July 14, 1691, and died February 6, 1695.

[3] *Munshiat es Selatin*, the *Correspondence of the Sultans*, is the title of a
valuable book which Feridun Bey, the secretary of Murad III., compiled from
18,000 original documents found in the imperial Ottoman archives. It has
recently appeared in print in Constantinople, with the addition of similar documents of a later date.

the favour and grace of God, the pride of government, Seïd
Subhankuli Khan,—may be greeted with endless salutations
containing everlasting friendship and unity, with countless
good wishes full of imperishable love and union. The end
of our cordial and distinguished command is as follows :
Thy honourable and musk-enveloped writing—I mean thy
letter penetrated with inward friendship—which thou hast
recently sent, arrived in the most favourable time, and at the
most auspicious moment. When its contents came to our
noble perusal from behind the veil of concealment, there
appeared from the eloquent text both the health and the
welfare of thy person inspired by fidelity and devotion, as
well as other events and circumstances clear to my wonderful
senses. Let it in turn be made manifest to thy bright
understanding, and to thy mind, rich in blessings, that, from
the times of our great ancestors of blessed memory, and of our
father now in paradise, we have chosen even unto the present
hour the path of the most beneficial wars of religion, that we
have especially held it an eminently godly occupation to exterminate from the face of the earth the Frankish unbelievers
and the miserable heretics of Kizilbashes. But the proverb
says that everything has its own season ; and that this work
has been delayed in consequence of certain hindrances is to
be attributed to the circumstance that we thought it best
first of all to finish with the Frankish unbelievers, and then
in full peace of mind to set out against the detestable Kizilbashes. Now with regard to our wars with the Frankish
unbelievers above referred to, although the complete extirpa-
tion of these hateful hordes belongs to the province of impossibility ; nevertheless, of the many hard battles that have
taken place, the final issue has been that, we, with God's
grace, have come out victorious, and many of the infidel
princes and chiefs have been captured, and the rest scattered in
every direction. But soon after the Frankish khans conceived
an evil purpose, they accumulated a mass of troops, and out of
the province Orkhan (?) attacked our well-defended empire,

seizing upon the property of the right believers ; and as they withal perpetrated many acts of violence, we also set out against them, and fell upon them. The unbelievers being unable to resist our countless armies, hastened in fear and anxiety back to their own land, whence they sent people of consideration, with promises of the cessation of further hostilities and submission, and with the ring of slavery in the ears, advancing on the path of obedience, displayed for a long time fidelity and devotion. But besides these the ring-leaders of another host of Frenghis of brutal nature, and proud of the multitude of their troops, had forced their way into our dominions. Quickly was a division of our troops sent against them also ; yet these had not yet arrived when our servants settled there upon the frontier had commenced the attack, and in one assault taken several of their distinguished men prisoners, and made themselves masters of their banners, their military music, and weapons. Only a few great men succeeded by wild flight in reaching their country. The soldiers whom we had sent against them had in the meantime united themselves with the troops of the frontier, and the inhabitants being pursued in their own land but few of them escaped with their lives, the rest were annihilated and stripped of all their property. A number of fortresses, whose strength is known through the world, and a mass of treasure and provisions, were with God's help thus easily won.

'And now we have filled our noble spirit with rest with regard to the infidels on this side, our fortunate star must daily shine ever brighter, our thanksgivings also soar up to the All-highest threshhold, and in full recognition of our deep devotion towards God the Almighty, our zeal and endeavour to extirpate the godless people of the Kizilbashes will from this time forward be disturbed and restrained by no consideration whatever. We, therefore, will immediately send our victorious troops into the sublime struggle, and in full trust in God, and with the intercession of Mohammed,

we will approach the castles and fortresses of those people,
and as soon as we have passed the frontier will communicate
the same to thee in a letter. Since thou art the Padishah of
Transoxania, and thy residence hath been known of old as
the dwelling-place of so many distinguished ulemas, pious
men, and sheïkhs, it seemeth to be thy duty also to draw the
sword for the maintenance of the laws of religion and for the
welfare of Islam. Thou shouldest decree a levy of the
Özbegs of the land ; so that most closely united with my
victorious army they may extirpate the sinners against
religion, and clear away thorns and thistles from the fair
valleys of Irak. We will not burden thee with aught more,
for only in order that thou mightest have opportunity to take
part in the holy duty of religious war hath this letter been
written.'

That Subhankuli, on the receipt of this inflated epistle of
the Kaisar-i-Rum, as the sultans are called in the distant
east, in spite of the unbounded respect which as a pious
Mussulman he paid to the Khalif, the Vicegerent of the
Prophet, could not answer it by sending countless hordes of
Özbegs over the Oxus is sufficiently explained by the
ruinous condition of his country. Nor was Subhankuli
the man to delight in the clash of arms. In his endless
troubles with his rebellious nobles, which were in some measure provoked by his unbounded but at the same time well-
placed confidence in Mahmud Bi, he was accustomed to
betake himself to violent measures only when pressed by the
most urgent necessity. In order to make an end of the civil
war in Belkh he was advised to place his son Mekim Khan
as governor in that town. But it was with difficulty that he
could be brought to comply with that advice, saying that
neither in years nor study was his son ripe for government.
For Subhankuli himself was greatly addicted to the study of
the sciences. He did not disdain, even at an advanced age,
to receive instruction from learned men of celebrity, and
wrote under the assumed name of Nishani verses that display

a more than ordinary poetical faculty. In secular learning he was especially devoted to medicine. Of this we have an eloquent proof in a medical book which he composed, and of which I was so fortunate as to procure in Herat a beautifully-written copy. In the short preface to the same the noble prince says: 'Observe that the wise men of medicine who have passed away have left behind them suitable works in the Arabic and Persian languages, but a book of medicine in the Turkish language has not as yet come into my hands. Therefore I, the submissive Seïd Mehemmed Subhankuli Khan, the son of the Seïd Mezr Mehemmed Khan (God rest his soul!) have written this book. For all possible diseases and failings is a remedy here given, and it will certainly be of service to many.'[1] By no means an every day example of a prince who in such wise cared for the health of his people! Subhankuli himself attained the great age of eighty years. When he perceived his end drawing nigh, after a short illness, he assembled his grandees around him, and exhorted them not to complain but to submit to the disposition of God. He expressed his regret that he could not take leave of his dear son Mekim Khan, who had long ago been marked out as his successor, and after he had named his elder brother Obeïdullah as regent till he should come of age, he departed this life in the first days of Rebiul akhir 1114 (1702), having governed thirty-one years in Belkh and twenty-four years in Bokhara, in all fifty-five years, partly as a powerful vassal, partly as an independent prince.

That the last will of Subhankuli Khan with regard to the succession to the throne was as stated above we assert on the authority of the author of the 'Tarikhi Mekim Khani.' Whether this really was the case, or that the writer made this statement in the interest of his master, is a point on

---

[1] I have communicated part of this book in my *Tschagataische Sprachstudien*. It is founded on the Arabic translations of Galenus (Djalenos), Hippocrates (Bokrat), and Ali ben Sina's (Avicenna) works, but there are still many wonderful cures related by means of the recitation of forms of prayer and the wearing of certain *muskhas*, or talismans.

which we are left in some doubt. One thing alone is certain, that a struggle for the throne broke out between the two brothers shortly after the death of their father, and raged for some years. When Mekim Khan in Belkh learnt the news of his father's death he first sent his brother a letter of condolence, and afterwards congratulated him on his accession to the throne. Obeïdullah, well aware of his brother's hostile feelings, received the embassy with ostentatious coolness, and the war between the two portions of the country, Cisoxania and Transoxania, at once began. Mahmud Bi espoused the cause of Mekim Khan, while the champion of Obeïdullah's interests was Rehim Bi Atalik, the chief of the tribe of Manghit. The struggle was in fact more a war of rivalry between the two Özbeg tribes than between the pretenders whose claims they asserted ; for the respect of the ruling family had already sunk very low, and after the death of Subhankuli the princes were but helpless puppets in the hands of ambitious nobles. After a struggle of nearly five years Obeïdullah at last gained the upper hand. He reigned as long as it suited the powerful Rehim Bi Atalik, but about the year 1130[1] (1717) he seemed to have attempted by means of a secret party to rid himself of his too burdensome protector and was consequently set aside by a violent death, and his brother Ebulfeïz Khan mounted the throne of Transoxania. This prince was characterised by the last degree of submission and weakness, qualities which the inhabitants of Central Asia disguised under the flattering appellations of ' religious mildness and the character of a dervish.' To these qualities, however, he unquestionably owed the length of his nominal government. For forty years he bore the title of sovereign, while the reality of power was in the hands of Rehim Bi and his tribesmen. The territory on this side of

---

[1] I here follow the oral tradition which I heard in Bokhara, but for want of historical authorities I cannot guarantee its correctness. It is very remarkable that modern times are just those of which we have the most imperfect records in the case of Bokhara.

the Oxus, namely, Bedak'hshan and Belkh, was governed by
another branch of the reigning family in the person of a
descendant of a daughter of Nezr Mehemmed Khan. Even
in the time of Subhankuli Khan, Salih Khodja, the head of
the family, had been engaged in sanguinary warfare for the
dominion of Belkh with Mekim Khan and Mahmud Bi.
When the latter at last retired from the field, it was easy for
Salih Khodja to make good his claims. A certain religious
character which he had contrived to lend to his pretensions
had long ago gained over the people of Belkh to his side.
Only Andkhoï and Meïmene, together with the Lebal[1] or
Ersari Turkomans, acknowledged to some extent the authority
of Bokhara on this side of the Oxus. Their adhesion, however, did but little in the way of retarding the process of
dismemberment and of ruin. By this time the slightest gust
of wind was sufficient to overturn the card house of the Ashtarkhanides; how much more the mighty storm which at that time
came from Persia in the person of Nadir Shah!

That this last of the Asiatic conquerors of the world[2] did
not turn his victorious arms against the east until after his
actual accession to the throne, is to be explained by the comparative weakness and unimportance at that time of the countries lying eastward of Iran. This was true not only of Transoxania, but also of India. Nadir would gain his first laurels
in a hard struggle with the powerful adversary in the west,
and it was not till he had defeated the Ottomans in Georgia

---

[1] Lebab Turkmen, or riverside Turkomans, so called because since their settlement in that neighbourhood they have dwelt on the left bank of the Oxus, from
Khodja Salih to Djihardjui. These Turkomans assert that they came thither
from Mangishlak.

[2] According to the account of Mirza Mehdi, his historiographer, Nadir, also
called Nadir Kuli, was descended from the Karakli branch of the tribe of Afshar,
or more correctly of Aushar. The latter is the pronunciation of the Turkomans.
It means one who holds together. The Aushars moved from Turkestan into
Iran during the dominion of the Mongols, and settled in Azerbaïdjan. In the
time of Shah Ismail Sefi they emigrated to Khorasan, where they dwelt in Yap
Köpken which belonged to Abiverd, and is situated twenty fersakhs to the north-
west of Meshed. Here, on the border of the steppe, Nadir was born, on
Saturday the sixth of Moharrem in the year 1110 (1698).

and Arabistan that he began to extend his empire eastward.
While he was still laying siege to Kandahar, his son Rizakuli
was despatched with a strong detachment towards Andkhoï,
by way of Badghiz and Martcha, formerly Mervitchak, to
punish the rashness of Alimerdan Khan, the master of
Andkhoï. This took place in 1149 (1736). The Turkish
nomads of the neighbourhood of Andkhoï, namely the tribes
of Kara and Djelair, appeared to have been soon gained for
the Persian cause by large sums of money. Without the
co-operation of these nomads a successful resistance was
impossible. Alimerdan was soon defeated, and sent as a
prisoner to Nadir. The same fate speedily overtook Aktche
and Shiborgan as had already fallen on Andkhoï. Only
Belkh, in which city ruled Seïd Ebul Hasan, the son of the
before-mentioned Salih Khodja, dared to oppose a serious
resistance to the formidable enemy. The road leading to the
ancient 'Mother of Cities,' [1] was barred by several deep
trenches, which, however, failed to prevent the approach of
Rizakuli, and his powerful park of artillery soon compelled
the fortress, only protected by a wall of earth, to capitulate.
Nadir was overjoyed at the capture of Belkh, and sent his
son as a recognition of his services twelve thousand ducats in
gold, three hundred dresses of honour, together with high-bred
horses, whose saddles and bridles were adorned with gold and
precious stones. Rizakuli felt himself urged to further
achievements, and as his troops had already begun to make
plundering incursions on the other side of the Oxus, he
crossed that river with his whole army, and attacked Ebulfeïz
Khan. The impetuous son of Nadir was, however, this time
mistaken in his calculations. Ebulfeïz, the weak-minded
ascetic, had sought the alliance of Yolbars (Lion) Khan, the
energetic and warlike ruler of Khiva, who, with an army of
valiant Özbegs, barred the way to the Persians at Karshi.
The invaders, it is true, succeeded in making themselves

---

[1] The Arabs gave to Belkh the name of Um el bilad, or 'Mother of Cities,' a
proof that they considered it of high antiquity.

masters of the neighbouring citadel of Shelduk, but it is
beyond all doubt that they sustained a defeat from the
united Tartar armies. Consequently Nadir, to avoid further
disaster, suddenly recalled his son, and at the same time
informed the princes of Central Asia and the Özbeg chiefs
that the campaign had been undertaken without his consent,
that he wished to live with them on a friendly footing, and
that it was not his intention to disturb them in their possession of the inheritance of Djenghiz Khan and the great
Turkoman houses.

This behaviour of Nadir was, as Malcolm in his 'History
of Persia' truly remarks, evidently dictated by prudence,
which, by affecting moderation, sought to carry out the plans
of his ambition, and in no degree the result of any jealousy
of his son's glory. In spite of the feebleness of the ruler of
Bokhara, united action on the part of the Özbegs might have
seriously hampered Nadir's operations in the south. Such
an event he wished to avoid, and in fact he succeeded by his
assumption of friendly behaviour in dissolving the alliance
between Khiva and Bokhara. While Yolbars took advantage
of Nadir's absence to ravage Khorasan, and give the governor
Rizakuli a great deal of trouble, the Özbeg chiefs in Bokhara,
at whose head stood Rehim Bi Atalik, were gained for the
service of Nadir by Persian gold and Persian promises.
They were won over all the more easily, since a good understanding with Khiva might not strengthen the power of the
Ashtarkhanides, but would certainly thwart the ambitious
projects of the tribe of Manghit. We do not know the details
of the breach between the khanates, but, when Nadir returned from his successful campaign in India he found the
ground so well prepared for him by Rehim Bi, that he was
not only able to approach the Oxus without striking a blow,
but was even received with demonstrations of respect. The
governors of Hissar and Karshi came to him at Kerkhi to pay
their respects. In a boat artistically carved and adorned
with mosaics, which the skilful artificers of Bokhara had

made for him, he crossed the ancient boundary of Iran and
Turan. The campaign of the Sassanide Firuz beyond the
Oxus is but obscurely revealed by the light of poetical
legends, so that we may consider Nadir as the first prince of
Persia wearing the cap of Keyyan who trod as a sovereign both of the silken[1] banks of the west river, to use the
expression of Rudeki. He pitched his camp four miles from
Bokhara, and there, under a splendid tent, awaited the visit of
homage from Ebulfeïz Khan. The crafty Rehim Bi Atalik
had been sent on to Bokhara to persuade the last of the
Ashtarkhanides to this act of submission. The task does not
appear to have been difficult, for he found the Djenghizide of
pure blood, as the Ashtarkhanides delighted to call themselves, in the society of devotees, absorbed in meditation
on the vanity of all earthly things. Accompanied by a
troop of mollahs, Ebulfeïz Khan betook himself to the camp
of the Persian on the 19th of Djemaziul akhir 1153 (September 12, 1740), and took possession of the tent that had been
erected for himself and his escort. The next day he performed homage to Nadir. On that occasion he received a
girdle adorned with precious stones, an Arab horse with
gilded saddle, and other presents. Nadir treated Ebulfeïz as
a brother sovereign, but at the same time required him to
cede all the territory on this side of the Oxus, and to furnish
him with a contingent of Özbeg and Turkoman troops. By
way of confirming the pact between them an alliance of
marriage was planned between the house of Afshar and the
noble race of the Djenghizides, and after a nephew of Nadir
had espoused a daughter of the pious prince, the Persian
king set out on his march towards Kharezm to settle accounts
with Yolbars, who now stood alone. In this expedition Nadir
was successful. On his return he received in Tchihardjui
renewed assurances of the submission of the prince of

[1] The distich of Rudeki here referred to is *Righ-i derya-i Amu ve durushtha-i
o—Ziri payem pernian ayed hemi*: 'Over the sand and flint of the Oxus' banks
my foot glides as over silk.' It occurs in a poem which Rudeki, the first poet in
the modern Persian dialect, composed in praise of Bokhara.

Bokhara. He made a triumphal entry into Meshed, where he had a padlock of gold adorned with precious stones made for Imam Riza, the patron of Iran, out of the spoils of the Turanians. This long formed the chiefest ornament of the massive silver cage which surrounds the last resting-place of that highly-honoured descendant of Ali.[1] From the Turanian auxiliaries was formed that terrible cohort, which, together with the Afghans, inspired with so much terror the Shiite Persians.

The advantages which Persia gained by Nadir's expedition across the Oxus disappeared, after the death of that victorious hero, as soon as the clouds of dust which had been raised by his hosts of cavalry. But the humiliation inflicted by him on the Ashtarkhanides proved fatal to that house. Ebulfeïz Khan sank even more and more to the position of an instrument in the hands of his ambitious vizir, by whom he was at last deposed and murdered, in 1150 (1737). A similar fate befell his son, who had married a daughter of Rehim Bi. And although a third prince, said to be an Ashtarkhanide, was raised to an illusory sovereignty, in point of fact Ebulfeïz, the youngest son of Subhankuli, closed the line of rulers of that dynasty. During his reign of nearly fifty years were extinguished the last sparks of that political greatness and social importance in which the little country on the Oxus had formerly surpassed so many peoples of Mohammedan Asia.

After what has been already said, what is to be expected of the civilisation of that period? During that period the Ottoman Empire, Persia and India had become acquainted with a powerful extra-Islamite civilisation, the courts of Constantinople, Isfahan and Lahore had been brought into

---

[1] A large portion of these costly ornaments were lost during the Afghan campaign of Ahmed Shah. Although Meshed was left in the possession of Shahrukh Mirza, the son of Nadir, still the greed of the Afghans wrought great havoc in the holy capital of Khorasan. Another portion of the treasures of Imam Riza was employed by the rebellious Salar against the present king of Persia. Such has been the case with many other saints. Devout persons lay treasures on their tombs, which ambitious men afterwards employ for the purposes of murder and war.

contact with the west by the visits of Europeans in the garb
of the diplomatist, the merchant or the missionary. Transoxania, isolated by its bulwarks of wild nomads, and un-
productive steppes, remained true to the spirit of past centuries, and even endeavoured to surpass the brightest examples
of those times in the practice of religious virtues. As has been
often remarked, by science was understood on the banks of the
Zerefshan only the exegesis of the Koran and dogmatic theology. The ideal of human perfection was the life of a sufi,
spent in contempt of human exertion, and the confession of
the worthlessness of all earthly objects. If men in Bokhara, as
in former days had been the case in Cordova, Damascus and
Bagdad, had known how to unite the noble instincts of enquiry and knowledge with a strict maintenance of the pre-
cepts of Islam, it might, perhaps, have been possible to have
preserved, even in her worst days of degeneracy, some traces
of old Mohammedan culture. But this was hindered on the
one hand by the exclusively warlike and consequently uncultivated character of the Turkish people, and on the other
by the isolated situation of the lands on the Oxus. Thus
it came to pass that of the offices and dignities of the courts
of a Harun ar Rashid or an Adurrahman II., the princes on
the Zerefshan only preserved that of the superintendent of
religious ceremonies. The sovereigns of Bokhara thought
that they had fulfilled their duties when the true believers did
not neglect the canonical prayers, and in all their actions
conformed to the customs of the *vakt-i-seadet* or 'golden
period of Islam.' Under the rule of the first princes of the
dynasty of the Ashtarkhanides a few poets and writers of
chronograms, who had survived the house of the Sheiba-
nides, still made a figure. Some of the Ashtarkhanides themselves gave unmistakeable signs of a real capacity for government and a genuine feeling for culture. Such were Imamkuli, the prince Kasim Mehemmed Sultan, and especially the
noble Subhankuli. What the first of these did for agriculture
may be seen even to-day, in the half-ruined irrigation canals

which bear his name; the poetical talents of the second is proved by his *divan* which is still extant; while the love of knowledge of the latter is shown by the book on medicine to which we have already referred. Still all this could do but little towards changing the narrow and uncultivated spirit of the people. That three sovereigns, one after another, exchanged the sceptre for the pilgrim's staff, and descended from a brilliant throne to pass the rest of their lives in the dust before the tomb of the Prophet—a thing without parallel in Mohammedan history—is in itself a sufficient proof that pietism and religious extravagance were the prevailing feelings of the age. That in spite of this less was done in the way of theological learning, that fewer colleges were founded, fewer mosques built in the days of the Ashtarkhanides than in earlier times, is to be attributed to the great falling off of the material prosperity of the country. According to the account of Seïd Rakim, Bokhara and Samarkand were already, in 1030 (1621), full of splendid buildings dating from the preceding century, and even then falling into decay from want of the necessary repairs. The buildings of the Ashtarkhanides themselves were only the following: The college of Yelenktosh, which was built in 1020 (1611) opposite to the already ruined college of Ulug Beg; a mosque and a college in Bokhara raised by the wealthy Nezr Divanbeghi in 1029 (1620); and lastly, two *körünüsh-khane* or reception saloons, which Baki Mehemmed Khan had built in Bokhara and Samarkand in 1014 (1605). Outside Transoxania Belkh was the place of which it is most often recorded that its governors undertook unimportant repairs of pretended tombs of Ali, which were always loudly trumpeted by the historians of the time. Still more melancholy is the picture presented by the state of literature during this period. Even theology and sufism, although they were sufficiently studied, did not produce any men of capacity, and in the gallery of so-called famous men we find at the best but a few ascetics and writers of chronograms hardly worth mention.

XVII.

THE HOUSE MANGHIT AND EMIR MAASUM.
1199 (1784)—1242 (1826).

WHILE our information respecting the fortunes of Asiatic countries during the last century becomes ever fuller and more trustworthy, the contrary is the case respecting Transoxania. The nearer we approach the present time the thicker is the veil which envelopes the unfortunate condition of that country. The annals of the neighbouring lands furnish no certain data on the subject, and as European travellers[1] did not dare to approach a country fast sinking into barbarism, we are obliged[2] for the time to be satisfied with the faint glimmer of a few scattered sparks. This obscurity is especially felt at that epoch when the dynasty of the Ashtarkhanides came to ruin, and the family Manghit[3] rose to power,

---

[1] European travellers of modern times only visited Bokhara in the beginning of this century. The brothers Polo stayed three years there in the time of Borak Khan, 1264-1274 ; and Anthony Jenkinson who, together with the brothers Johnson, travelled in Central Asia as agent for Russian cloth manufacturers, was in Bokhara 1558-59.

[2] From a friendly communication of Sir Henry Rawlinson, I learn that in the libraries of the East India Office and the British Museum there exist several oriental manuscripts referring to the later history of Bokhara. Unfortunately these can only be seen on the spot, and as this is impossible under my present circumstances, I can only hope to fill up the consequent *lacunæ* at a future time, in case these manuscripts contain anything really unknown.

[3] Abulgazi, in his *Genealogy of the Turks* (page 27 of the Kazan edition), asserts that the Manghits were so called because they lived in a dense forest when they were in vassalage under Djenghiz Khan. But I cannot understand how *manghit*, which the old Tchagatai authors write *mangkit*, can mean 'a dense forest.' The Manghits are at present divided into two parts. One of them lives in the district of Khiva of that name on the left bank of the Oxus, the other around Karshi.

an event of which the principal causes are easily explained, while a detailed account of it is still wanting.

That amongst all the numerous Özbeg families who had chosen Transoxania for their residence it was the Manghits who supplanted the falling house of the Ashtarkhanides is to be attributed not so much to chance as to the advantages which they had enjoyed from their first appearance in Central Asia.

Brought from their original forest-home in the north-east of Mongolia to the banks of the Oxus by Djenghiz Khan, they had mightily increased during the rule of the Djenghizide. Their new dwelling-place was in the wooded country on the left bank of the Oxus, where now dwell the Karakalpaks of Khiva. Here they had done good service to the princes of the khanate of Khiva. After the Kungrats, they were the most celebrated amongst the Turkish tribes for bravery and nobility of birth. For these reasons Sheïbani Mehemmed Khan took a portion of them into his pay. It was these who settled later in the khanate of Bokhara, on the steppe in the neighbourhood of Karshi.

They always exercised considerable influence over the court of Bokhara, not only on account of their warlike spirit but also on account of their loyalty towards the reigning family. As long as the princes of the Ashtarkhanide dynasty possessed any real power, the *bai* (superior grey-beard) of the tribe of Manghit was the devoted servant of his lord. But already, in the time of Ebulfeïz, as we have seen, Rehim Bi had given up this position, under pretence of the office of vizir usurped the real sovereignty, and not only had the last-named prince executed, but also his son, to whom he had previously given his own daughter in marriage. Rehim Bi was succeeded in the offices of vizir and of tribal chief of the Manghits by Danial Bai, who was related on the mother's side to the Ashtarkhanides.

Perhaps it was on this account that he was able to degrade the prince Abulghazi, a grandson of Ebulfeïz Khan, to a mere nominal sovereignty, while he made use of his name to give reins to the most disgraceful excesses of covetousness and tyranny. Abulghazi Khan, the last prince of Transoxania, in whose veins the blood of Djenghiz flowed, is said to have lived in such fear of his vizir and major domo that he did not even leave his house without permission. Danial Bai had on his side not only the *spahis* (military chiefs) but also the greedy sacerdotal class. It would have been the easiest thing in the world for him to have made himself prince, but that he left for his son Maasum, who, by means of his crafty and hypocritical behaviour, succeeded in bringing the people of Bokhara, weary of anarchy, to place the crown by force on his head.

In his childhoood Emir Maasum was called by his father Beg Djan [1] (Prince of the Heart), but as he entirely came up to his hopes and expectations, received in later years the name of Shahmurad (King's wish). He was the most characteristic specimen of the pietistic period of sufism in which he lived, and which reached in him its culminating point. Even in his youthful years he cultivated with marked preference the society of religious devotees, and exchanged the externals of his rank for the so-called khirkai de ervishan, i.e., beggar's cloak. While his brothers and relations lived in the fiercest feuds with one another, he passed whole days in the *khankas* [2] (cloisters) and mosques in pious meditations, during which time no one was allowed to disturb him. He even disdained to accept his paternal inheritance, saying, 'Give it to the distributors of the public alms; let it as far as it is possible indemnify those from whom it has been extorted; I for my part cannot bring myself to defile my hands with

---

[1] It is an old Turkish custom, which still prevails in Central Asia, to give a firstborn son the pet names of Baber djan (dear father) Khan djan (dear prince) Beg djan (dear chief). In the case of girls, whose birth it is well known never affords the same gratification to an Asiatic father, I have not observed a similar custom.

[2] Since that time it is customary in Central Asia for the great men of the country when they retire from public life to spend their days not on their estates but in cloisters or colleges.

money which force and violence have brought into my house.'
In order to give expression to his sorrow and contrition for
the iniquities committed by his father, he dressed himself in
penitential robes, hung a sword about his neck, and in such
guise passed weeping and crying through the streets, begging
pardon of all the inhabitants for the injustice which had been
done them during his father's government. We can imagine
what reverential enthusiasm this behaviour excited amongst
the people, and especially amongst the mollahs.   If Mir
Maasum had wished at once to realise the advantages derived
from his way of life, he might immediately after his father's
death have achieved a brilliant victory over his brothers and
the rebellious nobles of the country.   But he waited for some
time longer in order to base his future operations on a more
solid foundation.

Living in retirement in the fore-court of the Mesidjdi Kelan
(great mosque) he spent another year in religious meditations,
during which time he wrote his best work ' *Aïn ul Hilkmet* '
('The Fountain of Wisdom ').[1] He still contented himself with
favouring the great crowd of his admirers, who collected in
front of his house and accompanied him through the streets
with his *fatiha* (blessing), or with his wonder-working *ncfes*
(breath.)

Nevertheless, the disturbances in all parts of the country
continually assumed greater dimensions. The strife of parties
raged even in the capital itself.   On one of these occasions
nearly a thousand citizens, including some of his own brothers,
lost their lives.   The weak prince Abulghazi, who could himself do nothing to calm the disorders, betook himself, surrounded by a few grandees, to the mosque in which lived Mir
Maasum.   The prince implored the devotee to assume the
office of vizir which Mir Danial had so successfully occu-

---

[1] So far as I am aware Emir Maasum wrote only in Persian, and is thus the
first prince of Bokhara who on religious grounds neglected his mother tongue ;
for, although almost all his predecessors could write in Persian, the Turkish
language was the one in which they prefered to express themselves.

pied for years, he implored him to illuminate with the halo of
his sanctity the dimmed brilliance of the throne, and again
restore the peace of the country. But the holy man, at whose
commands so many thousands of human beings were afterwards murdered and whole districts laid waste, still shrank
from applying himself to earthly affairs. He only promised to
assist them with his counsels, and that too not before Niyaz
Ali Beg, the rebellious chief of Shehri Sebz, threatened
Bokhara with the last extremities of ruin. Then at last Mir
Maasum saw the danger of a longer delay. He placed himself at the head of an army, and not only drove the rebel over
the frontier of the khanate, but took from him Hissar and Karshi, which he had previously acquired by force. By this means
he gradually re-established order. Naturally enough the increase of Emir Maasum's political influence introduced into
every branch of the internal administration the strict Islamite
and hierarchical constitution towards which Bokhara had
always tended, and which had only been neglected under the
feeble government of the later princes. As long as the crafty
devotee laboured to procure for the rulers of Islam their former
respect, so long he left Abulghazi in the enjoyment of some
small measure of princely pomp. But after he had, partly by
the example of his own ascetic life, partly by rigorous severity, brought things into the order he wished for, he proceeded against the prince himself. The mode of life of the
latter furnished him with a plausible pretext for setting him
aside to enjoy as a private person a fixed pension, while he
himself in Sha'ban, 1199 (June 1784), mounted the throne of
Transoxania and commenced a career scarcely in accordance
with the patched mantle of a dervish which he still wore.[1]

The scene of his activity outside the border of Transoxania
was first Persia, or more properly speaking, its north-eastern

---

[1] Malcolm says, in his *History of Persia*, that Abulghazi was nominally king, and
his family was supported from the crown estates. But I can positively contradict
this view, for Mirza Sadik, the *munshi* (court-writer), speaks expressly of the date
of the accession of Emir Maasum.

provinces. Here from the times of past centuries, enthusiastic religious robbers had been accustomed to make forays as in the land of heretics, and here Emir Maasum would gather his first bays as a *gazi*.[1] This millennial road of Turanian forays was, however, at that time by no means so defenceless as it is at present. A few strong places, such as Merv and Sarakhs, were in the hands of the valiant Shiites, who often disturbed the pious Özbeg highwaymen in their occupation and placed serious hindrances in the way of their carrying out the Sunnite duty of devastating Khorasan and replenishing the slave-market of Bokhara. It is, therefore, not to be wondered at that Emir Maasum, or Begdjan, as he is called by the Persian authors—whose expedition, although his army consisted of thousands of horsemen, was really nothing more than a Turkoman alaman on a large scale—especially wished to sweep away these hindrances, in other words to make the road clear. In the very year of his accession he made an expedition against Merv, which since the rule of the Sefides had been entrusted to the tribe of Kadjar, and was commanded by the chiefs of the branch of Izzeddinlu. We have already mentioned that this branch of the Kadjars was related to the Ashtarkhanides.[2] Nevertheless sectarian hatred had fostered feelings of the bitterest hostility between the two families, and the purposes of the Özbegs and the Turkomans, when intent on more than mere plunder, had failed against the determination of the garrison at Merv. When Emir Maasum appeared before the walls of the fortress, its commander was one Baïram Ali Khan, a man who had for years held the robber hordes of the neighbourhood in check, but

---

[1] Properly speaking a man becomes *gazi* only in war against unbelievers (*kafir*), i. e., Christians, Jews, and Idolators ; but we have already mentioned that the Sunnites of Central Asia consider Shiite Mohammedans as unbelievers. The Ottoman Turks have never recognised this theory, considering the Persians as only heretics (*rafiz, mulhid*).

[2] I would here repeat that both families were fully aware of the relationship ; and in later times, relying on this circumstance, Shahrukh Mirza, a cousin of the present shah of Persia, when obliged to fly on account of treason or conspiracy, sought hospitality at the court of Bokhara.

now defended himself in vain against the overwhelming numbers of the enemy. Another member of his tribe, the ambitious and unwearied Aga Mehemmed Khan, was engaged in the south of Persia, in a struggle for the crown of the house Keyyan, against the valiant Lutf Ali Khan. Khorasan was divided amongst several princes, all seeking independence, and engaged in continual feuds with one another. Herat, the surest bulwark against Turanian invasion, was in the possession of Sharukh Mirza, a grandson of Nadir Shah, who, true to the alliance which, his grandfather had contracted with Ebulfeïz, now saw with pleasure the ruin that was falling on a Kadjar, one of the principal enemies of his house. Baïram Ali Khan, thus abandoned to his fate, was at last overpowered in spite of his heroic exertions, in spite of the bravery of his warriors, even now celebrated in song, who were accompanied in their desperate sallies by armed women and girls. Baïram Ali Khan fell beneath the walls of Merv,[1] and after the Özbegs had wasted the surrounding country, had carried off the whole population into slavery, and in order to prevent the future cultivation of the country had even broken down the dam of the ancient irrigation works of Bend-i-Merv,[2] their pious and god-fearing leader returned to Bokhara. This first invasion was only the beginning of a series of forays which Emir Maasum undertook one after another through several years of his reign.[3]

Merv, where after the fall of Baïram Ali Khan his valiant son, Mehemmed Huseïn, with some assistance from the Afghan Timour Shah maintained himself for some time, was at last laid entirely in ruins.[4] Its Turkish inhabitants were

---

[1] According to Mirza Sadik, Emir Maasum had the head of the fallen Baïram Ali severed from its trunk and fastened to a gallows in Bokhara.

[2] This dam, or more properly speaking the reservoir which it protected, was situated in a north-easterly direction from Merv, and derived its waters from the Murgab. Since its destruction, from want of the precious water, the whole agriculture of Merv has been reduced to a few fields of melons and vegetables.

[3] Mirza Sadik mentions four more important expeditions commanded by Emir Maasum in person.

[4] According to the *Rauzat es Sefa*, the ruler of Bokhara left behind him his son, Nasr-eddin, with a garrison in the citadel of Merv.

transferred by force to Bokhara, where they still bear the
name of Mervi.[1]   Since that time nothing remains of the
proud Margiana of antiquity to testify to its lost greatness
but a few mounds of earth rising amidst the monotonous
landscape of the steppe.[2]   In the year 1205 (1790) the
Sarik, and after them, about the year 1250 (1834), the
Tekke-Turkomans, who lived before that to the westward in
Akhal, took possession of the ruins.   In the place where once
had flourished Persian science and Persian industry are now
only to be heard, mingled with the rattle of their chains, the
Persian lamentations of those unfortunate Iranians, who, in
heavy bondage under the tents of the Turkomans turn their
longing eyes towards their near but lost country.   In the
following year came the turn of Meshed, but as the fortifications of that place offered an unexpected resistance, the pious
commander of the invading army declared that the saint
Imam Riza had appeared to him in a dream and had bidden
him spare Meshed, the place of his martyrdom, together with
its environs. 'I know that the Imam lives,' said Emir Maasum,
'and he shall not reproach me with having disturbed his repose.'   With that he retired, after visiting with still greater
devastation the villages of the neighbourhood.   Since the
incursions of Sheïbani and of Abdulmumin Khan the north-
east of Iran had never suffered so much from the Turanian
hordes as during the reign of this beggar-prince.   According
to the account of Mirza Sadik 20,000 was the smallest
number of Özbegs and Turkomans that took part in a foray,
and people in Bokhara relate that the slave-market was
so glutted that able-bodied Shiites could not be disposed

---

[1] In consequence of inaccurate information, I have mentioned, in my *Travels in Central Asia*, p. 370, Emir Saïd as the one who forcibly transferred the inhabitants of Merv to Bokhara.

[2] The ruins of Merv have been visited by Burnes, Wolf, Richmond Shakespear, J. Abbot, and Thomson—the two last-mentioned were entrusted with a
mission to the Khan of Khiva ; a Neapolitan adventurer of the name of Flores
Naselli, who, in spite of all advice to the contrary, went to Bokhara, and was there
executed ; and lastly Bloqueville, who spent a whole year there as a prisoner in the
hands of the Turkomans.

of for a few tenghes, or somewhat less than a franc, a-piece.[1] How many tears of ruined families were shed on account of this man, who rode on a sorry beast, clothed in filthy rags, by way of showing his contempt for earthly splendour, and under a miserable tent on a threadbare carpet was absorbed for hours in the contemplation of the Godhead! And this cruel course towards Iran the bigoted ruler of Bokhara carried on for nearly twelve yeaars. At last, in the year 1212 (1797), when Aga Mehemmed Khan, the founder of the present dynasty of Persia, had established peace in Fars and Azerbaïdjan, he betook himself to Khorasan, determined to put a stop to this terrible plague. But a campaign beyond the Oxus appeared to the Persian king neither prudent nor practicable, considering the insecurity of his position in the interior of his dominions. He therefore determined to try by diplomatic means to teach the Özbeg something better. He sent him, by the hand of Mehemmed Huseïn Izzeddinlu, the following letter, which is interesting, as in it we find for the first time an allusion to the national unity of the Turkish people.[2] The letter, as partially communicated by the ' Rauzat es Sefa,' ran as follows:—

. . . ' It is unnecessary to recapitulate the history of the Sefides and of the contemporaries of Mehemmed Sheïbani Khan, down to the Afshar Nadir Shah. I well know, and it is sufficiently well known to thee also, that Belkh, Merv, Zemindaver, Sistan, Kandahar, and Kabul, were from the earliest times integral portions of the Iranian empire. Well then, how has it occurred to thee to conquer Belkh and Merv,

---

[1] In modern times this has only happened once again in Bokhara, when Nasr-eddin Shah sent an army of 20,000 men against Turkestan, which was disgracefully defeated in the neighbourhood of Merv, by only 3,000 Tekke-Turkomans. Only a few hundred Persians escaped, the rest were taken prisoners, and sold for ridiculously low prices in the slave-markets of Bokhara and Khiva.

[2] The Mohammedan expression *Kulli muminin ihvetun*, 'all true believers are brethren,' has, it is well known, always made the idea of nationality impossible. So much the less should we have expected that a rough Kadjar, or his *mirza* (scribe), had an idea of the ethnical unity of the dynasties of China, India, and Rum.

and in the last-named place to slay Baïram Ali Khan the
kinsman of his illustrious house? Dost thou perchance wish
to renew the old wars between Iran and Turan? For such a task
thou art verily not sufficient.[1] To play with the tail of the
lion, to tickle the tiger in the ear, is not the part of a prudent
man. Yet all men are descended from Adam and Eve, and
if thou art proud of thy relationship to Turanian princes know
that my descent is also from the same. The origin and the
derivation of Kadjar Noyan[2] is not only nobler and more
distinguished than that of the family of Manghit and Kungrat,
but even surpasses in glory the renowned houses of Solduz
and Djelaïr.[3] We all of us owe thanks to God, the Almighty,
that he hath given the dominion over Turan and Iran, over
Rum, Rus, China, and India, to the exalted family of Turk.
Let each be content with the position that hath fallen to him,
and not stretch out his hand over the frontier of his own
kingdom. I also will dwell in peace within the ancient
boundaries of Iran, and none of us will pass over the Oxus.'

As we are told by another Persian authority, the document
in question was composed in an entirely different tone, for it
contained threats in case Mir Maasum did not immediately
send back the Persian captives. And the answer was of like
nature. Begdjan even allowed himself to trifle with the name
of the greatest of the Kadjars, for instead of Aga Khan, he
called him Akhta Khan, i.e., Eunuch Khan, and certainly
did not send back eighty thousand Persian captives, as the
author of the ' Nasih et Tevarikh ' would persuade us he did.
Aga Mehemmed Khan was at that time attacked by the
Empress Catherine of Russia, who would exact vengeance for

---

[1] What excellent irony to make an Efrasiab out of the monkish Emir
Maasum!

[2] Noyan is the title which was given to the superior officers in the Mongol
army. Whether the ancestor of the Kadjars really enjoyed this title is not made
out, for in Persia I have heard several Turks distinguish their original ancestor by
this title. The Kashkais in Shiraz are especially proud of this title.

[3] I do not know why Solduz and Djelaïr are described as renowned. Both
tribes have always dwelt in the land on the further side of the Oxus, and like
most of the Turks came with Djenghiz from the east.

the cruel fate of the Georgians under her protection. The Persian king was therefore obliged to direct his attention and his army to the banks of the Araxes, otherwise the world would have witnessed the strange spectacle of a bitter struggle for superiority between the two bizarre chieftains of the Mohammedan world of Inner Asia, one of whom was a eunuch, the other an old beggar-monk. But just then a third power intervened, which was later to overthrow them both, but which for the moment enabled the bigoted Özbeg to continue his plundering incursions into Persia. But it was not only on Shiite heretics that Emir Maasum stilled his religious lust for war. He found himself engaged with orthodox Sunnites, where he could not earn the merit of a *gazi*, and the weapon of conquest in vain sought concealment beneath the mantle of the dervish. The Afghans—a people of Aryan descent, who in the time of Mahmud the Ghaznevide formed but a small and inconsiderable clan in the mountain-chain of the Suleïman, but in the following centuries extended their frontiers until they occupied almost the whole territory between the Oxus and the Indus—had already begun to play an important part in the politics of Central Asia. Until the beginning of the eighteenth century of the Christian era they had, in order to defend themselves against the superior power of the Özbegs, paid tribute partly to the emperors of India, partly to the kings of Persia. But when in the last-named country the glory of the Sefide sovereigns had been extinguished, the Afghans, under the leadership of Mahmud, of the tribe of Ghilzai, overturned the throne of Isfahan. They had been driven out of Iran by Nadir, but after the fall of this last of great Asiatic conquerors, the ruin of the Mogul empire in India on the one hand, and on the other the weakness of the Özbeg government on the Oxus, enabled them to make their appearance as inheritors of that part of Nadir's dominion contained between the last-named river and the Indus. Ahmed Shah, of the Durani family, after making an alliance with Sharukh Mirza, the grandson of Timour, made himself master, in the year 1166 (1752), of all the possessions of the khanate of Bokhara on this side of the Oxus. Meïmene, Andkhoï, Aktche, Shiborgan, Serpul, Khulm, Bedak'hshan, Belkh, and Baïman, all did homage to Beg-i-Khan,[1] the general sent out for their conquest, who received for his achievements the title Sadraazam. The indolent ruler on the Zerefshan, or to speak more correctly, his all-powerful vizir, Danial Bai, cared little for the loss of these provinces, for the most part occupied by rebellious vassals. But to his son Emir Maasum the extension of the power of the Afghans had long been as a thorn in his side. So, when Timour Shah, the successor of Ahmed Shah, was, in 1203 (1788), engaged in the campaign of Bahaulpur, the Özbeg prince crossed the Oxus at Kilif, and re-conquered not all, but still the greater part of the above-named places. When Timour Shah was informed of this, he wrote a letter to his adversary in which he exposed in plain terms the ambition cloaked under a form of religious hypocrisy of Emir Maasum.[2] Timour Shah reminded him of the friendly relations which had always existed between the house of Durani and the Özbeg sovereigns, but, nevertheless, Emir Maasum, though intending the injury of the Duranis, had always got off with humble explanations as soon as affairs threatened an open war. Although no state is justified in waging war on the inhabitants of another country on account of their religious views, he had nevertheless conquered Merv, and had carried off its Shiite inhabitants into captivity, assigning as a reason that he would convert them to the right faith. But now the inconsistency of his conduct was plain and evident. If he cared so much about the conversion of unbelievers, why did he throw impediments in the way of the Afghans, through whose conquests in India so many unbelieving Hindus, Christians and Jews had been extirpated? And, further,

---

[1] See *History of the Afghans*, by J. P. Ferrier, London, 1858, p. 81.
[2] See *An Account of the Kingdom of Caubul*, by the Honourable Mountstuart Elphinstone, London, 1842, vol. ii. p. 315.

what mean his wars against the inhabitants of Shehri Sebz, of
Khodjend, and the Turkomans who were right-thinking
Sunnites? 'These people,' so continued Timour Shah in his
letter, 'have invoked my assistance, and I shall make their
cause my own, and at once march against Turkestan.'

In the spring of the year 1204 (1789), Timour Shah marched
at the head of a numerous and well-appointed army[1] to the
banks of the Oxus. He began by attacking Aktche, the
Özbeg commandant of which place, Rahmet Bi, gave way
before his superior forces and fled to the camp of his master
at Kilif. Emir Maasum was on the point of falling upon
Khorasan, where his efforts had in the preceding year been
unsuccessful, with a larger army. He felt himself unpleasantly
surprised by the attack of the Afghans, and would gladly
attempt to come to an understanding; but in order not to
display too openly his readiness to come to terms, he sent
Rahmet Bi, accompanied by Sultan Murad Bi, with a small
detachment back to Aktche, which gave occasion to a few unimportant skirmishes. As, however, he knew that it was with
reluctance that Timour Shah had undertaken this expedition,
he made proposals of peace through an embassy composed
of the most respected mollahs of Bokhara. As usual when
circumstances required it, he assumed an appearance of extreme humility and submission, and the Afghan chief who
had reproached him for this device in the above-cited letter
fell again into the snare, and not only concluded peace, but
even permitted him to retain possession of the places he had
conquered. As long as Timour Shah lived, Emir Maasum
respected the stipulations of the treaty and remained quiet.
But when in the year 1208 (1793) the Durani prince died
and was succeeded by his son Shah Zeman, he at once fell
upon the territory of Belkh, captured the governor together
with 4,000 of his best troops by means of an ambuscade,
and immediately invested Belkh, in the hope that the remain-

---

[1] Elphinstone, vol. iii. p. 305, gives the number of the Afghan army as 100,000;
Mirza Sadik says it was twice as numerous.

ing troops, terrified at the fate of their leader, would surrender. In this, however, he was disappointed. He threatened in case of prolonged resistance to execute the captive governor before the eyes of the garrison, and ultimately carried out this barbarous threat. But the Afghans held out until Shah Zeman had returned to Kabul from his successful campaign in Khorasan and they could hope for a speedy deliverance. Emir Maasum, too, expected such an event. But, as he perceived that it was delayed, he seized the opportunity of freeing himself from his dangerous position, and sent an embassy to Kabul with a promise of abandoning his claims on Belkh and its neighbourhood, and, in future keeping the treaty made with Timour Shah. Shah Zeman was fully occupied with his plans of Indian conquest and showed himself disposed to give way, so that Emir Maasum was again able to secure himself by his crafty conduct, but he did not thereby abandon his hostile intentions against his Afghan neighbour. When, in 1214 (1799), Shah Mahmud, a brother and rival of Shah Zeman, after several unsuccessful attempts to gain possession of the throne was obliged to seek his safety in flight, Emir Maasum offered him a place of refuge in Bokhara. Shah Zeman could make no open objections to the hospitality [1] of the Özbeg, but he privately sought to bring about the extradition of the fugitive by offering a large sum of money. If the Afghan sovereign had not just at that time entered into a secret alliance with the Kadjar Aga Mehemmed Khan, the old beggar-king of Bokhara would have had no scruples of conscience in violating even the laws held most sacred by Asiatics. As it was, he did not allow himself to be moved by the temptation, and, when the envoy of Shah Zeman requested him at any rate to keep a strict watch over his brother, he replied that he answered with his head, that Mahmud would not leave Bokhara. Nor would Mahmud have left Bokhara with his head on his shoulders if an

---

[1] Shah Zeman himself was later on obliged to seek refuge at the Court of Bokhara.

influential Özbeg had not enabled him to make his escape to
Khiva, where he was received in a friendly manner by the
ruler of that country, Mehemmed Rehim Khan. In the year
1217 (1802) Emir Maasum died, after a reign of eighteen
years, described by the inhabitants of Bokhara as the most
glorious portion of their recent past. As this period is still
fresh in the memory of the present generation, both Tadjik and
Özbeg are never weary of praising the just, pious, and
glorious government of this model Mohammedan prince. Of
course most stress is laid on the strict religious character of
the régime which he established. He it was who revived
the office of *Reïs-i-Sheriat* (guardian of the law of religion),
and that, too, at a time when it had been forgotten in the
whole of Islam.[1] The Reïs had to pass daily through the
streets accompanied by his police, who were armed with the
canonical four-tongued whip, to subject the people to a public
examination in religious matters. He who could not recite
the *Farz-ul-aïn* (principal duties), and certain enjoined
prayers in the Arabic language, or in the rolls of whose turban
the customary *kesek* (balls of earth)[2] were wanting, received
on the spot a sound beating or was thrown into prison for
several days. Negligence in attending the mosques, or of the
enjoined hours of prayer was visited on the first instance with
severe corporal punishment, the second time with death.
Drinkers of wine and smokers of tobacco[3] were treated in like
manner, while robbers, thieves and profligates were handed
over to the executioner without further ceremony. This
convulsive clinging to the rules prescribed by religion might
be observed in all the branches of political administration.
The true believer had only to pay the legal tithe of the pro-

[1] As I was told in Constantinople, this especial religious office never existed in
Turkey, nor did it exist in Persia, or northern India, but only occasionally during
recent times in Mecca, Medina, and some places in the east of Africa.
[2] On their meaning and application see my *Sketches of Central Asia*, London,
1868, p. 191.
[3] Smoking tobacco was for a considerable time strictly forbidden both in Persia
and in Turkey, as the doctors of religion reckoned the enjoyment of it among
the *musekkirat* (intoxicating pleasures).

duce of his land and of his cattle, and the *zekiat*, i.e., two-and-a-half per cent. of his income as a poor-rate, together with the duty on imported goods; while unbelievers, namely, Hindus, Jews, and Christians had to pay *djiziat*, or capitation tax. In his princely household Emir Maasum sought to conform to that strict religious and patriarchial pattern character by which the first khalifs gave an example to later ' Commanders of the Faithful ' of temperance and moderation.

As Omar was celebrated for having been so economical with the *Beït el Mal* (state treasury) as to be satisfied with the simplest food, and only allow himself a new dress once a year, so the fanatical ruler of Bokhara fixed one tenghe for his daily personal expenses. His cook, his servant, received the same sum, as did also the poorest inmates of colleges, which last were so numerous as to contain at one time more than 30,000 scholars thirsting for divine knowledge. But these measures imposed no restraint on the luxury and covetousness of his officers. While the prince himself lived in an old broken-down tent, and dressed in a frayed *tchapan* (a long upper garment) of camel's hair, and ate poor food out of a dirty pot, the officers of his army were dressed in silk, and bore richly-adorned arms, and were served, even in the camp, in vessels of gold and silver studded with precious stones. The contrast between the brilliant splendour of his officers and his own poverty-stricken appearance seems to have afforded him especial satisfaction. To his keeping up the sanctimonious appearance of a dervish he owed the great respect with which he was regarded, and it enabled him through eighteen years to use for his own purposes such restless elements as the Özbeg and Turkoman tribes. Although scarcely a year passed without his undertaking a campaign—for besides the wars of which we have spoken he was engaged in hostilities with the neighbouring princes of Khiva and Khokand [1]—the

---

[1] At this time, namely, 1202, died Alem Khan, the celebrated prince of Khokand, who, as I was told by Khokanders, held the Bokhariots in check for thirty years. With his death began the aggressive policy of the emirs of

khanate of Bokhara enjoyed under his government an unusual degree of prosperity ; for his people retain in their
memory not only the strictly religious character of his government, but also its mildness and justice. For us, the reign of
Emir Maasum is interesting because it forms the termination
of the old struggle between ·Iran and Turan. He was the
last prince who invaded Iran sword in hand.

His son and successor, Seïd Haidar Töre, mounted the
throne of Transoxania, under the name of Emir Saïd, in 1218
(1803). In religious mysticism, bigotry, and fanaticism, he
was not only a true child of his father, but even sought to
surpass him. But he inherited only a small portion of his
predecessor's skill in government and lust for war. He remained his whole life long a mollah, in the strict sense of the
word, consequently, according to the old Özbeg ideas, only
half a man.[1] This did not, however, prevent the devotee
from staining his heaven-blessed throne with blood at the
very commencement of his reign. The victim was his brother,
Nasireddin Töre, who had been entrusted during the lifetime of Emir Maasum with the government of the province of
Merv. As the new sovereign feared his rivalry, in order to
remove him quietly out of the way he required him to do
homage in person. As Nasireddin well knew the danger of
a fraternal embrace, instead of hastening to Bokhara, he fled
to the Persian frontier, and sought protection and assistance
of Feth Ali Shah. If the Kadjars had possessed real power
instead of the vain and ridiculous show of sovereignty, this
would have been a favourable opportunity for giving a severe
lesson to the predatory neighbours who laid Khorasan waste.
As it was the fugitive prince received only empty promises,
and Emir Saïd, the weakest prince of the house of Manghit,
had not the slightest reason to fear the anger of Feth Ali

Bokhara against their eastern neighbours, until Russia imposed peace upon both
the combatants.

[1] An Özbeg proverb says 'Two mollahs make a man, one mollah only a
woman.' See my *Tchagataische Sprachstudien*, p. 57.

Shah, who felt himself happy in the possession of the longest beard in the country, and the richest diamonds in his girdle. Emir Saïd enjoyed for twenty-three years the peaceable possession of his dominions. He spent several hours every day in the cloisters performing his devotions, or attended the exegetical lectures of distinguished professors. When his western neighbour, Mehemmed Rehim Khan, of Khiva, would avenge the death of his father, Iltazar Khan, and, plundering and burning, advanced by way of Tchihardjui and Karaköl to the very gates of Bokhara, even then Emir Saïd did not allow himself to be disturbed in his pious mode of life, as he exclaimed : *Akhir Rigistan amandur*, i.e., ' The Righistan (the place in which the palace is situated) is still safe.' In the absence of any great or glorious achievements, the Bokhariots praise highly the strict clerical character of their prince. The servile herd of the capital on the Zerefshan are said to have wept with joy when the Emir passed through the streets, with head bowed low and supported on a stick, not from any bodily weakness, but by way of acting the mollah. Nay, they even attributed to him miraculous powers, although it is known of this living saint that he violated in the most flagrant manner the holiest of Asiatic laws, to wit, those of hospitality, by violently carrying off the beautiful daughter of the blind fugitive at his court, Shah Zeman, and when the blind father broke out in just complaints would have had him put to death. What a melancholy picture of a prince who would maintain an ascendancy over his people by religion and morality ! If the state of morals in Bokhara was bad in earlier times it became still more abandoned and horrible under the rule of these uncultivated Özbegs of the house of Manghit. Under the Sheïbanides and Ashtarkhanides a spark of enlightenment and education was here and there to be found, but the Manghits, those diligent pupils of the ambitious and greedy mollahs, would bring about the improvement of their people by no other way than that of bigotry and fanaticism. The melancholy result may easily be conceived. Thus, for instance, the prohibition of wine and tobacco led to the enjoyment of the much more injurious opium, and the draconic laws respecting the separation of the sexes produced the most disgraceful vices. These were even publicly tolerated, and the hire of a *betche* [1] was settled by the kadi in open court. Yet even then Bokhara boasted that she was *Kuvveti islam u din*, i.e., ' the support of Islam and religion.'

[1] Juvenis imberbis.

XVIII.

EMIR NASRULLAH.

1242 (1826)—1277 (1860).

IN no country and among no people of Mohammedan Asia has the proverb ' The princes of the time are the mirror of the time ' [1] been so applicable as in the case of Nasrullah Bahadir Khan, the son and successor of Emir Saïd, who, on the death of his father in 1242 (1826), mounted the throne of Bokhara. One must be able to form to oneself an idea of the society of the Bokhara of that day, crippled by boundless hypocrisy, crass ignorance, and unscrupulous tyrrany, and sunk in the swamp of immorality, in order to imagine the mixture of cunning and stupidity, of pride, vain-glory and profligacy, of blind fanaticism and loathsome vices which made up the character of Nasrullah Khan. The way in which he obtained the throne marked him as a remorseless fratricide. As a younger brother he could make no claim to the throne, he therefore began during the lifetime of his father, while he filled the post of commandant of the district of Karshi, to win over the most influential persons in his interests. Of these the most important were the Koshbeghi Hakim Bai,[2] and Mumin Bai, the governor of Hissar, who, although they were in the service of Emir Huseïn, the rightful heir, and afterwards prince, were nevertheless the principal causes of his fall and of his death. It is with reason supposed that he was

---

[1] This is an old Uigur proverb, which occurs in the MS. *Kudatku Bilik*, and with a slight alteration is still used by the Özbegs and Turkomans.

[2] Bai corresponds to the Ottoman Bey. The Tadjiks, and occasionally the Özbegs also, say Bi.

put out of the way by poison, at the instigation of Nasrullah, after a reign of scarcely three months. This murder, however, called a third claimant into the field, namely, Omar Khan, a brother of Huseïn, with whom Nasrullah had now to contend in open war. With the fetva of the great kazi of Karshi in his hand, and accompanied by a small but devoted band, Nasrullah threw himself upon Samarkand, which opened its gates without a blow. After he had received ceremonial homage on the köktash,[1] he hastened towards Bokhara. Kette Kurgan, Kermineh, and the other strong places lying between the two capitals submitted one after another. Bokhara itself made an obstinate resistance for forty days, but hunger and the want of water—for Nasrullah had made himself master of the principal canals—and especially the treachery of Hakim Bai, brought the place into his hands. On March 22, 1826, Nasrullah entered the palace on the Righistan. Omar saved himself by flight, and died soon after of the cholera in Khokand, the khan of which place had received him hospitably. After he had executed in cold blood, on the banks of the Oxus, three of his younger brothers and a great number of the adherents of his former rivals, Nasrullah arrived at the undisputed possession of power, and during his long reign of thirty-four years afforded the world an example of how many atrocities a prince of Mohammedan Asia can commit, and what amount of tyranny a people enslaved by religious bigotry can· endure. In the years immediately following his accession, while still under the control of the influential Hakim Bai, it seemed as if, following in the footsteps of his father,[2] he would make the strict supervision of religious observances and the happiness of his subjects his highest end and aim. It

---

[1] Köktash is the blue stone in Samarkand of which we have already spoken. It recovered its former importance in the ceremony of coronation under the Ashtarkhanides. The Sheïbanides, in order to get rid of all traditions of Timour, had made Bokhara their capital, and the custom of raising the throne on the köktash was discontinued during their dynasty.

[2] Although people in Bokhara were of opinion that Nasrullah was guilty of his father's death, which, considering his character, is by no means quite improbable.

was about this time that Alexander Burnes visited Bokhara,
otherwise he could not have said of Nasrullah that he had re-
deemed the atrocities by which he came to the throne, and
governed his subjects with a just and impartial hand.[1] Afterwards, when all fear of rivals had been banished, and he felt
himself secure in his seat, the mild animal dropped the mask,
appeared as a savage tiger, and tried his claws on the very
man to whom he especially owed his power, namely, on
Koshbeghi Hakim Bai. This man had used the favour at first
shown him by his master to procure not only great honour for
himself, but also immense riches. We are told that more
than a thousand slaves were employed on his estates. Of the
numbers of his camels, horses, and sheep, I have heard the
most fabulous reports. He is even said to have trafficked with
caravans of his own with Russia, and when Nasrullah (I use
the words of the Bokhariots) raised his hand to strike the gnat
whom he had allowed to grow fat on his blood, he was certainly full to bursting. As nothing is easier than for a tyrant
to declare his own servant guilty, Koshbeghi's trial was soon
ended. He was accused of embezzling the public treasure,
was deprived of his office, and sent into exile, at first at
Karshi and afterwards at Nurata. That he might not at
once make enemies of the powerful party of Koshbeghi, Ayaz
Bai,[2] the grey-haired father-in-law of the latter, had honours
and distinctions heaped upon him. But as soon as the odium

---

[1] See *Travels into Bokhara*, by Lieutenant Alexander Burnes, London, 1834,
vol. ii. p. 361. The same author rightly observes, in a book which appeared
seven years later, under the title *Cabool, a Personal Narrative of a Journey to
and Residence in that City*, p. 250: 'His (Nasrullah's) acts of tyranny are so
audacious and so numerous, that I have never ceased to congratulate myself at
having passed so successfully through his kingdom.'

[2] Ayaz Bai filled the post of a *toptchibashi* (*chef d'artillerie*), and had amassed
great riches. In order that Nasrullah should not lose these riches by a sudden
announcement of his displeasure, he called the grey-haired servant to him, gave
him a robe of honour, and a richly-caparisoned Turkoman horse, and when
Ayaz Bai would withdraw escorted him to the gate, and would even help him to
mount. The old man observed the malice concealed by these perfidious favours,
flung himself at the feet of his master, and begged that he might be punished at
once. Nasrullah raised him up, embraced him, and thus treacherously calmed
the just apprehensions of the unfortunate man.

excited by his tyrannical treatment of Koshbeghi had in some
measure subsided, Ayaz Bai was cast into prison, and in the
spring of 1840 both of them were executed. Not only had
Nasrullah coveted the wealth of his vizir, but also hoped,
when once freed from the distasteful guardian, to give reins to
his manifold abominable passions. He now began to exhibit
himself in his true light to the terrified inhabitants of Bokhara.
The remorseless robber, Maasum Birdi, a Turkoman hireling,
was appointed *reis*, or chief of the police, not to serve his
master as counsellor, but as a blindly-devoted catchpoll.
Occasionally, too, some scoundrel was dignified with the title
of vizir, but often only for a few hours. In 1839, however,
Maasum Birdi expiated under the axe of the excutioner the
long-continued favour of his lord, who from that time forward
remained sole master of his country, nay of the lives and fortunes of his subjects. Who can make out the long list of
atrocious and violent acts with which this debauchee stained
his rule? All classes of his subjects, but especially the foreign
merchants, were continually exposed to his insatiable greed
for money. Even Bokhariots themselves who had a reputation for being in easy circumstances, were induced by fear to
propitiate his favour by frequent presents. An almost incredible number of secret reporters and spies were always on
the alert to denounce everything, however trifling, that took
place in the bazaar or the school, in the mosque, the public
promenades, or the bath.[1] These members of the secret
police would intrude even into the family circle, and, under
the pretext of a strict supervision of the ordinances of religion,
spy out everything that might gratify the lust or avarice of
their master. As he, in the midst of his profligate life, took
care to spare the interests of the influential and hypocritical
priests, these were on their part so abandoned as not to
oppose his arbitrary proceedings. As their veto was at all

---

[1] I was told in Bokhara that these spies, with their arms crossed before them,
took advantage of the loose wide sleeves of the Bokhariot dress to write unseen,
taking down word for word what they heard.

times an effectual check upon tyranny, for them not to resist the tyrant was to render him assistance. Religion was continually used as a pretext. Whoever sought to rescue his property, his slaves, his beautiful children of either sex, from the foul hand of the tyrant was at once accused of rebellion against the ' Prince of the true believers,' against the ' Shadow of God upon earth,' and had to expiate his daring by the most horrible punishment. In order to put such offenders to death with all conceivable torture, they were tormented for days in a pit full of sheepticks,[1] were flung down from high walls or towers, were flayed alive, or burnt in glowing ovens. Yet the wretch who inflicted these punishments without any form of trial, himself wallowed in the pool of vice without fear of God or man.

Such was the prince who sat on the throne of Transoxania, when the foreposts of European power and the European mind, which had already penetrated so many regions of Asia, began to knock at the gates of that country, in old times so renowned, but at that time almost entirely unknown. From the north Russia, advancing century after century on her long way through warlike and savage hordes across barren deserts, had reached the banks of the Yaxartes. From the south, the Britons, who in less than a hundred years had developed a few unpretending factories into a gigantic Indian empire, cast the eagle glance of a conqueror over the mountain-chain of the Suleïman towards the banks of the Oxus, from which they were distant but a few days' journey. The first contact of an Asiatic country with the West is always of high importance for its weal or woe, in fact, for its future existence. Where fanaticism and self-conceit render anything like improvement impossible, a violent breach and consequent ruin must necessarily follow ; while in other countries, a certain amount

---

[1] This horrible prison is known under the name of *siah tchah*, ' the black well ;' also *kenne khane*, ' the house of ticks.' It swarmed with those insects, which, in default of living victims, were fed with the offal of slaughtered animals. The delinquent who was cast in to them was first bound so as not to be able to defend himself against their attacks.

of compliance, a cheerful acquiescence in a better direction of political and social life, bring as their consequence moderation of treatment and even friendly advances. In the latter category may be placed, Turkey, Persia, Egypt, nay, the whole northern coast of Africa, while in the former, we must reckon as yet the Mogul Empire in India and Transoxania. In Bokhara, the scrupulous observance of the least tittle of Mohammedan law, the narrow views of its inhabitants, shut in by a girdle of steppes, perhaps also the halo of departed glory, from the first rendered the people indisposed on principle to all commerce with the Christian West. But even were it otherwise, what awakening to new life, to taking any part in the new movement of the world, was to be looked for under such a ruler as Nasrullah? We shall see presently how Nasrullah met the first contact with the Christian West, what ideas he had of the power and influence of European countries. The reader will then see that Transoxania, unlike the other countries of Mohammedan Asia, was from the first averse to reform, and that its fall as a state has not been caused by the recent conquest of Samarkand by the Russians, but was decided thirty years ago by the behaviour of Nasrullah Khan. Before, however, we pass on to that point, it is necessary first to discuss to some extent his political relations with the neighbouring countries.

That the vicious son of the bigoted Emir Saïd aspired to play the part of a great conqueror, has been already mentioned. The town of Shehri Sebz and the surrounding country afforded him in the first place the best opportunity of satisfying his ambition. The Özbegs of this part of the khanate belonged to the tribes of Ming, Atchmaili and Kungrat. Already, in the time of the earlier Ashtarkhanides, they had often revolted against the supremacy of Bokhara, and had given those princes all the more trouble as they had four strong fortresses serving as the basis of their operations, while their country was protected by its marshy character. The bitterness which inspired them dated from the last century, namely, from the war between the brothers Mekim Khan and Oberdullah Khan, or, more correctly speaking, from the mutual rivalry of the tribes of Manghit and Kungrat. This bitterness was naturally enough augmented by the fact that the tribe had not only the upper hand, but had actually raised itself to the throne. Consequently, we find the Özbegs of Shehri Sebz constantly opposed to the princes of the house of Manghit. Emir Maasum had tried his strength on them. During the reign of Emir Saïd they lived for years in complete independence, and Nasrullah undertook his first expedition against them. The tyrant had a long and obstinate struggle to maintain against the defenders of the place. He took the town more than once, after sieges of several months duration, and the inhabitants were compelled to submit. But scarcely had he withdrawn with his troops, when the whole affair began over again. Nasrullah attempted at one time by means of the influence of the priests, at another by bribery and assassination, to make himself a party in the plan. Nay, he once married the sister of his principal enemy, Velina'am Khan, who stood at the head of the movement. But all in vain. Shehri Sebz continued to revolt till the death of the tyrant.

Equally obstinate, but not distinguished by any important success, were the wars of Nasrullah against Khokand, the name by which Fergana had been known since the accession of the dynasty of the Ashtarkhanides. As we have seen in the course of this history, this little eastern country lost its independence after the last defeat of Baber, and, if I have been rightly informed, recovered to some extent its existence as a state after the fall of the Sheïbanides. When the last-named dynasty was in the height of its power, there arose in the eastern part of what is now Khokand, from Oosh to the neighbourhood of Khodjend, a family which set up as rivals of the Sheïbanides. This family was of Mongol origin, and its chief, Yunis Khan, was grandfather of Baber on the mother's side. The power exercised by the earlier Sheïbanides made their rivals keep to the mountainous country in the north of Khokand, and but seldom attempt to give effect to their claims to the throne. It is true that the sons of Yunis Khan deprived the usurper Tenbel [1] of the possession of Endidjan, and, with the assistance of the Kara-Kirghiz and Kiptchaks, struggled energetically against the Özbeg influence, but their descendants did not come into the actual possession of Khokand until the time of Subhankuli Khan.[2] On the other hand, it is asserted that even then the name of the ruler on the Zerefshan figured on the coins and in the prayer. But in the same degree that the princes of Bokhara declined in power and influence, the khans of Khokand enlarged the borders of their dominions. Nay, as descendants of the family of Kaidu, they had extended their claims over the whole of the land on the banks of the Yaxartes, over the province of Turkestan, properly so called, and from the beginning of the present century they continued to subject Khodjend to their rule till they had advanced far beyond Tashkend. More than five centuries had passed since Kaidu, the grandson of Oktai, waged war with the descendants of Tchagatai for the possession of Turkestan. But, in spite of the complete absence of all written documents, the conscious- ness of their hereditary rights lived on among the Mongol princes of this house and afforded them a never-failing reason for renewing the contest. The rulers of Khokand were but little disturbed by the later Ashtarkhanides, but the accession to power of the house of Manghit altered the posture of affairs. Emir Maasum had waged a sanguinary war for the sake of Khodjend, and his grandson Nasrullah fell upon Khokand because its prince Mehemmed Ali Khan had, through his victories over the Chinese in Eastern Turkestan, made his name as glorious throughout the whole world of Islam as

---

[1] Tenbel had revolted against Baber, when the latter went to Samarkand to fight against Sheibani, and had seized on Endidjan, but was soon afterwards defeated by Baber's relations on the mother's side.

[2] I here follow the oral accounts given me by my Khokander fellow-travellers, for we have no historical accounts of the state of Khokand during recent times.

that of the profligate Nasrullah was hated and dreaded.
Mehemmed Ali Khan was also well known for the justice of
his government, and the consequent happiness of his people.
Nasrullah's lust of conquest was considerably increased by
the appearance of Abdul Samed Khan, a crafty and worthless
Persian adventurer. This man, or rather, this inhuman
monster, who, even in Persia, was condemned as a rascal—
and, considering the character of the modern Persians, that is
saying a great deal—had wandered about for a long time in
India and Afghanistan, supporting himself by means of a few
ideas of European military science which he had picked up in
his youth. Afterwards, in 1835, when Hakim Bai was at the
helm of affairs, he came to Bokhara to try his fortune. The
Koshbeghi would employ him as military instructor, but on
the principle *similis simili gaudet*, he was taken up by
Nasrullah, who showed him peculiar favour, and, conferring
on him the title of *Naib*, placed him at the head of the army
of Bokhara. As he certainly knew how to manage cannon
better than did the Özbegs, and as he had learnt two or
three French words of command, his master thought that he
had acquired in him a paragon of military capacity, with
whose assistance he would soon acquire the eagerly-coveted
title of 'Conqueror of the World.' In order to show himself
off in this capacity first of all to his brother sovereign in
Khokand, a campaign against Mehemmed Ali Khan was
commenced in 1839. The frontier fortress of Pishaghir served
as a primary *casus belli*, although it had been erected by the
Khokanders in 1819. Nasrullah demanded that it should be
razed, and receiving a refusal, marched thither with his army.
Here Abdul Samed had the satisfaction of first displaying his
capacity, as he saw the mud walls crumble to pieces before
his parks of artillery. The army returned home proud of
their victorious campaign. According to the accounts current
in Bokhara, Mehemmed Ali, well knowing the hostile disposition of his western neighbour, and not wishing to be
surprised, himself assumed the offensive in 1841. He drove

the Bokhariot garrison out of Oratepe, which rightly belonged
to Khokand, and made himself master of the place and
of the surrounding country. Nasrullah took the field a second
time with a superior force of Özbeg horsemen and 500
men of the newly-organised militia (*serbaz*), and took
Oratepe after a three months' siege. Here, as usual, he
executed a bloody vengeance, in consequence of which the
inhabitants of the town became his bitterest enemies. He
had scarcely retired to Samarkand, before they rose, and in
concert with the Khokanders, fell on the Bokhariot garrison
and massacred both officers and soldiers. It may be imagined
with what haste and fury Nasrullah returned to fall again
upon Oratepe. As the khan of Khokand had to detach a
considerable portion of his forces to watch the Russians on
the lower Yaxartes, he did not dare as yet to risk a battle, but
retired along the road leading to Khodjend. Nasrullah, however, followed him closely, and near the last-named place
forced him to fight. Mehemmed Ali was defeated, and as
he saw his capital in danger, he sent a flag of truce to the
conqueror, with whom he made peace at Kohne Badem. He
submitted to the suzerainty of Bokhara, and ceded Khodjend
together with several other places. Of course this peace did
not reconcile the enemies to one another. In order the more
to annoy his conquered foe, the malicious Emir of Bokhara
appointed to the governorship of the newly-ceded province
a brother and rival of Mehemmed Ali, who had previously
been a refugee at Bokhara. This time, however, he made a
mistake. The mother of the prince of Khokand still lived,
and she reconciled her two sons to one another. Thus
Khodjend passed again into the possession of Khokand, and
Nasrullah had now two enemies instead of one. The wrath
of the tyrant of Bokhara knew no bounds, and his thirst for
vengeance urged him on to more than usual exertions. Besides his ordinary army, which was composed of 30,000
horsemen and 1,000 *serbaz*, he hired 10,000 Turkomans
of the tribes of Tekke and Salor. Hastening by forced

marches to Khokand, he surprised Mehemmed Ali so that he had to fly from his capital. He was overtaken in his flight near to Mergolan, and ten days afterwards was executed [1] in his own capital, together with his brother and his two sons. Even the wife of the unfortunate man and her unborn child were not spared. After the greater part of Mehemmed Ali's adherents had been handed over to the executioner and their property had been confiscated, Nasrullah returned to Bokhara. As garrison in the conquered city, one Ibrahim Bi, a Mervi by birth, was left behind with 2,000 men.

Although the success of the Bokhariot arms is to be in a great measure attributed to their numerical superiority, yet at the same time the intrigues, by means of which Nasrullah divided the powerful and influential tribe of the Kiptchaks,[2] contributed in no small degree to bring about that success. For some time he succeeded in inducing this warlike people to hold aloof from all political action, but the insolent conduct of the Bokhariots soon put an end to their neutrality. They overpowered the garrison, made themselves masters of the town, and set on the throne Shir Ali Khan, a son of Mehemmed Ali,[3] who had taken refuge among them. As everybody in Khokand was aware that Nasrullah would exact vengeance, the most energetic preparations for resistance were made at once. For the first time Khokand was surrounded by a stout mud wall ; this was hardly finished, when an army from Bokhara, consisting of 15,000 men led by a pretender to the throne, an old protégé of Nasrullah, arrived before the town. Musulman Kul—such was the pretender's

[1] In order to justify this act of cruelty Nasrullah had the report spread abroad that Mehemmed Ali maintained illicit relations with his own mother, and therefore deserved death according to the laws of the Koran.

[2] The Kiptchaks, who still maintain themselves, though few in numbers, in the north-east of the khanate of Khokand, are the bravest and most warlike of the Turkish tribes, and are held to be the descendants of those Mongols who, under the name of Djete-mogul, waged such obstinate war against Timour, and afterwards, under the leadership of the sons of Yunis Khan, made themselves masters of the eastern part of Turkestan.

[3] On the genealogy of the family of Mehemmed Ali Khan, see my Travels in Central Asia,' p. 391.

name—seems, however, to have come to an understanding with his countrymen while on the way. The gates of the city were thrown open to him, and he at once openly revolted against Nasrullah, although the latter had sent him thither with the intention of making him khan. In conjunction with his fellow-countrymen he put the Bokhariots who had accompanied him to flight. Nasrullah fell ill with rage and vexation, but sent a fourth expedition under the command of Shahrukh Mirza to Khokand. He, however, did not penetrate further than Oratepe, for the death of the tyrant, as we shall presently see, put an end to the war. The results of the machinations against Khokand were only so far disadvantageous to the latter country, that Russia met with less resistance in her advance along the lower course of the Yaxartes. In Khokand itself everything remained as before.

The relations of Nasrullah Khan with his western neighbour, the Khan of Khiva, were not more friendly. In this case, to the old feud which had existed between Khiva and Bokhara, a new *casus belli* had been added since the accession of the house of Manghit. While the Russian army of conquest, whose operations were carried on without ostentation, and with occasional interruptions, pushed its outposts ever nearer and nearer to the right bank of the Yaxartes and the shores of the Sea of Aral, bodies of Kazaks, both of the 'little' and 'middle' hordes, discontented with Russian rule, retired towards the inhabited portions of the oasis lands of Turkestan, to shelter themselves, so to say, in the shadow of those independent Mohammedan states. As we shall have occasion to observe, they found the very contrary of protection; but their mere approach towards those khanates proved a source of misfortune to the latter. Both Khiva and Bokhara claimed to have received them to allegiance, and not only were the Kazaks heavily taxed by two masters, but they formed an object of contention between them, which gave rise to a war every ten years. During the reign of Nasrullah these hostilities were perennial. Even when the Russian expedition under General Perowski placed Allahkuli Khan, the ruler of Khiva, in a position of the utmost danger, the prince of 'holy Bokhara,' extended his forays as far as Hezaresp, and thus rendered assistance to the common enemy in the west as well as in the north-east. The hostility of the Bokhariots lasted all through the reign of Rehimkuli Khan, who ruled in Khiva from 1841 to 1843. Only the strong arm of Mehemmed Emin Khan (1843–1855) availed to check the madman on the Zerefshan, but Nasrullah remained always the bitterest enemy of his kinsmen and co-religionists on the lower courses of the Oxus.[1]

At no period could Bokhara reckon on the friendly relations of Persia, least of all during the reign of Nasrullah. More than 20,000 Persians groaned in captivity in Bokhara. For the most part they belonged to the north-eastern pro- vinces of Iran, and, although many of them rose to high offices of state, still the picture of the misery caused by the utter depopulation of whole towns and villages, was too horrible to allow Abbas Mirza to remain an unconcerned spectator. This prince, the active and worthy son of Feth Ali Shah, lived at that time in Khorasan. He had driven the Turkomans from Sarakhs and Merv, and his position in the latter place, at the head of a large and powerful army, inspired the emir of Bokhara with well-grounded fears. Indeed, had it not been for the opposition presented to the Persians by the Turkomans, who were stirred up by Allahkuli, khan of Khiva, it is probable that the glory-loving Abbas Mirza would have sent a detachment of his forces, if not against the capital, at any rate against the nearest towns of the khanate of Bokhara. As this hostility of Khiva and the Turkomans prevented the Persian prince from doing anything more than

---

[1] Although both are Özbegs, and belong to the same tribe, the Turkish inhabitants of Bokhara and Khiva have lived for centuries in a state of mutual hostility. The Özbeg of Bokhara considers his relation at Khiva a rude and unpolished barbarian, and is in turn held by him to be crafty and deceitful—in one word as a man stained by Tadjik vices.

threaten, Nasrullah thought that the projected attack was
not carried owing to the fear entertained of his own power,
and became in consequence bolder than ever in his behaviour
towards Persia.   Nor was the state of affairs in Afghanistan
less favourable for the gratification of the lust for plunder
and dominion of the bloodthirsty tyrant.   The Afghan
empire, founded by the first princes of the house of Durani,
had almost fallen to pieces, owing to fraticidal strife that
raged there continually.   Rendjit Singh, the 'Lion of the
Punjab,' had, after the battle of Nutcherov, so fatal to the
Afghans, extended his boundaries as far as Peshawer.   Persia
had not only reconquered a portion of Khorasan, but even
sought to compensate itself for former losses by the acquisition of Afghan territory, and attacked Herat.   During the
reign of Rehimkuli Khan, the Khivans had triumphed over
the Djemshidis, a nomad people of Iranian descent, living on
the upper waters of the Murghab.   It were therefore no
wonder if Nasrullah Khan, taking advantage of these favourable circumstances, extended his power and influence on the
left bank of the Oxus, so as to revive the old claims of
Bokhara.   It is true that he did not succeed in actually re-
incorporating Belkh, Khulm, Andkhoï and Meïmene, nor did
it seem to him particularly desirable to do so, considering the
terrible state of desolation into which those districts had
fallen.   Nevertheless he exercised, until the campaign of Yar
Mohammed Khan altered matters, full rights of suzerainty
over these miniature khanates, which gladly paid a small
yearly tribute, so as to be secured under the protection of the
Emir of Bokhara against the attacks of Persians or Afghans.

We thus see that Nasrullah was as much as possible encouraged by circumstances in his vain dreams of greatness.
In spite of several occasional humiliations, he still saw himself
surrounded with the glory of a shehinshah (king of kings).
Of course this was a foolish, even a ridiculous, delusion ;
but it was quite sufficient to induce the barbarian, who felt
himself secure behind his deserts of sand, and knew nothing

whatever of the outer world, to behave towards the great powers of Europe with the same insolence and daring as if he were dealing with Khiva and Khokand. In presence of the political combinations with which Russia and Great Britain approached the borders of Transoxania, he was allowed to play his bold game with impunity, although he did not require much penetration to convince himself that the shadow of the great power approaching Turan from the north would grow longer as time went on, and darken the existence of his nearest successors.

As regards Russia specially, this power had carried on political intercourse with Bokhara in former centuries. The old commercial route followed in the middle ages, leading from the heart of Asia along the course of the Volga to Moscow and Novgorod, had necessitated an occasional communication between the grand dukes of Russia and the khans of Bokhara. But mere agents entrusted only with commercial interests passed between those rulers. The first diplomatic embassy, in the European sense of the word, sent from Russia to Bokhara was the one conducted by M. Negri in the year 1820. From Baron G. von Meyendorff, a member of this mission, we receive the first authentic report of Bokhara. The columns of the Russian army of conquest then first began, as it were, to rise out of the sand on the southern edge of the steppe. Then they engaged in disputes concerning boundaries with the neighbouring khanates of Khokand and Khiva. With Bokhara, on the contrary, the Russians cultivated friendly relations. They wished to spare this the largest and most important khanate, until they had done with the smaller and weaker ones. This line of policy was certainly a sound one, if Great Britain had not in like manner appreciated the importance of Bokhara, only from an opposite point of view—not to conquer, but to protect those exposed to conquest—and displayed an inclination to enter into relations with the state on the Zerefshan. This competition between two Christian European powers excited, as we shall presently see, Nasrullah's imagination of his own power and importance, till he became little less than mad. The competition was opened in 1832 on the English side, by the semi-official journey of Alexander Burnes, to which Russia attributed more importance than it actually had. In 1834 the envoy Demaison, in 1835 the political agent Vitkovitch, left St. Petersburg for Bokhara ostensibly, in order to procure the liberation of Russian slaves, really to assure the Emir in the style current in his country of the unfeigned friendship, nay, the devoted service of the Russian Czar, the proud Nicholas. Otherwise, this assurance of friendship was very seasonable, for, while the Russian diplomatic documents tickled the haughty Nasrullah behind the ear with pompous titles,[1] the Russian arms drew ever nearer to the cultivated portion of the steppes, and the people in Bokhara paid no attention to the sound of the Russian cannon on the Yaxartes. With regard to the manner in which the Emir answered the Russian embassies the Russians showed a remarkable indulgence and patience. If Nasrullah wished to confer on a chamberlain (*mehrem*) or any other officer of his house a lucrative post, he sent him as his representative to St. Petersburg, there to gather in a harvest of rich presents, of which he, his master, received his share. On another occasion, such a pseudo-diplomatist was commissioned to beg from the Russian Government military instructors, skilled miners or other intelligent artisans, whose services the

---

[1] Russia judiciously kept before her eyes the principle *Si fueris Romæ, &c.*, and strictly observed the rules of Oriental etiquette in her communications with oriental sovereigns. In Zalesoff's memoir relating to the diplomatic relations between Russia and Bokhara in 1836–1843, there is given as a specimen of the official correspondence a letter of General Perowsky, at that time military governor of Orenburg, in which the Emir is entitled as follows : ' To the expounder of wisdom and law, the esteemed, all-perfect, glorious and great Emir' (namely Nasrullah !), ' descendant of the benignant Hakan, the centre of learning, order, and glory, and the disseminator of happiness, we offer our most sincere respect and warmest devotion. May the all-high and powerful God secure you on the throne of dominion and prosperity, shield you from its tempests and evil destinies, and grant you a long life.' See *The Russians in Central Asia*, translated from the Russian by John and Robert Mitchell, London, 1865, p. 409.

Emir promised to reward liberally. Of course such ideas were only the abortive expressions of some passing whim, for the suspicious Emir could never endure to have his country travelled over and examined by foreign officers.[1] At last, however, even Russian patience reached its limits. The party in Afghanistan opposed to the British had been defeated. Its leader, Dost Mohammed Khan, was obliged to fly to Bokhara. On receipt of the report that the English outposts had already approached the left bank of the Oxus, Russia desired to come to a definite understanding with Bokhara, and in 1840 sent Major·Butenieff at the head of a politico-scientific mission to that city. This plenipotentiary was in the first place instructed to convince the Emir of the pure and disinterested affection which the court of St. Petersburg bore to the Mohammedan states, for instance, to the Sultan Mahmud II., in his difficulty with Mehemmed Ali of Egypt, as also to Mohammed Shah of Persia—an affection of which Nasrullah too would receive a share, provided that he subjected himself to certain obligations. These were as follows: 1, to engage in no hostilities against Russia either openly or in secret ; 2, to keep no Russian in slavery, and to protect both the persons and properties of Russian subjects ; 3, not to confiscate the property of Russian subjects dying in Bokhara, but to send it intact to Russia ; 4, to forbid the Bokhariots in the most positive terms to commit any acts of robbery and violence on Russian subjects, and to punish at once all who should so transgress ; 5, to subject Russian merchandise to a single uniform duty which should not exceed five per cent. of the real value ; 6, Russian merchants to be subjected to no vexations and annoyances, but to receive the same protection in the territory of Bokhara that Bokhariot merchants receive in Russia. Russia on her part

---

[1] Afterwards, during the mission of Butenieff, a Russian scientific expedition made, it is true, a short excursion in the mountainous country near Samarkand, but the explorers' every footstep was dogged as carefully as if they had been spies, so that it is really wonderful that Lehmann and Jakovleff accomplished a much as they did.

offered advantages and concessions corresponding to those which she claimed, and when we consider the cost of this embassy, and the ability of individual members of the same, we cannot be surprised at the expectations entertained in St. Petersburg of its success.

Even Russia, this Asiatic Russia, was inexperienced enough to abandon itself to certain illusions with regard to Nasrullah. What could the mad debauchee on the throne of Bokhara know about the difference between the mission of a mere agent and that of a plenipotentiary? Or was it to be expected that his former minion and now vizir, Abdul Khalik, a youth only nineteen years old, could give his master information respecting the contents of the imperial handwriting and Count Nesselrode's despatch? The reception and hospitality accorded to the Russian embassy left, it is true, nothing to be desired, but in the way of business they effected nothing. Nasrullah graciously received the presents and friendly messages of his imperial brother on the Neva. He even took advantage of the knowledge of mineralogy possessed by some members of the mission. But he could not be drawn into negotiations with regard to the treaty so much desired by Russia. At one time he was in a hurry to place himself at the head of his victorious army in Khokand; now he had this and now that to attend to, until, after a stay of eight months in Bokhara, during which time Major Butenieff had repeatedly requested an audience, but always in vain, he was at last summoned to hear the 'gracious words' of the Emir. The latter made his appearance in the court of his palace booted and spurred, ready to mount his horse to proceed again to the campaign in Khokand. In all haste the ambassador extraordinary and plenipotentiary of the Emperor Nicholas was informed that the settlement of his business had been entrusted to the superior *desturkhandji* or 'table-coverer.'[1]

---

[1] *Destur Khan*, *i. e.*, 'Ceremony of the table,' properly means the tablecloth on which the food is laid in Central Asia, but it is also used to denote the custom whenever a guest enters a house of laying a table from which under all circumstances he must eat something. The man who attends to the duty is called *Desturkhandji*.

Then calling out 'Farewell,' Nasrullah rode out through the gate of his court. Then for the first time the Russian ambassador perceived with what disrespect he, or properly his imperial master, had been treated by the barbarian. The Russians were justly indignant at this treatment, but of course Nasrullah cared nothing about openly violating the rules of international intercourse. His victories in Khokand had excited his vanity more than ever, and he already dreamed of playing the part of a Djenghiz or a Timour. He was freed from his anxiety about an English invasion by the news of the catastrophe in Kabul, of the slaughter and expulsion of the English. When he saw that the Afghans, in comparison with whom he considered himself an Alexander the Great, could triumph over the vaunted regular army of one of the great powers of Europe, he considered that he had nothing to fear from the anger of his northern enemy whose headquarters were at such a distance from the frontiers of Bokhara.

After this no one will wonder that England, which firmly clung to the principles of European morality, even when dealing with the most prejudiced and obstinate of Asiatics, should reap even less profit from her transactions with Bokhara, nay, be even worse insulted than was Russia. The events which brought the British government into communication with the capital in the Zerefshan, are too recent, too well-known to make a detailed account of them necessary in this place. From the moment the Anglo-Indian troops crossed the Indus, intercourse with Central Asia and an approach to Bokhara, its hierarchical and political centre, became inevitable. There were, in fact, two principal grounds for this intercourse. In the first place, in spite of its internal corruption and decay, Bokhara was still the state which took the lead among the other states of Central Asia: the glory of former rulers of Transoxania even now surrounded the khans on the Zerefshan with its reflection. What Bokhara praised was approved of; what Bokhara favoured, found favour.

England was therefore obliged to seek the friendship of Bokhara in order to consolidate her position beyond the Suleïman Mountains—a position, unfortunately, taken up prematurely[1] and with too much haste, and which had consequently to be abandoned with loss. In the second place, the fact that another European power, to wit Russia, pursued a similar end in Bokhara, made that city the scene of a struggle of rivalry—a struggle which excited the more anxiety in England, as it was supposed that not so much the position in Afghanistan as the fair Empire of India was at stake. Whether this apprehension was groundless or perhaps exaggerated, is a question which it is as yet difficult to answer decidedly, and must be left for future decision. In this book we have merely to register the existence of such apprehensions, and, without reference to my own views, which I have expressed elsewhere,[2] I shall set them down as the second cause of the English mission to Bokhara. The travels of Alexander Burnes were not of an official character, and can only be regarded as a sort of secret political reconnaissance. Thus the mission of Colonel Stoddart to Bokhara in 1838 was the first which brought the English government into communication with that of Bokhara. Stoddart received from J. MacNeil, the British ambassador in Teheran, instructions to assure the emir of Bokhara that he had nothing to fear from the influence of the British in Afghanistan, that England was much rather disposed to enter into friendly relations with Bokhara, and to render the Emir assistance in case his country was attacked by a foreign power. But while

[1] I say 'prematurely,' for, if the English had first crossed the Sutlej, established their power in the Pendjab, and made themselves better acquainted with the Afghans by several years of immediate contact, the campaign would not have had so unfortunate an end. Besides, in all probability it would then never have been undertaken.

[2] I have expressed my own opinions on this subject amongst others—(1), in the last chapter of my *Sketches from Central Asia*, 1867; (2), *Unsere Zeit; Deutsche Revue der Gegenwart*, in the numbers for November and December 1868, for July 1869, for February, May, and November 1870, and in that for November 1871. Also in the *Globus; eine durch Dr. K. Andrée redigirte geographische Zeitschrift*, vol. xx. pp. 81, 105, and 122.

it was sufficiently unpractical to make offers of friendship to a fanatic like Nasrullah, to whom every Christian was an object of detestation, the choice made of the person who should conduct the negotiations was still more unfortunate. Colonel Stoddart was indisputably an excellent officer, adorned with all the virtues of his profession, but his violent temper, his rough military manners, and his want of pliability, were of more service at the head of his regiment than in a diplomatic mission. With such qualifications he could, of course, do nothing with a tyrant like Nasrullah. He at once excited the Emir's aversion and anger by his ridiculous obstinacy in refusing to submit to certain ceremonies customary in Bokhara. An unbeliever who dared to prance about the 'noble Bokhara,' nay, even in the Righistan, where everybody had to dismount, who refused to the prince of the faithful the reverence due to him, and appeared before the steps of the throne without any present in his hand—all this was too much for the irritable tyrant. Two days after his audience with the Emir, Stoddart was seized in a disgraceful manner and thrown into a horrible dungeon. As a tiger secure of his prey, the Emir played with the unfortunate officer. At one time he had him tortured in prison, at another time he was set free and overwhelmed with tokens of honour, for his treatment varied according to the reports that arrived from time to time from the British camp in Afghanistan. But neither the intercessions of the Sultan nor of the Sherif of Mecca, the Shah of Persia and the neighbouring princes, availed to save the unfortunate captive; nor even the mediation of Russia, which power, through the before-mentioned Major Butenieff, in vain gave itself trouble to rescue the agent of its rival from certain destruction. Stoddart, compelled to the profession of Islam, nevertheless publicly disavowed the doctrine of the Arabian prophet, and endured during a period of nearly four years every kind of torture and humiliation, until he received, in the person of a fellow-countryman, a companion in suffering, in whose company he trod the last way to execution.

C C

Captain Arthur Conolly— such was the name of Stoddart's fellow-prisoner—set out from Kabul on September 3, 1840, on his diplomatic mission to Central Asia. The English politicians had gradually acquired the conviction that the diplomatic correspondence between London and St. Petersburg could lead to no result, and that Russia would continue to pursue her aggressive policy against the three khanates. There remained, therefore, no other course open to them but to apply directly to the princes of those khanates, to attempt to open their eyes to their imminent danger, and induce them to enter into an offensive and defensive alliance. The idea of making an alliance between these countries, which had lived for centuries in the bitterest mutual hostility, was the most unfortunate and the most unpractical that can well be imagined, and again the choice of an agent to carry it fell on another unsuitable person. Conolly was a man of the noblest and tenderest feelings, whose soul was penetrated with the purest Christian ideas, before whose mind's eye hovered the emancipation of the slaves of Asia, nay, of the whole world! And this dove of universal peace was to enter into negotiations with the black vultures on the thrones of Central Asia. In Khiva he had been preceded in the humane mission for liberating Russian slaves by the English officers Abbot and Shakespear. There Conolly was received in a friendly manner by Allahkuli Khan, but his efforts in the political field were as little successful as his endeavours to procure the emancipation of slaves. For the warlike Özbegs, slaves and irrigation canals are alike indispensable means for procuring their daily bread.

With regard to the question of the alliance with Bokhara and Khokand, the Khan was of opinion that he did not require the advice of foreigners, and demanded subsidies and arms as an expression of British friendship. Conolly consequently went from Khiva *re infectâ*, to Khokand. Avoiding Bokhara, he passed through the northern steppe—a road which, as far as I know, comes out at Djizzak, and had at

that time not been visited by any European. The reception
which he received in the eastern part of Turkestan was not
less cordial than that accorded him in Khiva. Mehemmed
Ali was just then at war with Nasrullah. Consequently, the
arrival of an officer acquainted with European weapons and
tactics was exceedingly welcome to him, and the hope that
he might derive some military advantage from his presence
led him to receive his guest with splendid hospitality. To
what results the negotiations with Mehemmed Ali came we
do not know, for all the notes he took in Khokand were lost.
The results were certainly not of importance, for the critical
position in which the sovereign of Khokand was placed by the
war must have deprived him of all wish for forming plans for
the future. Conolly, finding no promise of success in Khokand, was so imprudent as to accept the treacherous invita-
tions of Nasrullah and visit him in his camp at Mehrem, not
far from Khokand. The suspicious Emir had persuaded himself that Conolly had instigated his eastern neighbour to war
against Bokhara. In order to draw him into the snare, Stoddart was employed to urge his fellow-countryman to this step.
In spite of the warnings of his Khokander friends to beware
of the malice of the Emir, Conolly determined on visiting his
camp, where he was at once seized, plundered of all his
effects, and sent to Bokhara to share with Stoddart his
terrible captivity. The Anglo-Indian author, j. W. Kaye, a
man of great knowledge and a powerful writer, has in his
book, 'Lives of Indian Officers,'[1] published some fragments
of the diary written by Conolly in prison. They are but
slight sketches of the melancholy picture, but of a deeply
affecting character, and sufficient to give the reader an idea of
the tortures and sufferings which the unfortunate Europeans
had to endure during their confinement for nearly six months
in a dark, damp, noisome hole. During all that time they had
not only to endure cold and damp, clad in a few miserable
rags and covered with vermin, but were in constant expecta-

[1] In two volumes, Strahan and Co., London, 1867.

tion of death. As long as the Russian embassy under
Butenieff, whose humane exertions for the liberation of the
prisoners are not as well known as they deserve, remained in
Bokhara, a ray of hope still penetrated to their dungeon, but
its last spark was extinguished by their departure. By this
time Nasrullah had received authentic information with regard to the catastrophe at Kabul. He saw that he had no
reason to fear vengeance from any quarter. He therefore had
the captives, to whom death must have appeared as a welcome
deliverer, executed on June 17, 1842,[1] in an open place in the
presence of curious bystanders. First Stoddart's head was
struck off. Then the executioner paused as Conolly's turn
came, for it was said that his life would be spared if he embraced Islam. But the honest man observed with abhorrence,
' Stoddart became a Mohammedan and still you have executed him ; I prefer to die.' With that he held out his neck
to the executioner, who with one blow separated his head
from his body. The corpses of the two martyrs were placed
in one grave, which had been dug before their eyes.

Thus the first ambassadors of the Christian West who had
entered Transoxania since the time of Clavijo met their
end. We may call them the first apostles of a new world,
for, whatever may have been the motives which led the
British Government to interfere in the affairs of the states
beyond the Oxus, it was certainly no lust of conquest that
dictated that policy, but a humane endeavour towards the
civilisation of Central Asia, in which was sought the best
rampart against the attacks of the northern rival. That the
wretched Nasrullah dared to insult so disgracefully a great
European power which has the reputation of not shrinking
from the greatest sacrifices in defence of its subjects, is at-

[1] This is the date given by Kaye in the work before-mentioned. General
Ferrier, in his *History of the Afghans*, p. 46, places it on the 24th of June, and
that on the evidence of Akhundzadeh, who, on the strength of conjecture, assigns
as the day of the execution the second of Djemazi ul evvel or Djemazi ul sani,
which is, however, an error, for the beginnings of those months in the year 1258
of the Hidjra fell on May 12 and June 10.

tributable in the first place to the unfortunate events that took place in the valleys of the Hindoo Kush. With the British remaining in Kabul, Nasrullah had not dared to carry out what, according to Mohammedan rules, was a sinful violation of international law. And if he had, just retribution in the form of an advance of the British army by way of Belkh and Karshi would have certainly followed. In the second place the tyrant was indebted to the rivalry between the two European powers for his immunity from punishment. No state could have been more suitably employed in chastising the Emir than Persia, hundreds of thousands of whose subjects were kept as slaves in Transoxania. But Persia was always in want of the necessary funds, and, as its predilections for the Russian alliance were no secret, England could not strengthen the instrument of her rival.

Favoured by these circumstances, Nasrullah could continue after these tragical events to pollute his throne with his infamous misdeeds. Besides the two Englishmen,[1] there fell as victims to his murderous cruelty the Italians Giovanni Orlando and Flores Naselli, and the Greek Joseph. The first of these was induced by his love of travel to accompany an envoy from Khokand, whose acquaintance he had made in Constantinople, to that distant city, and he fell with it into the hands of Nasrullah. For some time he was employed as court watchmaker. But on one occasion, the machinery of the tyrant's watch having come to a stand-still, Orlando was summoned to the palace, and by way of punishment, the machinery of his life was brought to a standstill by the executioner. The second Italian, Flores Naselli, was a soldier by profession,

---

[1] The missionary Dr. Joseph Wolff, an eccentric, but certainly a courageous man, reports in his book *Mission to Bokhara*, that Lieutenant Wyburt was seized on his way to Khiva, brought by Turkomans to Bokhara, there detained for years in prison, and executed shortly before the arrival of Stoddart. Accounts of his fate from other sources do not agree with that of Wolff. Wyburt flung himself into the Turkoman steppes without any knowledge of the languages or customs of Central Asia. In vain was he warned at Teheran of the certain death he was encountering. He followed his passionate wish, and met his end in the desert.

probably attracted to the East by the splendid career of his
countryman, General Avitabile, in the service of Rendjit
Singh. Flores came to Bokhara some time after the execution of the English, and would place his military science at
the disposal of the Emir. As he had, however, no acquaintance with the languages of the country, and the treacherous
Abdul Samed Khan, a great enemy of Europeans, feared
to find in him a rival, he was arrested as a spy within a
week of his arrival and executed. The third was a servant
of Conolly, and although he had established the fact of his
being a subject of the Sultan, he had none the less to precede
his master in death. What did Nasrullah care about the
Sultan, whom he recognised from religious necessity as his
hierarchical superior, but whom he believed himself to surpass
in wordly greatness ? Nay, even a Mohammedan subject of
the Sublime Porte fell a victim to his thirst for blood. Mustafa Tchaush, whom Reshid Pasha had, at the request of the
Emir, sent to Bokhara in the capacity of military instructor,
was after a month's stay found to be irreligious in his conduct
and thrown into prison, where, on his · complaining of the
severity of the law, he was put to death. Nothing was
sacred enough in the eyes of the miserable tyrant to restrain
the excesses of his lust and cruelty. When Dost Mohammed
Khan, flying before the English, sought refuge together with his
family at the court of Nasrullah, the beauty of Sultan Djan,
a boy of fourteen years old, the youngest son of the fugitive
prince, excited the foul passion of the Emir. In spite of the
sanctity of the laws of hospitality respected by the wildest
barbarians of Asia, he dared to ask the son of the father.
Dost Mohammed attempted to save his child by flight,
but unsuccessfully. Sultan Djan and his eldest brother
Ekber Khan were overtaken, and, in spite of a desperate
resistance, taken back to Bokhara. Dost Mohammed
himself escaped with great difficulty out of the claws of the
monster. The pure spring of Bokhariot Islamism did not
probably seem to him very attractive when later he was able
to compare the honourable confinement in which he was kept

by the British at Loodianah with the hospitality afforded him by his neighbour and fellow-believer. As we shall see in the next chapter, he determined in his old age to take vengeance for this disgraceful behaviour.

This just vengeance did not, however, reach Nasrullah. His external enemies were not in a position to call him to account, and his successor had to suffer for the sins of Nasrullah. In the interior, namely in Bokhara, everybody was paralysed with fear. Fathers saw their sons and daughters carried off by force into the ' Ark,' as the palace was called, without daring to breathe a word of discontent, for according to the teaching of the mollahs the prince could deal as freely with his people as the shepherd with his flock. About the year 1840—I could not ascertain the exact date—a large party of the discontented. was formed, and it was suspected that Mozaffar-eddin, the eldest son and presumptive successor of Nasrullah, was at their head. The slightest suspicion was sufficient to doom to instant death. More than forty of the conspirators were handed over to the executioner, and Mozaffar-eddin was removed from the governorship of Karshi to that of Kermineh, where he had not only a more limited field of operations, but was more under the eye of his father. The more Nasrullah advanced in years, the more frequent and violent became his paroxysms of rage, which in 1860 put an end to his life after he had reigned thirty-four years. Besides the repeated revolts of Khokand, the obstinate struggle maintained against him by his brother-in-law Velinaam of Shehri Sebz embittered his last years. He was already in his last agony when the news arrived that that fortress was taken. Scarcely able to express his meaning, he yet gave orders to put to death his rebellious brother-in-law and all his children. But as he could not satiate his eyes with their blood, he had his own wife, the sister of Velinaam, brought to his bedside. This poor woman, the mother of two children, trembled, but that did not move the dying tyrant: he had her beheaded before his eyes, and gazing on the blood of the sister of his principal enemy he breathed out his detestable soul.

XIX.

EMIR MOZAFFAR-EDDIN AND THE HOUSE OF ROMANOFF.
1277 (1860)—1287 (1870).

THE ancient Eastern proverb 'The fathers have eaten sour grapes, and the children's teeth are set on edge' has seldom been so entirely or so rapidly verified as in the case of Mozaffar-eddin Khan, the son and successor of Nasrullah.

The Nemesis did indeed advance, borne on the wings of the north wind, towards the shores of the Oxus, even in the lifetime of the offender, but before she could overtake him death had forestalled her, and the sins of the father were visited on the son by the loss of his crown, and on the country by the loss of its independence. Mozaffar-eddin had spent his early youth at Karshi, in the Dauphiné and chief seat of the Manghits, in order to learn the art of government in the midst of his own tribe, as his father had done before him. He was early remarkable for the industry with which he attended to his studies, no less than for his brilliant capacity, and the author of these lines can vouch from his personal knowledge for the fact that he was a thoroughly cultivated Mohammedan, of course in the Turkestan sense of the word. In spite, however, of this Mozaffar-eddin seems to have been from the first a thorn in his father's side. The latter, judging by the standard of his own shameful conduct to his father Emir Saïd, always feared to find a dangerous rival in his own child; he was haunted by perpetual visions of a conspiracy at Karshi, and to get rid of this constant nightmare he appointed his son governor of Kermineh in order to fix him in his own immediate neighbourhood, and thus be able to keep a constant watch over his movements. Mozaffar remained there, in comparative retirement and disgrace, from 1842 until the death of his father, and then ascended the throne of Transoxania to be known in history as the last of the long list of independent sovereigns of many different dynasties, who, commencing with the Samanides, had ruled on the Zerefshan for the space of a thousand years.

It cannot however be confidently affirmed that Mozaffareddin was personally entirely free from blame regarding the misfortune which overtook his family. Often, and in all countries, a vast difference has been noticed between the character of the heir to the throne and that of the eventual sovereign. In Mozaffar-eddin's case too, he seems to have entirely lost as emir the peaceful mollah-like disposition of the former *kette-töre* [1] and to have recommenced immediately on ascending the throne the struggle with the rebel Shehri Sebz, where the standard of revolt had been set up soon after his father's death. It was his first deed of arms, but his exertions proved as fruitless as his father's had been ; he was occupied with the siege of Tchiraktchi, one of the fortresses of Shehri Sebz, when he found himself involved in a fresh war by the events in Khokand, and compelled to pursue there the same policy which had already brought such disastrous results to his father and to all Central Asia. Musulman Kul, whom my readers will remember as having seized on the government in Khokand, was got rid of by assassination, planned by Bokhariot intrigues, and the crown reverted to the third grandson of Mehemmed Ali, Prince Khudayar Khan. This weak and cowardly prince was brought up under the eye of Nasrullah himself amidst all the vices of the Bokhariot court. He was consequently devoted to Bokhara and even longed to exchange the throne of the primitive and still uncorrupted country of Khokand for the gilded vice of the hypocritical

---

[1] This word, which has only lately become known in the Western world, is synonymous with the *Veli Ahd* (crown prince) of Western Mohammedans : *kette*, great, *töre*, prince, i.e., *great* or *elder* prince, who is according to custom heir to the throne.

capital on the Zerefshan. If the possession of the white felt of old Fergana was distasteful to him, the fulfilment of the obligations of his royal position, which forced him personally more than once to lead his armies to check the advances of the Russians on the lower courses of the Yaxartes, was still more distasteful, especially as he had received more than one blow from the northerners, and had lost one fortress after another. An attempt was to be made to retake Ak Mesdjid, on which the Russian flag, the *Karakush* (black bird, bird of ill omen, eagle), was floating, and which had been re-christened . Fort Peroffsky ; but when Khudayar returned from one of his religious campaigns; which had as usual proved fruitless, he found the gates of his capital closed against him, for during his absence his elder brother Mollah Khan had taken the throne from him, and he was obliged to fly to Bokhara. If Mozaffar-eddin, instead of thus giving the lie to his own former peaceable professions, had remembered the Arab proverb ' *Peace* is the best of all sentences,' and endeavoured to smooth down the quarrels in the family of Mehemmed Ali, contenting himself with offering quiet hospitality to the protégé of his house, he might have avoided many difficulties ; but, like all Asiatic rulers, he was ambitious of the title of a 'World Conqueror,' and thinking to make capital out of Khudayar's cry for help, he hastened to leave Shehri Sebz at the head of a large army, intending to conquer Khokand. In this first campaign, the dagger of the assassin was again resorted to in order to attain the objects of the war ; Mollah Khan was murdered one night in his bed by Bokhariot partisans, including some of his own servants ; his adherents the Kiptchaks, then in power at Samarkand, endeavoured to set their nominee Shah Murad, a younger brother of Khudayar's, on the throne, but Mozaffar-eddin forestalled them, reinstated Khudayar, and then returned himself to Bokhara.

His protégé, however, was not able to maintain himself above four months in his position, and when the emir of Bokhara saw his protectorate treated with such utter contempt,

he had no alternative left to retrieve his position but to proceed against Khokand with a still greater display of force,
and to pursue at any price the policy on which he had em-
barked. He first sent forward Shahrukh Khan, his serdari-
kul (commander-in-chief) with 4,000 men, and Mehemmed
Hasan Beg with 30 guns, and then hurried eastwards himself
accompanied by a few hundred Tekke-Turkomans, fully
determined never to return until he had subdued everything
between himself and the Chinese frontier. In consequence, Khokand on its part had armed to the teeth. The
Kiptchaks, the most warlike element of the last-named
khanate, declared themselves ready to defend to the uttermost
the cause of the pretender who had thrown himself on their
protection; they avoided coming into collision with the
superior numbers of the enemy, especially with the Emir's
artillery, which enjoyed a great reputation in Central Asia, so
that he was enabled to advance unmolested as far as Oosh;
but, nevertheless, the success of Mozaffar-eddin, however pom-
pously proclaimed, was but a very illusory one. The total loss
of men on *both* sides during this 'fearful' campaign amounted
at most to *one hundred*, and although the ruler of Bokhara
fancied himself a second Timour, his troops had barely
evacuated any place before the Kiptchaks re-occupied it, and
obliterated every trace of Bokhariot authority; the upshot of
the whole affair was that Khokand was divided into two
parts. The east of this khanate, from Oosh to Mehrem, fell
to the share of the protégé of the Kiptchaks, whilst the
north, from Oratepe to beyond Tashkend, was subject
to Khudayar Khan, who took up his residence at Samarkand,
so as to be in the immediate neighbourhood of his protector.

Mozaffar-eddin's attack on his neighbour's territory might
have been in some measure justified if his policy of conquest
over and 'protectorate' of others had been based on any idea
of a general alliance or union of forces to oppose the foreign
invader on the lower courses of the Yaxartes. But he was quite
incapable of any such far-seeing policy, and the real motive

of his actions, the absurd ambition and covetousness by which he was inspired, far from securing him against the future, only accelerated his ruin, for his protectorate of Khudayar Khan only served to bring him into collision with an adversary with whom neither he nor Central Asia, nor even all Islam itself, could hope to cope.

Russia, after the failure both of Peroffsky's expedition in 1839 and of all her diplomatic missions, had changed the base of her operations from the south-east of the Sea of Aral to the banks of the Yaxartes, and had by this time advanced as far as the inhabited regions of the territory of Khokand. The fort of Orenburg on the river Turghai was built in 1847, and that of Karabutak on the Karabut in the following year.[1] The expectation that the Oxus would prove the great channel of communication and the best highway by water to the interior of Turkestan [2] had not been realised, and the Yaxartes had therefore to be chosen in its stead.

General Peroffsky, Governor-General of Orenburg, had caused the fort Aralsk to be built by Captain Schultz at the mouths of the last-named river in 1847 ; this was naturally enough a thorn in the side of the Özbegs of Khiva, which they were, however, unable, in spite of many remonstrances, to get rid of, and they were therefore forced to remain passive spectators while the Russian eagle, his shadow ominously threatening their future, spread his wings further and further on the left bank of

---

[1] *The Russians in Central Asia*, by John and Robert Mitchell, London, 1865, p. 320.

[2] The able and otherwise accurately-informed Sir Alexander Burnes was the first to propagate the notion in Europe that the Russians would use the Oxus as their chief channel of communication with Turkestan. Admiral Butakoff, in his studies carried on on the lower courses of the Oxus, and at its mouths, between 1848 and 1859, proved directly the contrary. It is clearly evident from investigations that no one of the four arms into which this river finally divides is navigable. In the first place the bed of the river is in itself shallow, and besid_s, the accumulation of sand causes an alteration of the current almost daily when the water is low. It might possibly be made navigable as far as Kiptchak, if some canals, partly artificial and partly natural, which draw the water off in the plain beyond Kungrat and Tchortanköl, could be filled in. More details on this question are to be found in the *Journal of the Geographical Society of London* for 1867, in an Essay by Admiral Butakoff himself.

the Yaxartes. As the fort Aralsk, afterwards called fort 1, proved a good point of departure, it was easy to predict that forts, 2, 3, and so on would shortly follow, and that the advancing Russian columns would soon come into collision with Khokand as the power which, nominally at least, ruled over these territories. At first the garrison of the Khokand fortress of Ak Mesdjid took upon itself the ungrateful task of obstructing the outposts of the northern Colossus by attacking now the Russians themselves, now the Kirghizes placed under their protection ; but, as usual, they were repulsed with heavy losses. Their skirmishes lasted for years ; the Khokanders mostly had to deal with small detachments of the Russian army, so that they never were sufficiently impressed with the immense superiority of the enemy; whilst the Russians, on the other hand, becoming accustomed to the various stratagems and general local habits of conducting war in these parts, went through a most valuable preparation for their conquest of Turkestan. Meantime, the steamers intended for the navigation of the river had arrived on the dark green waters of the old Khahrezmian lake, having been transported by land from Sweden to the Aral. For want of coal the wood of the gnarled shrubs, called *saksaul*, had to be used for fuel, but in spite of all the difficulties encountered by these, the first steamers ever seen on those ancient classic waters, they fully answered their object. In the year 1852 Colonel Blaramberg set out with a corps on a reconnaissance towards the fortress of Ak Mesdjid, and penetrated with a handful of men under the very walls of the fortress ; this daring act, for he had ventured 250 leagues away from the Russian frontier, led to no immediate result, but the grand attack of the following year was all the more successful. This expedition was planned on a much larger scale.[1] The Russians in an unusually warm spring pushed across the most barren part of the great

---

[1] The expedition consisted of 2,168 men, including officers, with 2,442 horses, 2,038 camels, and 2,280 oxen, used for transport. *The Russians in Central Asia*, P. 339.

steppe of Orenburg as far as fort 1, intending thence to reach Ak Mesdjid on the right bank of the Yaxartes. The steamer 'Peroffsky' followed up the river. Neither the intense heat, nor the swarms of grasshoppers and locusts, nor the glow of the desert sand, sufficed to intimidate the hardy northerners. Ak Mesdjid was invested, and the struggle for the possession of this, the first fortress on Turkestan ground, commenced.

General Peroffsky first summoned the Khokanders to surrender peaceably,[1] but the tenor of their reply was that they should resist so long as they had a grain of powder in their flasks, or a *kesek* (clod of earth used as a missile for want of stones) in their streets, or until the hilts of their swords and heads of their spears were all shattered. The fighting was obstinate on both sides, and it was not until the earthworks had been shattered at many points by the Russian artillery, and the garrison had suffered grievously from the bombardment, that the first storming column, led by a Hungarian, Lieutenant Erdélyi,[2] penetrated into the fortress, Aug. 8, 1853.

[1] It appears by the document containing this request, that when needful, the Russians communicated with the Central Asiatics in a correct Özbeg style. The letter ran thus :—

'From the Governor-General of Orenburg to the Commander of the Fortress of Ak Mechet.

'By order of my master the Emperor of all the Russias, I have come here to take possession of the fortress of Ak Mechet, which the Kokandians have erected on Russian territory for the oppression of the Kirghizes, subjects of His Imperial Majesty.

'Ak Mechet is already taken, although you are inside it, and you cannot fail to perceive that, without losing any of my men, I am in a position to destroy every one of you.

'The Russians have come hither not for a day, nor yet for a year, but for ever. They will not retire.

'If you wish to live, ask for mercy; should you prefer to die in Ak Mechet, you can do so. I am not pressed for time and do not intend to hurry you. I here repeat that I do not come to offer you combat, but to thrash you until you open your gates.

'All this I would have told you on the first day of my arrival, when I approached the walls of your fortress unarmed, had you not traitorously opened fire on me, which is not customary among honourable soldiers.'—*Russians in Central Asia*, p. 348.

[2] In the above-mentioned English work, the name is spelt Erdeli, but I imagine that the unfamiliar Hungarian diphthong *ly* (equivalent to the Italian *gl*) has been altered. Erdélyi (signifying Transylvanian) is a common name in Hungary,

The Khokandians continued to defend the ground by inches with extraordinary courage, although their commander Medveli (Mehemmed Veli) was killed at the very beginning, and most of the superior officers had fallen. A very few only escaped. It was the first place of any strategical or political importance taken by the Russians on the northern borders of the steppe, and it was also both the first and the last place where the Central Asiatics displayed real heroic self-sacrifice in their endeavours to repel the foreign invader.

Each year after the fall of Ak Mesdjid, the Khokandians made frequent and often very serious attempts to retake the fortress,[1] but without any success, although the period from 1853 to 1856 might have been thought especially favourable to them, for just then Russia had had to strain every nerve and concentrate all her forces in the Crimea. She could not in this crisis attach supreme importance to her possessions in Southern Asia, and if the princes of Central Asia, who were by no means unaware of the contest going on before Sebastopol, could have made up their minds in face of the imminent danger threatening their common interests to unite cordially with each other, they would then have had little difficulty not only in taking the forts but in driving back the Russians to the northern borders of the steppe; more especially as the Kirghiz chief Izzet Kutibar[2] had just then succeeded in undermining the Russian supremacy in the 'little' and 'middle' horde. The best proof of the total unfitness

and the first man to enter the chief fortress of Central Asia was therefore my countryman.

[1] One of the most serious attacks of the Khokandians was made from December 14 to 17, 1853, on which occasion the Khokandian army of 12,000 men was not only kept in check but put to flight by six hundred Russians.

[2] Kutibar (the Lucky one), a perfect specimen of the knight-errant of the Kirghiz steppes, had distinguished himself as far back as 1822 by his bold attacks and daring robberies. He used in former days to enjoy the protection of Russia, while engaged in plundering the rich caravans from Khokand and Bokhara, and he received a gold medal (surely not the one for art and science) from St. Petersburg in recognition of his services. He afterwards however turned against his patron and was only subdued and made harmless after a tolerably long and obstinate struggle.

of the sovereigns to rule, and of the people to be independent
in Central Asia, is afforded by the fact that they took a precisely opposite course, for in her great difficulties Russia found
her policy less endangered in the Oxus countries than anywhere.
It was in vain that the Porte had striven to impress on the
envoys from Khiva and Bokhara, accredited to her for years
past at an enormous expense, to return home at once and
draw the attention of their respective sovereigns to the excellent opportunity now offering for exerting themselves to
secure the safety of their own dominions and the independence
of Islamism. Khiva, instead of assuming the offensive, sent
envoys to Ak Mesdjid with professions of friendship. At
Bokhara, the reprobate Nasrullah was still on the throne and
took advantage of the weakened condition of his unfortunate
eastern neighbour to invade Khokand, and thought himself
fortunate in being able to incorporate one place after another
with his own dominions. Under these circumstances, it was
but natural that Russia, as soon as she had concluded the
treaty of Paris, should resume all the more eagerly and
successfully her plans of conquest. The little fortress of
Tchölek was taken in 1859, and two years later the fort
Yenghi Kurghan on the Yaxartes ; the Russian outposts on
the left bank of the river advanced further and further into
the already tolerably populous parts of the north of Khokand ;
and in the month of June 1864, the town of Turkestan,
or Hazreti Turkestan, the resting-place of the celebrated
ascetic Khodja Ahmed Yesevi fell into their hands. This
news sent a thrill of terror through the Central Asiatics,
and inflamed their religious fanaticism. Khodja Ahmed is,
next to Bahaeddin, the second patron saint of Turkestan, and
especially venerated in Khokand. It had been expected
that the Kiptchaks would now make common cause with
Khudayar Khan, and that they would together attack the
unbelievers. But envy and hatred carried the day as they
always had done in Turan, and the Kiptchaks, far more
warlike than any other Khokandians, were well pleased to

see the Russians after the victory of Djemkent,[1] advance by Sairam against Tashkend and take possession of this place, which is both commercially and politically the key to Central Asia, at least from the northern side.

Mozaffar-eddin Khan now at length realised that it was high time to look into the affairs of his protégé, Khudayar Khan, and try, at least indirectly, to put some impediment in the way of the Russian army of occupation. He first marched on Khokand (in May 1865) for the purpose of chastising the Kiptchaks, a false report having been spread in Bokhara that they had, by their passive attitude, assisted the plans of the Russians. This was, however, a purely malicious invention, for it was the Kiptchaks themselves who had offered the most courageous resistance; their brave leader Alemkul had lost his life before Tashkend. After the death of this resolute opponent, Mozaffar-eddin found the conquest of Eastern Khokand an easy matter. The puppet, Mir Saïd, a son of Sarimsaks, was carried prisoner to Bokhara, and Khudayar Khan, who had lost nearly all his own possessions by the advance of the unbelieving enemy, was raised to the throne of Khokand. He sent at the same time an insolent letter to General Tchernayeff (who had succeeded General Peroffsky in command of the Russian army), summoning him to evacuate the conquered territory, and threatening, in case of default, to bring all the faithful in Turan[2] into the field against Russia; and by way of enforcing his argument he confiscated the property of such Russian merchants as happened at that moment to be in Bokhara. The reply from the Russian head-quarters was no less courteous; but when the Russians, undisturbed by the Emir's threats, proceeded to reprisals on the Bokhariots at Orenburg,

---

[1] See note 2, p. 2 of this book.

[2] It will be seen by this that the Emir had still at that time a very high opinion of the superiority of his own army, and of his own spiritual supremacy over all the Moslems of Turkestan. It had never become known in Bokhara that the Russians had routed the Khokandian armies on the Yaxartes, ten, and even twenty times stronger than themselves. No one would have dared to relate these disasters, and even if they had been related no one would have believed them.

he, on his part, before the correspondence had ripened into open hostility, sent the Khodja Nedjm-eddin on a friendly mission to St. Petersburg, to complain to the Czar of his general's aggressions. The intention of the Emir was by this to gain time, and put down the rebellion at Shehri Sebz, but he was outwitted by the Russian authorities. Nedjm-eddin was arrested on his road and confined in the fort of Kazala, and, as the ruler of Bokhara still kept the Russian subjects there imprisoned, although the Bokhariot merchants had been released, General Tchernayeff sent off Colonel Struve, accompanied by several officers, to Bokhara,[1] to try and bring about a friendly solution of the differences, as it seems the general was either not authorised to maintain the offensive, or not in a condition to do so. It might have been foreseen that the Emir would treat Colonel Struve no better than the Russians had treated Nedjm-eddin.[2] Neverthelesss Tchernayeff expressed himself as much offended at the indignity offered him, crossed the Yaxartes in 1866, and, avoiding Khodjend, marched across the desert on Djizzak, the first place within the actual territory of Bokhara. This time, however, the Russians were at fault in their calculations. They reached the last-named place after severe forced marches through a perfectly arid waterless country, then found themselves confronted by a force, not as usually only ten, but at least *twenty* times more numerous than themselves, and only dis-

[1] The mission consisted of the astronomer Councillor Struve (according to others Colonel Struve, and not the well-known man of science), with Lieutenant-Colonel Tatarinoff of the Engineers, and two other officers, Captain Gluchoffsky and Ensign Kolesnikoff. (*Die Russen in Centralasien. Eine geographisch-historische Studie von Friedrich von Hellwald.* Vienna, 1869, p.65.)

[2] The Russian mission remained from the time of their arrival up to February 1, 1866, confined within the four walls of their house. They were then summoned by the authorities of the town to give up their arms, which they peremptorily refused. The result of this was a ' scrimmage,' in which an Aksakal and five Bokhariots were severely wounded ; nevertheless the Russians, in spite of their valour, which was on this occasion greater than their discretion, had to give way. (*Edinburgh Review*, January 1867, p. 40. This article, on ' The Foreign Policy of Sir John Lawrence,' was due to the able and well-informed pen of Mr. Wylie, whose early death is much to be deplored. It was one of the best articles published on the subject by the English press.)

covered too late that they had no option but to retire. A rapid but orderly retreat was therefore organised, and in the course of it the Russians were able to assert themselves against the countless hordes hovering along their line. The modern descendants of the once-terrible Turanian warriors are but cowards indeed !

Tchernayeff received his well-deserved rebuke, and was replaced by Major-General Dimitri Ilyitch Romanoffsky. The failure of the Russian plans had encouraged the Özbegs to assume the offensive, and on April 5 of the same year they established themselves, after rather a serious action, at Tchinaz, a small fortress on the left bank of the Yaxartes, and Emir Mozaffar-eddin, fancying that he should dispose of the Russians as easily as he did the Khokandians, set out at the head of an army of 5,000 Serbazes, 30,000 Kirghizes, 10,000 Turkomans, with 21 guns, to wrest the northern part of Tashkend from the unbelievers. Under these circumstances the Russian general could not remain inactive. Romanoffsky himself tells us in a pamphlet published by him upon this campaign,[1] that he had with him on his expedition against the South but 4,000 out of the 15,000 men composing the army corps operating in Turkestan; he was forced to accept the challenge. A decisive battle was fought on May 20, 1866, at Yirdjar, on the left bank of the Yaxartes, some miles northwest of Khodjend ; the Russian artillery opened up a way through the serried ranks of the Özbeg cavalry, and when the handful of Russians charged, their mere appearance was enough to throw the enemy into confusion, and cause a precipitate flight southwards.[2] The whole camp, including the

---

[1] I am only acquainted with this pamphlet through extracts from it published in the *Times* of March 16 and 26, 1869, in the letters of its Berlin correspondent, whose information on Central Asiatic politics is of inestimable value. General Romanoffsky appears by these extracts to be thoroughly well acquainted with Asiatic affairs, and to be himself a man of exceptionally sound judgment.

[2] The best and most detailed account that has as yet appeared of the decisive battle of Yirdjar is in F. v. Hellwald's above-mentioned work, p. 68. His book is distinguished throughout by a thorough knowledge of the subject and an agreeable style of writing ; the only drawback to it is that his zeal for Russian interest has led him occasionally into unfairness in judging England.

Emir's magnificent tent and the entire park of artillery, was abandoned, and Mozaffar-eddin himself escaped with difficulty to Djizzak. The loss of the Bokhariots amounted to about 1,000 men ; the Manghits of Karshi, the *élite* of the army, suffered most severely of all ; but the Russian killed and wounded were only about 50. This battle of Yirdjar proved the *Cannæ* of Turkestan, for it cost her her independence as a country which she had successfully asserted during a thousand years, her reputation and her influence on the other peoples of Central Asia, and the whole cause of Islamism in the interior of Asia may be said to have received at the same time a deadly blow. The Russian general might have continued his march at once on Samarkand, favoured by the panic spread by the news of the great catastrophe, but he contented himself with calling up a few reinforcements from Fort Körütchi, and occupying, on May 28, the small fortress of Nau ; and as this place, south of Khodjend, is the point to which the roads converge from east and north, the fate of the latter town and fortress, thus entirely cut off from Bokhara, could not long remain doubtful. Khodjend, protected on two sides by the Yaxartes, on the south-east by the main stream, and on the south-west by an arm of the same river, had always been deemed impregnable by the Asiatics. Though belonging to Khokand it was held by a Bokhariot garrison, which offered resistance. The civil population, chiefly merchants, impressed with a belief in Russian supremacy, were in favour of surrendering, but the garrison, egged on by their fanatic mollahs, defended themselves obstinately for seven days, at the end of which time the place was taken by an assault which cost the Russians more men than the decisive battle, whilst the loss of the Özbegs themselves was reckoned at 2,500 men.

Thus, as M. v. Hellwald truly says,[1] the principal places of Khokand had all fallen into the hands of the Russians, and the puppet Khudayar Khan slipped helplessly from the protecting arms of the Emir of Bokhara, under the shadow of

[1] See his above-mentioned work, p. 70.

the wings of the Russian eagle, accommodating himself, as time has already proved, easily enough to his new situation. The Muscovite arms would scarcely have attained their victory thus cheaply if a more energetic prince had occupied the throne of Khokand, or if the warlike elements of the country, such as they were, had not just then been ranged under the banners of Yakub Kushbeghi in Eastern Turkestan. As it was, their rapid success took the Russians themselves by surprise, and Khudayar might well deem himself lucky in being allowed to retain the ancient seat of Baber under the sovereign protection of the 'white czar.' He had to surrender the valleys of the Yaxartes from Mehrem onwards down the whole course of the river, to open his cities to Russian subjects, and give security for their property, and over and above all this to pay over to the Russian treasury a war indemnity which will most undoubtedly cripple him for years to come. His power is reduced to a perfect shadow, and at his death the whole of this, the easternmost khanate, will, as a matter of course, be incorporated with the dominions of the Russian Empire.

What could Mozaffar-eddin, himself isolated and weighed down by misfortune, have done to save him? He in vain implored assistance on all sides; no one dared to join him, the vanquished one, against his powerful conqueror. His pride, even more than their old long-standing enmity, forbade him to apply to his nearest neighbour at Khiva, even if this little country, divided against itself as it was, had not been powerless to assist. Afghanistan in the south, just then convulsed by civil war, had enough to do at home, and although some of the descendants of Dost Mohammed Khan might possibly gladly have joined him, others had inherited their father's old grudge and were well pleased to see the humiliation the proud Özbeg prince had undergone at the hands of the unbelievers. The idea of a united polity never seriously occurred to the princes of Central Asia, bent as they really were solely on individual conquest; the Afghans were at heart delighted to see Bokhara so much weakened that it would be an easy matter to wrest from her the miniature khanates on the left bank of the Oxus. This they will proceed to do, provided Russia does not hereafter claim them as integral portions of Bokhara. The only person who would for his own interest have been glad to ally himself with Bokhara was the new ruler of Eastern Turkestan, Yakub Kushbeghi. The shadow of the Russian columns near Narin, within a few days' journey of his capital, weighed heavily on him, but he had had experience in his youth of the superiority of the Russian arms,[1] and was therefore very careful in the expression of his sympathies; in addition to which united action was rendered practically impossible by the wedge the Russian conquest of Khokand had inserted between him and the ruler on the Zerefshan. Mozaffar-eddin's more distant prospects were no less desperate. Whatever suspicions the Russians may have harboured,[2] it is absolutely certain that England never thought of assisting in its last struggles the country which had inflicted on her the greatest of diplomatic indignities, where two of her envoys had died the death of martyrs. Turkey was as little inclined to rouse the storms ever lowering on her political horizon by machinations in the far East. Indeed the great men of the Porte know no more about Özbegs, Tadjiks, etc., about Khiva, Bokhara, Khokand, the Oxus and the Yaxartes, than they do about the island of

---

[1] Yakub Kushbeghi, now Prince of Eastern Turkestan, served his apprenticeship to the art of war in the battles against the Russians on the lower courses of the Yaxartes, and gained a great reputation, recognised by the Russians themselves, by his heroic conduct as commandant of the fortress of Ak Mesdjid. If Turkestan scandal is to be believed, his zeal for the cause of Khokand was cooled by the application of Russian ducats; and he is accused of the treacherous surrender of one or two places.

[2] The Russian press has taken the opportunity of spreading the reports of the presence in the capital on the Zerefshan during the Bokhariot-Russian war of English diplomatists (!), who encouraged the Emir in his hostile attitude by providing the Özbegs with Enfield rifles, etc. etc. A Turkestan correspondent of the *Invalide russe* (English translation in the *Times* of October 19, 1869) goes so far as to put into the Emir's own mouth the declaration that England had kindled the war between himself and Russia. Everyone who knows the modern apathy of Englishmen will perceive that this invention is as absurd as it is malicious.

Haiti ; no trace remains among the modern generation of Osmanlis of the animated diplomatic intercourse existing in the days of the Sherbanides and the Ashtarkhanides ; and even if there had been any, how could the Osmanlis, themselves fighting for their life, have rendered any material assistance to their kinsmen and brethren in the faith in the far East ? Neither could the Shiite Persians, with thousands of their countrymen pining in Özbeg slavery, and accustomed from time immemorial to connect the very name of Turkestan only with ideas of terror, be expected to ally themselves with Mozaffar-eddin. Some distant relationship exists, indeed, between the Kadjars and the rulers of Bokhara, but their hatred of each other is only the more intense, the more savage, and, on the part of Iran, the more justified ; they rejoiced heartily at the Russian successes on the Oxus and Yaxartes, and the last thing they would dream of would be to impede the course of their benefactor.

In the midst of his complete abandonment Mozaffar-eddin must have felt more bitterly than all the conduct of his subjects, his *spahis* (chief officials), and most of all his own relations. A few years before, at the time of my stay in Bokhara, he was not only feared, but generally respected and loved ; and now in the bazaars and at the Righistan, he had to hear himself openly and loudly accused of cowardice before the enemy, and of having precipitated the catastrophe by his flight from the battle-field of Yirdjar. He was also accused of malversation in his dealings with the national treasury, having, in his extreme need, first altered the standard of value, then had recourse to the secular property of the priests ; and finally, the terrible sin was laid to his charge that he, the former 'Prince of the Faithful,' had entered into secret negotiations with the unbelievers, and had received the price of the sale of the 'noble Bokhara.' He could only venture out at night or in disguise, for fear of the insults offered him by the populace, egged on by the mollahs, and the curses and abuse of the women. It is almost impossible for anyone not acquainted with Bokhara, its insane vanity, ignorance and fanaticism, to understand the consternation and fury caused by the blow dealt by the Russians to the self-conceit of the dwellers on the Zerefshan. Their Emir was no Timour,[1] not invincible ; their *serbazes* and the famous warriors of Karshi were no Rustems ; the intercession of the saints whose tombs surrounded them had proved useless against the unbelievers. These terrible experiences were too much for them, and might well drive the nation out of its senses. Beys, sheïkhs, sufis, dervishes, merchants, mechanics, beggars, were all up in arms, united only in one thing, the determination to renew the war, and carry it out to the bitter end. A *djihad* was proclaimed, such as had never yet been seen in any country or under any circumstances in Islam ; old and young, mollahs and soldiers alike took part in it, naturally increasing the confusion, but the Emir had to give way, and the war with Russia was renewed. It need hardly be said that this insane behaviour of the Bokhariots and the folly of their prince were just what the Russians could desire for carrying out their objects.

After the fall of Khodjend the Russians only allowed themselves to rest till the necessary reinforcements and additional ammunition could be brought up. A change in the command also took place, Romanoffsky was succeeded by Count Dashkoff, who continued the victorious progress begun by his predecessor further south, and took the important fortress of Oratepe at the beginning of October, 1866. Djizzak, the frontier fortress between Bokhara and Khokand, fell shortly after, and the conqueror found in both places considerable stores of arms and ammunition. The great losses suffered by the Emir, and the narrow limits within which he was now driven, led to the hope that the tumult of war might shortly

---

[1] As a small proof of this extraordinary vanity, I may mention that the Emir himself once seriously asked me if the Sultan of Constantinople's army was really as large, as well equipped, and as brave as the one I had seen pass through on his return from Khokand to Samarkand. I do not know what the heroes of Balaklava would have said to this assumption ?

be appeased in the valleys of the Ak-Tau mountains; but, unhappily, the attitude of both parties rendered this impossible. Mozaffar-eddin, as we have seen, was forced by his own subjects to renew the struggle. Djura Bai of Shehri Sebz, had promised his assistance in this *gaza* (religious war), in return for the recognition of his independence. Turkomans and Afghans had also rallied in considerable numbers round the banner of Bokhara, but in spite of all this, we can hardly be surprised to find Mozaffar-eddin watching behind the ramparts of Samarkand the danger bearing down on him from the north, with less confidence in himself than that with which the Khahrezmian prince of yore awaited the Mongolian invasion. The Russians on their side could not well avoid pressing forward from their position at Djizzak. In the first place there can be no doubt that, in spite of occasional denials and official disavowing of over-zealous generals, the policy of the Court of St. Petersburg then was, as it still is, never to lay aside the sword until, by the subjection of all three khanates, the natural frontier of the Oxus is obtained; in the second place, the Bokhariots, by their raids on the newly-acquired territories of Russia, and their irritating conduct altogether, had themselves precipitated the prosecution of this policy. During 1867 hostilities were confined to a few skirmishes, in the course of which the Russians under General Kauffmann, an excellent and energetic officer, took the little fortress of Yenghi Kurghan, and threw out their outposts as far as Tashköprük, a stone bridge half way between the latter place and Samarkand. On May 13,[1] in the following year, the order was given definitely to march on Samarkand; the army was set in motion, but Col. Petruschewsky, who was leading the advanced guard along the right bank of the arm of the Zerefshan, was met by the Bokhariot envoy already mentioned, Nedjm-eddin, with

[1] Captain F. Trench, in his book on *The Russo-Indian Question*, London, 1869, p. 81, gives April 30 as the date of the Russian march. This must be according to the Russian calendar, as, otherwise the variation from all the other versions would be inexplicable.

propositions of peace from the Emir, and a request to halt
during negotiations. But for the fact that a large proportion
of the 40,000 men forming the Bokhariot army was drawn up
on the steep opposite bank, the Russian general might have
been accused of rejecting by force all thought of an amicable
settlement; but as the whole transaction was merely a
clumsy blind, instantly detected by the Russians, General
Kauffmann was perfectly right in replying to the Emir's overtures with his guns rather than with his pen. His forces,
consisting of 21 companies of infantry, 16 guns, a division
of engineers and 450 Cossacks, altogether about 8,000
men, were drawn up in order of battle and commenced
crossing the Zerefshan under the eyes of the enemy; the
left wing, commanded by Major General Golowatscheff, spent
a quarter of an hour wading breast high in water, regardless
of the heavy fire of the enemy's artillery, before they could
find in the marshy ground a favourable spot for reaching the
opposite bank. The Özbeg army, outnumbering them five or
six fold, had barred the passage at various points but in vain,
for as soon as the Russians approached they abandoned
their most favourable positions on the heights and ran away,
leaving all their guns behind them. The whole affair took
place within a short distance of Samarkand; the inhabitants
of the town fearing worse consequences from the panic of
their own countrymen than from a Christian occupation,
closed their gates against the fugitives of their own army,
and sent a deputation of their principal mollahs and aksa-
kals to invite the enemy into the town. The next day part
of the Russian army went into Samarkand; General Kauffmann made his entry at the head of a numerous suite, including the Afghan prince Iskender Khan, son of Sultan
Dsans of Herat. He is said to have gone at first to the
assistance of the noble Bokhara, out of zeal for the threatened
cause of Islam; but when the noble Bokhara could not pay
him the price he had stipulated for, he recited a *fatiha* for the
health of his soul, and passed over to the service of the double

cross. A splendid specimen of the Central Asiatic defenders of Islam!

In this fashion, on May 14, 1868, the Russian Christians took possession of Samarkand, the once-splendid capital of Timour, the birthplace and the grave of so many men distinguished in the annals of Islam, and the brilliant centre of old Mohammedan learning. With Samarkand the best part of Transoxania was transferred from the hands of the Özbeg dynasty of Manghit to the house of Romanoff. The first conqueror of the country, so far as we know, was Alexander (the Macedonian), and another Alexander (II. of Russia) has been the last. Two thousand years ago Samarkand paid tribute to a small country in the south of Europe, now it is governed from a northern capital of the same continent; and if we take into consideration all it has gone through in the interval during the struggles of so many different dynasties, at the hands of Greeks, Arabs, Turks, Mongolians, and Özbegs, it would be difficult to find another spot in Asia with so chequered a history of sunny and stormy days to compare with it. Although the furthest countries of the East were made known to us in the course of the last century, and the remotest corners of Cathay and Zipangu could not escape the researches of western explorers, Samarkand has remained veiled in all the romance of mystery almost up to the present day. Her fall consequently took Europe by surprise, and the opening up of the country has destroyed the most interesting field for the imagination to revel in, whilst recalling the traditions of mediæval Asia. After the catastrophe of Samarkand, the Emir escaped as fast as he could to Kermineh. His son, the Kette-Töre (Crown Prince) Abdul Melik Mirza, a youth of nineteen, had run away during the battle to Bokhara, and the panic was so general that whole caravans of peaceable inhabitants of the district of Miyankal, abandoned house and home, and escaped by Karshi and across the Oxus to Andkhoï and Meïmene. As regards the Russians, they had first to make themselves secure, and began by putting the small mound on which the citadel stood in a state of defence, but at the same time they continued their march along the road to Bokhara, partly in pursuit of the Emir, partly in order to subdue the places in the immediate neighbourhood.   Major General Golowatscheff, with fourteen companies of infantry, eight guns, and three sotnias of Cossacks, first advanced on the fortress of Kette Kurghan (Great Fort) on the Zerefshan, which, when I passed through, was declared to be impregnable, and which did, in truth, possess tolerably strong outworks; but in spite of this, and of its numerous garrison, the gates were opened without even an attempt at resistance. The Emir seemed anxious to concentrate his last forces and set up his head-quarters at Mir,[1] whence he sent out occasional bodies of light horse to harass the Russians at Kette Kurghan, until General Kauffmann, tired of these constant though but petty annoyances, determined to march straight on Bokhara and annihilate the remaining fragments of the Özbeg army. Still the Bokhariot self-conceit was not entirely broken, for the Emir, whether of his own accord or egged on by the crowd of fanatics is uncertain, prepared to resist once more, and marched against the Russians.   The battle between the family of Manghit and the house of Romanoff for the crown of Transoxania was fought at Serpul, on the same spot, at the same season of the year, possibly on the very anniversary of the day on which 379 years before Sheïbani Mehemmed Khan and Baber had fought the battle of their dynasties. As may be imagined, the result was very much against the Özbegs. The Russians began by storming with their accustomed bravery the heights on each side of the road occupied by the Özbegs, and the panic was so general and uncontrolable that the whole road as far as Kermineh was strewn with the arms thrown away by the fugitives. In the general

---

[1] Mir is a pretty little village on the road from Bokhara to Samarkand, a half-way house between Kermineh and Kette Kurghan. See my *Travels in Central Asia*, p. 200.

disaster, Mozaffar-eddin's own fate was the cruellest of all. He dared not retire on Bokhara, for his son, always an obstinate and rebellious boy, had there placed himself at the head of the malcontent fanatics, and sought to deprive his father of the miserable fragment of a throne remaining. He dared not advance, for the Russians seemed now seriously bent on carrying the banner of the black eagle straight into the 'noble Bokhara.' A treacherous attempt to attack Samarkand in the rear of General Kauffmann was defeated by the marvellous bravery of the Russians,[1] and the Emir had now no alternative left him but to make peace with the victorious enemy, and to retain for the period of his own life-time the shadow of sovereignty, on condition of paying a war indemnity of 125,000 tilla (500,000 thalers), which, only out of consideration for his feelings, was not called tribute. By the conditions of the treaty of peace the Emir bound himself, 1st, to allow all Russian subjects without distinction of creed to trade freely in all parts of the khanate, and to become security for their property and persons ; 2ndly, to allow Russian merchants freely to appoint trade agents in all parts of the khanate ; 3rdly, to fix the tariff on all Russian imports at two and a half per cent. of their nominal value ; and 4thly, to allow Russian merchants a free passage through the khanate to all neighbouring countries.

[1] When General Kauffmann and the main body of the Russian army had left Samarkand in their rear, the citadel of the latter place was treacherously attacked by 25,000 Samarkandians and Üzbegs from Shehri Sebz and placed in the greatest peril. The Russian garrison, commanded by Major Baron v. Stempel, consisted of 685 men, including sick and non-combatants, and the heroic exertions of this handful of men, many of whom left their beds to take part in the defence, are deserving of the highest praise. The struggle lasted six whole days, from June 12 to 18, and cost the Russians forty-nine dead, and 172 wounded. The enemy set fire to one of the gates and opened a breach, but in the end effected nothing. Night and day the storming columns rushed against the walls with unearthly yells, but the Russians flew from one point to the other, invariably repulsing their bloodthirsty enemy, and inflicting heavy losses, until at length, General Kauffman having after much delay learnt the state of affairs, hurried back by forced marches and delivered them from their perilous position. This episode of the Russo-Bokhariot war gives us the most striking example both of the impotence and of the rascality of Asiatic hordes.

Peace was thus made with Russia, but Mozaffar-eddin found he had thereby only incurred the bitter hostility of his own subjects. All their defeats, all their disasters, the loss of so many fortresses, and of so many lives, all had failed to bring the vain, fanatical, half-insane mollahs of the capital on the Zerefshan to a true understanding of the state of things. People, who but a few years back were firmly convinced that Bokhara, in the strength of her army and in the purity and perfection of her Islamism, was a match for the Sultan of Constantinople himself, far more for Christendom, had now to realise that a handful of Christian unbelievers had over-powered an army of Moslems ten or fifteen times stronger than themselves, and that the devilish inventions of the modern Europeans in the art of war, had proved more effi-cacious than the blessings and holy breath of their own *ishans* (chiefs of religious orders). No Mohammedan fanatic could be brought to believe this! As is generally the case in mis-fortune, their leader was accused of treachery; the furious crowd did not dare to turn on the Russians, so they fell on the Emir, excited the populace against him, and endeavoured to place the Kette-Töre on the throne. The latter, in addition to a strong party in Bokhara and Karshi, was supported by Djura Bai and Baber Bai of Shehri Sebz; the northern dis-tricts of Gidjdovan, Nurata and Khatirdja also coquetted with him, and when, leaving his father, he retired to Karshi, he lost no time in getting himself proclaimed sovereign, and, in this capacity, entered into alliance with the Khan of Khiva. His cause became so popular that in an astonishingly short time he found himself at the head of an army of nearly 10,000 men. Under these circumstances, Mozaffar-eddin could no longer remain a passive spectator. He collected together the scanty remnants of his forces and marched on Karshi to put down his own son, but when half way there, he learnt that the standard of revolt had also been raised in the northern part of the khanate, probably with the connivance of the Kette-Töre, and that Sadik Bai the chief rebel of that

neighbourhood was marching on Kerminch. As the enemy
had thus suddenly appeared in the north, and the danger
seemed more pressing in that quarter, the Emir gave orders
to turn back, and made the best of his way home to his
capital. The Kette-Töre, encouraged by his father's retreat,
wanted to pursue him, and would probably have successfully
carried out his well-concerted plans, if the Russians, to whom
all these troubles could scarcely be agreeable in the uncon-
solidated state of their newly-acquired province, had not
interfered at the request of the Emir, and checked the further
advance of the prince by concentrating a small force [1] under
Colonel Abramoff near Djam. Meantime, Mozaffar-eddin disposed of Sadik Bai in the north-east, routing him utterly ; and
in order to carry out his operations with equal success in the
south, where he was confronted by Shehri Sebz, as well as by
his rebellious son, he invoked the co-operation of the Russians,
who readily granted it. Colonel Abramoff marched from
Djam with the corps of observation alluded to above. Preceding the Emir by a few miles, he encountered the Kette-
Töre's troops in October (others say in November), defeated
and scattered them; the Russians occupied Karshi, the second
city of the khanate, for two days, and then, to the extreme
astonishment of the Central Asiatics, handed it, with its
citadel and all the arms stored there, back to the Emir of
Bokhara. Mozaffar-eddin intended to employ the Russians
further to assist him against Shehri Sebz, his chief object
being the destruction of Djura Bai, and not that of his own
son, whom he regarded as a mere catspaw of the former.
General Kauffmann did not, however, think himself bound to
add more to the proofs of friendship he had shown his new
ally, and after evacuating Karshi, sent his troops into winter
quarters to Djam . . . As regards the Kette-Töre, his pretensions to the throne would not allow him to rest, and his
adventurous career often caused uneasiness to his father,

---

[1] It consisted of seven companies of infantry, two sotnias of Cossacks, six
rifled guns, six pieces of heavy artillery.

to the Russians, and to the English. With his band of Ersari and Tekke-Turkomans, who were all devoted to him, he would suddenly re-appear from the steppe, now in one part of the khanate, then in another ; next he allied himself with Khiva, again he was heard of in Kabul, trying to stir up Shir Ali Khan to go to war with the Emir, but all in vain. There was no lack of hospitality and expressions of sympathy, and Shir Ali Khan gave him his own daughter in marriage. But no one dared to take up his cause, and at last Abdul Melik died during his wanderings in Khiva, most likely a violent death.[1]

By the time the Emir saw himself thus relieved from this terrible nightmare, peace had been restored in the part of Bokhara he was still allowed by an act of condescension to call his own, and he had learnt, taught by necessity, to accommodate himself to his hard fate. The instalments of the war indemnity were paid in hard cash at Samarkand with tolerable punctuality.

A regular communication was established between the Ark at Bokhara and the citadel of the city of Timour, and in order to give a further proof of his devotion to his suzerain, he sent a mission to St. Petersburg, headed by his youngest and favourite son, Abdul Fettah Mirza, a boy of twelve years old. This fourth son had been designated by Mozaffar-eddin as his successor, and he sought to have this arrangement sanctioned, if possible, on the banks of the Neva. This was of course a doubtful point. Nicholas did, indeed, formerly give the present king of Persia his first lessons in love for Russia when he nursed him as a child on his knees at Tiflis, but Alexander II. may spare himself any similar trouble, for, his tutelage over, Abdul Fettah is far more absolute in his nature. The mission from the distant shores of the Zerefshan was received at the Russian Court on November 3, 1869, with every mark of respect. The Czar was unbounded in his protestations of

[1] According to another more recent version, he still lives as the guest of Yakub Kushbeghi in Kashgar.

friendship for his 'good brother'—who might have been more truly described as his vassal—in Turkestan, and received, accompanied by the empress, the following presents from the Emir: 1, a ring with a remarkably large diamond; 2, a lady's head-dress set with precious stones; 3, sets of silver harness studded with turquoises for the four horses which were shortly to arrive from Turkestan; 4, three robes of black horses-skins, lined with Cashmere; 5, three robes of grey lambswool lined with the Bokhariot stuff known as 'shali'; 6, two Cashmere dresses; 7, a piece of wonderfully fine and beautiful cachemire; 8, eighteen pieces of silk manufactured there; 9, eighteen pieces of the stuff known as 'Attres,' half silk, half wool.[1] The usual number of *nine* presents, according to the custom of Turko-Tartaric nations, was adhered to on this occasion; suitable gifts were sent in return, and this exchange of presents naturally brought about a certain amount of good understanding if not of actual good-will. In point of fact, Mozaffar-eddin has abstained from any sign of hostility towards Russia ever since the taking of Samarkand by General Kauffmann. It is very probable that attempts are secretly made to conclude an alliance with the mighty ruler of Eastern Turkestan, and that overtures are occasionally ventured on at Constantinople and at Calcutta, for the Emir of Bokhara has not as yet absolutely given up all hope of regaining his former power, but, as far as we can judge, all his endeavours are likely to prove fruitless. No instance has yet been known of Russians ever retracing their steps backwards in any part of Asia, and Mozaffar-eddin seems destined to be the last of his race and the last of those princes who, from the Samanides downwards, have reigned as independent sovereigns in Transoxania.

Thus my History of Bokhara is brought to a conclusion. The moment that the Russian flag was hoisted on the citadel of Samarkand, this ancient and distant country of Asia

---

[1] From F. v. Hellwald's essay in the *Ausland* of March 11, 1872, under the head of 'New Explorations in Central Asia.'

entered on the path of the modern world and of modern ideas. Towns and countries hitherto unknown to the denizens of the Western world have been thrown open, and places where the European traveller could only venture in disguise and at the peril of his life are now not only free and safe but actually governed and administered by Christians.   Churches and clubs have been opened at Tashkend, Khodjend, and Samarkand ; in the first-named city there is even a newspaper (' Turkestanskia Wjedomosti '—' Turkestan News '), and the melancholy monotony of the Muezzin's chant is broken by the cheerful sounds of the bells of the Greek churches, more terrible to Mohammedan ears than the roar of artillery. Popes, soldiers and merchants now move with the proud steps of conquerors through those very streets of Bokhara, where, a few years ago, the author of this work only dared to venture about chanting Moslem hymns.   A Russian hospital and storehouse is established in the once-splendid palace of Timour, whither in olden times, embassies from all the princes of Asia came to do homage and bring offerings, whither the proud King of Castille himself sent his ambassadors humbly to sue for friendship, and where the descendants of the Turanians came with pious reverence to touch with their foreheads the ' blue stone,' the pedestal of Timour's throne! Whether, and how, this marvellous revolution of things will contribute to the welfare of the people of Central Asia, is a question far exceeding the limits of the present work, and I can only refer the reader to the opinions I have expressed regarding it in other publications.[1]   I must, however, here briefly allude to one very important circumstance, and that is, that the Russian successes in Central Asia have dealt Islamism the severest blow it has ever received from Christendom in the course of their thousand years of struggle. In modern days, the powerful influence of Christian Europe had permeated and filled all parts of Mohammedan Western Asia, the holy places of Mecca and Medina themselves had

---

[1] See note 2, p. 384.

not escaped the innovating spirit of the times, but for a while the Mohammedanism of the distant parts of Central Asia retained its primitive character pure and undiluted, the faith flourished unopposed and uncontroverted. Bokhara, and not Mecca, had become practically the spiritual centre of Islamism. Thither came the ascetic, the pious member of a fraternity, and the enthusiastic theologian; and though not generally known, it is an undoubted fact [1] that zealous Moslems in all parts of the Ottoman Empire, in Egypt, Fez, and Morocco, received thence the inspirations which excited their religious enthusiasm. The sight of this holy ground profaned by the presence of unbelievers, and ruled by them, must be intolerable to all pious souls of the Islamite world, and the dust raised by the fall of this chief pillar of Islamism, as Bokhara has always been called, will long hang as a dark cloud, over-shadowing for many a day, if not for ever, the horizon of the future prospects of Islam.

[1] Amongst others I may mention the Bokhariot *tekkes* or convents, in fact refuges for Central Asiatic dervishes and hadjis, maintained at Constantinople by the contributions of pious Osmanlis. The best known are in the Eyub quarter, at Scutari, and near the Aya Sophia. As regards the spiritual intercourse with Western Islam, I may observe that there are a considerable number of Turks and Arabs who give themselves out as *murid* (pupils) of the sheïkhs of Bokhara, and I have myself received letters of recommendation to these spiritual superiors from Turks at Constantinople, Engürii, and Erzerum.

LONDON: PRINTED BY
SPOTTISWOODE AND CO., NEW-STREET SQUARE
AND PARLIAMENT STREET

WS - #0037 - 250724 - C0 - 229/152/25 - PB - 9781330388457 - Gloss Lamination